BOTTLED

SARA BYALA

Bottled

How Coca-Cola Became African

OXFORD
UNIVERSITY PRESS

OXFORD

UNIVERSITY PRESS

Oxford University Press is a department of the
University of Oxford. It furthers the University's objective
of excellence in research, scholarship, and education
by publishing worldwide.

Oxford New York

Auckland   Cape Town   Dar es Salaam   Hong Kong   Karachi
Kuala Lumpur   Madrid   Melbourne   Mexico City   Nairobi
New Delhi   Shanghai   Taipei   Toronto

With offices in

Argentina   Austria   Brazil   Chile   Czech Republic   France   Greece
Guatemala   Hungary   Italy   Japan   Poland   Portugal   Singapore
South Korea   Switzerland   Thailand   Turkey   Ukraine   Vietnam

Oxford is a registered trade mark of Oxford University Press
in the UK and certain other countries.

Published in the United States of America by
Oxford University Press
198 Madison Avenue, New York, NY 10016

Library of Congress Cataloging-in-Publication Data is available

ISBN: 9780197758427

Printed in the United Kingdom by Bell & Bain Ltd, Glasgow

For David Byala

CONTENTS

LIST OF ILLUSTRATIONS

LIST OF ILLUSTRATIONS

LIST OF ILLUSTRATIONS

PREFACE

Rwanda, June 2016

The day is clear and bright, the colors of the landscape vivid: chestnut earth, electric-green hills, aqua sky. We make our way in a kombi two hours east of Kigali and into the Rwandan countryside. The closer we get to our destination, the more another color starts catching my eye. Bright red, now dotting the vista. There, men in overalls are painting new signs. Those look fresh, too. All are offering the same product: Coca-Cola.

I've spent the past two hours on the press bus headed for the village of Ruhunda, though I am no reporter. The formal invitation arrived the day before in a woven envelope, hand-delivered to my hotel room. My research assistant and I are staying at a friendly outfit perched atop a supermarket in the city's old center, where crowds assemble to watch the Euro Cup throughout our stay.

I am here to witness the relaunch of the EKOCENTER, one of Coca-Cola's most visible sustainability initiatives. When I was invited to the event while doing research at Coca-Cola's global headquarters in Atlanta, I rerouted an upcoming trip, flying into Kigali from Nairobi, arriving just as Coca-Cola's executives from across the global system did likewise. They are staying at the much swankier Mövenpick Hotel that I was fairly certain my research funds would not cover.

At the time I visited, there were 127 EKOCENTERS, mostly in Africa, but this one is the flagship: the model of all that the project could be, seeking to aid an underserved area through the comingling of commerce, healthcare, and sanitation. It is Sunday, and we are heading to Ruhunda for a tour; tomorrow, we will come back for the official launch. I have spent the ride chatting with the global directors of the project. They speak about the endeavor in near-religious terms, avowing that if Coca-Cola was to stop supporting it, they would look for employment elsewhere to continue this important work. I wonder, not for the last time, who besides Coca-Cola has the footprint, will, and money to do something this ambitious in Africa. No one that we can think of, we all acknowledge.

Unlike Coke's other sustainability initiatives on the continent, which are barely branded, if at all, the EKOCENTER screams Coca-Cola, in its red splendor. But, selling Coke is just one sliver of the EKOCENTER's purpose. The Ruhunda EKOCENTER provides 25,000 nearby residents with clean water, 3G internet connectivity, and a regulation football field, the only one that exists outside of the capital, used for the beautiful game and, on Sundays, for church services. This EKOCENTER also includes a medical center backed by a solar-powered generator, which means that babies who arrive during the brown- and black-outs that plague the region will no longer have to be delivered by flashlight. Electricity and purified water are sold to the community, as are consumer goods (including Coke products), by female entrepreneurs whose empowerment is part of the scheme's design. EKOCENTER is not the work of Coke alone: a group of other multinational companies have lent their time, money, and expertise to it, all brought to the table by Coke's convening power. As Coca-Cola's then Chief Executive Officer

Muhtar Kent put it at the luncheon following the launch, Coca-Cola's work here should not be mistaken for charity. Rather, this was 'pre-competitive collaboration' that hopes to promote healthy communities, since healthy communities, he explained unabashedly, become consumer communities.

I've seen enough of Coca-Cola's sustainability work by now to put this project in context, and I am impressed. Still, I have questions, many of which will go unanswered on this trip. Is this project really sustainable, or will it disappear in a few months' time, the Coke signs once more fading? What do the locals think of it, and of Coke in general? Most importantly, where does this project fit into the larger story of Coca-Cola in this country and on this continent? Some of these questions I ask at that night's cocktail party. Most, I keep to myself. I am an anomaly here: an Africanist historian working on a book on Coca-Cola's history in Africa. I almost feel bad admitting that my book will take years and not the weeks to complete that the Coke folks who invited me here hoped for.

When the day for the official launch arrives, we again ride the minibuses eastward. We are intermixed with personnel from the other companies participating in this endeavor—Tigo and Ericsson, MedShare and Philips, Solarkiosk and Pentair, as well as a who's who of global Coca-Cola executives working on sustainability. As we near Ruhunda, we are stopped at a makeshift checkpoint. Our bags are scrutinized, our bodies put through metal detectors and pat-downs.

Once inside security, the area is brimming with thousands of guests from the region. We are ushered to a dais on the side of the soccer field, while local dancers enact what I imagine visitors are expecting from their African hosts. The tone is festive but orderly, a controlled celebration. From the stage, I watch the backs of the VIP speakers brought in for the occasion: Kelvin Balogun, president of Coca-Cola's Southern and East African

PREFACE

Business Unit; Odette Uwamariya, Governor of Rwanda's Eastern Province; Muhtar Kent, Coca-Cola's CEO; Paul Kagame, President of Rwanda; and, incongruously, American civil rights icon, Reverend Jesse Jackson. All offer similar takes on the same message; in its capacity to assemble businesses, government, and NGOs in the service of African betterment, Coca-Cola is doing essential work here.

Though there are boxed lunches on hand for the ride back, once in Kigali, a catered meal awaits us. Kent talks again, this time off the cuff. Then Reverend Jackson gets up, also speaking, it seems to me, with more abandon in the more intimate setting. 'Coca-Cola is known as the refreshment drink,' he muses, 'but the Coca-Cola Africa story is untold. And it concerns me; its value is so great, we need the story told.'

When I meet Jackson later that evening at the hotel bar, we chat about his fraught history with Coca-Cola in the United States, about his knowledge of Coke's hidden political work across the African continent, and more. I marvel how it is that he—a man who once led a boycott of Coca-Cola—came to this place, both ideologically and physically. Not for the last time, I wonder how Coca-Cola came to have such a vast presence on the continent and question if this multinational company selling carbonated sugary water can, in fact, have generative powers, and, if so, upon what balance sheet.

I spent the lunch after the EKOCENTER launch talking to Jackson's children as well as a Dutch fellow who works for Bralirwa, the local Heineken bottler that also bottles Coke in Central Africa. I'd been trying to tour a plant in this country—as I had done in every other African nation I visited—but my contacts all seemed too busy to make it happen. When he offered to run me over to the plant for an impromptu tour, I jumped at the opportunity, snapping a picture of his business card and sending it via WhatsApp to my husband on the other side of the world, as one does when one is a woman researcher about to get into a stranger's car. The plant, I find, is meticulous, and even though we are the only ones there, he carefully follows the global safety protocols. We walk through all the usual spots— the fillers and purifiers and mixers—before pausing at a plaque commemorating the Tutsi who were killed in this facility in 1994. This difficult past, I have found, is forever present in this nation, in billboards, on the radio, and in quiet memorials like these.

I leave Rwanda not long after the EKOCENTER launch, intrigued with a country that is able to live with its brutal past while letting technical innovation drive its future. I am enamored with the trash-less streets and cheered by the country's ban on plastic bags. As we drive, I think of the Rwandan expert who suggested that this orderliness is at once impressive and unsettling, that this too could be a sign of a rising dictatorship. The story is always beneath the surface, I remind myself.

We pass a twenty-foot-tall Coca-Cola bottle on our way out of town and I pause. On closer inspection, I note that it is a kiosk from which cold Coca-Colas are sold to passersby, the first of its kind I've seen. It reminds me of those Russian nesting dolls: bottles in a bottle. Coca-Cola, I think, is a product no one needs. Yet its bottles are the outward face of a company that is and has been doing work on this continent—much of it necessary—that no one else either can or will do, for better or worse, and for longer than most of us would imagine. This book tells those stories in a story.

INTRODUCTION

The Sahara Desert, Mali, June 2003

When the jeep is running, hot, dusty air floods the open windows as we rush northward. I have been traveling in West Africa for several weeks with other history graduate students, and Timbuktu, the famed ancient city of learning at the crossroads of the Sahara, is to be the pinnacle of our trip. But it is proving harder to reach than we anticipated. Held together by duct tape, the dilapidated blue and silver Patrol we are in is no match for the desert. The breakdowns become more frequent. The hours spent idling roadside expand. Our supply of warm water dwindles.

Then, out of nowhere, a gleaming white Land Rover appears. Three men, dressed in boubous as pristine as their vehicle, emerge to survey us: four ragtag women, immodestly clad. We find surprising common ground when they announce that they, too, are historians. They proclaim it unsafe for us to stay where we are, with night approaching. We leave our bags with our driver and head with them to a homestead, where we sleep on colorful mattresses under an impossibly wide sky. Dawn breaks, and we bid our gracious hosts farewell. We trek on foot to a shack where, again, we wait. Hours pass before we are able to hitch a ride atop a green rice truck piled high with sundry. It deposits us at a ferry stop along the Niger River, Timbuktu within reach at last. Boarding, grimy and parched, we are offered—as if in a dream— ice-cold Coca-Colas.

***

Like travelers before and after me, I marveled at the presence of a cold Coca-Cola that day. How is this here, I recall musing. Where was this bottled, how was it transported, and, most importantly, how was it cooled? Cynically, I questioned whether there was anywhere beyond the reach of American consumerism. Yet I also remember how happy the vendor was to make that sale and how I—thirsty and wary of unsafe water—was so pleased to drink that Coke.

Later, when I learned the jaw-dropping statistics about Coca-Cola's African footprint, I would come to understand that an ice-cold Coke far up the Niger River was as much about Mali as it was emblematic of an American corporation's reach. I would come to see that Coca-Cola—and its sister products like Fanta, Sprite, and bottled water—were regarded as local just about everywhere in Africa, and had been for roughly a hundred years. I would see the drink's ubiquity reflected in the material culture I have long collected in a new light, too: the Coca-Cola picture frames and Fanta toy airplanes from South Africa that line my desk; the cloth with a repeating Coca-Cola pattern I was gifted from Mozambique; the Coca-Cola-bottle-shaped coffin I coveted from Ghana all seeming to take on new import. Africa was Coke country. But, I came to understand, so too was Coke African. More than a decade after my Malian journey, when I decided to write this book, that moment on the ferry surfaced in my mind to epitomize what I hope these pages expand upon. In its profound breadth and depth, Coca-Cola offers an unequaled lens onto modern Africa.

INTRODUCTION

The Kola Nut

There would be no Coca-Cola without the African kola nut, so that is where our story begins.

'He who brings kola brings life,' Chinua Achebe wrote in his classic novel about the advent of colonialism, *Things Fall Apart*. Throughout the story, the kola nut is broken and eaten, offered or withheld, as a measure of culture's shifting norms. Today, as in Achebe's 1959—or the book's early twentieth century setting—the kola nut continues to embody hospitality and community.[1]

The kola nut is not a nut at all, but rather the seed kernel of indigenous West African trees of the *Sterculiacae* family, genus Cola, primarily of the species *Sterculia acuminata* and *nitida*. Kola-bearing evergreens can measure upwards of twelve meters. Their waxy green leaves and star-shaped flowers frame the fruit pods in which the white, red, or pink nuts are nestled. Though bitter at first bite, chewing mellows the flavor while releasing more caffeine than coffee and yielding a mild psychoactive stimulant. 'Neither food nor medicine,' historian Edmund Abaka explains, the kola nut is a 'peculiar substance,' whose little-known history has much to teach us about the spread of indigenous knowledge throughout, and out of, Africa.[2]

People across West Africa have been cultivating and ingesting the kola nut for centuries. The nut was known to stave off hunger and thirst, to aid digestion, and to improve the flavor of food and water. It was used as a restorative, a gift, and a ceremonial offering. Kola trade spread with the expansion of Islam in West Africa, particularly during the eighteenth- and nineteenth-century jihads there, since it was deemed exempt from Muslim dietary restrictions.[3] Kola cultivation impacted land use in Liberia, enriched the Asante in Ghana, and enhanced trading networks, playing a central role in the histories of diverse societies across West Africa for the last several hundred years, at least.[4]

With kola's popularity and versatility, the world of kola was bound to widen. Kola cultivation spread to the islands of São Tomé and Principe, throughout Africa to the DR Congo, Angola, and Tanzania; it moved to Mauritius, the Seychelles, and, further afield, to Sri Lanka, and more.[5] With the advent of the trans-Atlantic slave trade, kola was transported across the Atlantic by enslaved Africans.[6]

The earliest written mention of the medicinal powers of kola outside of the continent dates to the twelfth century, when an Arab doctor, El-Ghafeky (or Gafiki), published a description of nuts capable of addressing stomach ailments and colic.[7] By the sixteenth century, travelers to the continent were describing kola by name. We find it in the 1556 writings of Grenadian Leo Africanus, the 1591 accounts of Portuguese slave trader Odoardo Lopez, and the 1594 recollections of Cape Verdean Andre Alvarez of Almada.[8] In the late seventeenth century, French traveler Jean Barbot described 'a fruit called "cola" … which quenches the thirst and makes water delicious to those who make use of it,' likening it to 'a kind of chestnut, with a bitter taste.'[9] By the middle of the seventeenth century, interest in the nut had been piqued in the Caribbean, with cultivators in Jamaica clamoring for it.[10] From the turn of the nineteenth century, European and American naturalists began to record kola's components.[11] By the 1880s, scholarly information on kola's properties gave way to military studies on the efficacy of kola use for soldiers.[12] At the same time, enterprising merchants started disseminating kola samples in Europe and the United States to grow a market for them.[13]

The cumulative effect of all this effort stirred interest in the global north. In 1885, *The New York Times* reported on 'That Nut from Africa,' noting that 'It is superseding all stimulants in medical practice.'[14] Three years later, one Dr. Charles Yarbough published 'Therapeutics of Kola,' claiming kola's usefulness in treating an astonishing range of ailments, from cardiac disease to melancholia and uterine inertia.[15] In his 1906 *Diet and Dietetics*, French biochemist Armand Gautier further sang the praises of kola, noting how it 'increases the number and energy of the muscular contractions, prevents fatigue and overwork, renders respiration more free and more powerful,' in addition to having 'exciting and aphrodisiac properties,' which can be useful in treating a host of ailments, from 'intestinal agony' to 'affections of the liver.'[16] By the last decades of the nineteenth century at least, knowledge about this peculiar food-medicine (some sound, some inflated) had found its way—via travelers, enslaved people, slavers, scientists, and more—out of Africa.

Alongside the dispersion of kola knowledge out of Africa, the end of the nineteenth century saw the emergence of another would-be health movement. This was the era of patent medicines and nerve tonics—over-the-counter, heavily advertised products that promised to treat an often-impossible range of ailments. One of the most well-known nostrums of the day was a tonic created by Corsican pharmacist Angelo Mariani in 1863. Vin Mariani, as it was called, was a potent mix of Bordeaux wine and cocaine, a Peruvian drug that had recently come into fashion as a cure-all for Gilded Age ailments. Vin Mariani purported to do much: increase appetite, stimulate the heart, and alter moods. Mariani, who came from an elite family of chemists and physicians, used his personal connections to promote his product in often ingenious ways.[17] Evocative ads for Vin Mariani featured testimonials from such disparate celebrities as Pope Leo XIII, the Czar of Russia, Sara Bernhardt, and Buffalo Bill Cody, as well as American president Ulysses S Grant, who found it helped ease the pain of end-stage cancer.[18] Mariani produced his nostrum in France and his brother did likewise in New York; the two set up a string of distribution centers that included such far-flung locations as Egypt and China.[19] In its heyday, Vin Mariani soothed drinkers around the world.

It was Vin Mariani, then, that Dr. John Stith Pemberton, a chemist and patent medicine maker in Atlanta, Georgia, sought to emulate. In 1884, Pemberton's French Wine Coca hit the market as a 'direct imitation' of the real thing.[20] Pemberton's was not the only copy of Vin Mariani around, but, historian Mark Pendergrast tells us, it was a really good one, which Pemberton readily marketed with 'an Americanized, supercharged version of Mariani's claims.'[21] Yet, before a demand for his product could emerge, the temperance movement arose. Pemberton made two interventions that influenced both his product and its subsequent history, partly in light of the social turn against alcohol. Driven by a desire for a single-serve product and motivated to keep costs down, Pemberton replaced wine with still-water. Then, Pemberton added a small amount of kola nut to his recipe, having come to the conclusion that the caffeine in kola was superior to that found in coffee or tea, no doubt the result of the steady stream of kola enthusiasm that peppered public discourse in the years preceding his invention.[22] Kola joined the coca leaf, water, sugar, and caramel (to color and mask impurities) to form the basis of Pemberton's earliest copper-cauldron brew. Thus, in 1886, as Europe was scrambling to carve up the African continent, half a world away, John Pemberton created the earliest version of a beverage that would soon be called Coca-Cola, a drink whose name and whose origin came, in part, from Africa.

'In its fledgling days,' journalist E J Kahn wrote in 1950, 'the Coca-Cola Company used to stress the two ingredients that give the drink its name... the wonderful COCA PLANT and famous COLA NUT.'[23] When, in the end, cocaine turned out to be a far more powerful drug than initially thought, the company swiftly removed what were, by then, already de-cocainized leaves, incapable of rendering an effect on drinkers. Its relationship with kola was subtler and tinged with notions of exotic Africa. 'Playing on racial mythology, some manufacturers [of kola] brazenly asserted that kola—native to Africa—was the source of the physical strength of black people,' historian Frederick Allen writes, citing an 1897 Johnson & Johnson ad for its kola extract Kolafra as evidence.[24] Perhaps kola's African origin enhanced Pemberton's insistence on it, and nothing else, as his source of caffeine. Yet transporting kola nuts proved to be too costly and too complicated to sustain in the long run and so, in its stead, the makers of Coca-Cola started to use synthetic materials.[25] Abaka laments this turn, bemoaning that, in the end, 'Kola was... the unsung hero of Coca-Cola and an African initiative that failed to make a mark on the international market.'[26] Somewhere along the way, the amount of kola nut that could be found in Coca-Cola became close to, if not, negligible. Certainly, by the middle of the twentieth century, Kahn could write that 'Coca-Cola contains only perhaps a hundredth of one percent of cola—so little of it, in fact, that it cannot be detected by laboratory analysis.'[27] Yet, ever wary of appearing to advertise itself falsely—and under threat of lawsuits should it be found to do so—Coca-Cola maintained traces of both ingredients long after they had given their names to the brand.

Ninety years after Pemberton's creation, in May 1976, The Coca-Cola Company—by then one of the most powerful multinationals in the world, available throughout Africa and beyond—launched a global campaign that paid inadvertent homage to the humble kola nut, from whence it came. 'Coke adds life,' the advertisements proclaimed, echoing Achebe's pronouncement and affirming that the mystique of Coca-Cola as more than a simple beverage lived on.[28]

Soda

There would also be no Coca-Cola were it not for the advent of soda.

Humans have long been intrigued by water that bubbles up from the ground, often believing carbonated springs to be magical.[29] As early as 400 BCE, the father of Western medicine, Hippocrates, suggested that sparkling water could cure disease, a notion that persisted in the West.[30] When Europeans identified what we now call carbon dioxide in the seventeenth century, they made the first step in recreating sparkling water. A further breakthrough came in 1767 when British chemist Joseph Priestley identified how to make this 'fixed air,' as carbon dioxide was then known. Tinkering over vats of fermenting beer, Priestley then determined how to put carbon dioxide into water, creating a barely fizzy drink that nonetheless captivated European scientists.[31]

Two years after Priestley published his *Directions for Impregnating Water with Fixed Air*, in 1772, chemist John Mervin Nooth debuted an apparatus for making mineral water that improved upon Priestley's innovations.[32] Then, in 1781, Manchester apothecary shop owner Thomas Henry put out a pamphlet describing an even better device. Henry was the first to recognize the commercial, rather than medicinal potential of fizzy water; his machine could make greater quantities of carbonated water, while his pamphlet contained recipes for different aerated drinks.[33] Swift on his heels, in 1783, Swiss scientist Johann Jacob Schweppes used a hand-crank to refine the carbonation process even further, launching the (still extant) Schweppes Company. The quest to impregnate water spread across Europe, while scientists continued to grapple with how to keep the carbonation in the water, a problem that was partially solved in 1813 by Charles Plinth's invention of the soda syphon, but that would not be adequately resolved until the invention of the Crown Cork at the end of the nineteenth century.[34]

While Priestley escaped religious persecution by fleeing across the Atlantic to America in 1791, so too the race to carbonate water took hold in the New World. In America, as elsewhere, the fascination with natural mineral springs yielded attempts to recreate carbonated water, with inventors facing many of the same logistical problems as their European counterparts. One visitor to natural springs who would successfully impact the course of mineral water's history was Benjamin Silliman, who, having spent a week at a spring in upstate New York, became convinced of its healing power. After finishing legal studies at Yale University, he decided to forego law in favor of becoming the university's first professor of chemistry, itself a budding field of inquiry at the time. Fearing poverty, Silliman sought to augment his income by mimicking British aerated water. He purchased a Nooth Apparatus and began to sell his bottled water in a New Haven apothecary in 1807. Immediately, the inadequacy of American glass and stoneware bottles presented a roadblock to bottling. Though Silliman decided that importing British bottles would suffice, a congressional ban stymied his plans. So Silliman turned to selling carbonated water by the glass, first at a local drugstore and then in larger premises in New York City. While Silliman would not reap the fortune he rightly believed that mineral water could bring, this intervention—selling fizzy water at apothecaries by the glass—would impact the course of what was to come in America and, later, the world.[35]

During the first half of the nineteenth century, pharmacies selling soda water took hold in America, almost overnight and almost without regulation. This era saw drinks that included such ingredients as cannabis, opium, heroin, morphine, and cocaine.[36] Soda jerks, as the operators were known (on account of the jerking movement they made) became like bartenders, especially as the temperance movement gripped the States. Though Americans—like many around the world—once believed cold drinks were harmful, when Irish pioneer George Usher began selling his water ice cold in the hot New York summer of 1809, a new age of beverage consumption was born, bringing with it additional challenges in the era before refrigeration.[37]

Soon, sparkling water became known as 'soda,' a misnomer rooted in original recipes that included sodium bicarbonate, that nonetheless stuck.[38] And, soon, it was not just plain soda.[39] Enterprising soda jerks started adding flavors to their fizzy water. By the end of the eighteenth century, mixtures of wine and sparkling water had become popular in Europe; by the 1830s in the United States, lemonade appeared, followed by a string of berry-flavored drinks. Shortly thereafter, ginger ale emerged, with ice cream soda not far behind. Before the turn of the century, Americans were drinking Sarsaparilla and Root Beer, in addition to the 1886 creation, Coca-Cola.[40] Just as sodas became more diverse, the medical profession was coming to understand that there were no real health benefits to carbonated water. In 1831, soda was removed from the US Pharmacopeia.[41] Increasingly, the drinks were marketed as affordable treats, though dubious health claims remained entwined in their promotion well into the twentieth century. Soda fountains spread rapidly across America in the second half of the nineteenth century. So too did soda manufacturers. In 1860, there were 123 plants bottling soft drinks. By 1900, there were 2,763.[42] Globally, soda came to be known as America's national drink.[43]

It was not long before soda—and soda fountains—emerged in Africa, too. As early as 1899, one F J Bryne, chemist, was advertising 'Cool Iced Drinks' and 'Ice Cr'm Sodas' at his 'American Soda Fountain' in Bulawayo, in what is now Zimbabwe.[44] By 1901, the South Africa *Cape Times* carried ads imploring readers to 'Meet your friends at the American Soda Fountain, where cold beverages and the famous "Ice Cream Soda" are dispensed.'[45] Similar announcements ran in the *Rand Daily Mail* as well as in Mafeking (now Mahikeng, near the Botswanan border with South Africa), Harare, Zimbabwe, and further afield in southern

Africa.[46] In 1913, *The Lagos Standard* ran an ad for 'Coca-Kola wine,' said to contain quinine and available at a local dispensary in what is now Nigeria.[47] By 1920, soda fountains appeared to be in many large African cities. That year, *The Uganda Herald*, the *Sierra Leone Weekly News*, the *Gold Coast Leader*, and the *Dar Es Salaam Times* all contained adverts for aerated water, soda, and soda fountains, showing that by the time Coca-Cola officially arrived in early twentieth-century Cape Town, the continent was primed for a sweet, carbonated drink.[48]

Why Coca-Cola in Africa?

'Who knows when the first sip of Coke was enjoyed on African soil?' the magazine *African Business* once asked, imagining—as I have—that it 'could first have arrived on the dockside of an African seaport in a sailor's kitbag or passenger's portmanteau, or maybe even wrapped in a rug on an Arab caravan,' but that we would not know, since that 'event,' if it happened, 'is not catalogued in The Coca-Cola Company's long history.'[49]

Coca-Cola narrates its African story as one of unstopped progress that begins with its first bottling in 1928 South Africa, moves through its entry into northern Africa during World War II and subsequent expansion across the continent mid-century, and peaks with its full entrenchment in Africa today: present in every African nation as the continent's single largest private employer with a multiplier effect that means that for every formal job that exists within the Coca-Cola system, roughly ten other people are supported.[50] As elsewhere in the world, Coke's existence in Africa began as exported concentrate that, before long, was bottled and distributed by local franchises. Eventually, company-owned bottling enterprises were set up as well. After bottles came cans and plastics, and after them came larger bottles. So too did Coca-Cola's product line expand. After Coke red, the flagship, came Fanta and Sprite, before the company moved into juice, water, tea, and more, making it into, as it now calls itself, a 'total beverage company' that boasts two hundred product lines.[51] Though Coca-Cola red will forever be the company's mascot, the company's recent advertisement campaign declared that there is but 'one brand,' and that brand is Coke.

Coke is everywhere in Africa, and has been for longer than most people would imagine. But ubiquity alone is not a reason to write a book. Still, it was a starting point for the type of inquiry I hoped to make. Motivated by David Armitage and Jo Guldi's *History Manifesto*, which calls upon historians to ask big questions in order to speak to broad audiences, I wanted to write a history that captures a continent-wide story over a tumultuous century.[52] Staking such a vantage point is not without risk. Any attempt to write about Africa as a singular entity chances effacing regional differences, at best, and replicating a flattening gaze, at worst. Keenly aware of this and other pitfalls relating to the long time-frame, I have endeavored in the following pages not to present a single African story, but rather to render the broad contours of manifold African stories, all via the world's most recognizable bottle.

My chosen vehicle for this project was biography, in this case of a commodity. Through biography, we see the life of a thing, from its earliest iterations, through its reinventions, to the present. We understand that its trajectory is only knowable in relation to its surroundings, that the two necessarily exist in tandem. Biography compels us to ask not why something is as it is, but rather how it is, and to examine what this explanatory question can tell us. Surely, Coca-Cola is not just any object worthy of such biography, but rather the product for this time, what Slavoj Žižek calls 'the perfect commodity' and Daniel Miller dubs a 'meta-commodity,' 'the quintessential commodity,' to use Arjun Appadurai's term for a singular item that encapsulates the contradictions and complexities of life late in the era of capital (or Capitalocene), arguably better than anything else.[53]

With Coke's biography as my window onto Africa, I trace the corporation's uneven spread across the continent to expand our understanding of how capitalist systems interact with political, cultural, and environmental forces. I write against the backdrop of Africa wrenching its freedom from colonialism (apartheid included) and a planet bending under the weight of climate change. I examine the ways Africans have engaged this multinational to counter simplistic understandings of the capitalized, that is, the people who participate in capitalist systems. As such, and as much as the sources allow, I try to center African agents in this story. In sum, I show how a seemingly mundane product hides truths in plain sight, how a beverage no one needs, but that is everywhere, serves as a vehicle to traverse both space and time to capture a macro-history via a micro-lens.

In setting myself the task of writing the history of Coca-Cola in Africa from the early twentieth century to the near present, I did not want to rehash arguments about so-called Coca-Colonization and how it homogenizes the world.[54] Those positions have been more than adequately staked by more than a few scholars by now. If anything, my experiences on the continent have shown the opposite, in any event. It is precisely how Africans make use of outside items—including this drink—that is worthy of study in its particularities. Coke may be everywhere, but that does not mean everywhere is the same. Simultaneously, I did not want to rehearse arguments against globalization or write about the ills of big business, which, too, have been equally laid out by others.[55] To be sure, I do still wrestle with these issues in the following pages. Nor did I come to this book to write a treatise against sugar, water, energy, or plastic use. Though I am not blind to the crises of our time, I was not driven by the kind of single-minded activism that forestalls critical inquiry.

Conversely, I did not want to write a paean to Coca-Cola, my fondness for the occasional soda notwithstanding. Instead, I have taken a position similar to that of economist Pietra Rivoli, whose inquiry into global capitalism by way of a white T-shirt served as a model. She writes, 'certainly the world does not need another tome either defending or criticizing globalization and trade as abstract concepts, as the cases on both sides have been made eloquently and well.' Like her, I wrote this book, 'not to defend a position but to tell a story.'[56] And, like her work, the story I tell is not nearly as neat as some would expect.

Method

I began researching this book in archives. Coca-Cola is famously committed to its own past and, unsurprisingly, houses a vast, state-of-the-art business archive at its corporate headquarters in Atlanta. Though closed to the public, I was granted rare access to this treasure trove. In the Coke archives, I combed through thousands of pages of internal memos, speeches, correspondence, reports, and more. I pored over videos and advertisements and listened to hours of audio files. I marveled at the wealth of Coke ephemera stored on site and scrutinized whole runs of internal publications and entire boxes full of archival photographs. I conducted additional archival research at Emory and Clark Atlanta Universities and plumbed national, business, and personal archives across Africa.

After documents came corporate interviews, facilitated by my contacts in Atlanta. I interviewed dozens of Coke employees for this book, executives and leaders of the global teams for sustainability, energy, water, soccer, marketing, and more. I spoke to public relations personnel and risk assessors, to advertisers and engineers, and to personnel based in America, Europe, and Africa, alike.

INTRODUCTION

I also undertook fieldwork in eight countries in Africa: Egypt, Eswatini, Ghana, Kenya, Nigeria, Rwanda, South Africa, and Zimbabwe. In each, I conducted interviews with Coca-Cola personnel and Coke bottlers, mapping Coke's imprint on the ground. From my base at the University of Pennsylvania, I also guided six research assistants who undertook supplemental interviews and data collection in eleven African nations—Egypt, Ghana, Kenya, Morocco, Mozambique, Senegal, South Africa, Tanzania, Uganda, Zambia, and Zimbabwe—adding to the wealth of information about Coca-Cola in Africa I accumulated.

Throughout my research, I met everyone from billionaires to the folks who work on the lines; I toured plants, traveled to depots, visited betterment schemes, saw water and energy initiatives, spent hours with small-scale vendors, and more. I spent a day with the marketing team behind Coke Studio, the company's musical enterprise, and conversed with Coca-Cola-supported soccer players. I engaged folks who make the labels for bottles and interviewed an artist who uses discarded labels as his medium. I met the chemists who make concentrate at one of the two concentrate plants on the continent (out of the seven that exist worldwide), and was schooled on the chemistry of quality control. I watched Coke bottles and cans be upcycled into art objects and interviewed Africa's biggest collector of Coca-Cola kitsch, whose house boasts an illuminated Coca-Cola-bottle-shaped doorway. I have seen remnants of Coke waste on roadsides and spent time at plastic and glass recycling centers. I got used to donning helmets and earplugs and plodding along in borrowed hard shoes that were always too large. I rode tuk-tuks and had police escorts. And, I drank a lot of Coke.

Early in my research, I realized that while my project had been sparked by a desire to account for Coca-Cola's remarkable reach—illuminated on the Niger River years before—there was something greater at play than mere omnipresence. I understood this when I arrived in Johannesburg one night to a surprise dinner with a sugar activist, who heard I was coming and wanted to speak with me, but did not want to go on record as having done so. Another day, my cell phone buzzed: one of the most well-known political activists in South Africa had tracked me down to explain what she saw as the political problem with Coca-Cola on the continent. As encounters like these multiplied, I began to weigh them against my considerable time spent investigating Coca-Cola's innovations in empowerment, water access and purification, waste collection and repurposing, and energy acquisition, the likes of which I touched upon in the preface. That work, at the forefront of sustainability and driven by capitalist techno-optimism, offered a compelling counternarrative. At the same time, as I met with aspiring politicians across the continent, I heard about the useful intersection of Coca-Cola management and governance, again countering naysayers. The more I researched and spoke to people, in other words, the more the story of Coke in Africa appeared as a parable for late capitalism, full of both cause for concern and seeds of optimism.

I began to see Coke, then, not merely as a commodity worth investigating for its ever-presence; it is also a powerful vehicle by which the most salient anxieties of our time—those around the environment, politics, equity, and health—are embodied. In the following pages, I tell this biography of African Coke, moving chrono-thematically from its African birth to the near present. In doing so, I make the case that Coca-Cola grew and thrived in Africa by becoming African, which I define as a range of adaptations, responses, and positions that put Africa and Africans central to the company's work on the continent and even beyond. Telling this history, I reveal much about how The Coca-Cola Company works. At the same time, and perhaps more importantly, I bring a new lens to modern African history.

INTRODUCTION

Chapter 1 traces the arrival of Coke in South Africa before the advent of the apartheid state, explaining how the company's method of doing business in that tumultuous climate helped create a blueprint for it to use elsewhere on the continent. Chapter 2 begins with Coca-Cola's arrival in Morocco and Egypt to set the stage for the company's continent-wide expansion, describing the multiple logistical difficulties that it faced along the way. Chapter 3 maps several mid-century advertisement campaigns that served to enmesh the Coke business in Africa and co-brand Africa at the same time. In Chapter 4, I examine instances where Coca-Cola protected its license to operate—including how it maneuvered the Arab boycott and centered itself in the Egypt–Israel peace deal—by creating mutually beneficial agreements, particularly important as Africans began to win their independence. Chapter 5 unearths the hidden role Coca-Cola played in helping end apartheid in South Africa, providing another rare glimpse into the company's political work and setting the stage for its involvement in fully post-colonial Africa. Chapter 6 continues to move in time by taking up three Coke endeavors meant to woo the hearts and minds of Africans at the dawn of the new millennium, those around sport, marketing, and music. Finally, Chapter 7 explores Coca-Cola's twenty-first-century sustainability efforts, highlighting those around water, women, and energy. The book's Conclusion weighs the balance of this history against the two biggest threats facing this company—and, arguably, the world—today: those relating to the human body and the environment.

Taken together, the book telescopes from one location to another across the continent. While rooted in company-produced documents and interviews, it strives to capture the voices of people who altered the company from below, suggesting that ordinary Africans have had as much a hand in bending the will of Coca-Cola as the converse. In these pages, I pay attention to the racial makeup of the Coke business at any given time and place, an important, if complicated barometer of localness. I purposely efface the Saharan divide here as well, reclaiming North Africa's history alongside that of sub-Saharan Africa. South Africa and, in particular, the fight to end apartheid, feature prominently here, since South Africa features prominently in the Coke business, and the end of apartheid is central to how we reckon with this era. Nowhere can I claim exhaustive coverage; this book is necessarily a compression of vast places and rich stories. And, everywhere, this history is colored by my perspective: that of a white, South African-born historian, who was raised by parents whose own childhoods in Durban, South Africa, and Bulawayo, Zimbabwe, were full of Coca-Cola, and whose fascination with Coke in Africa dates to childhood trips to the continent. In the end, if I have succeeded, the book will demonstrate that the biography of Coke in Africa impacts what we know about The Coca-Cola Company and Africa at once.

***

In the middle of the twentieth century, Coca-Cola executives loved to tell this tale: Two tourists, setting off to drive across the Sahara Desert, asked their guide, 'When do we run out of civilization,' clarifying, 'When will we reach the point where there's no more Coca-Cola?' to which the guide cried, 'Never!'[57] A few years earlier, Coca-Cola's internal organ reprinted a contrasting story, then hitting news syndicates, to make the point in reverse. When the assistant press counselor of the Egyptian Embassy, one Samir Souki, brought his personal cook to Washington, DC, his chef was surprised to find similarities between Egypt and America. '[W]hen Mr. Souki came home one night carrying a carton of "Coca-Cola" the Egyptian woman's face registered complete amazement and her eyes gleamed,' the story went. '"Do you mean," [the cook] asked, in apparent disbelief, "Do you mean they have 'Coca-Cola' here, too?"[58]

This book is written against the worldview that emerges from these anecdotes, where a sugary American soda is the harbinger of progress and Africa is a blank slate. Still, they remind me of when I was in Egypt in 2016. When I asked if Uber might be a good way to get back to my hotel, I received an incredulous laugh from my guide. 'You have Uber in America, too?' he chuckled. Putting aside what makes these stories problematic, there is a naiveté here that strikes me as a fine beginning for this book, since it points to something universal in the human experience. Ultimately, we all desire to see ourselves at the center of our worlds and to imagine that which we have to be unique. This history, I hope, demonstrates the opposite.

1

ALL THAT SPARKLES

HOW COCA-COLA ESTABLISHED A FOOTHOLD IN SOUTH AFRICA

In 1953, the Coca-Cola Bottling Company of Johannesburg released a new advertisement. 'When you're tired and a little weary,' it implored, 'enjoy a delicious ice cold Coca-Cola. You'll feel fresher, more relaxed. Yes, sparkling,' since, it claimed, 'Coca-Cola—so pure and wholesome—adds sparkle to life.'[1] By the early 1950s—the dawning days of the apartheid regime—Coca-Cola was offering effervescence throughout the troubled nation of South Africa. Why the company had come to the bottom of the African continent to do so is less certain than how it did. Building upon existing sparkling mineral water operations—themselves rooted in subterranean mineral extractions of the nineteenth century—Coca-Cola had woven itself into South African life, thus securing its first foothold on the African continent.

The Coca-Cola Company's official narrative puts its South African arrival at 1928. In fact, there is evidence that the drink made a brief appearance there nearly two decades earlier, in 1909, only twenty-three years after it was created in America.[2] Coca-

21

Cola lore also suggests that everywhere the drink went, it was speedily embraced. In reality, nothing about the introduction to South Africa of what would become the world's most iconic sparkling drink was easy. It would take false starts and floundering before the company was able to secure its business there. Along the way, Coca-Cola would have to work closely with existing and new bottlers, who would have to come up with ingenious tactics to make the sale of this bottled soda profitable. Full entrenchment in the country could not be achieved solely from afar. The company would also have to set up local operations under the auspices of a subsidiary, the Coca-Cola Export Corporation. Crafting its business in South Africa, Coca-Cola would, in turn, create a blueprint for use elsewhere on the continent. This chapter tells this story.

Sparkling Water in South Africa

While Africans, like people the world over, were drawn to naturally sparkling mineral waters, the first impetus to recreate such waters on the continent arrived with imperialists. Information about carbonated water—alternately called mineral, sparkling, aerated, soda, club, or table water—moved with Europeans as they came into contact with water unsuitable for their consumption across Africa. Once dissolved in carbonated water to make tonic, quinine—which naturally works as an anti-malarial, and which was once believed to cure such disparate ailments as scurvy and fever—was one reason for this spread.[3] Another was the emergent belief that the mere process of aerating water rendered it safe for consumption.[4] Just as carbonated water was gaining traction in the United States and Europe, so too did it spread through Africa until it began to take root, first at the Cape.

In 1820, the Schweppes company began shipping to the South African Cape from Switzerland.[5] By mid-century, a string of local manufacturers emerged, including one run by Thomas Mulvihal, an enterprising Irish immigrant who has until now escaped inclusion in the story of how Coca-Cola got to Africa, but whose family played a role, as will later become apparent.[6] With his two sons, Tommy (Thomas Jr.) and James, Mulvihal operated various water enterprises with related names throughout the second half of the nineteenth century. As hoteliers and water manufacturers, the Mulvihals capitalized on Cape Town's growth. Mulvihal's sons later expanded their beverage operations, both at the Cape and further afield in South Africa, as the demand for aerated water accompanied mineral discoveries in the country's interior.[7]

Sparkling water production spread northward with the discovery of diamonds in Kimberley and then gold around Johannesburg on the Witwatersrand, or Rand.[8] Right from the start in Johannesburg, water was a weak point. When the city emerged out of a makeshift mining camp, the fact that there is neither a river nor an ocean nearby was felt acutely. A burgeoning mining industry required significant amounts of water, as did a growing populace. In 1887, the first water concession was awarded, followed by a steady stream of water syndicates jostling for power. These made use of springs and river water, which had to be transported long distances. When an 1890 drought set off a number of water-related crises, the local Transvaal (ZAR) government set up a water commission, whose board traveled to Egypt and Europe and studied the Mississippi River Basin for guidance on how better to make use of limited and distant resources.[9] Without ready access to water, proper sanitation was challenging. The early years on the Rand were rife with outbreaks of disease; government and civic interest in cleanliness intensified. By 1896, the ZAR Sanitary Commission was keeping track of the numbers of workers engaged in finding and storing well and river water, in addition to the more than two dozen men who were making effervescent water.[10] There is no doubt that their product was in demand in Johannesburg's early days. The high expense for still, potable water meant that many preferred to use bottled soda water, even for cooking.[11] The Second South African War of 1899–1902 further increased demand for mineral water, particularly among the military.[12]

To meet growing demand for their product, Cape-based mineral water manufacturers, like the Mulvihals, began shipping their product north, just as a host of small soda water factories sprang up around the Rand as part of the secondary industry that emerged alongside industrialization. Some grew alongside pharmacies or butchers. Most were run by European immigrants. In 1898, two such men, Goldberg and Zeffert, launched an aerated mineral factory that operated in Johannesburg as part of the Niagara (sometimes Niagra) Mineral Water Works and that will later factor into our story significantly.[13] By 1903, Goldberg and Zeffert's Niagra was advertising daily deliveries to town and suburbs, alongside competitors Castle Mineral Water Works, Central Mineral Water Works, and the Van Riebeek Natural Mineral Water Company, which, unlike the others, bottled naturally occurring carbonated water from the Tygerberg Springs.[14] By the turn of the century, South Africa was awash with water manufacturers.[15]

The water industry was not an easy one anywhere in South Africa in the years surrounding the turn of the century, giving early bottlers a taste of the kinds of problems endemic to the bottled beverage industry.[16] Questions around brand integrity and copyright control plagued water manufacturers such that many went out of business.[17] Those that endured struggled to keep people from filling their empty bottles with pollutants, like petrol, and to get them to return empties for refilling. Mostly, water manufacturers fought to make sure that their own products remained in their own bottles.[18] By the time word of a product called Coca-Cola reached South African shores, there was a bustling bottled soda water business, but it was one working hard to stay solvent.

A Brief False Start

When exactly did Coca-Cola arrive in Africa? The answer is not so simple. By Coca-Cola's accounting, the company awarded Goldberg and Zeffert of Niagra the first bottling concession in the late 1920s or early 1930s. Sometime before then, perhaps in 1925, the imprecise story goes, a shipment of ten gallons of Coca-Cola fountain syrup found its way to one Waldorf Café, on St. George Street, in Cape Town, a claim for which I have yet to find any evidence.[19] Yet, in the summer of 1909, roughly two decades before Goldberg and Zeffert were appointed by Coca-Cola to bottle its drink in Johannesburg, a series of newspaper advertisements ran in the *Cape Times* that complicate this story. The ads were produced by the Mulvihals—the water proprietors from the Cape who had expanded their reach across the country— to promote the various sparkling beverages, beyond water, that they had come to sell, drinks like the New Zealand creation Zolakone, then popular in Australia,[20] and something called Nectrona, a self-described 'drink of the gods.' Their ads also enticed readers during 'this warm weather for cool drinks' to try something new, 'Mulvihal's Coca-Cola,' which they described as 'Refreshing and Stimulating.'[21] Could this have been a cheater brand? Maybe. Those certainly emerged in these years in America. But the early date makes it unlikely. It is more plausible that this advert refers to the ten gallons of Coke fountain syrup that the company claims was shipped to the Cape at some previously unspecified date. If that is the case, then this 1909 advertisement is, in fact, the earliest evidence of Coca-Cola for sale on the African continent.

What supports this theory? From 1901, the same year that the notion of a soda fountain—that quintessential American creation—started showing up in the South Africa press,[22] Tommy Mulvihal took ownership of the St. George Hotel in Cape Town.[23] By then, the St. George Hotel had achieved some degree of fame for its long bar facing St. George Street, which eventually came to include—as a kind of novelty—a separate entrance to a café, supposedly for women who did not want to pass through the bar on the way to the drawing room. Mulvihal ran this hotel alongside his family's sparkling beverage enterprises until his financial ruin, at the hands of horse betting, in 1910, mere months after the last Coca-Cola advert ran.[24]

So, what might we suppose from this history of the Mulvihals and their advertisements for Coca-Cola? Perhaps the Mulvihals were tapped into global trends in the emergent soda industry and had gotten wind of Coca-Cola. Perhaps they imported it in fountain syrup form. Maybe it was just ten gallons, as Coke lore suggests. Maybe it was more. And perhaps they offered it for sale, both via their newspaper ads and also maybe in their hotel, on St. George Street, adjacent to the Waldorf Café, on the very street, if not the very establishment, where Coca-Cola says it first appeared. Maybe they set up a nascent soda fountain through their separate entrance, which their fast-approaching insolvency thwarted. Maybe there was yet no appetite for the drink. Or maybe there was, but there was no way to meet demand. What is sure, in any event, is that despite the Mulvihals' well-established water distribution networks across South Africa, the drink was not to take off, either on St. George Street or elsewhere in the country. The entire, short-lived Cape Town adventure would be little more than a false start for the beverage, though it does tell us something about the entwined growth of global knowledge about and interest in sparkling beverages in the earliest days of the twentieth century. It also gives us insight into what would later become apparent. The strength of this beverage aside, as a product, Coca-Cola's penetration into Africa, begun at its bottommost tip, was never a foregone conclusion.

A Second Attempt

How and why The Coca-Cola Company set its sights on South Africa in the 1920s is impossible to say. In 1920, South Africa was a ten-year-old country whose future remained uncertain. Union and the subsequent 1913 Land Act, which served to dispossess the Black majority, caused irreparable damage to most South Africans. Throughout the 1920s, Black South Africans continued to agitate for paths to justice by way of legal means; the colorblind Cape Franchise remained law in that province and would continue to provide a beacon of hope for Black activists who had watched Britain renege on its promises as it exited its colonial hold. The 1920s saw whites, who until then considered themselves to be part of different races—English and Afrikaners—begin to heal the wounds of the brutal Second South African War by forging a singular identity of whiteness through a deliberate process known as South Africanism. The country was still largely agrarian, with the mines continuing to pull migrants from throughout the subcontinent and beyond; cities were already segregated, though the darkest legislation compelling separation lay in the future, beyond the rise of the apartheid state in 1948. In the 1920s, there was no major tourism industry in South Africa, and retail remained small-scale. But that was starting to change by the end of the decade. In 1927, Kruger National Park opened. A few years later saw the founding of the giant retailer OK Bazaars. Cars were sparse in the 1920s; hence, few petrol stations existed. Travel to the country took two weeks by boat from Europe; it would not be until the 1930s that travel by air was possible. Railways did run across the nation, and beyond.[25] Yet, even with connections, South Africa was already beginning to see itself as separate, and somehow apart from, the continent it called home.

In 1900, The Coca-Cola Company began shipping its syrup outside the contiguous United States, first to Canada. Jamaica and Germany followed next, in 1901. By 1902, Hawaii was added, followed by Bermuda, Mexico, Puerto Rico, and, in 1904, the Philippines. In 1915, the famed hobble skirt bottle was invented and, though it would not be patented until the 1960s in the United States, it fast became a guard against imitators as the beverage moved beyond its country of origin. When, in 1926, the Foreign Department of The Coca-Cola Company was established, there were only nine bottlers of the product outside the United States and Canada. At that time, the company decided to send concentrate, not syrup (which is made from the concentrate and sugar) to overseas bottlers, setting the stage for the use of local forms of sugar and establishing an embryonic system of franchise bottlers. In 1930, the Coca-Cola Export Corporation, a wholly owned subsidiary of the parent company, eclipsed the Foreign Department and took charge of all expansion beyond the United States and Canada.[26] Again, why the Foreign Department and then Export Corporation trained their sights on South Africa during the interwar years is hard to say. But, that is what happened.

Sometime around 1928, Goldberg and Zeffert of Niagra, by then well-established South African bottlers of mineral water, were appointed by Coca-Cola's Foreign Department to bottle its product. The company sent concentrate from Atlanta. Without existing secondary industry to meet the company's needs, imported bottles and crates were required. Six-and-a-half-ounce green hobble skirt bottles arrived from Owens, Illinois; yellow crates of pine wood were imported from Canada.[27] Over the next two years, Goldberg and Zeffert published effusive Coca-Cola advertisements in the *Rand Daily Mail*. A 21 November 1928 advert mimicked a commentator introducing a new fighter to the ring. 'And now—a new drink for South Africa,' it opened. 'After achieving an amazing success in America and Europe,' the ad boasted, 'Coca-Cola, the new soft drink, has arrived in South Africa.'[28] Advertisers made much of the fact that the drink was American. 'Try this great drink from America,' readers were implored a week later. 'In America, a land of long, hot summers, the favourite drink is Coca-Cola. People drink it to refresh themselves.' Explaining that the beverage was equally popular in Canada 'where the weather is colder,' the advert argued that with over eight million sales a day, this was a drink worth trying in any weather.[29] Advertisements also asserted that Coca-Cola had taken off in Europe; the reality is that the drink was only just beginning to gain access to European markets. '"You've heard of it?' another from 1929 asked, 'Well, just try a glass... It's the favourite soft drink in America and has "taken on" in Europe. Just the right thing for this country, too.'[30] 'Its subtly blended flavor has made it the most popular soft drink in America,' readers were told. 'On the Continent there is a large and growing demand for it. In South Africa it is voted "Absolutely toppin."'[31] Marketers also underscored the drink's unique flavor, which, they were told, 'supersedes the old drink' and which 'satisfies thirst as nothing else can.' 'Sole South African distributors, Goldberg & Zeffert, Ltd.'[32] assured readers of the product's quality, too. Coca-Cola is sold 'in sterilized bottles, with the goodness and purity sealed in for you,'[33] they guaranteed, noting that, 'Even the Coca-Cola bottle is distinct.'[34] They called the drink 'delicious,' 'stimulating,' 'cooling,' 'enticing,' and, yes, 'sparkling.'[35] 'Have a bottle to-day,' they suggested: 'You, too, will like it.'[36]

Yet, for all their flurry of advertisements from 1928 to 1929, global economics were not in their favor. In 1929, the United States stock market crashed, setting off the Great Depression, which would, before long, reach South Africa, too. Disillusioned,

Goldberg and Zeffert would lose faith in this product around the same time as the Coca-Cola Export Corporation would lose faith in this duo to adequately promote Coca-Cola. It appeared that it would take more to get this drink off the ground in Africa than just shipping concentrate to established bottlers. It was time for American Coca-Cola men to step in.

Despite the havoc wrought by the Great Depression and a 1933 South African drought, not to mention the ominous signs of rising German and South African authoritarianism, by the end of the 1930s, the climate for white-owned businesses in South Africa was looking up. That year, The Coca-Cola Company transferred its American sales manager for Belgium, Howard Patterson, to South Africa.[37] When Patterson arrived in 1938, he found signs of a recovering economy. Manufacturing was booming, particularly in the major cities of Johannesburg, Durban, Cape Town, Pretoria, and Port Elizabeth, as industrialization helped diversify an economy that up until then was dually dependent on farming and mining. While the noose tightened around Black South Africans, white South Africans' quality of life was improving. Bioscope theaters were fast spreading, while a tourism industry took hold amidst rising white consumer spending.[38] Patterson liked what he saw. Thus, when Goldberg and Zeffert relinquished their Coca-Cola concession in 1938, Patterson took control on behalf of the company, rather than lease it to another franchisee, creating what would later come to be known as a Company Owned Bottling Operation.[39] Patterson became the first Managing Director of Coca-Cola (Pty) Ltd., the first operation dedicated solely to Coca-Cola production on the continent.[40]

In June 1938, when Patterson took over the bottles and syrup from Goldberg and Zeffert, he immediately started bottling the product using the premises of the existing Benoni Mineral Water Works.[41] A production engineer from England was brought in to supervise operations. Each day, the engineer would travel to Benoni from the company offices in Johannesburg's central business district to prepare syrup from two units of concentrate. Given that they were operating in borrowed facilities, production would occur during the night shift only. Every night, the bottles were then transported to a company warehouse in Johannesburg, where a young salesman by the name of Les Forbes would load the route truck he was to drive.[42] After the war interrupted his employment with Coca-Cola, Forbes would return, eventually working his way up to becoming Managing Director of Peninsula Beverages, one of the largest independent bottlers of Coca-Cola in Africa, still in existence.

The earliest days of the company's presence were fraught, as Forbes would recount for his family. According to his son-in-law and longtime Coca-Cola bottler Dave Lewis, Forbes often spoke about going door to door selling Coca-Cola by the 200 ml bottle in these early years, trying desperately to convince a skeptical white public that a brown sparkling liquid was safe for consumption.[43] Likewise, E Neville Isdell—future CEO of The Coca-Cola Company who cut his teeth in South Africa and Zambia, and who plays an important role in future chapters—recalled the early struggle to get the product off the ground. 'When they launched Coca-Cola, it was not something that was popular right at the outset,' he recounted. 'So, what they used to do was they would sell a case of mixed drinks and then slip two Coke bottles in the case, so they could get it into the store. It wasn't an easy sell at the start.... It was a slog.'[44]

Despite challenges, Patterson spearheaded Coca-Cola production. He started purchasing glass bottles locally from the newly created Pretoria Glass Works, which produced a hobble skirt six-and-a-half-ounce bottle, that, while not green, still met the company's standards.[45] He opened company-owned bottling plants in Johannesburg and Durban, followed by a third in Pretoria. The Johannesburg plant started operations first, in 1939, producing 500 cases a day, with one white and five Black employees. Patterson took over distributing Coca-Cola himself in Pietermaritzburg.[46] Then, Patterson started to award franchises, turning first to existing mineral water manufacturers, no doubt because they already had the premises and wherewithal to meet the company's needs. Between 1939 and 1951, Patterson awarded franchises to the Witbank Mineral Water Company, Worcester Minerals, Ryley's Mineral Water Factory, precursors to what would become Suncrush, and more. The fraternity of early franchisees was interwoven, with many connected in some way to the pioneers of effervescent water.[47]

There would come to be other franchisees, of course, with little to no connection to the early water industry. The third franchise ever awarded went to Peninsula Beverages—the one that Les Forbes would later come to head—in Cape Town.[48] In 1948, Tom Cook, a World War II fitter in charge of munitions, had a chance encounter that likewise led to him getting a franchise for Nigel, then but a small, sleepy, industrial town. Later, Tom, along with his sons, Richard and Alan, would be influential to this story as the creators of the line of drinks called Sparletta, a rival brand that would paradoxically come to sustain a flagging Coca-Cola through difficult times.[49] But that lay in the future.

Of more immediate importance was a franchise awarded by Patterson to a man who not only had no roots in the South African mineral water industry, but who was also not even South African. William Donald Hyde, the aptly-named leather tanner from the equally well-named town of Gloversville, New York, had at that stage maintained an office in South Africa for many years, from which he purchased sheepskins for his glove manufacturing business.[50] In the late 1930s, Hyde began to expand his interest in South Africa, importing such well-known American items as

Campbell's Soups and Scott tissue. He began to wonder if Coca-Cola would do well there as well. Hyde contacted the Canadian office of Coca-Cola, which in turn connected him with Patterson. At the time, Hyde was unaware that Patterson was already in South Africa establishing the Coca-Cola business there. Hyde was awarded a franchise for Port Elizabeth, Bloemfontein, and Brakpan, which he assembled under a new company, the South African Bottling Company (Pty) Ltd., in 1940. He appointed his two sons to run his businesses; Gordon Byron Hyde ran his importing business while William Donald Hyde Jr. ran the Coca-Cola side of operations. Bottling began in 1940 on an old Dixie unit that could produce seventy-five cases an hour. When The Coca-Cola Company no longer wanted Patterson involved in distribution, it broke up his franchise control over Pietermaritzburg. Hyde then stepped in and, along with a young employee named Philipp Rowland Gutsche, who had joined his South African Bottling Company in 1940 as a driver, purchased this enterprise. Gutsche would buy out Hyde in 1960 and, eventually, set up the South African Bottling Company (Sabco) that, under his son, Phillip H Gutsche Jr., would become the single largest bottler on the African continent, which it remains to this day. But, again, that lay in the future.[51] Before any of that could happen, World War II intruded.

World War II was a pivotal moment for Coca-Cola, both in South Africa and globally, for it was during these years that the company exploded on the world stage. During the war, Coca-Cola moved rapidly into markets in Europe and beyond, expanding swiftly. This obtained in South Africa, too, as many franchises were awarded in these years. With the spread of franchises came the spread of product. Tom Cook—future owner of the Nigel franchise—would later recall that enlisted army men were regularly treated to Coca-Cola during their training in South Africa.[52] Likewise, bottling employee Lynn Coggin remembered that he was one of many children who tasted his first Coke in wartime South Africa.[53] Along with its spread, Coca-Cola came to take on a meaning beyond simply that of a beverage during the war. From World War II onward we see the symbiosis of Coca-Cola and America, both the country and the concept, in the world's imagination.

World War II deprivations—felt throughout much of the world—handicapped the fledgling bottling industry in South Africa, too. The War Measures Act sought to conserve resources. Engine batteries and electric light bulbs had to be turned in to the state for replacement. All newspapers were collected at special depots. Metal crown caps were in short supply, leading bottlers to collect and refurbish old ones. Petrol was rationed; baking white bread was forbidden; meat was in short supply. Glass—for bottles—was in such demand that bottlers treated their existing bottles with kid gloves. Likewise, it became illegal to destroy old car tires, making route drivers extra cautious. Lack of supplies meant that whatever advertising was produced was simple and small, all in the days before radio adverts—much less television ones—had arrived in South Africa. Perhaps the biggest problem of all for South African bottlers, much like that faced by their American counterparts, had to do with procuring adequate sugar. In those days, sugar was imported from Cuba. Wartime naval operations meant that shipments were sporadic and subject to enemy fire. When they did arrive, the sugar shipments came in linen, rather than hessian, bags, which, at least, was fortuitous. To save funds, the bags were used to make worker overalls. As another workaround, bottlers would trade extra Coca-Cola product with customers who happened to have extra bags of sugar.[54]

Thus, for the early South African Coca-Cola men—and, yes, they were all men in these years—World War II figures significantly in their origin stories, which were notably marked by struggle and, as they tell it, a need for ingenuity born of the times. Donald Hyde Jr., for instance, used his clout to help the industry survive wartime travails. Rumor has it that Hyde used his connections to convince ship captains to transport Coca-Cola concentrate in their personal cabins on passenger, rather than merchant, ships, thus increasing the odds of goods escaping enemy torpedo.[55] Phillip Gutsche Sr., then a low-level driver doing what he thought was temporary work in a fledgling business, spent the war years tasked with 'opening up' the market around the small town of Brakpan.[56] Nothing was simple about this job. In fact, the original machinery meant for Brakpan never arrived. It was sunk off the African coast by, presumably, enemy ships, prompting a complete rethinking of his haphazard enterprise, run in those days out of a garage.[57] Only when the war ended was Gutsche able to import a small Dixie production line in 1948 that filled one bottle at a time, slowly launching his business.[58]

While rationing ended in 1948, two other government initiatives presented potentially insurmountable obstacles to Coca-Cola's growth in South Africa. The first had to do with travel by road. In those days, the Motor Carrier Transportation Act stipulated that no product could be delivered beyond a certain distance by motor vehicle. This was, ostensibly, to protect the railroads. To get around this, bottlers had to establish depots between locations, incurring additional expense. These depots had to be bona fide places of business, rather than just fronts. The emergent apartheid state, ushered into power in 1948, watched carefully to see that bottlers were complying with this regulation. This hawkish attention to transport regulations also partially explains the granting of so many franchises in these years.[59] The second—and arguably far more damaging—government intervention was the imposition in the post-war years of an excise tax on soda, meant to generate revenue for empty government coffers. Imposed in 1952, this tax nearly crippled the industry. To survive it, Coca-Cola bottlers would have to unite. They would also have to do something creative: invent and then promote a product line other than Coca-Cola to sustain their industry.

Sparletta, the Line that Helped Save Coca-Cola

'In the late 1940s and 50s,' Dave Lewis recalled, 'the Coke business did not make money, at all. No, dead serious. My father in law, [Les Forbes, told me that] the only way they could survive was to introduce a fighting brand... called Sparletta.'[60] While Coca-Cola spread throughout South Africa from the late 1930s onward, the business was not an easy one. Tom Cook, the bomb fitter turned bottler, recalled in a 1983 letter that during his early bottling years he was advised by Coca-Cola that his Nigel—like other bottling franchises of the day—would need to sell 50,000 cases of product a year to show a profit. This was easier said than done and, after three years of sustained losses, the Cook family was down more than half on its initial investment, a situation that was not unique to them.[61] The years 1948 to 1950 were difficult for soft drink makers in South Africa. At the time, there were no fewer than 428 different manufacturers of flavored sparkling beverages, with fourteen on the Rand alone. This was perhaps an outcome of the Motor Carrier Transportation Act. Or maybe it stems from the early history of prolific sparkling water manufacturing. Or maybe it just reflects the global explosion of flavored soda in these years. In any event, the field was a crowded one. And that was not the only problem Coca-Cola bottlers, in particular, faced. In those days, Coca-Cola produced but one SKU, a 200 ml bottle. At the time, sugar and crown (or cap) supplies were closely controlled by the government, while the price of Coca-Cola was fixed at three pennies a bottle and governed by a Coca-Cola policy that 1/3 of the retail price went to Coca-Cola, 1/3 went to the bottler, and 1/3 went to the retail outlet.[62] The result was that bottlers were struggling to turn a profit. At a 1951 Coca-Cola bottlers meeting, the South African Coca-Cola bottlers signed and sent a petition to Atlanta, asking for help. J Paul Austin, then head of Export, was sent out, but the best he could do was cut down on the cost of advertising for the next few years; according to New York, where Export was based, the price of concentrate was not negotiable.[63] Without an ability to negotiate down either the price of concentrate or the price of the 200 ml Coke, both of which were deliberately stable across the globe, the bottlers' position seemed untenable.

Faced with this situation, Cook's plant in Nigel sought to expand its market share in 1950 by introducing, with Coca-Cola's permission, a line of what were known as bar drinks, or generic sodas, called 'National Bar.' These were produced in 8 oz bottles, meant to be easily stacked in the trucks of the day. When the bottle size proved to be problematic—in a world where most drinks were 6 oz—and when bar drinks proved less profitable than initially imagined, Nigel quickly moved on to what was called the rainbow flavor market. Such rainbow drinks were, literally, named after the colors of the rainbow. So, there was a red and a green, and so on. 'This move proved highly successful,' Cook later wrote, 'and other Bottlers of Coca-Cola began to show great interest in the Nigel product.'[64] By controlling their own concentrate, which cost much less than that of Coca-Cola, Nigel was able to increase its profit margin. At the June 1951 bottlers' meeting in Johannesburg, seven other small Coca-Cola bottlers expressed interest in the Rainbow line. A committee was formed that included Phil Gutsche Sr., Les Forbes, and Tom Cook, who handled the organization. An agreement was reached. They would all use Nigel's National Bar bottle and recipes, which combined saccharine and glucose to supplement sugar, which was still rationed. The new line would be produced under a newly invented name, Sparletta, with 'spa' meaning water. Sparkling rainbow water. Over the course of 1951, the dire bottling situation spurred the committee to work swiftly. In letters throughout the year the trio agreed to standardize concentrate units, bottles, and labels, and to create uniform crates with room for individual bottlers' names. Later, they would convince the Board of Health to allow a single address for all Sparletta products, regardless of where in the country they were bottled.

Immediate problems abounded: glass was in short supply and sugar remained rationed. Still, they persisted, sending out their first letter on Sparletta letterhead in January 1952. 'About this time,' Cook recalled, another problem arose. The bottlers had attracted the ire of Coca-Cola. 'I was summonsed to appear before Mr. J H Smit and Mr. Harold Patterson of the Coca-Cola Export Corporation who accused me of creating an independent Franchise Company amongst their Bottlers,' he reminisced. Though the 'argument became very heated,' Cook stood his ground, insisting that it 'had been for the benefit of the Bottlers who were in sore need of this help.' As a result of this encounter, Cook put forward a resolution at the first annual Sparletta meeting that stated that even if a bottler lost the right to bottle Coca-Cola, he could retain the right to bottle Sparletta.[65]

Then, in 1952, the government introduced the mineral water excise tax of one shilling per case for all soda manufacturers (mentioned above) that could have brought the industry down. This, coupled with the fact that sparkling mineral water prices had just gone up, sent some smaller bottlers out of business. The situation was bleak. By the second annual Sparletta conference, twenty-two bottlers had joined Sparletta, hoping that this b-brand line would help save their businesses. Then, in July 1954, the Sparletta board met with Coca-Cola Export men Smit and Pasea. The board asked Coca-Cola Export if it would take over manufacturing and selling Sparletta in the main commercial centers of the country, to broaden its reach and, presumably, appease Coke. Coca-Cola had no interest in this, preferring at that stage to stick to its own products. In turn, Sparletta asked if it might do so. According to Cook's recollection, to this Export replied by producing a letter from New York saying that while they could not stop Sparletta from expanding thus, the company would consider this move to be nothing short of 'immoral,' arguably because it skirted a conflict of interest line.[66] Sparletta appeared undeterred, expanding its advertising to radio and standardizing its products. By its fourth annual board meeting, in June 1955, the company now included thirty-five bottlers, with others clamoring to get on board. By then, rumors started to spread amongst bottlers that Coca-Cola Export was worried about Sparletta's growth and that, as a result, the company was considering launching a rival line. Gutsche, then president of the Sparletta board, reached out to Austin for clarity. Austin assured the South African bottlers that was not Coca-Cola's intention, though the company was planning to roll out a would-be competitor named Fanta, which Sparletta bottlers could choose whether or not to bottle. Eventually, an agreement was reached between Coca-Cola Export and Sparletta. Sparletta agreed to confine itself to South Africa, Southern and Northern Rhodesia (now Zimbabwe and Zambia), Swaziland (now Eswatini), Lesotho, and Botswana. In turn, beginning in 1966, it ceded world rights to Sparletta to Coca-Cola for use elsewhere. Affirming this agreement in 1966, Austin penned a letter that included a little-known piece of trivia. That year, Austin wrote, the company planned to use the 'Trademark "Sparletta" ... on a low-calorie carbonated citrus base drink ... presently being marketed in the United States under the name "Fresca."'[67]

Sparletta grew from strength to strength. In 1954, the excise tax was lifted, opening up an era of expansion.[68] Within four years, the long-existing and powerful Suncrush bottling company joined Sparletta, further strengthening it.[69] Sparletta began to promote its brands individually, rather than as a rainbow-colored range. Ads began appearing for Sparberry Red or Pine Nut (red and yellow, respectively). Yet, as it matured, tensions between it and Coca-Cola lingered, especially as Sparletta's market share grew, at times up to and even exceeding 20% of the carbonated beverage market in South Africa. At the global Coca-Cola bottler convention in 1983, The Coca-Cola Company began to look askance again at Sparletta. That year, Alex Reid of Amalgamated Beverage Industries, a Coca-Cola-owned bottler, demonstrated that the Independent Bottlers (those not owned by corporate Coke) reaped hirer profits than those owned by Coca-Cola, precisely because of Sparletta. In response, Don Keough, then Chief Operating Officer of The Coca-Cola Company, based in Atlanta, declared that Sparletta should not, under any circumstances, exceed 30% of total bottler volume. 'I know the history of Sparletta,' Keough reportedly said. 'Sparletta is a companion to Coca-Cola and the products of the Coca-Cola Company, not an adversary.' Still, he cautioned, 'Don't ever forget who you are and what you are. You are a member of the most exclusive club in the world. You are Coca-Cola,' before adding the warning: 'When I am dead and gone and you are dead and gone, there will still be Coca-Cola.'[70] This temporary détente aside, Coca-Cola was not willing to let Sparletta exist independently for long, especially not when some of its drinks, like Iron Brew, rivaled Coca-Cola sales. In 1994, The Coca-Cola Company all but forced Sparletta to sell its master franchise to the company, bringing this chapter of internal tension to a close.[71] While Sparletta products like Green Cream Soda and Stony Ginger Beer are still available in South Africa (and even further afield), they are now wholly owned and bottled by Coca-Cola.

Looking back on the charges that he was a Sparletta bottler first and Coca-Cola bottler second, Tom Cook recalled the pragmatism—rooted in a belief in Coca-Cola—that had compelled him and his compatriots to create Sparletta in the first place. 'It is a recognized fact,' he penned in 1983:

> that by bottling Sparletta the Coca-Cola Bottlers in South Africa have been able to suppress all opposition and allowed Coca-Cola in South Africa to achieve a higher share of market than in any other Country in the World today. Further, due to Sparletta's policy of passing the maximum profits to Bottlers, and provided a Bottler maintains Sparletta sales at one third of his overall volume, he would receive a profit equal to that on the two third volume of his Coca-Cola products. Our Bottlers, having this double profit, are in a strong position to finance the heavy costs of building new factories and purchasing bottles and cases, trucks, machines, etc., to meet our rapidly expanding market.[72]

By bottling Sparletta at a high rate of return, bottlers increased their profits, thus enabling them to subsidize their production of Coca-Cola. Sparletta, in other words, was the very boost that Coca-Cola bottlers needed to start making their businesses profitable, setting the stage for South Africa to grow into, as it would, one of the top ten Coca-Cola markets in the world. This colorful, carbonated soda range, fully born in and of Africa, did much to assure Coca-Cola's start at the bottom of the African continent. Yet, it could not do everything. Alongside the growth of Sparletta, corporate Coca-Cola was itself working to secure the business's entrenchment in southern Africa. Importantly, the method it established would do more than just work in South Africa; it would become a model for expansion elsewhere on the continent.

Coca-Cola in South Africa in Action

After World War II, while Coca-Cola franchises were being doled out, now under the auspices of J H Smit, who replaced Patterson upon his return to the United States, the company itself moved to secure its presence in South Africa.[73] In 1952, the Coca-Cola Export Corporation registered a branch in South Africa, taking over the operations of Coca-Cola (Pty) Ltd. Two years later, it sent J Paul Austin to lead its operations on the ground. Austin was a Harvard-educated lawyer who had interrupted his employment with Coca-Cola's legal department to fight in World War II before rejoining the Export Corporation after the war. Austin would stay in South Africa for four years. During this time, he helped root the foundering business, while his experiences shaped his view of the possibility and limits of Coca-Cola in the world. After leaving South Africa, Austin became Vice President of the Coca-Cola Export Corporation in New York in 1959. Then, in 1962, he was appointed President of The Coca-Cola Company. The immediate post-World War II years in South Africa thus saw the full establishment of the Coca-Cola system in South Africa, which, in turn, impacted the company at large for years to come.

How did the Coca-Cola Export Corporation function, exactly? As already noted, Coca-Cola spread rapidly during World War II, such that by 1962 it was operating in 112 countries, all of which, save the United States and Canada, were steered by Export.[74] The goal was clear: produce a universal product of comparable standards through partnerships with local, independent bottlers or, where necessary, company-owned bottling plants. The secret to its budding success, as told in a 1962 article in an internal publication, *Coca-Cola South of the Sahara*, was extensive training. By that year, executives culled from the more than 6,500 overseas personnel—less than one per cent of whom were American— were already being brought to New York City from five continents to undergo training. Materials were assembled in no fewer than fourteen languages to teach trainees how to operate modern food-processing facilities, which required purifying water in the process. Operating through local bottlers, Coca-Cola relied upon secondary industries as well, such as those used for crowns, carbonic gas, advertising materials, coolers, and bottles; often these industries arose in response to Coca-Cola's needs. The two processes—supporting strong franchises and encouraging secondary industrial growth—were closely entwined and closely related to what Coca-Cola Export, under Austin, started to see as a healthy world economy.[75]

And how exactly did its franchise system work, on the ground? Coca-Cola chose its bottlers carefully and revoked franchise agreements where necessary. Those granted a franchise were required to invest in the machinery and infrastructure needed to meet the company's stringent global standards. They were required to meet the fiduciary and procedural demands of the company, as we saw with the mandated concentrate price, even if these presented obstacles to quick or easy growth. Franchisees were meant to service a predetermined territory. In each country, there would be what was called a master franchiser meant to handle advertising campaigns, which were often done in conjunction with the New York office, to ensure quality control. Master franchises were also supposed to control access to Coca-Cola concentrate.[76] From 1952 until divestment in the 1980s, this role was inhabited by the Coca-Cola Export Corporation in South Africa. While there was always some degree of tension between franchisees and corporate Coca-Cola, more often than not they understood themselves to be partners.

The entrenchment of Coca-Cola Export in South Africa demonstrated corporate Coca-Cola's faith in the country's potential, despite its struggles in the immediate postwar years. Export arrived just as Johannesburg opened a new, larger production plant, one based upon over five years of joint planning. The size of the plant was meant to reflect Johannesburg's 'status in the economy of the country' as well as the 'golden dream,' from which this mining camp grew. It also stood as a harbinger of a diversified healthy economy, according to S A Lombard, the Provincial Secretary to the Administrator of the Transvaal, who spoke at the plant's opening ceremony.[77] That the plant only grew in production capacity throughout the early 1950s as the largest in the southern hemisphere seemed to prove his point.[78] 'I appreciate all the more the privilege of performing this opening ceremony,' Lombard had concluded, 'because this concern is financed by South African capital for products of South African material.'[79] Lauding the local products and local capital, Lombard showed the degree to which Coca-Cola was coming to be seen as home-grown, something the company was quick to point out as happening around the world: 'In Europe, Africa, Asia, Latin America, and the far islands of the Pacific, as well as in the United States and Canada,' *Coca-Cola South of the Sahara* reported, 'the business of Coca-Cola is accepted everywhere as a local enterprise because the plants are locally-owned and operated.'[80] This was also the case in South Africa, even with the arrival and entrenchment of Coca-Cola Export to run the show. And, just like elsewhere, in South Africa, Coca-Cola came to make use of political connections and to integrate itself in local development in order to make its business work.

Coca-Cola's expansion in South Africa and elsewhere remained predicated on secondary industries, another tenet fast becoming central to its business model. Les Forbes, then managing director of Vaal Bottlers, described the men who peddled Coca-Cola on red tricycles in an article for *Coca-Cola Overseas*, the official mouthpiece of the Export Corporation, as but one example of the new employment opportunities the business created. He further recounted the fact that Coca-Cola had spurred significant infrastructure growth in Vanderbijl Park, crediting the Coca-Cola plant there with boosting the iron and steel industries, helping expand water, lights, sewage, and macadamized roads, as well as promoting the growth of retail outlets, in this town at least.[81] In 1949, Smit penned a similar piece, praising the growth of secondary industry in post-war Krugersdorp and thanking, in particular, the 'sympathetic' town council that provided access to 'water and lights at reasonable rates.'[82] In an iterative process, the local government enhanced utilities, just as businesses called for them. Coca-Cola helped spur on other sectors as well. By 1956, the timber business outside of Port Elizabeth was booming, in large part in response to Coca-Cola's needs. By that year, timber manufacturers were diverting water to use in plants to produce 'hundreds of thousands of "Coca-Cola" cases,' for use in South Africa, Kenya, and elsewhere.[83]

As Coca-Cola grew and, in turn, encouraged the growth of related industries, Export and independent bottlers worked to integrate their business into society in more subtle ways. Often, they welcomed consumers into their factories to see just how the product was made, thus furthering the company's reach. Likewise, dealers—those who sold the product—were encouraged to tour plants.[84] Plant managers often extended invitations like this one: 'To all interested a cordial invitation is extended by the management to visit the factory and get a close-up view of the conditions under which Coca-Cola is prepared and bottled.'[85] Coca-Cola also took its product to the people, regularly setting up sampling sessions, particularly among schoolchildren.[86]

At the same time, Coca-Cola Export and Coca-Cola bottlers also made sure to have the product present at all major festivals, such as the South Africa Rand Show of 1949. At this week-long agricultural show, nearly 450,000 people, mostly white South African farmers, were treated to images of tractors and sheep. They were also served Coca-Cola, and lots of it, as Ira Emery, then director of public relations for the company, recounted:

Realizing that here was a golden opportunity to demonstrate the delight of delicious and refreshing Coca-Cola, our South African organization went all-out in a special events promotion for the Rand Show. Ball park carriers, coolers, fleets of vans from the supply depot to the showground kept Coca-Cola moving to meet the constant public demand. It was all day and every day service. Queues were everywhere—especially at the Coca-Cola kiosks. In the showground bars, cases were stacked high to accommodate the onslaught of crowding customers. There never was a need for a 'sold out' sign. In sprawling Milner Park, the back veldt farmers—most of them making their annual trip to the golden city of Johannesburg from sheep and cattle stations—readily acquired a liking for the pause that refreshes with ice-cold Coca-Cola. So did their wives and their bonny children.[87]

Here as with other such festivals, Coca-Cola made its presence known, all the while introducing its product to potential customers, young and old. And, here, as elsewhere in the early days of apartheid, the company showed a willingness to work within the rising authoritarian, racist system. Coca-Cola established a visible presence at the Dingaan's Day Celebration of 1949. That year, 250,000 white South Africans, largely Afrikaners, gathered to see the unveiling of the new Voortrekker Monument outside Pretoria, commemorating Afrikaner victory over the Zulu, often considered to be the defining moment in Afrikaner history. Reporting from South Africa, Emery affirmed that 'Coca-Cola was there—and in force' with 'Coke stands everywhere,' noting that this 'was the greatest Coca-Cola promotion drive ever seen in South Africa.'[88] The cumulative effect of all its fervor meant that, from factory and secondary industry jobs to school sampling and public fairs, Coca-Cola was becoming enmeshed in South African life. This fusion paid off. By the time Austin was to leave his South African post in 1958, he was credited with turning what a company historian termed a 'dismal' market into one of Export's biggest success stories.[89]

For his part, J Paul Austin was to leave South Africa with an appreciation for what the business looks like on the ground in a fledgling industrial environment. Later, he would turn his attention to initiatives that seem, in part, to have been influenced by his time there. One was his enduring interest in nutrition, particularly as it obtains in the global south. As President of Coca-Cola, Austin spearheaded a project aimed at fighting world hunger. It included the development of three protein-rich drinks, called Saci, Samson, and Tai, for sale in Africa and South America, which, while planned, were never realized. Austin was also keenly devoted to clean water initiatives, well before that became en vogue in the business world.[90] Both nutrition and water fed into Austin's larger world view, itself a kind of mission, articulated by him often after his days in South Africa, about corporate responsibility in what he advocated as a free world market.

In 1951, Howard Patterson came back to 'the Golden City,' Johannesburg, after a five-year break. There, he found himself amazed by the growth of Coca-Cola in his absence. 'Upon my return here,' he wrote, 'I found that the trade mark Coca-Cola is a household word everywhere,' celebrating the 'Astonishing progress [that had] been made with Coca-Cola...now available in even the smallest villages, or dorps, as they are called here.'[91] Here he noticed that the hot climate, sports, and incessant promotion had helped impel Coca-Cola's growth, particularly among white consumers. Though he did not credit it as such, so too did the hard work of Sparletta bottlers, Export, and Coca-Cola franchisees. No longer were salesmen battling to get customers to try this strange, dark, carbonated brew, slipping bottles of Coca-Cola alongside other, more colorful drinks. Now, Coca-Cola was visible across the country, and its presence was only growing.

Conclusion

The April 1957 edition of *Coca-Cola Overseas*, the Coca-Cola Export Corporation's shiny monthly magazine, commemorated Coca-Cola and Johannesburg's shared anniversary. 'The year 1886 marked the birthdate of Johannesburg, South Africa and of *Coca-Cola* in Atlanta, Georgia,' the piece remarked. At the Johannesburg Festival that year, the city celebrated its birthday with a parade. To participate, Coca-Cola created a float with a cake fashioned on it. Seventy king-size bottles of the iconic beverage stood in for candles, and signs brandished a 'Happy birthday Johannesburg and Coca-Cola, 1886–1956' message that celebrated '70 Years of Progress.'[92]

By then, Coca-Cola king size (a 300 ml package) was in circulation in South Africa. Fanta Orange (1960) and Sprite (1961) were soon to be launched by the company, with Tab coming shortly thereafter (1963) and canned sodas arriving in the next decade. Coca-Cola concentrate was being produced near Tzaneen, in today's Limpopo Province, along with the finished product, then being made under the auspices of twenty-one bottlers. Thousands of employees toiled on the lines in both company and independent bottling plants, not to mention the thousands more who were busy selling the product in the 21,000 retail outlets where it could then be found.[93] Their individual stories have been lost to time. But, we can see them still, in the faded pictures of old factories running lines, washing, filling, and loading bottles, helping make liquid gold out of this fizzy water; and we can imagine them and the hard work it took to do what they did.[94] It was these men—and, again, they were largely men at this time—who helped make Coca-Cola what it had become in South Africa. In service to both independent bottlers and those controlled by Coca-Cola Export, these workers helped entrench Coca-Cola in virtually all manner of South African life, entwining the business with politics, secondary industry, resource allocation, cultural events, and more, such that as apartheid solidified, Coca-Cola appeared to be along for the ride, something clearly part of this nation. This model of comingled commerce and corporate citizenry would be exported with the beverage throughout the continent, becoming the defining feature of its work and presence there.

On the corporate side, change was afoot. In 1956, Patterson passed away; the same year as his successor, Smit, was transferred to Atlanta. Thereafter, A E Killeen took over control of what was, by then, called the southern African region. For, by this time, Coca-Cola had spread far beyond the Limpopo River, into much of the African continent, which it mapped into southern and middle regions, along with its growing northern African business, each of which was quickly becoming a key point of operation for the company. In fact, Coca-Cola's operations outside of South Africa caused something of a headache for the company in 1957 when the apartheid government, spurred onward by the Police College, the Defense Force, the Pretoria Technikon, and other institutions, called for a boycott of Coca-Cola because the company was believed to be assisting African states in their fights for independence. Pointing to Kenya, Tanganyika (now Tanzania), Northern Rhodesia (now Zambia), Nyasaland (now Malawi), and the Belgian Congo (Zaire, now the DR Congo), the government raged against the supposed involvement of this company in other countries' affairs, supposing that the corporation was funding African independence struggles, an assertion that, as will be explored in the coming chapters, seems plausible.[95] After twelve months of appeasement, Coca-Cola South Africa was able to stave off a boycott. This episode alerts us, in part, to what we will see later in various ways: that the company had to navigate life under the authoritarian apartheid state and through the tumultuous waxing of independent African nations in innovative, often clandestine ways that tested the boundaries of its dual identity.

In March 1960, the South African police opened fire on peaceful protestors at Sharpeville, outside of Johannesburg, killing sixty-nine and wounding more. This brutal display of government might presaged what was to come during the heyday of apartheid, then dawning. Whatever future still felt possible throughout the 1950s was reconceived from then onward. That same year, Coca-Cola launched the largest animated billboard the country had ever seen: a forty-five-foot-long, ten-and-a-half-foot-tall clock attached to the Merchandising Center in Johannesburg. Every ten seconds it displayed an alternate call: Drink Coca-Cola and Be Really Refreshed.[96] From 1960, South Africans were increasingly constrained by the brutality of apartheid, just as their neighbors began to win independence. Coca-Cola would be there, yoked to its city of twin origin. In this city of gold and sparkling minerals, as the brutal apartheid regime emerged, the most iconic sparkling mineral beverage was finally, and firmly, home.

2

FROM CAPE TO CAIRO

THE SUN NEVER SETS ON COCA-COLA

The February 1929 edition of *The Red Barrel*, the official monthly organ of American Coca-Cola bottlers, celebrated Coca-Cola's spread beyond the United States. Showcasing far-flung operations from Mexico to Italy, from Spain to Burma, the publication noted that Coke was now 'even [in] South Africa,' boasting that with this African addition, it could be 'truthfully said that the "The Sun Never Sets On Coca-Cola."'[1] Fourteen years later, Coca-Cola arrived in Morocco, this time to meet the needs of American military personnel stationed nearby during World War II. After Morocco came Egypt. Later, both countries' plants would be converted into civilian operations, initiating Coca-Cola's proliferation across North Africa. At the same time, the success of the stabilized South African business meant that after World War II Coke began spreading upwards from the bottom of the continent. At the war's end, the Coca-Cola Export Corporation remarked on its promising African presence. Where twenty years before there had been only a budding South African business, 'The phenomenal development in Egypt and the

Moslem world [and]... paralleled in South Africa,' anchored the company's continental presence and suggested the potential for future growth. 'They call Africa the dark continent,' the Export Corporation publication noted with no small amount of racism, 'but for Coca-Cola there is plenty of light at both ends of it.'[2] Those lights, the beacons of emerging northern and southern African Coca-Cola businesses, would eventually bookend the company's continent-wide entrenchment.

Throughout the 1950s and 1960s, Coca-Cola would spread from one end of Africa to the other, establishing itself across the continent as it encountered worlds far less dark than its racist publication suggested. Still, the company, and its growing cohort of local franchise bottlers, would face a host of difficulties along the way—relating to water, electricity, transportation, capacity, and more—which necessitated ingenuity. Coke and its bottlers met these and other problems by extending the model it created in South Africa, establishing its reach into both business and civic life as its footprint widened. By the end of the decade, just as African countries were starting to break free from the yoke of colonialism, Coca-Cola was nearly everywhere from Cape to Cairo, awash in African sun.

Coca-Cola and World War II

World War II was a pivotal moment for Coca-Cola. While the half-century-old company had secured its presence in a few countries across the globe by then, the vast majority of the world remained beyond Coke's reach when the war began. Robert Woodruff, longtime CEO of the corporation, favored expansion, believing in the global potential of his quality American product. When the Japanese bombed Pearl Harbor, Woodruff committed the company to putting a Coca-Cola within—in Coke's advertising language—'arm's reach' of all servicemen.

Roadblocks existed. World War II initiated sugar rationing in the United States, thwarting production, while wartime naval procedures stymied the overseas shipment of non-military goods. Coca-Cola quickly came up with work-arounds to both obstacles: by maneuvering itself onto the sugar rationing boards that controlled American policy at the time, the company was able to get itself exempted from rationing, provided that some of its product was earmarked for military outposts (be they training or active, domestic or international).[3] Here the company went to great lengths to suggest that making its product available to soldiers was the least a grateful country could do for those willing to fight for its freedom. Then, the company began establishing overseas production plants to service servicemen more easily. In total, Coke created sixty-four production plants near all wartime theaters and dispatched 163 Coca-Cola technical observers—nicknamed Coca-Cola colonels—to oversee global expansion.[4] The military welcomed Coca-Cola's presence, empowering commanders to order Coca-Colas just as they might military equipment.[5] It was not long before servicemen began to function as emissaries for the beverage, introducing it to locals around the globe.[6]

Expanding alongside American military presence, World War II saw Coca-Cola's image become entwined with that of its country of origin. Here, the company actively pushed the notion of the drink as a stand-in for home, arguing that providing soldiers stationed abroad with cold Cokes was akin to bringing a piece of America to the frontline. Simultaneously, The Coca-Cola Company's growing overseas production expanded America's reach. Before long, the idea that Coca-Cola was quintessentially American took hold at home and abroad. Coca-Cola became America's emblem.

Axis and Allied powers alike took note of this conflation between company and country. Axis propaganda machines regularly denigrated Coca-Cola as evidence of American—and by extension, democracy's—failings.[7] On the other side, Allied powers—led by the company—embraced Coca-Cola as drinkable democracy. At the first bottlers' convention held after World War II in Atlantic City, New Jersey, 5,500 bottlers, including representatives from thirty-two countries on five continents, met to plot a unified path for the business. A celebrated poster at the event spoke to their budding view of themselves as spokespeople not just for a business, but also for an ideology. It read: 'When we think of Nazis we think of the Swastika, when we think of the Japs we think of the Rising Sun (that set), and when we think of Communists we think of the Iron Curtain, BUT when THEY think of democracy they think of COCA-COLA.'[8]

Yet, Coca-Cola was not always immediately understood to be a metonym for democracy or America. In places where Coca-Cola already existed before the war (like Germany or Cuba), people often saw the beverage as local. Some of that was deliberate, a product of purposeful dissociation, as was the case in Germany.[9] Mostly, though, Coca-Cola came to be seen as local by virtue of the fact that its plants were operated by local people with real ties to their communities. An early edition of Coca-Cola Export's glossy magazine, *Coca-Cola Overseas*, reported on how surprising this could be for soldiers, noting that upon finding locally produced Cokes in far-flung locations 'many servicemen were astonished to discover that something they considered exclusively American was likewise an established custom in many other lands.'[10] While perhaps unexpected for outsiders, making Coke native was part and parcel of the company's expansion plan. The goal of the franchise bottler system was to employ locally owned and operated bottlers to run successful businesses selling an American product whose American-ness was beside the point. When Coca-Cola began its North African foray, landing on Moroccan shores at the start of 1943, it may have been an American company making an American product for American soldiers. Before long, though, it would come to be seen as a Moroccan company producing a Moroccan product for Moroccans.

Coca-Cola's North African Arrival

Morocco

In 1942, the United States army stationed itself along the Atlantic and Mediterranean coastlines of North Africa in preparation for its entry into World War II. Coca-Cola followed the next year, launching its first bottling plant in the Atlantic coastal town of Casablanca in then French Morocco to serve American military men. That same year, as Coke began meeting wartime demand from this perch, Franklin Roosevelt and Winston Churchill met in Casablanca to plan their countries' unified war strategy. Arriving in Morocco, Roosevelt stayed at the home of Kenneth Pendar, the American vice-consul in Casablanca and an associate of the Sultan of Morocco who would, at the war's end, petition Coca-Cola to take over the equipment used in its army-only plant. With this equipment, Pendar created the first Coca-Cola bottling company in the country, Compagnie Des Boissons Hygiéniques.[11] While there were 400 'European' and 576 'Moroccan' outlets selling Cokes to both populations in 1947, six months later, under Pendar's direction, there were over 3,000, the vast majority located in medinas.[12] By 1949, iconic yellow and red trucks advertising Coca-Cola in both Arabic and French crisscrossed Casablanca; dual Dixie production lines running twenty-four hours a day could not meet swelling demand. In 1951, Pendar presided over the opening of a new, larger factory that included then state-of-the-art bottle washers, water purifiers, and filling machines capable of producing 160 bottles a minute. That same year, a second facility opened in

Marrakech, this one pink, in keeping with local regulations. The Marrakech plant also contained cutting-edge Coca-Cola technology, culled from across the globe: an American carbocooler, or carbonation machine, a French filler and syruper, a British mixer, an American-patented but French-made soaker, and Moroccan inspection lights, in addition to a water treatment plant, conference rooms, and syrup storage facilities.[13] Swift on its heels, a third plant was opened in Safi.[14] Before long, a second company, the Atlas Bottling Company, was licensed to spread Cokes throughout northern and eastern Morocco (then an international zone) from new plants it opened in Tangier and Fez.[15] Less than a decade after Coca-Cola's arrival in Morocco, the business was established.

Yet, the entrenchment of Coca-Cola in Morocco was not all smooth sailing. The first problem related to Kenneth Pendar. Pendar's status as an American vice-consul—sent to Morocco to work undercover in advance of American arrival—raised questions about his motives, while his ties to Moroccan monarchy raised even more.[16] Some saw Pendar's presence as an affront to French authorities that helped foment Moroccan nationalism, while Pendar himself felt his American citizenship left his business—like that of other American expats—open to French discrimination.[17] Writing in the 1950s for *The New Yorker* magazine, E J Kahn recounted that Pendar's peculiar status as consul-come-bottler fed a popular conspiracy theory that Coca-Cola was a front for US espionage.[18] Yet, Pendar—and the image he created for the business—was not the only problem Coke faced in Morocco.

The most challenging obstacles encountered by Coke in Morocco had to do with its ingredients. Coca-Cola is famously secretive about what goes into its product, designating most ingredients as 'merchandise,' each with its own number, in order to cloak it in secrecy. When the company began shipping concentrate to Morocco, it faced the scrutiny of French customs agents keen on understanding exactly what it was they were allowing into the country. Confidential archival correspondence reveals that while in 1948 the company was able to get around intense scrutiny by paying a 'present' to a sympathetic customs officer, this arrangement was short-lived.[19] In 1949, the Moroccan business was forced to submit merchandises two and seven to lab analyses, but was able to save merchandises five and eight from scrutiny.[20] This was crucial since it helped maintain 'complete secrecy' about the solvents, which, as the Casablanca Export office recounted at the time, 'prevent[ed] the spreading of rumors which could have a disastrous effect.'[21] Here secrecy was important not because Coke contained dangerous ingredients or because the company was worried about cheater brands. Rather, the company was concerned that any reporting on or mislabeling of its products could ignite passions, particularly if any part was found to contain even a trace of alcohol.[22] 'The question of Customs classification for merchandise No8 [and No5] in Morocco is especially important,' A M Eshaya of Coca-Cola's Export branch in Paris wrote to his colleague in Casablanca in 1949, 'because we are dealing with a Moslem country' that forbids alcohol consumption.[23]

Despite—or perhaps because of—its attempts to shield its ingredients from scrutiny, towards the end of the 1940s, rumors emerged in Egypt that soda, and in particular Coca-Cola and Pepsi, then present there too, contained pig intestines, violating the laws of Halal and sparking a boycott that soon made its way across North Africa. By the time the boycott landed in Morocco, Coca-Cola bore the brunt of this misinformation.[24] 'I must say I am somewhat surprised by the violence with which the campaign has broken out in North Africa,' Eshaya lamented to the New York Export office in 1951.[25] The boycott, which came to include targeted attacks on Coke vehicles, emerged in response to false rumors about Coke's ingredients. But it was also stoked by a budding anti-American sentiment, where American—and American businesses in particular—were seen to bolster European colonial aspirations.[26] Coca-Cola felt the need to act and act swiftly. Coca-Cola Export began pumping money into newspaper advertisements, collecting international endorsements of its products' safety, and imploring the Sultan to speak about the drink in order to forestall the 'whispering campaign' then spreading.[27] These efforts began counteracting misinformation.

Coca-Cola Export and independent bottlers continued to promote their product as local and safe for Moroccans at the November 1951 opening of the new Compagnie Des Boissons Hygiéniques plant in Casablanca, then the largest and most modern plant in North Africa. Presiding over the opening was Prince Moulay Hassan—brother to His Majesty the Sultan of Morocco, and now president of Pendar's bottling company.[28] Prince Hassan's role in the company did much to assure Moroccans of the product's safety. The following year, in November 1952, Coca-Cola Export in Casablanca further recast its public persona by positioning itself as central to the Feast of the Throne, the celebration marking the anniversary of the Sultan's ascension to power. According to a participant, Export's involvement in the event was part of a deliberate plan to dispel 'the last traces of anti-Coca-Cola campaign in the minds of the native population,' by aligning itself with this nationalistic, anti-colonial event.[29] Through product sampling, prizes, and aggressive endorsement that included a complete scholarship to university, the company achieved a prominent place at the multi-day festivities, bowing out on day one when the soda's presence would have jarred with tradition. After the days' long celebrations, Coke then commissioned local writers to pen poems and prose for a commemorative magazine, which it issued free of charge. According to its own self-praise, 'in some villages, the natives literally fought for' the magazine, proving that 'this review is the best thing we have yet produced,' and suggesting that 'from the standpoint of effectiveness in the Arab market, it seems as if indirect publicity might be more useful to us in this field than direct advertising.' According to Coke, Moroccans accepted the publication as a 'friendly gesture' of a friendly business.[30]

Coca-Cola's acceptance as part of modern Morocco was all but assured when Prince Moulay Hassan became King Hassan II of Morocco in 1961. The following year, Coca-Cola took advantage of its long history with the King to query a recent Dahir (or royal order) calling for all non-alcoholic beverages to be labeled as belonging to one of three categories—none of which readily fit its product.[31] Faced with this situation, Coke personnel panicked, supposing that they may need to start tweaking their formulas to include the requisite fruit juice needed for rebranding. Not only would such tinkering undermine the flavor and consistency of Coca-Cola (and, by then, Fanta, which had entered the market), but adding fruit juice would also make gassosa—as sodas were known there—unaffordable for most Moroccans. Before taking such drastic measures, two representatives from Export went to visit the King; one of them even stayed at the royal palace. They found the King receptive to their requests. On 27 January 1962, the Dahir of 10 December 1960 was amended so that 'soda' now included beverages with natural plant extracts, which is precisely how Coca-Cola started labeling its products.[32]

By the time the Casablanca bottler gave a case of Coca-Cola to a pilgrim ship bound for Mecca in 1958, the company was well on its way to being accepted as local, judging from per capita consumption and the business's expansion.[33] By then, Coca-Cola in Morocco was producing not just finished product, but also concentrate, which turned out to be the most cost-effective way to move the product beyond Moroccan borders.[34] From 1949, Coke expanded into Tunisia. In 1950, it moved into Algeria.

Later, in 1962, it spread to Libya.[35] From 1950, the company moved farther afield from Morocco into Senegal and Côte d'Ivoire in French West Africa. Eventually, concentrate made in Morocco was also sent to Egypt, whose nascent Coke operations mirrored those of Morocco.

Egypt

Coke's story in Egypt paralleled that of the company in Morocco. In 1944, Coca-Cola set up a single temporary bottling machine in Cairo to service the needs of military men, which it did until 1945. During that time, it was not unusual for American servicemen to treat their friends to Coca-Colas, thus extending the product's reach.[36] Civilian operations began in earnest in Cairo in 1946. Within three months, old army trucks were put to work, makeshift salesmen were trained during the night, and new kiosks were constructed around the city. Existing outlets were given red coolers free of charge and instructed to sell Coca-Cola ice cold. Hundreds of walls were painted Coke red and dozens of neon lights were strung across Cairo, all to announce the arrival of Coca-Cola. Within three months, 100,000 cases had been sold.[37] Within ten months, the company had sold a record-breaking million cases.[38] The next year, a second plant was opened in Alexandria. In 1946, the annual per capita consumption of Coca-Cola in Alexandria was five bottles. One year later, it was more than four times that. Running two bottling machines twenty-four hours a day, the business struggled to keep up with demand. In 1947 the company erected the country's largest neon sign atop Alexandria's tallest building. Visible from fifteen miles out at sea, this neon Coca-Cola bottle announced in Arabic and English that Coca-Cola had arrived in Egypt.[39]

Within three years of its civilian start, by 1949, there were five permanent plants and one provisional one producing Coca-Cola in Egypt as well as four warehouses and twenty distribution centers serving all major cities. The business employed over 2,000 people and made use of more than 300 vehicles to transport its product along 200 routes, many of them served daily.[40] A central Coca-Cola Export office in Cairo oversaw production across the nation, ensuring standard procedures that would produce standardized products. But it did not micromanage production. Each bottling plant was left to run its business in compliance with Coke procedures. Between the central office, the bottling plants, and the distribution centers, by 1949, an estimated 1% of the population of Cairo was 'living on, because of and off Coca-Cola,' not to mention 'the many ice manufacturers and dealers supplying the thousands of coolers, nor all those engaged in the side industries for Coca-Cola,' according to a Coca-Cola Export article.[41] And this makes no mention of Coca-Cola employees living outside of Cairo.

Yet, like in Morocco, the introduction of Coca-Cola to Egypt was not without bumps. There were mundane problems, like a shortage of glass bottles. In 1949 Cairo reported that it was not uncommon to see the same bottle returned to be refilled twice in one day.[42] Bigger obstacles attended sanitation. When the Alexandria plant opened, for instance, it did so amidst a local cholera epidemic. As a result, no celebratory party was held. Instead, and in response, the Coca-Cola plant opened by celebrating its cleanliness. An Export article reported that 'the whole medical staff of Alexandria... all public health departments, hospitals, doctors, nurses, etc., were invited to visit and inspect the plant during the first week of operations,' in the hopes that upon seeing the plant's state-of-the-art water purification system and overall cleanliness, they would 'spread their favorable impressions all over the country.'[43] By casting its business as clean and its company as open to ample employment, Coke appealed to Egyptian hearts and minds. From Cairo, the central Coke office implemented what was known as 'the Domestication program,' a plan aimed at heightening goodwill by making the business 'genuinely Egyptian, in terms of capital investment, management, labor and local purchases benefitting local side industries.'[44] By using Egyptian money and Egyptian labor to produce a product Egyptians enjoyed, Coca-Cola became Egyptian.

Along the way, Coke faced problems in Egypt, from perception to logistics. Yet these were solvable by using local know-how. Vehicles were purchased, products sourced, routes drawn, and product moved, all by tapping into existing systems of knowledge. In total, this early successful expansion, which mimicked that found in South Africa and Morocco, enhanced the company's belief in its franchise/Export model.[45] It appeared that Coca-Cola, the quintessentially modern, American, and clean product, could be profitable—and profitable for people up and down the value chain—anywhere, even in a land, as the company saw it, as ancient as Egypt. The 1964 cover of *Coca-Cola Overseas* celebrated this particular juxtaposition between old and new. It showed a woman on a camel receiving a bottle of Coke, with the Giza pyramids and iconic Sphinx in the background.[46] With this cover, Coca-Cola Export declared its North African presence and was ready to expand elsewhere.

Coca-Cola's Spread from the South

By the time Coca-Cola operations gained traction in North Africa, the business had made inroads northbound from South Africa. In 1948, the Salisbury Bottling Company Limited in Southern Rhodesia (now Zimbabwe) became the first bottler of Coca-Cola in the 3,000 miles between Egypt and South Africa.[47] From there, the business spread through Central Africa, later renamed by Coke 'Middle Africa' for administrative purposes (and inclusive of West and East Africa). In 1949, operations began in Kenya, with Congo following the next year. Mozambique and Zambia were next in 1951. Then came Tanganyika (now Tanzania), Mauritius, and, in 1954, Nigeria, from where operations spread to the Gold Coast (now Ghana) in 1956. By then, Coke was being bottled in Sudan, Nyasaland (now Malawi), Zambia, and Uganda.[48] From 1957, Coca-Cola concentrate was being produced in Durban, South Africa, for use elsewhere on the continent.[49] The same would happen in Casablanca, Morocco. The late 1950s saw a proliferation of bottling plants across West Africa—in Côte d'Ivoire, Réunion, Senegal, and Sierra Leone. The central African nations of Angola and Burundi were next, while eastern Africa's Ethiopia followed towards the end of the decade. Then Gambia, Niger, Togo, and Upper Volta (now Burkina Faso) cemented the product's presence in 1967 West Africa. By the end of the 1960s, Coke operations spanned the continent.[50]

From an administrative perspective, Coca-Cola Export regarded the Sahara as a dividing line across Africa, much like many would, then and now.[51] From its main office in New York, Export parsed the continent into regions: northern, middle, and southern, each administrated on the ground from a local office. By the 1970s, northwest Africa was grouped under the administrative domain of Europe, while northeast Africa fell under Mediterranean and Middle Eastern leadership; sub-Saharan control rested in the middle and southern area units, housed in Nairobi and Johannesburg, respectively. These Export offices oversaw vast terrains, but they also drew upon shared strategies. This put them in tension with local bottlers, who tended to feel that there was no single method of establishing and entrenching bottling operations that was guaranteed to work in all situations. This strain between corporate Coca-Cola and its bottlers was a hallmark of the business.[52] There is no question that each country created unique circumstances requiring unique solutions. Still, patterns were discernible.[53]

As we saw in Morocco and Egypt, the birth of local bottling enterprises was not without pain. First, there were tangible problems. The business required machinery, which had to be brought in from overseas. Importing machinery meant paying duties, which meant navigating local import regulations. Coca-Cola Hellenic, today the third largest bottler of Coke worldwide, now based in Greece, understood the need to negotiate with local governments from its earliest days in West Africa. Hellenic got its start in the then British colony and protectorate Nigeria in 1951, when a Greek businessman named A G Leventis established the Nigerian Bottling Company (NBC).[54] When, in 1954, NBC was considering expanding into Ghana, it fought to have import duties waived by the British colonial government. The company successfully argued that since such duties were already waived in Nigeria, there was imperial precedent. It further asserted that Coca-Cola was good for the local temperance movement and, most significantly, that the business was sure to bring jobs and industrial development to the region. Here, NBC was hoping to import American, rather than European equipment, since, in its view, American equipment tended to hold up better in the tropics.[55] Often, emergent bottlers did not have much choice. While early bottlers tended to be immigrants (or second-generation citizens) with access to capital, they did not tend to be exceedingly wealthy. Many imported small or secondhand bottling lines, which broke down or became obsolete quickly. Case in point: in 1958, the ten-year-old Salisbury Bottling Company was finally able to replace its original, dated Alpine bottling unit, capable of producing a mere thirty bottles a minute, with a Meyer-Dunmore bottle washer and forty-spout liquid filler able to turn out five times this amount. This brought the Salisbury plant into line with the most up-to-date Coke factories in the world and made that facility the largest single production plant in southern Africa at the time.[56] Such upgrades relied on sufficient capital and product demand. They also relied upon large facilities.

In order to house bottling lines, bottling facilities needed to be built, which required time, money, and manpower. Logistical and transportation difficulties meant that multiple factories were often needed to service a single country. In Ghana, for example, NBC originally contemplated serving the entire country from one factory in Accra, before transport costs suggested it would be both cost effective and simpler to move the product from three smaller bottling plants situated around the nation.[57] Something similar happened in Nigeria. In 1954, The Nigerian Bottling Company opened its first plant in Lagos. Kano followed in 1961 to service northern Nigeria. NBC's third plant, in Ibadan, was opened in 1962 to cater to the western part of the country. All were met with government fanfare, since officials saw the introduction of the Coke business as a boon for jobs, industry, and tax coffers.[58] Across Africa, new factories were generally regarded this way. That is why they tended to be opened with ceremony, often involving local politicians and celebrations. It was not uncommon for openings to include parades with floats bearing giant Coca-Cola bottles surrounded by local musicians or beauty queens, all performing for politicians, army, church, and civic administrators.[59] Notable politicians were often asked to open new plants, such as when Simon Ronde, administrator of the Congo, opened the Matadi plant in 1961, or when Mayor S Everett and Deputy Mayor M P Ondiek—the first Black African to hold this high office in Kisumu, Kenya—presided over the opening of the new plant there, or when Haile Selassie inaugurated the Addis Ababa plant in 1959.[60] Everywhere, politicians and civic administrators seemed to welcome the presence of Coca-Cola bottling plants and the promise they brought.

Facilities required both transportation vehicles and transportation strategies. When, in 1951, Tanganyika Bottlers

Limited began operations in Dar es Salaam, the company learned that while standard rack trucks could move the product throughout the macadamized capital, more remote areas required smaller trucks to navigate unpaved, palm-tree-strewn paths.[61] The budding business in Umtali (now Mutare), Southern Rhodesia, faced a similar situation in 1953: while a three-ton Bedford rack-bodied truck could maneuver downtown, a seven-ton Leyland diesel was needed for country routes.[62] By 1957, the Tanzanian business expanded beyond motor vehicles and began using dhow ships to move product more easily along the Indian Ocean coastline.[63] Elsewhere, hand- and animal-drawn carts, mules and donkeys, and bicycles and tricycles would come to be used for distribution—as they remain to this day. Many areas relied on humans to move product, particularly within crowded outdoor markets or other areas where vehicles were prohibitive. One famous *Coca-Cola Overseas* snapshot from 1960 showcases a Ghanaian woman with a crate of Coca-Cola balanced upon her head delivering Cokes to dealers in the Selwyn market.[64]

As Coca-Cola radiated outward from urban centers in nations across the continent, additional needs arose. First, the business required warehouses to store its product between bottling facilities and remote points of sale. In 1961, The Ugandan Bottlers, Ltd., of Kampala, for example, was given extra-territorial sales rights to cover a 150-mile radius, in which it built warehouses; the result: sales grew ten-fold as the product's reach was expanded.[65] As depots and warehouses were built across vast terrains, transport routes fed the need for petrol stations. Before long, Coke distributors worked to put these stops to use by championing the comingling of refreshment and filling stations with, for instance, vending machines like those that arrived in the Congo in 1955.[66]

The expanding business called for other tangible products. The first, of course, was water. In some places, water was scarce. In others, it was available from local municipalities, but it was not up to Coke's purity standards. Such was the case in Oran, Algeria in 1950. That year, the new Société Oranoise de Boissons Gazeuses was forced to purchase a remote tract of land that contained a well for use in its plant.[67] Nearly everywhere, bottlers installed water purification systems to clean what water they could access. Bottles themselves were also essential, if also often scarce in the early years. In 1957 Umtali, for instance, Allen Lang—whose uncle was first awarded a franchise for the area in 1951 and who was managing director of Mutare Bottlers until 2018—recalled that even seven years into operation, the company had only enough bottles to fill a few trucks at a time, halting production until the trucks could make it back from the market with empties.[68] Since these bottles were not manufactured locally, but rather shipped almost 1,000 miles from South Africa, they were neither easily replaceable nor their numbers easily augmented.[69]

Tommy Hagan, who started at Mutare Bottlers in 1960, drew upon early ledgers to reconstruct just how precarious the business's start was. In the first ten months of production, the bottlers were only able to put out about 9,000 bottles, roughly as much as the fastest plant in the 1950s could put out in an hour. Part of that had to do with machinery. But more had to do with how difficult it was to source not just bottles, but also the other requisite components for Coca-Cola. Carbon dioxide, water, crowns, sugar, and concentrate were all needed to make Cokes. Early on, Mutare Bottlers would collect gas for carbon dioxide from a local distillery, testing its purity by, as the bottlers tell it, smelling it before use. Sugar was brought in from Salisbury, while dry ice and concentrate were imported from South Africa.[70] Water, which was clean, but expensive, and crowns were both purchased locally. Using what was called a pre-mix machine, the bottlers would mix concentrate with sugar to make syrup. This would be bottled and then topped with carbonated water.

The crate filled with bottles was then rolled to the end of a line, where it was inverted to mix the syrup with the carbonated water—an arduous, labor-intensive process then being mirrored at small-scale bottling operations across the continent.[71]

More than any other limiting factor to the spread of Coke, the advent of Coca-Cola operations across Africa necessitated a way to keep the product ice cold, as Coca-Cola demanded. E Neville Isdell—eventual CEO of The Coca-Cola Company who got his start as a route salesman in 1964 Zambia—recalled how unappealing (and thus hard to sell) warm Cokes are. According to him, Fanta could more readily be drunk warm, which is why he attributes the successful proliferation of the Coca-Cola business across Africa at this time to its sister product, Fanta orange, introduced throughout the region in the 1960s.[72] To sell Cokes, they had to be cold, meaning that electricity or ice was needed. This limited where Coke could go. In Liberia in 1953, for instance, Coca-Cola bottled at Harbel, headquarters of the Firestone rubber plantation, was transported sixty miles daily to the capital, Monrovia; along the way, it could be found only in stores that were able to run refrigerators off private diesel generators.[73] Mutare Bottlers' early accounting records show just how high their expenditure was for coolers in their starting years, typical for other bottlers at this time who wanted to extend their product's reach. There were of course innovative ways to cool drinks where electricity was scarce or nonexistent. A favorite from the Congo entailed putting a warm Coke in a wet sock and allowing the water's evaporation to cool the drink.[74] Still, this was not ideal. As bottlers expanded, they spent considerable time and effort spreading cooling technology along with their product, which eventually came to include petitioning governments to extend electricity grids, procuring their own generators, or—most often—simply by giving coolers to dealers, which often entailed producing and providing ice. The proliferation of cold drink was perhaps the most obvious tangible evidence of Coke's spread. But the spread of Coke also entailed hidden intangible processes.

In order to entrench Coca-Cola across Africa, the company and its bottlers first had to gain the trust of locals. This was done deliberately and in large part through relentless attention to quality, as we will see below, and marketing, as we will see in the next chapter. Trust was also attained through the method the company laid out in South Africa—comingling civic engagement with business. In late colonial Africa, this engagement often involved aligning itself with colonial powers, again harkening to the business's work in South Africa. When Bulawayo, Southern Rhodesia, housed a festival to honor the centennial of Cecil Rhodes' birth in 1954 with an exhibition that was opened by Queen Elizabeth, the Queen Mother, all local bottlers were on hand. For this grand imperial event—which included building a village to house the 2,500 visitors who came from across the empire—the local Bulawayo bottlers transported their entire factory piece by piece to the exhibition premises. The large cost was borne by multiple bottlers of Coke in the region—DB Aerated waters of Lusaka, the Rhodesian Bottling Company of Kitwe, Crystal Mineral Waters of Gwelo, and the Salisbury Bottling Company. Beyond distributing 32,000 miniature bottles of Coca-Cola free of charge, the exhibit factory allowed 250,000 people to witness how Coca-Cola was made. In helping to celebrate Rhodesia's founding colonial father, Coca-Cola spread goodwill towards its product, which its bottlers were quick to point out required local manpower and local products.[75] Coca-Cola's imperial alliances were on display again in 1956 when the Queen arrived for a twenty-one-day tour of Nigeria, which came to include a tour of the local NBC Lagos plant.[76] Though Coca-Cola was present at these large-scale events, the product—by way of its local bottlers—was also coming to be ubiquitous in more mundane ways.

Coca-Cola came to rely upon relentless advertising, merchandising, and product placement to weave itself into everyday life, thus creating demand amongst all races and religions. As a 1955 Coca-Cola Export article explained, 'Thirst knows no time, locality, season, economic circumstance, color or creed.' The plan, bottlers were instructed, was simple, but deliberate. Create and distribute coolers and signs that clearly marketed Coca-Cola, both in color (red) and in script (Spencerian). Ensure ubiquity— 'Having "Coca-Cola" within arm's reach—not only makes it easy and convenient for people to try "Coca-Cola" for the first time, but it also indicates leadership and popularity.' Then, advertise both outside shops—'Clean, dominant, outside advertising attracts the attention of potential customers and suggests popular demand, quality and leadership'—as well as inside stores, where 'Clean, fresh, dominant, inside advertising gives potential drinkers of "Coca-Cola" the impression of goodness, purity, enjoyment, wholesomeness, popularity and actually creates a desire to try it.' Seal the deal with the cooler, one capable of keeping the beverage at the ideal thirty-three to thirty-eight degrees Fahrenheit: 'A clean, polished, bright-red "Coca-Cola" cooler, placed where it can be easily seen and conveniently reached, attracts a prospect's attention, suggests outstanding quality and purity, and makes the impulse to go over to the cooler simple and inviting.' In short, bottlers were told, 'The same effort, skill, cleanliness and painstaking attention to detail that goes into the manufacturing and bottling of "Coca-Cola" must also go into the marketing and merchandising of our outstanding product.'[77] It was not enough to make the product. It had to be taken to market, too.

Bottlers took their product to the people, primarily in an effort to capture new Coca-Cola drinkers.[78] The easiest way to reach new customers was to target young customers, often via their mothers. In Brakpan, Coca-Cola hired 'sampling crews' to spread awareness of Coca-Cola during school holidays with samples and coupons, particularly hoping to set up a 'buying pattern' among targeted housewives.[79] Bottlers also marketed directly to children in those days. School children were often invited to tour plants or given free samples of what some called this 'elixir of life.'[80] In June 1949, D O Jones published in *Coca-Cola Overseas* a 'A step by step report on how to capture the youth market' via 'school sampling' from his experience in South Africa. It details how a successful sampling entailed working with local headmasters and empowering special salespeople to spread information amongst students and teachers about the 'pure and wholesome nature of our quality product' as well as 'the care and cleanliness around every phase of its manufacture,' all during a brief school break. And, of course, it entailed giving out a lot of cold Cokes.[81] Bulawayo 1953 ran an aggressive two-part school sampling that seems informed by this strategy, targeting both white and Black school children, addressed in English and Ndebele, respectively. The goal was to establish brand, trademark, and bottle recognition amongst the 1,500 participants who were treated to music during this midday break.[82] Importantly, the goal was to reach both white and Black consumers. In 1958, Coca-Cola bottlers went into Alexandra Township, outside Johannesburg, in another effort to capture Black consumers. Alongside the Mayor of Johannesburg, who was there to preside over 'Road Safety Week,' all township students were present. All were treated to King Size, or large, bottles of Coke, which had recently entered the market.[83] Whether it was Eid, a boy scout festival, a holiday event, industry fair, or just a regular school day, bottlers across Africa found ways to give free samples of their product and, in so doing, activate—as it is now called—new customers from across all demographics. How did they know how to do this? They were trained and trained well. For the spread of Coke was only possible with the concomitant spread of knowledge about the business.

Spreading Coca-Cola Knowledge

The final component that attended the spread of Coca-Cola across Africa after World War II was the dissemination of Coke know-how. The publication of *Coca-Cola Overseas*, the Coca-Cola Export publication quoted often above, was one way that people within the Coke system shared information on everything from local anecdotes to global problems. A 1949 letter to the editor from the young bottler in Nairobi, then Kenya colony, affirmed the lifeline that this magazine seemed to provide for those at the drink's frontier, often cast as the frontier of civilization itself.[84] While *Overseas* relied upon material sent to New York for publication, other regional magazines emerged. In the 1950s, the Southern Africa Export Division office began producing the *South African Coca-Cola Bottler*, an organ that shared information about such topics as water treatment plants, vehicle operating costs, seasonal resort commerce, and other pressing concerns for bottlers across the sub-continent.[85] The next decade, *Coca-Cola South of the Sahara*, *Coca-Cola Southern Africa*, and *Coke in Middle Africa*, also locally produced magazines, would emerge to speak to local audiences as well.

Besides ingesting information in print, bottlers and bottling employees often went overseas to receive training. As early as 1949, bottlers from around the world convened in Trinidad to attend a two-week-long 'production school.' The agenda included the history of the product and all of the intricacies involved in a successful bottling operation: treating water, including purification and carbonation; creating syrup from concentrate; making and storing carbon dioxide; controlling quality and cleanliness; maintaining refrigeration and water cooling; filling, crowning, and inspecting bottles; sourcing and storing materials; training crews, and more. At that session and others like it, participants were given manuals to take home with them.[86] In

1960, twenty-eight engineers and chemists from around the world—including representatives from Johannesburg—met in Atlanta and New York. There, they discussed innovations in bottles, cases, and cartons, concentrate plant design and operation, and how best to exchange technical data, in addition to conducting taste tests.[87] At these and other global sessions, bottlers and their employees gained the technical know-how to run their African plants just as their colleagues did around the world.

Moving through the world to gain such expertise, bottlers based on the African continent (whom I call 'African bottlers'), followed in the footsteps of Coca-Cola Export employees. Most Export offices were peopled by a mixture of American and European ex-pats and locally born white Africans (by the end of the 1960s, avenues for Black Africans to rise to prominence in the company were emerging, as we will see in Chapter 4). From the start, Export employees traveled.[88] In 1948, the first group of Export graduates completed four months of training in the United States before taking up their posts abroad. This training session, which mimicked ones that would continue for years to come, included spending time in New York, Atlanta, and the Midwest, where attendees witnessed how both large- and small-scale bottling plants operated. 'The purpose of this training,' Coca-Cola Export explained, 'is a refresher course for old employees of the Company and an indoctrination program for newcomers to our organization,' whereby 'On completion... graduates will be familiar with all phases of Coca-Cola.'[89]

African bottlers also met in person to train regularly on the African continent. At a ten-day Bottlers Conference in 1950 Johannesburg, for instance, more than seventy bottlers arrived by plane, car, and air from throughout South Africa as well as from as far afield as Tanganyika, the Rhodesias, and Mozambique. Many had never traveled that far beforehand. Together, they heard lectures, watched demonstrations and films, toured plants, and studied copyright control, plant management, customer relations, and more. A key area of focus at this conference was expanding into the 'Native Market.'[90] A Northwest African Bottlers' Meeting in 1959 Morocco similarly brought together a wide swath of bottlers, many of whom had never met before, from Côte d'Ivoire, Senegal, Tunisia, Algeria, and throughout Morocco, for similar discussions.[91] In 1961, Near East Bottlers likewise convened in Cairo.[92] Some regional meetings drew across different Export regions; at a 1959 sales meeting in Johannesburg, bottlers came from as far as Nigeria. These disparate bottlers were shown per capita comparisons to augment competition and standardize knowledge about the latest technologies.[93]

Conferences that drew from wide areas were complemented by local meetings. In 1955 Cairo, Egyptian salesmen convened at night to stay up to date on sales methods.[94] In 1957, South African bottlers did the same, meeting at central locations to spread information about the 'new look' for newly introduced king size Coke.[95] Bottlers met in 1960 to discuss spreading 'goodwill' to their bigger product, as well as to address tangible topics like efficiency, managements, cold technology, and home consumption.[96] Beyond sales, bottlers got together to learn how to run their plants efficiently. In 1958, thirty-four delegates arrived from Central Africa, Uganda, Mauritius, and throughout South Africa to attend the first 'Production and Plant Management School' in Johannesburg for just this purpose. Once there, bottlers were schooled in making Coke, each leaving with copies of the 'Production Man's Creed' and a 'Production Manual' covering quality control and plant management.[97] That same year, route managers—the men in charge of expanding the reach of Coca-Cola into remote corners of the continent—traveled from Uganda, Kenya, and South Africa to a Route Managers Training Course in Southern Rhodesia. There, they attended training sessions on how to run delivery routes efficiently. Each participant went home with a certificate.[98] It was at these and countless other meetings like them that Coca-Cola bottlers—often in conjunction with Coke Export—learned the minutiae of the business, through collaboration and comparisons.

Additionally, senior Coke employees—normally from South Africa, the oldest African operation—traveled the continent to spread knowledge about the system. Often, this travel happened in conjunction with a new plant opening, such as when the heads of quality control and engineering from South Africa went to Nairobi to help make the first bottle of Coke there in 1949, or when South African chemists established the first carbon dioxide plant in 1956 Ghana in advance of that country's first bottling plant.[99] The area quality control chemist for southern Africa, D Meijer, traveled regularly for just such reasons in these years. Meijer documented for the global Export audience a six-week tour he undertook to check regional operations in 1955, that gives a sense of what the circulation of regional knowledge entailed at this time. After a three-hour flight to Livingstone, Northern Rhodesia from Johannesburg, Meijer took another five-and-a-half-hour flight to Entebbe, Uganda. From there, he drove twenty miles on a macadamized road to Kampala to see the newest Ugandan Coke plant in action. After spending two weeks ensuring that this plant was up to Coke's standards, Meijer rode a slow train through the Ugandan countryside, watching cotton, coffee, and tea plantations give way to the Rift Valley and the greens of Kenya from his window. From Nairobi, he boarded an Air France plane to Arivonimamo, Madagascar, from where he drove another forty-five minutes to Tananarive, the site of a nine-month-old Coke factory, then struggling to get off the ground. After four days of counseling these new bottlers on basic operational logistics, Meijer made his way to the airport on windy dirt roads. Then, it was onward to Mauritius, where he was met by a bottler with a thriving business. Meijer spent three days there, testing the product's consistency. From Mauritius, he re-crossed the Indian Ocean, this time on a ten-hour flight. Back in Nairobi, he helped sort the bottlers' quality control and supply problems, before heading to Dar es Salaam in Tanganyika. After that, it was back to Kenya to visit Mombasa and, finally, home to Johannesburg. What problems was Meijer addressing along the way? He left no complete record. But, we can surmise from his brief notes. For all the training around Coke systems at the time, the business was not an easy one. Along the way, much could go wrong in the mixing, bottling, quality control, and shipment. Water could be unclean in any number of ways. Carbonation could be off, bottles sealed improperly. In those days, most of the work that went into making a Coke was manual, requiring careful attention to detail, whether that meant mixing syrup from concentrate, cleaning bottles, eyeing filling lines for imperfections, or loading crates, not to mention delivering product.[100] Meijer's quality control inspections aimed to smooth the multiple rough edges he found on the ground and, above all, ensure the product's uniformity, no matter the circumstances of its production.

Meijer was not the only Coke man to make such dizzying tours to ensure that African operations were functioning at international Coke standards across the vast African continent in these years. Representatives from Coke Export regularly toured operations, as they did on a 1957 circuit through Nairobi, Mombasa, Johannesburg, Pretoria, and Leopoldville, as well as the concentrate plant in Durban. That same year, J Paul Austin, then head of Coke Export in South Africa, similarly toured Nairobi, Mombasa, Dar es Salaam, and Zanzibar.[101] Later that year, Austin toured farther afield in Central and West Africa—to places then named Elizabethville, Usum Bura, Stanleyville and Leopoldville, Congo, Brazzaville, French Equatorial Africa, as well as Accra, the capital of then newly independent Ghana, and Lagos and Kano, Nigeria.[102] Such trips were not uncommon.[103] The goal everywhere was the same: make sure all Coca-Cola plants, whether locally or company owned, were operating at Coke's international standards. Make sure, in other words, that Coke know-how had landed successfully on the ground.

Conclusion

In 1944, amidst World War II, Coca-Cola—then a fifty-eight-year-old company—announced that it had sold its billionth gallon of Coke syrup. In 1953, only nine years later, the company revealed that it had sold its two billionth, evidence of Coke's rapid, global spread in these years.[104] This was played out in Africa, as we read above. By 1961, Coke was being bottled in every country across North Africa, while sixty-nine plants south of the Sahara, operating in twenty-three countries, were doing likewise. Of those, Coca-Cola Export ran but five; the rest were run by locally owned and operated franchise bottlers.[105] By 1952, Coca-Cola seemed to be ubiquitous: 'Wherever you go, there is "Coca-Cola,"' the common traveler's quip became in Africa, much like elsewhere in the world.[106] This ever-presence owed itself to the spread of Coke operations and Coke know-how as well as to the rise of a veritable army of local Coca-Cola workers guided by local Coke bottlers and a near religious belief in the product.

The 15 May 1950 cover of *Time* magazine captured this moment. Captioned 'world & friend,' it showed a round, smiling Coca-Cola icon serving a bottle of Coke to a smiling anthropomorphized globe. Inside, the cover story opened with the reflection that, by then, 'The Sun Never Sets on Cacoola,' referring to the beverage's Egyptian nickname. According to *Time*, with 50,000 daily servings worldwide, Coca-Cola had become both 'the essence of America' and the world's product.[107]

The same could be said in Africa. Between the Cape and Cairo, as Coca-Cola landed, it became African, in one of the many iterations of the term. This meant that Coke came to adapt to local realities—paying attention to how its product interacted with the laws of kashrut in Morocco, Ramadan in Egypt, Christmas in South Africa, and more.[108] It also meant that Coca-Cola operations quickly became multiracial ones. While the bulk of Export personnel and top bottler leadership was white in these years—owing to experience, access to capital, and racism—the spread of Coke meant that the category 'white' was a diverse one that included both immigrants and people who were born locally but who came from a range of countries. While top leadership may have been white, from the start, Coke employed scores of Black employees as everything from bottle fillers and washers to route drivers, syrup makers, and more. These jobs, as well as those within the secondary industries the business spawned, were largely considered to be good, stable jobs with decent pay and room for growth. Ultimately, it would be this footprint capturing the broadest swath of people that would ensure Coca-Cola's lasting presence on the continent.

The multiracial nature of the business—obscured from a top-down analysis—is essential to understanding how the business became accepted locally. By way of one example: when Tanganyika Bottlers Ltd. began operations in 1951 Dar es Salaam, the company was managed by A Cassolis, a Greek citizen who had arrived in the country five years earlier. Cassolis's initial management team was typical for a Coke bottling operation at this time and place: his first accountant was Goan; his production foreman was Czech; one machine operator was Chinese, while the other was Indian. The production team were Swahili speakers. The company's three salesmen spoke Gujarati, Arabic, Swahili, and English.[109] Here, as elsewhere, Coca-Cola revealed itself to be, as D J Walker wrote in *Overseas* in 1961, 'truly a "Citizen of

Africa,'" in all its complexity.[110] Throughout the 1960s, as the continent began to break free from colonialism, so too would the nature—and color—of Coke operations change, as we shall see in future chapters. As increasing numbers of Black employees were able to access positions of power within the business, Coca-Cola started to accurately reflect African demographics.

In 1960, ten years after its *Time* magazine cover, Coca-Cola had reached the corners of Africa. In June of that year, this became apparent when tragedy struck a chartered flight that had originated in Luxembourg bound for Johannesburg. During the Cairo-to-Entebbe leg of its journey, one engine aboard the plane caught fire, prompting a crash-landing in the Egyptian desert, near the Bedouin village of El Badary. Witnessing the crash, villagers promptly made the one-mile trek to find all sixty-seven passengers alive, if shaken, waiting outside their enflamed aircraft. The villagers hastily used all available vehicles to take the passengers to El Badary to await further transport. There, much to the passengers' delight, the villagers made their inadvertent guests feel at home by serving them something that was as much a piece of their home as it was the Egyptians': ice-cold Coca-Colas.[111] The world and Coke had become friends, in a desert in a corner of Africa no less than anywhere else.

3

KNOW YOUR COUNTRY
HOW COCA-COLA BRANDED A CONTINENT AND ITSELF

The November 1958 edition of *Harper's Magazine* arrived on American newsstands just as Africans were winning independence across much of the continent.[1] By then, declining settler colonialism and its concurrent fascination with big game hunting had added to centuries-old notions of an imagined Africa full of wild animals and wilder people. Historian Laurence Lafore's 'Elephants get the right of way,' a sarcastic first-person account of his recent Kenyan safari, spoke to *Harper's* readers at this moment. After extolling the 'uncommonly handsome' 'mud and thatch huts' of traditional 'villages,' Lafore looked askance at the 'prefabricated sheet steel' abodes and other instances 'where Western civilization had touched,' and, by implication, spoiled, Africa, quipping by way of example that 'where there are trading posts, there are always Coca-Cola signs.'[2] That same year, *Coca-Cola Overseas* published a letter from a traveler who had likewise just returned from hunting in Africa. In it, the author writes that he took 'quite a few shots of deepest Africa showing natives in their primitive villages,' similarly writing that always 'in the background will appear a Coca-Cola sign.'[3] In both instances, the message is the same: Coca-Cola, found by the middle of the twentieth century dotting African landscapes far and wide, was somehow out of place in its environment, an anomaly that jarred with what 'Africa' was supposed to be. Here Coca-Cola—by then one of the four most recognized brands in 109 countries worldwide—meant modern civilization, while Africa remained the generalizable land of timeless tradition.[4]

The history of Coca-Cola is, on some level, a history of branding. Few companies have done as good a job of marketing themselves or their products. And the history of Coca-Cola in Africa is also, largely, about visible markings, about the ways in which Coca-Cola signs—both red and small-scale and oversized and neon—came to pepper the continent, creating what some have termed, derisively, 'the red rash.' This chapter takes up the story mid-century to describe how the dual branding of a drink and a continent came about. What we see is that, faced with political changes across much of the continent, the company—from its Export base in the United States—embraced a new advertising strategy, one that was attuned to local realities, just as its local Export offices and bottlers aimed to both capture and empower local populations. The result was a series of African advertisement campaigns—described here—that blended product and location branding in new ways. These mid-century ads shared a common denominator: they all celebrated the natural, knowable world. Spread predominantly across sub-Saharan Africa, they aimed to open new markets by purposely contributing to a particular branding of the continent, against the backdrop of, and inexorably tied to, waning colonialism.

Coca-Cola in Mid-Century Africa

By the middle of the twentieth century, Coca-Cola's work on the continent had been parsed into southern, middle, and northern units, where North Africa was aligned eastward for administrative purposes and where South Africa fancied itself as distinct from its home continent. In the Coke universe, Africa proper meant sub-Saharan Africa at this time. This would change again over time, as administrative units shifted. Yet, at mid-century, Africa for Coke was Black Africa. By then, the likes of Ernest Hemingway, Teddy Roosevelt, Karen Blixen, and others had done much to solidify an imagined Africa full of unspoiled farms and bountiful, huntable animals, of heroic white outsiders conquering a dark wild. In the Western conception, Africa had been cast in binary terms, ones that had come to characterize the colonial enterprise and, indeed, Westerners' sense of themselves: Westerners were civilized while Africans were savage; they were modern and rooted in history versus tribal and rooted in tradition; most importantly, they were European versus African, which, at the time, was conflated as white versus Black, since there was no room, intellectually, for a white African or a Black European (let alone Indian, Asian, or biracial Africans) in this reductive global imagining of identity. While Coca-Cola—as a company—did not purposefully work to uphold these rigid racial conceptualizations, it did not purposefully work against them either.

In Coca-Cola's internal publication for American bottlers, *The Red Barrel*, this is the Africa we find. A July 1930 edition includes the recollections of one Mrs. W B Seabrook, who, along with her husband, had just returned from a six-month visit to her father, then working at a Coca-Cola office in the Ivory Coast, a place she describes as 'Cannibal Land.'[5] The following year's edition includes a transcript from the radio show 'The Coca-Cola Hour' about wildlife photography in Africa. In it, photographer and Coca-Cola enthusiast Martin Johnson is asked to talk about 'three things about wildlife in Africa—lions, pygmies, and gorillas,' casually lumping people and animals together.[6] In these instances of casual racism and others like them, wild Africa comes alive for American readers, validating the Africa they already imagined.

It is therefore unsurprising that American-based Coca-Cola ad executives would employ familiar tropes about the continent in their advertisement initiatives. This worldview is epitomized in *Wonderful World*, a forty-three-minute film created by Coca-Cola that was first screened in 1959 at a meeting of overseas ad executives in New York City, where representatives from all over the world met for two weeks to discuss innovations in marketing and advertising, both American-born and those created elsewhere. An extended advertisement cast as a documentary, with footage from Chicago to China and from San Francisco to Singapore, *Wonderful World* evidences the stereotypes that guided Coca-Cola's post-war global marketing philosophy. We are first told by way of voiceover that as humans progress beyond the pursuit of basic necessities, everywhere there is 'a universal desire for something beautiful.' This something, we infer from the film's none-too-sly product placement, is Coca-Cola. The film suggests a linear sense of progress, in which contemporary America stands at the pinnacle of achievement. While the entire non-Western world is cast as 'other,' Africa emerges in the film as 'other' in exactly the way we expect it would. After journeying through the 'modern cities' of Casablanca and Cairo, cities, we learn, that are heavily influenced by Islam (code here for outside), we find ourselves taking a ride in a felucca up the Nile, which is likened to journeying 'up the corridor of history.' Minutes later we are staring at Victoria Falls and hearing that 'Africa is a continent of striking contrasts.' Beyond the falls, we learn, 'there are miles upon miles of dense jungle and uncharted veldt' as well as 'the greatest reserve of wild animals in the world.' The film then jumps to a dance scene, and we hear that 'Here also lingers such primitive art forms as the tribal dance' complete with 'Symbolic animal skins, feathers, amulets, [and] the markings of tribal ritual.' 'Almost within earshot of these tribal drums,' we are told—and here comes the contrast—just as in North Africa, 'there are great modern cities like Johannesburg in South Africa,' cities made possible by white colonizers, we infer. Africa in this film is timeless, beyond history. It is vast and empty, tribal and Black. And it is dotted with some imperially created cities. The film ends with the Statue of Liberty and praise for American 'rights, privileges, and responsibilities.'[7] By 1961, *Wonderful World* had received special mention at the International Exhibition of Documentary Films in Venice, had been voiced over in at least nine languages, and had been seen by millions worldwide.[8] By that decade at least, Coca-Cola's global advertisements represented where the company saw its product—and its home country—in the world.[9] For The Coca-Cola Company understood perfectly well what a film like this could do to promote its viewpoint and product. As an article from a few years later put it, with regard to advertising's objective: 'Advertising cannot be a completely disinterested service of consumer information.' Rather, the author made clear for his audience of Coke employees south of the Sahara, 'it is salesmanship on a mass scale, it is the truth well told.'[10] If done correctly, in other words, advertisements both render a product known and shape the knowable.

Freedom and Advertising

From its earliest days, The Coca-Cola Company understood that the way it marketed itself was just as important as the products it marketed. Under the direction of leading American agencies, Coca-Cola's advertisements became icons of product branding—think of rotund red-and-white Santa Claus and Norman Rockwell's idyllic Americana.[11] The marketing choices that drove its advertisements were deliberate. The goal, a 1948 article in *Coca-Cola Overseas* noted, was to show how Coca-Cola, an inexpensive impulse purchase, 'logically' fit into one's life and to promote the idea—as the earliest ads did—that the drink is a quality product that 'relieves fatigue,' is 'delicious and refreshing,' and, lest anyone think it was only for the summer, that 'thirst knows no season.' At the close of World War II, Coke's marketing also came to reflect the company's recent global expansion. 'Around the Corner from Anywhere and Whoever you are, whatever you do, wherever you may be, when you think of refreshment think of Coca-Cola,' consumers were implored.[12] Increasingly available everywhere for everyone, Coca-Cola offered itself up to all in the post-World War II world.

Coca-Cola's visual advertising aimed to sell the product and the American worldview with which it had become conflated. Reflecting on 'Freedom and Advertising' in 1949, ad executive Will Grant voiced his sense of Coca-Cola's grandiose global role. 'The bright red signs for Coca-Cola that appear all around the world are playing a greater part in the gradual progress toward a better way of life than one may think at first glance,' wrote Grant: 'In an almost human way, the signs for Coca-Cola have become a part of the dramatic struggle of man for a better way of life. In the many languages of the world... they embody the way of life based on the freedom of every individual to make his own choice. They are a cheerful acceptance of the premise of free enterprise.'[13] For Grant and others like him, Coca-Cola signs did more than just peddle product; they spoke to local aspirations, proclaiming that a good life—by way of a good drink—was within arm's reach for all. By the end of the decade, this concept would dominate Coke marketing, with ads declaring the beverage itself to be a 'sign of good taste.'[14]

In the post-World War II world of the soda's expansion, Coca-Cola advertisements thus promoted not a drink, but an idea. The notion was a simple one: that people are fundamentally the same no matter who or where they are. We can take this to mean that people are all potential consumers. Driven by the same human desire to live the best lives possible, they all deserve access to the same products. Coca-Cola promoted this democratic idea by keeping its price stable and low, hoping to render its drinks attainable luxuries. During its initial years of global expansion, the company also focused on using singular advertisement campaigns, created in America and distributed globally. This is why we find the same print ad in different languages from Cairo to Kansas City in the first half of the twentieth century. Such a system ensured standardization of font, message, and image, reflecting a belief in the overall superficiality of human difference. Still, it often played out to surreal effect since the default models were always Americans who often appeared out of place outside of America.[15]

In the 1950s, Coke's growing global presence demanded a different advertising strategy. In response, The Coca-Cola Company started to distribute 'pattern' ad campaigns that could—and should—be adopted to meet local realities on the ground. Previewing the mockup of the 1957 'Let Coca-Cola put you at your Sparkling Best' campaign in *Overseas*, readers were assured that 'Local situations, problems of reproduction and translation, varying space sizes—all have been taken into consideration,' such that one template should suit all situations. Writing to places grappling with, as the article termed them, 'native situations,' the author noted that 'Illustrations can be easily adapted to the needs of different countries where different races must be featured.'[16] This is precisely what happened in Africa. The 1950s saw the rise of marketing on the continent that portrayed African consumer cultures using

African models, such as a 1952 Arabic-language Moroccan ad picturing a fez-clad man, a 1957 French-language Ivory Coast ad with a Black model, and a 1959 South African ad featuring the iconic singer Miriam Makeba imploring consumers to 'Be smart: choose Coca-Cola.' These campaigns and others like them were rendered locally, making advertising another secondary industry strengthened by Coca-Cola.[17] As 'the pause that refreshes' gave way to 'Coke refreshes you best,' as 'Things go better with a Coke,' gave way to 'Things go better with big, Big Coke' upon the unveiling of larger packages, African advertising agencies took global campaigns and localized them.[18] While local advertisements were careful to reflect both the company's overarching mission, as seen in *Wonderful World*, as well as whatever the reigning global campaign was, local rendering attuned the ads to target audiences. In turn, these ads became another way that Coca-Cola came to be seen as local wherever it landed, of particular importance during the upheaval that attended the end of colonialism.

Africa, Emergent

At a 1960 meeting of central and southern African leadership, A E Killeen, then Export Vice President and Area Manager for Africa, spoke about what he called 'The Challenge of the Sixties.' According to reports, 'Mr. Killeen emphasized that we [Coca-Cola bottlers] have everything to lose if we do not take a firm hand now and decide to carry out business operations with skill and determination, whatever the challenges the future holds.'[19] The challenge, we can assume, was how to steer the Coke business through the coming of African independence, then embryonic.[20] Judging from a photograph of the meeting, he gave this speech to a room full of white managers from across the continent, suggesting that, regardless of where these people came from, the vast majority of Black Africans were as of yet excluded from these positions of power in the business. This would soon change. So too would it later become apparent that the way Killeen and others framed this moment would inform global Coca-Cola policies for years to come.[21]

Killeen is an interesting figure. Born in Iowa in 1912, he served in World War II in India before moving to South Africa to work for Douglas Aircrafts. He first joined the Coca-Cola business on the bottler side, managing a plant. In 1953, he crossed over to Export, working his way up to positions of power within both the southern and central business units, before becoming Vice President of Export in 1964. In 1974, he moved back to Atlanta as Senior Vice President of Export, before being elected Executive Vice President of Marketing for the entire company.

Killeen's time in Africa was formative, both for him and for the company. During his many years on the continent, he traveled widely: 'In Africa,' he reflected, 'I used to get everyone from our offices out into the trucks, riding routes, talking with dealers—all in an effort to keep us in touch with the realities of the marketplace, and to sell more Coca-Cola.'[22] Under a program called 'operation customer,' Coke employees across Middle Africa would journey to various parts of their markets in order to understand what motivated stakeholders.[23] Killeen insisted that 'fact, not fiction,' govern the Coke business, championing extensive research on markets, products, and operations that accompanied this travel.[24] The result was that he—and those under him—seemed to understand that Africa on the ground was nothing like Africa was imagined to be from outside. During his time in Africa, Killeen would spearhead not only the diversification of products and packages, but also manpower development and equal employee benefits programs aimed to correct racial disparities within the business.[25] To be sure, such high-minded initiatives were not solely born of activism. Rather, they reflected a belief that a free market—unencumbered by racial policies—was better for business.[26]

When asked in the mid-1970s about how he was managing his transition back to America, Killeen pushed back against what he understood to be his interlocutor's false sense of the continent. 'That question makes me wonder if, in fact, I had been committed to the remotest village in the densest jungle of darkest Africa,' he began. 'The reverse of that desolate picture is the truth. During my stay in Africa, I had the opportunity to visit most African countries and most of the major and secondary cities and their marketplaces, plus the up-country and rural areas. Remember, please, that the people, terrain, cities, climate, marketplaces, cultures, life-styles, and standards of living differ as widely in Africa as they do in the United States, and perhaps more so.'[27] In this exchange, Killeen seemed to say, Africa is not what you think it is. It was precisely because Killeen and others like him saw both the complexity of the continent and the humanity of its inhabitants that they were able to steer the business there as politics changed. Starting in North Africa and moving downward, Coca-Cola had to navigate the continent's transition to independence. With the exception of Egypt and Libya, which were already independent by the time Coca-Cola landed there, Coca-Cola operations across North Africa had weathered each nation's transition to independence.[28] The company, by way of its bottlers, now sought to do likewise across sub-Saharan Africa as freedom dawned mid-century.

In 1960, *Coca-Cola South of the Sahara*, another of the company's internal African publications, put out a special supplement celebrating Ghanaian independence, achieved three years earlier, as a way to mark the company's renewed commitment to the changing continent. Titled 'Ghana: New Africa Emergent,' it praised the new nation and extolled the extant Coca-Cola business—and embeddedness—there. Further company publications suggested that not only did Coca-Cola stay in Ghana through its political transition, but that it also grew there. In 1960, Fanta was introduced. By 1962, six-packs were on the shelves.[29] Coke king size and Sprite were not far behind. Repeatedly, readers were given glimpses of the beverage's alignment with the new nation, starting at the highest office, with President Kwame Nkrumah. Upon the opening of the first Coca-Cola plant in Accra, Nkrumah reportedly said he was pleased 'a wholesome product like "Coca-Cola" was now available in Ghana to refresh thirsty throats.'[30] In 1963, *Overseas* ran a picture of Nkrumah's presidential garden party that included a shot of his three-year-old toddler, Samia Yaba Nkrumah, drinking from a large glass bottle of Fanta orange.[31] In 1965, Coca-Cola bottling trucks participated in a parade to mark Nkrumah's birthday, now known as Founder's Day, boasting banners that wished the president—and, by implication, the beverage—long life in this free nation.[32]

Coca-Cola was likewise present as other countries on the continent achieved independence from colonial rule. In 1960, the business celebrated its continued work in newly independent Senegal, boasting for its readers that it abounded under the 'modern skyline' of Dakar as well as 'the most remote corners' of the country.[33] That same year, Coke marked its new operations in the new nation of Burundi, noting the rapid acceptance of both Coke and Fanta there.[34] Across the continent, Coca-Cola bottlers staked a visible presence at the events that marked the emergence of post-colonial Africa. This work was deliberate, steered often from Export leadership and its awareness of how businesses should position themselves in independent Africa. In June 1963, Chairman of the Board of the Coca-Cola Export Corporation, James Farley, along with other Export members, received certificates for attending a talk at the United Nations by Ambassador S O Adeho, Nigeria's permanent representative to the United Nations, about corporate responsibility overseas. The implication of the talk was that along with responsibilities came benefits.[35] Events like these helped underscore the business's sense that entrenching itself in post-colonial countries was a good idea that had the benefit of looking like a high-minded idea.

On the ground, Coca-Cola's commitment to a changing Africa could also be seen in the company's deliberate attempt to weather what were often tumultuous transitions. Its point of pride in 1960 was that it did not abandon its work during the so-called Congo Crisis that followed 1960 independence in what is now the DR Congo. According to Coca-Cola Export's internal newsletters from that year, during the upheaval that attended independence, the Congo Bottling Operation was able to keep its plants operating in both Leopoldville and Stanleyville; the company was particularly proud of what it saw as the 'bravery' of its Congolese District manager who returned from a European furlough to cross the Congo River in order to 'salvage the District office records and Company car.'[36] Not only did Coca-Cola maintain operations during this crisis, but its sales also increased during it.[37] It is possible that this profitability helped set a precedent, proving that political unrest does not preclude money-making. Coke's tenacity was also celebrated in an Export newsletter from May 1961. In this, the travails of the African Area engineer and his assistant were recounted. During the Congo Crisis, the men had been caught in Matadi when they were precluded from boarding the ferry to leave the troubled area. That is, until they told the guards that they were 'civilians on Coke business,' at which point 'the attitudes of the guards changed completely' and the two were 'smilingly allowed to board the ferry.' Coca-Cola, in other words, provided them with a ticket to operate with a kind of impunity.[38] This too became a hallmark of Coke work in a transitioning continent, demonstrating the power of business.

For its part, Coca-Cola cast its perseverance as commitment. When its new plant opened in Congo in 1961, the company noted that this bottling plant 'is a living symbol of confidence in a country on the way to complete recovery.'[39]

Where the transition from colonial to postcolonial rule involved invoking so-called traditional leaders, Coca-Cola was similarly deliberate in its alignment with these loci of power. In 1963, Princess Buyisiwe Dlamini of Swaziland, daughter of Paramount Chief Sobhuza II, graced the cover of *Overseas*. The occasion: the opening of the Swaziland Bottling Company, the first and only Coca-Cola bottling plant in what was still a British protectorate (full independence for Swaziland was won in 1968). Prince Sifuba Dlamini presided over the opening, with both Killeen and Chief Manyakatane Mdluli present. For the occasion, Killeen spoke about 'how prosperity can come to Swaziland through industry.'[40] The following year witnessed the royal wedding of another of Sobhuza's daughters, Princess Gcinaphi, to Nkontinophondo Khumalo, a director of the Swaziland Bottling Company, further entwining the royal family with the Coke business.[41] On the other side of the continent, in Nigeria, a 1965 *Overseas* edition included a picture of recently installed Oba Kobiowu, the Olubadan (king) of Ibadan, presiding over the opening of a 'Total Garden,' which served only Coca-Cola, owned and run by Prince Sijuade, heir to the throne.[42] That same year, the Coca-Cola Bottling Company of Durban was on hand playing a similar role in apartheid South Africa, where endorsing tribal authority simultaneously ingratiated the company with said tribe and the apartheid state. Alongside Durban's mayor, bottlers brought thousands of cold Cokes, Sprites, and Fantas to the opening of the Zulu Paramount chief Cyprian Bekhuzulu's official residence in KwaMashu Township.[43] In each case, the business of Coke gained credibility and support from local sources of royal power. And in each case, the company took tribal authority at face value, undoubtedly because the notion fit squarely with its sense of authentic Africa.

Coca-Cola's New Strategy

Coca-Cola's multi-prong strategies seemed to work. Whether freedom was won, freedom was being fought for, or colonialism/ apartheid continued unabated, Coca-Cola found a way to stay, maintaining enough goodwill to continually grow its business. In fact, 1963 marked an all-time high for Coca-Cola sales outside of the United States. The following year, fifty Export officials from twenty countries convened in Atlanta at the 'Woodruff Fortieth Anniversary Meeting of the Management of the Overseas Business' (named in honor of the man who launched Coca-Cola beyond American shores) to reflect upon this accomplishment. At the meeting, Export president Lee Talley attributed the landmark growth of the business overseas to two processes: the diversification of Coke products and new marketing techniques. Both were playing out in a changing Africa, as attendees learned. Fanta and Sprite had been particularly successful, thanks to planning, extensive sampling, and innovative marketing, as you will see in the text that follows.[44] Beyond the introduction of new product lines, attendees at the Woodruff meeting were told that the launch of larger bottles of Coke red had been a huge success, demonstrating the potential for both king and family size packages.[45] King size (or 10 ounce) Coke had already risen in sales across the continent, beginning with its roll-out in Dar es Salaam in 1957.[46] Family packs followed suit. Consumer thrift and the allure of convenience led to increased demand for bigger packages, a trend that was not unique to Africa. At the same time, the larger packages, by design, were meant to be consumed at home, broadening where and how people drank soda.[47] Tied into all was the growth of supermarkets and the marketing push to convince people to drink Coca-Cola while eating food, again something that was not unique to Africa.[48] The African area sales meeting from 1960 responded to this trend with the catchphrase 'King Size Coca-Cola has more for you.'[49]

Along with the roll-out of new products and new sizes was the deliberate attempt to reach more Black consumers. In 1960, manager of the southern Africa region, R H Pasea, spoke to a meeting of salespeople with just this message. While 1961 would be a time where 'Politically, socially and economically, the whole of Africa, south of the Sahara, was going to be severely tested,' bottlers' best bet, he said, was to train their sites on the 'vital' 'non-European market.'[50] Here, as elsewhere, non-European meant Black people. New products and larger packages could only do so much. Now, Coca-Cola bottlers had to deliberately focus on capturing the bulk of Africans and activating them as consumers.

Closely related to reaching Black consumers—a story I pick up in the next chapter in more depth—was the deliberate empowering of Black workers within the Coca-Cola system. In the early 1960s, internal Coke publications began to devote space to instances of Black worker advancement, which, in these years, took place most often under the auspices of local bottlers. The same special edition of *Coca-Cola South of the Sahara* that praised emergent Ghana and Coke's perseverance through the Congo Crisis devoted some attention to a recent sales training course that had been organized by Leopoldville Bottlers. The course, readers learned, was put together for a select group of Black salesmen to discuss pressing local issues. The high point was the 'passing out dinner,' where each man received a diploma, credentialing him in the Coke system.[51] The message of the special edition seemed to be that, in 1960 Africa, Coke was celebrating independence, weathering harsh traditions, and turning its attention to the newly empowered majority all at once.

In a 1961 edition of *Overseas*, readers were again reminded that Black empowerment was on bottlers' agenda with a story about how the opening of a new Coca-Cola plant in Kenya included information about 'the welfare and advancement of Africans in locally-owned Coca-Cola bottling plants.'[52] Two years later, *Overseas* profiled L M Chaponda, a director of Nyasaland Bottling Company, the only licensed bottler of Coke and Fanta in what is now Malawi, no doubt to celebrate a Black employee who had risen through company ranks. Chaponda, readers learned, 'is an example of the hard-working and ambitious Africans who are striving for success for themselves and their emerging nations.' His story is an impressive one. Born in 1929 and educated at Scottish missions and by correspondence course, Chaponda worked his way up from being an accounts clerk at a transport company to owning his own service station (the first Black Malawian to do so) as well as his own fleet of trucks that came to transport everything from bricks to Coca-Cola. In 1958, he convinced his brother to join the company as the first Black salesman, making his work there a family affair. 'Being a shrewd businessman and seeing the rapid expansion of Coca-Cola in Nyasaland,' readers learned, 'Chaponda, in 1960, bought several shares in the local bottling company. Subsequently, he showed such an interest in the Company that he was asked to become a director in 1962.'[53]

Though an outlier in terms of his achievement, Chaponda was not alone in finding a path to betterment via Coca-Cola. In 1964, *Overseas* readers were introduced to Peter Ngugi, a fast-rising salesman for the Nairobi plant (who also happened to be a star golfer).[54] That same year, Espin Mlandle, a route salesman for Phil Gutsche's operation in Port Elizabeth, was profiled. Educated only up to standard six, Mlandle had nonetheless risen swiftly through company ranks since he joined the business two years earlier. His current salary, readers were told, was twice what it was when he worked as a tax collector. Mlandle's charge was to serve the densely populated areas of New Brighton and Kwazakela townships outside of Port Elizabeth, servicing 'small shops serving lesser developed areas' and helping open up the Black market. 'It's a tough assignment,' readers learned, 'But Espin Mlalandle is tough,' repeatedly winning sales contests and catapulting himself to the forefront of sales for the plant.[55] The following year, Prince Elliot Zulu, of the Zulu royal family, was the guest of honor at a party thrown for the Black staff of the Coca-Cola Bottling Company of Durban. At this braai, or barbeque, awards were given to more than two-dozen long-term employees. Among those to receive awards were Dabuyana (Charlie) Hlongwana, who had worked for Coca-Cola Export for twenty years, and Mvungazeli Faya, who had clocked in fifteen years, during which time each man rose through the system, suggesting that for every successful Black employee who was profiled in an internal company publication—and thus captured for the historical record—there were more who went unnoticed.[56] These vignettes and others like them demonstrate some of the avenues for (almost exclusively male) Black betterment that were extant or emergent at Coca-Cola plants across the continent by the 1960s.

Marketing to Emergent Africa

At the same time as Coca-Cola was augmenting its sales by deliberately targeting Black consumers and empowering Black workers, its marketing and advertisements—now touting Coca-Cola, Sprite, and Fanta, as well as some local products—were similarly evolving.[57] A strong move for localizing ads had occurred since the end of World War II, as documented earlier. From this push now emerged a series of African ad campaigns in the 1960s and into the 1970s that sought to accomplish multiple goals at once: broaden the products' reach with a highly localized message that, in turn, gave consumers a sense of ownership over the product and home itself, a particularly important concept in the shifting terrain of mid-century Africa. These ads also sought to comingle product promotion with a kind of activism centered around the natural and the knowable.

In 1961, Coca-Cola Export launched the first such promotion in Mombasa, in then Kenya colony. Called the 'Animals of Africa,' this campaign asked consumers to collect and then exchange six specially marked crowns, or bottle caps, plus one cent, for any of twenty ivorine figures of African animals. These tiny plastic animals were meant to stand against a three-dimensional backdrop, which was available for purchase separately. The campaign landed in Nairobi a few months later with elaborate sales displays that entreated consumers to find 'your own fabulous big game collection.' But the pursuit was not just selfish, consumers learned. 'Every time you refresh with ice-cold Coca-Cola, you help a wild animal survive,' they were told, since proceeds went to the 'Water for Wild Animals Fund.' It was the conservation aspect of the campaign that appealed to various charities, first in Kenya and then beyond, leading other countries to call for its expansion.[58] By 1962, the promotion had arrived in Uganda, where a young boy named Aminsi Katumba was photographed receiving a full set of animals for having the good luck of claiming the 200,000th figurine distributed.[59] Two years later, the animals arrived in Réunion, where they were photographed being used by a teacher during a lecture, as well as in Mauritius, where sales teams were photographed distributing them along with product samples in a hospital for children with disabilities.[60]

The strength of the Animals of Africa campaign was two-fold. Firstly, the campaign appealed to children, aiding in product sampling and market growth. The promotion also seemed educational, which, again, gave it longevity. In 1962, Nairobi Bottlers ran a follow-up promotion that asked schoolchildren to paint sets of figurines and matching dioramas in which to house them. The director of the Royal National Parks of Kenya and a secretary of the National Arts and Crafts Committee judged entries from a wide range of Kenyans, awarding transistor radios to the winners (a young Sikh boy and a teenage white boy, as seen in the published photographs and their captions). Besides being good fun and good marketing, this spin-off promised 'to interest school children in wild animals and national game parks, both so important to the life and economy of Kenya,' as *Overseas* readers were told.[61] Something similar was at play in Bulawayo, then Southern Rhodesia. When two lion cubs were orphaned by a hunter in Uganda, the manager of Bulawayo Bottlers took up the lions' cause. At his insistence, Coca-Cola Export arranged for the animals to be moved to and preserved in the Johannesburg Zoo. For the Bulawayo manager, this cause was 'a most fitting climax to the "Animals of Africa," promotion' there; he awarded four child winners the chance to travel to Johannesburg to witness the cubs' relocation.[62] That same year, Animals of Africa kits were given to Johannesburg Zoo curators to give as host gifts on their tour of European zoological gardens, demonstrating the degree to which the promotion had spread beyond mere marketing.[63]

Herein lies the second strength of the Animals of Africa campaign: by appealing to a budding notion of conservation aimed at protecting natural Africa, Coca-Cola aligned itself with an emergent, seemingly apolitical cause. The preservation and upkeep of animals as well as the notion of reserving land for their free movement were nascent ideas in these years, marking a distinct shift from Africa as huntable to Africa as savable.[64] Coca-Cola was fast on board with this move. As early as June 1962, a year into the campaign, Export earmarked a check for $22,400 to the Water for Game Fund that was turned over to the Wild Life Protection Society of Southern Africa.[65] And that was just the start. By 1967, Export had donated $100,000 for wildlife protection, funds raised exclusively through the Animals of Africa campaign. A portion of these funds went towards supporting still-young national parks, something of a pet project for Coca-Cola. In 1962, Export funded 100 underprivileged South African children to visit South Africa's Kruger National Park, all of whom had never seen a wild animal outside of a zoo.[66] A few years later, Coke money was put towards digging bore-holes and erecting a memorial library in the park itself.[67] In a similar vein, in 1963 the Kampala Coke bottler sponsored a student trip to Uganda National Park, where students were photographed taking a break from animal viewing and drinking Cokes at the monument marking the Equator.[68] Cast in ivorine, a plastic meant to look like ivory (which was not yet considered anathema to the cause of conservation), tiny plastic animals helped ensure the protection of large flesh-and-blood animals.

The Animals of Africa figurines were highly sought after at the time of this widespread promotion. They remain so amongst collectors today. During his tenure, CEO Muhtar Kent had a complete set on display outside his office high within Coca-Cola's flagship office in Atlanta. *Coca-Cola Journey*, the company's online magazine, reflected on this novel campaign in 2012, noting that at the time of launch, the company wanted 'a large-scale promotion which would not only offer to the public interesting and attractive premiums for the purchases of Coca-Cola, but would be of direct assistance in a cause of national importance, namely, the protection of the wildlife of Africa.'[69] What is interesting here is the idea that the preservation of wildlife was of great concern to most Africans in 1961. I suspect it was not. This was the first year of independence for seventeen countries in Africa. More continued to fight for their freedom. Some, like South Africa, were just seeing the darkest days of oppression dawning. It strikes me as highly unlikely that in any of these countries would we find a majority who was worried about preserving nature. More likely, the preservation of nature and animals was a minority concern, rooted in anxiety about changing political landscapes. As such, I would suggest, the promotion of African animals allowed The Coca-Cola Company to skirt difficult questions of citizenship and colonial legacies in order to market an Africa—to itself as much as to outsiders— that was benign and natural. The two concepts, in fact, seemed to merge.

The success of the Animals of Africa meant that it was not to be the last of its kind. In 1962, dignitaries in Durban, Port Elizabeth, and Cape Town, South Africa released carrier pigeons carrying with them specially issued promissory notes from Fanta-bottlers that were redeemable by wildlife authorities, thus announcing that the Birds of Africa campaign had arrived. Like its precursor, this campaign entailed print ads that showed up in newspapers and on trucks, in addition to cinema slides and promotional point-of-sale materials. This time, consumers exchanged specially marked Fanta crowns (plus one cent) for any of twelve replica ivorine birds.[70] Like Animals, Birds entailed product sampling and youth appeal. And like the Animals, it too spread beyond its country of origin. It was kicked off in 1965 Mauritius, for instance, in the island's schools, where ice-cold Fanta Orange was sampled and kids were given one free miniature bird to seed their collections.[71] Here collecting functioned as it always did within colonialism, as a way to assert power, and thus ownership, over the outside world.[72] Again, whether deliberately or not, Birds served to position Coca-Cola as central to a matrix where belonging in the nation equaled knowledge about and control over the natural world.

After animals and birds came flora, with a campaign launched exclusively in South Africa. The Kirstenbosch Flower Campaign, named after Cape Town's eponymous garden, began in 1964, as a follow-up to both Animals and Birds. Coinciding with the garden's Golden Jubilee, Coca-Cola Export promised the garden that a minimum donation of $14,000 would result from the campaign. Like its predecessors, the Kirstenbosch Flower Campaign invited the public to collect 100 card illustrations of flowers that would then go into an album (available for purchase separately), written (in both English and Afrikaans) by then director Professor Brian Rycroft. This was a robust campaign: flower-clad floats announced its launch across the country while a partnership with South African Airlines brought a Viennese model to the country to peddle clothes and flower albums in participating department stores. Redemption centers were set up in supermarkets while the Boy and Cub Scouts sold albums door-to-door and schools competed for a special scholarship. To spur them on, a competition was launched amongst salesmen, too. To ease the process, Export officials contacted salesmen's wives, sending these 'surprised recipients' a letter imploring 'them to be tolerant when their husbands arrived home late due to the extra effort they would be exerting.'[73] Unlike the other campaigns, which had appeal beyond their countries of origin, Kirstenbosch Flowers stayed in South Africa. Like Animals and Birds, this too had a colonial flavor to it, to the extent that we can see apartheid as a form of colonialism.[74] As the apartheid state was solidifying, Flowers skirted politics entirely, using sexism to appeal to an undoubtedly white, female segment of the population—those able to shop at department stores and who had the time and wherewithal to collect pictures of wild flowers. Here again, the natural became a safe place for Coca-Cola from which to promote its products in a way that urged a portion of the citizenry to feel a sense of ownership over part of the country's natural heritage.

Towards the end of the decade, South African Coca-Cola bottlers initiated a campaign that picked up where the Flowers left off, once more tying product promotion to a kind of narrow patriotism. 'Know Our Country,' described in *Overseas* as 'an unusual national consumer campaign with strong public relations overtones,' ran from September to December 1967, in collaboration with the state-run Springbok Radio. The promotion included a checkerboard map of the country (available separately), where participants would place square stamps as though filling in a puzzle. The map reflected the most up-to-date boundaries and ecological information about the country as well as, in the corner, a small Coca-Cola insignia. Participants, who had to be between the ages of eight and eighteen, exchanged six removable liners from crowns in return for a map square. Then, each week, radio personalities would ask listeners questions about the map, questions that presumably queried how well they knew their country. Of the reported tens of thousands who participated, there were 165 winners. Each won one of four impressive free vacations: a trip by coast from Cape Town to Durban and then overland to the Umfolosi Game Reserve (now Hluhluwe); a trip to Etosha Game Park in then Southwest Africa (now Namibia); a trip by air to Victoria Falls and Kariba Dam in then Southern Rhodesia (now Zimbabwe); or a trip to Swaziland (now Eswatini) and Kruger National Park. According to *Overseas*, government support was nothing short of 'enthusiastic,' given the 'campaign's tremendous educational' value to children and adults alike.[75] Reflecting on the campaign before its launch to Killeen, J Paul Austin wrote 'If this promotion is not a great success I will be dumbfounded. It seems to have every element.'[76]

There is much that is interesting about this campaign. The timing, for one. The year 1967 was the height of apartheid, a dark era when ten state-declared Bantustans (euphemistically called homelands) were used to negate Black South African citizenship and as justification for calling South Africa a country of whites only. Then there were the pronouns. The objects of 'your' and 'our' are unclear. If it is any indication of just who was being spoken to, in the above article celebrating the campaign, all eight child winners photographed are white. At the same time, we also have to wonder about the word 'know' and what it meant to have knowledge about your country. The ability to place markers on a map, to name, and thus assert ownership reeks of colonial space-making and a literal surface-level knowledge about a place. Then, of course, there were the prizes. In exchange for knowing about terrain and boundaries, children were sent to view animals and nature; with the exception of Umfolosi and Kruger, these trips took the children outside of the Union of South Africa proper, making us wonder if country was being elided for continent. Did being able to locate a country on the map grant ownership over the rest of the region? In apartheid South Africa, desperate to exert control over the frontline states that threatened its existence, maybe. Or were animals simply the prize—the idea that knowledge affords the chance to luxuriate in an Africa unspoiled, an Africa populated not by troublesome people but by intelligible animals. More than the other large-scale mid-century campaigns, this one reified the logic of colonialism and apartheid, seemingly ignoring the bulk of South African consumers. Yet, it was this campaign that traveled—albeit in changed form—beyond South African boundaries.

By the middle of 1969, 'Know Your Country' had been picked up by bottlers across the continent. A newspaper ad from Liberia showed how the contest worked there. On offer was $7,000 worth of prizes, $750 for first place plus twenty-five Phillips transistor radios and 100 prizes of ten dollars each. To enter, consumers had to send six stickers (found in specially marked Fanta caps) along with a completed form answering six multiple-choice questions ranging from identifying important buildings to estimating the country's total square mileage.[77] Everywhere, the contest entailed identifying national landmarks on bottler-created forms, according to the *Overseas* story 'Middle Africa Knows.' The piece included photographs of one Michael M Aselo, who won a Honda motorcycle in 1968 Kenya, and one Mrs. Adetokunbo Olafenwa, who was runner-up in the Nigerian contest that year, showing that beyond South Africa, the campaign reached Black consumers. Still, the naming and locating of landmarks aligned Coke bottlers with nationalist programs, whatever the context. Nowhere does Coca-Cola seem to grapple with the deeper questions at play. 'The contest not only increases interest in the product,' *Overseas* happily reported, 'but it generates excellent goodwill for Coca-Cola bottlers as it helps people know more about their country.'[78]

By 1969, Know Your Country had been eclipsed by a new campaign urging consumers to 'Discover Africa with Coca-Cola.' In a joint print ad for Coca-Cola, Fanta, and Sprite, co-sponsored by bottlers in Kenya, Uganda, and Tanganyika, consumers learned that there were 150,000 shillings worth of prizes on offer, including three cars. The contest followed the familiar form, where consumers had to send in stickers from specially marked caps (of all three products) along with a completed multiple-choice questionnaire (seen at the bottom of ads). The difference: these questions were no longer country-specific, but instead jumped from the pyramids in Egypt to the headquarters of the Organization of African Unity to Mt. Kilimanjaro.[79] By 1970, Discover Africa had reached Ghana. Posters on the backs of trucks advertised the campaign, urging consumers to try their hand at naming a handful of countries outlined on an otherwise blank map of the continent. In an article for the internal magazine *In Middle Africa*, this campaign was noted as being 'among the most popular promotions ever.' Two photographs that accompanied the piece showed several winners, one Mrs. Patience Museun, who is seen receiving her prize from salesman Vincent Katseku, and two unnamed young male winners in Takoradi, seen receiving their awards from the local depot manager, K Wiafe.[80] Telescoping from one country to tackle 'Africa' more generally, this campaign focused on capturing consumers by imploring them to discover their continent.

Beyond asking consumers to Discover Africa with Coke, from the late 1960s the company's internal publications devoted increasing space to helping readers in the larger Coke world discover the continent virtually. Company magazines filled with pieces extolling the landscapes of everywhere from the Seychelles to Madagascar, Uganda, and more.[81] Gone were articles about modern cities and citizens. The pages were now filled with broad spreads of oceans and mountains and animals. What was interesting about Africa was once more what was most natural about it. A 1968 piece went so far as to describe Southwest Africa as the 'edge of the world.' In this long essay, Southwest Africa was cast as a place without people, awaiting discovery by, in this case, the Coke-drinking travelers whose pictures accompany the story.[82] A similar piece, titled 'East to Eden,' extolled the beauty of the Seychelles, yet to be 'spoiled.'[83] The implication was that free Africa remained wild Africa. By the early 1970s, Coca-Cola executives were similarly focused on nature, underwriting the production of a film, 'Africa's Big Five,' meant for use by bottlers across the continent.[84] In settler colonies in particular, bottlers were particularly trained on the natural. In South Africa, they were championing the plight of cheetahs, calling for preservation as opposed to hunting. In Kenya, bottlers were running a wildlife essay contest for schoolchildren as part of what was called the Big, Big Five Contest.[85] Where settler colonialism was being eclipsed, rising anxiety about whites' continued presence on the continent mapped onto bottlers' anxiety, leading to increased attention not to African people, but to African wildlife.

Coca-Cola's interest in Africa as wild—as seen in its internal publications—persisted into the era of late colonialism (1975 onward) and into the postcolonial era. As with the animals, birds, and fauna, with the knowing and then the discovery of a country or the continent, the focus was on collecting, owning, and naming space, of comingling the beverage with that which is beautiful, natural, and, as such, authentically African, without any hint of irony. Always, this was a fraught, uneven endeavor, aligned with nationalistic goals, in South Africa's case, placing the company firmly within the logic of apartheid. At root, these campaigns seemed to suggest that Coca-Cola could stand as an arbiter of knowledge, that it could judge what was both correct and worth knowing about an animal or a bird or a country. In so doing, the business seemed to cast itself as both outside of Africa—knowing more about the continent than it did about itself—and inherently of Africa, attuned to local wisdom. Here the company seemed to echo Jacob Dlamini's sense of how conservation functions in the colonial logic: '[T]o know the African wild,' he writes about Kruger National Park's directors, 'was to know the African subject.'[86] To know nature was to know Africans, since Africans were closer to wild than civilized. And to know Africans—to transplant Dlamini's statement into business—was to be able to sell to Africans. Since, ultimately, all marketing was just packaging to create truth well-told.

Kariba Dam

Here is where the rub of Coca-Cola's work in Middle Africa in the middle of the century becomes most clear. In attempting to broaden its market share and engender goodwill, Coca-Cola tried to be everything to everyone, to align itself with whatever loci of power seemed ascendant, ignoring others, all in the name of being both above and of Africa. Cloaked behind a wall of supposedly democratic red signs, driven by the expedient notion that anyone and everyone can be a consumer, the company was shrewd in its positioning, difficult work on a continent where power dynamics were rapidly shifting. Sometimes, Coca-Cola found itself on the right side of history, as when it threw its weight behind emergent independent nations. Other times, it did not, aligning itself with despots of one sort or another. Always, there was a slipperiness to its work, a sense that if and when the power shifted, so too might Coca-Cola's allegiance, or, put another way, that casting itself as democratic meant that it was open to all, good and bad, all the time. Most often, the strength and weaknesses of Coca-Cola's co-branding were ambiguous at the time and remain so in hindsight.

Take, for instance, Coca-Cola's relationship to Kariba Dam, the most dramatic infrastructure project undertaken on the continent mid-century. Built between 1955 and 1959 on the Zambesi River under the auspices of the Central African Federation (a ten-year-long federal dominion of the British protectorates of Nyasaland and Northern Rhodesia and the self-governing British colony of Southern Rhodesia—now Malawi, Zambia, and Zimbabwe) and funded by the World Bank, this hydroelectric power station 400 km from Victoria Falls was meant to electrify the Zambian Copperbelt and growing Zimbabwean industry; it provides power to both countries to this day. With Kariba Dam came Kariba Lake, the largest manmade lake in the world, whose construction entailed flooding previously dry land. The entire project was steered by Italian architects and sub-contractors and actualized by 6,000 laborers—the vast majority local—to do the difficult, often dangerous work entailed in building a structure four times the size of the Hoover Dam. A village was built around the project that included family housing for white workers, a school for white children, bachelor quarters for Black workers, a hospital, a radio station, a post-office, a bank, canteens, and an airfield.[87] The massive undertaking required a related five-year-long mission, called Operation

Noah, to move thousands of animals from Kariba Gorge. Tens of thousands of Tonga people who lived in the area were forcibly moved without consultation—and without such a cutely named mission.[88] To them, the dam remains a breakage point in their history to this day.

The June 1957 edition of *Coca-Cola Overseas* celebrated Coca-Cola's enmeshment in the dam's construction. During the long construction years, readers learned, the Salisbury Bottling Company made sure that the soda was consistently available, regularly shipping it to retail dealers and canteens there. Even a flood could not stop this process. Under those extreme circumstances, Coca-Cola was transported manually on the heads of workers across a narrow foot bridge, a scene photographed to local delight.[89] When, in 1960, Queen Elizabeth, the Queen Mother arrived to inaugurate this 'Colossus of Africa,' Coca-Cola was again visibly present along with the 3,000 people there to mark the occasion. 'Of course "Coca-Cola" and "Fanta" were no strangers to Kariba,' readers of *Coca-Cola South of the Sahara* were told, as 'many millions of bottles of our famous beverage have gone down the thirsty and appreciative throats of the many workers from the country and overseas, who have contributed to the successful completion of the Kariba Dam.'[90] The creation of Kariba Dam was a modern engineering feat. It was also an old-fashioned colonial endeavor. All of the usual markers of a colonial undertaking were at play: segregation by race, privileging of white family and welfare over Black workers, low regard for indigenous homelands, and the exaltation of animals over people. Bottles of Coca-Cola were there, too, refreshing the throats of those who could purchase them, creating a pull for worker salaries in much the same way as the company's mid-century ad campaigns did. Here we see Coca-Cola doing what it always did, striving to remain within arm's reach of anyone and everyone's desire, seemingly neutral, but ubiquitous. The ambiguity in this engineering feat—

at once empowering and devastating—is ultimately the ambiguity of Coca-Cola in Middle Africa mid-century.

Conclusion

Classic Coca-Cola red led the company's global expansion after World War II. But by 1965, the company offered 250 products in over 500 different packages worldwide, proving its own assessment that product and package diversity were key to the company's growth. Driving this expansion was also the business's sustained commitment to advertising. That year, the company earmarked $55 million for Coke red alone, with more devoted to sister products like Sprite and Fanta.[91] Much of this advertising had become localized, trained on regional consumer cultures, as seen here. Beyond print ads, localization was also achieved through local language campaigns, particularly those that ran on the radio. In Africa, Congo led the way in terms of diversity mid-century. By 1960, ads for Coca-Cola were running there in Kiswahili, Kikongo, Lingala, and Tshiluba, in addition to French and Flemish.[92] By the next decade, Coca-Cola South Africa rivaled this list, with radio ads in Sotho, Tsonga, Tswana, Venda, Xhosa, and Zulu, in addition to English and Afrikaans.[93] Diversification and relentless local advertisement grew the business, just as the proliferation of Coke signs enhanced its visual presence across the African continent. Many signs were professionally made and distributed by bottlers to local outlets; the business's internal publications are rife with ads for them. But by the early 1960s, African dealers were also creating makeshift signs for Coca-Cola from whatever they could find, prompting bottlers to respond. In Ghana, bottlers began selling premade kiosks advertising the drink. When demand swelled, they partnered with a local furniture maker, selling over 150 'drink Coca-Cola' kiosks in one year, sprinkling Accra's landscape red.[94]

By the middle of the century, Coca-Cola increasingly considered its business to be at home across the African continent; its visual presence and growing profits bolstered this view. Yet, outside observers continued to look to Coca-Cola signs in Africa as evidence of something out of place with what they imagined the continent to be. Perhaps this was just a kind of cheap wit, as when a self-described Italian posse recounted for an Italian newspaper their exploits looking for Mau Mau freedom fighters in 1953 Kenya colony. Though they encountered no fighters, in their translated words, 'The thing that we discovered on the top of a native hut, the only one for hundreds of miles, was a coloured square of tin tied to a pole as if it were a flag, and bearing the words "Coca-Cola."' This sign was a symbol of outside modernity in a place assumed to have been ancient and uncivilized. 'Dear reader,' the author explained, 'it seemed as if the whole of our surroundings had suddenly been transformed. There was no longer silence, impenetrable woods, but something warm and human... friendly voices speaking from the red and white piece of tin.' Pressing their guide about how rare a sight this Coca-Cola sign was, our Italian writer 'turned to the interpreter and said: "Has that thing got as far as this?"' to which 'He answered: "There are millions of those all over Africa."'[95] Innumerable Coca-Cola signs dotted the African landscape by then, jarring with what either Africa or Coke was meant to be in this Italian imagining.

While the unnamed Italians took these signs as friendly beacons that evinced a familiar humanity, the signs undoubtedly meant something very different to the people who had put them up and whose huts they adorned. To them, these signs signaled local opportunity, a way to make a buck, and, if you were lucky enough, to better yourself and your family. They signaled electricity, coolers, or ice; they were markers of other items for sale and other opportunities. They meant upward mobility, embodiments of what Pierre Bourdieu theorizes as symbols of social capital and good taste, in this case, literally, for a sweet, carbonated drink.[96] Least of all, they meant Italy or America. Though the historical record is inadequate when it comes to recapturing the voices and the experiences of those who hoisted either official Coca-Cola signage, provided by a local bottler, or, just as often, makeshift branding, we can imagine the smarts it took to harness a new product deliberately, just as we might celebrate the hopefulness that it took to compete for a radio or a bicycle or some other marker of middle-class status by mailing in stickers or answering trivia.

Coca-Cola signs that peppered African landscapes were not there as flags of safety for travelers ill-at-ease on the continent. Nor were they there because Africans were dupes who allowed an outside corporation to corrupt their pristine landscape. Rather, the red signs were the signs of an African modernity—a phrase so antithetical to colonial binaries as to seem nearly absurd to contemporaneous observers. The signs made visitors think of Africa as like, but not quite like what they were used to, and this was both humorous and unsettling. Reading these quips—in *Harper's* and elsewhere—should remind us, as Homi Babha does, that it is precisely hybridity—that almost but not quite the same—that challenges the polarizing knowledge of colonialism.[97] A widely circulated cartoon from 1962 seemed to make the same point. In it, a man is seen kneeling and peering through a magnifying glass, presumably trying to decode lines of hieroglyphics etched into stone, with pyramids visible in the background, when he comes upon the final line: 'Coca-Cola.'[98] Here the binary is effaced and Coca-Cola—code for modern, civilization—is rendered at home in an ancient landscape. One could argue that a Coca-Cola sign on a hut in mid-century Kenya does the same.

4

THE LINK BETWEEN OLD AND NEW

SECURING A LICENSE TO OPERATE

At the 1973 Kenyatta Day celebration in Nairobi marking a decade of freedom from British rule, throngs of citizens waited behind Coca-Cola-branded barriers to witness the presidential cabinet perform that year's Loyalty March. Profits from the sale of Coca-Cola at the rally went to the ruling Kenyan African National Union, demonstrating how enmeshed the business was in free Kenya. 'As leaders in the commercial field,' internal coverage of the event proclaimed, Coke bottlers 'have an obligation to share the burdens of modern society.'[1] Such obligation was also self-serving. Coca-Cola's position was never preordained, its significant roots notwithstanding.[2] To secure their continued ability to operate, Coca-Cola bottlers and Export personnel fell back upon old strategies with renewed vigor, broadening the company's work beyond beverages as freedom was both fought for and attained. Across the emergent postcolonial landscape, Coca-Cola assumed the role of civic cheerleader in ways grand and small. Through its bottlers, the company became involved in everything from the quotidian to the essential, often eliding the line between business and government. This activity was deliberate, part of a long-standing commitment to secure its license to operate by being an upstanding corporate citizen, whatever the situation demanded. Speaking about the drink's decidedly 'modern' growth in 'ancient' Egypt, a company article explained that "'Coca-Cola" is a link between the old and new world,' a theme I explored in the last chapter.[3] In a similar vein, Coca-Cola now stood as a visible marker of the transition from colonial to late/postcolonial orders. Yet, Coca-Cola was not simply witness to both moments. Rather, by committing itself to easing the many burdens of changing societies, the company stationed itself at the center of civic activity, shaping personhood and national life in diverse ways.

While African nations won their freedom at different times, most countries on the continent achieved independence after 1960. This meant that similar themes were at play across much of the continent throughout the 1960s and 1970s, even in places where oppression still reigned. What Coke did in unfree nations echoed what it was doing elsewhere to different ends, creating continuity. Yet, everywhere, the drink's existence was only as assured as its specific work at a precise time and place. In much of the continent, Coca-Cola bottlers and employees sustained the business's ability to operate through civic endeavors, mapped here. These activities were not always successful. Egypt stands as a prime example of the company's fraught existence in this era. From 1968 to 1979, Coca-Cola was forced to leave Egypt, as the country joined a larger Arab boycott protesting Coke's business in Israel. To return to Egypt—seen as a gateway to Arab nations more broadly—Coca-Cola Export would amplify the tactics used by bottlers elsewhere on the African continent, revealing a truism about the business: Coca-Cola's goodwill work worked if and when it created benefits not just for itself, but also for its host country.

THE LINK BETWEEN OLD AND NEW

Creating Goodwill

The Coke system, as we know, functioned precisely because the vast majority of bottlers and bottling employees were local, from the very communities they served. As a result, their involvement in civic life occurred in response to local needs, most often those close to home. A good deal of this work was conspicuous, done on grand display in order to co-brand the drink with one sort of celebration or another. Take, for instance, civic parades like the Nairobi one that opened this chapter. Coca-Cola's participation at such an event was typical across much of the continent. For instance, we see Coca-Cola bottlers supplying product for Cape Town's annual 'Coon Festival' in 1964 as well as to the local town and country parade that moved through Salisbury (now Harare) in 1966.[4] We see a large Coke-branded float as part of Blantyre's 1967 Malawi Republic Celebrations, marking eleven years of 'prosperity and progress.'[5] And we see the bottlers of the Letaba District of Tzaneen, South Africa showing off their newest Chevrolet as part of the local Republic Day Parade there in 1971, and more.[6] Virtually wherever and whenever a parade or festival moved through a city or town, you could be sure to find cold Coca-Cola products there.

In addition to parades, Coca-Cola bottlers increasingly staked a prominent role when it came to the emergent movie industry. In part, this was driven by a larger, short-lived Coca-Cola Company initiative to get involved in film more generally. In 1964, Nairobi cinema opened with a promotion that included free Coke-branded cooler bags.[7] Before long, Coke bottlers would come to sponsor matinees that included free beverages.[8] Elsewhere, Coca-Cola bottlers would lend the company's name to local film festivals.[9] The company was also particularly keen to celebrate when its product made its way onto the set of motion pictures being filmed on the continent, such as when international star

Stewart Granger and local actor John Sekka were filmed drinking Cokes on the set of Paramount Pictures' 'The Last Safari' or when daily supplies of Coca-Cola went to the set of the film 'Mr. Moses,' filmed at Lake Naivasha, Kenya.[10] Likewise, Coke was happily supplied to the set of the 1964 film, 'Zulu,' then being shot with 250 Zulus and fifty white Active Citizen Force soldiers lent by the South African government to serve as extras, as well as chief Mangosuthu Buthelezi channeling his nineteenth-century forebearer, Cetewayo.[11] 'Far from the anachronism it would seem to be,' a company magazine reported, 'the presence of Coca-Cola amongst Queen Victoria's redcoats and Cetewayo's warriors is a mirror of mid-twentieth century progress.'[12]

There was no question that parades and co-branding with cinema and films garnered the Coke business visibility at grand events, but it would be the company's ubiquitous presence at small happenings that would entangle it in everyday life. Here we find Coca-Cola enmeshed in everything from gas stations to schools to restaurants and markets. As the 1960s drew to a close, A A Parrisis, manager of Coca-Cola Middle Africa, called upon his workers to go further, making 1970 the 'Year of Enthusiasm and Initiative by Bottlers.' Applauding bottlers' ability to 'identify themselves with the aims of the communities in which they operate,' he underscored that such work was 'essential to maintaining goodwill everywhere,' urging bottlers not just to continue, but in fact to augment their civic work, of particular importance as African countries underwent swift changes.[13]

The middle of the twentieth century brought rapid urbanization and industrialization to many African countries, particularly those that anchored the business on the continent— places like Nigeria, the Rhodesias, Kenya, and South Africa. In turn, urbanization and industrialization induced related stressors. As people moved to cities in greater numbers, infrastructure was challenged, and urban space was repurposed. Coca-Cola bottlers responded to new challenges with new campaigns meant to alleviate local hardships while cushioning the business against criticism and creating ever-more consumers. Making consumers meant shaping wants and changing tastes. This the company tried to do with goodwill activities that gained access to people's taste buds with clever brand exposure. Coca-Cola bottlers first began engendering goodwill in a gendered way by sponsoring a series of beauty pageants. In 1960, one Vivien Lentis, a white woman from Kitwe, Northern Rhodesia, was named the first bottler-sponsored 'Miss Federation' and elected to represent the three countries at the annual Miss World contest in London.[14] Giving their name to the competition, Coke bottlers aligned themselves with aspirational beauty, receiving a spokesperson in the process. The success of this competition meant that, in the following year, Coca-Cola bottlers sponsored pageants across all of Middle Africa. This time, the bulk of the winners were Black women.[15] Each winner received money, clothing, and publicity, as well as unspecified 'career opportunities.'[16] In both southern and West Africa, the competitions were run in conjunction with *Drum* magazine, the famed publication 'for Africa,' known for its portrayal of pinup girls as central to mid-century African urban culture.[17] Like *Drum*, Coke's pageants celebrated urban Africa and its attendant shifting norms. At the same time, the competitions tied female beauty and empowerment to consumerism. Beauty pageants extended Coke's reach by embracing the same spirit of competition that motivated some of the last chapter's campaigns, focusing on what seemed to be but lighthearted fun. It was not long before bottlers turned to more substantive endeavors.

Coca-Cola bottlers focused on improving social well-being. Since well-being often meant health, the most vulnerable citizens were often the first ones Coke bottlers championed. Such was the case when then Ruanda-Urundi (now Rwanda) bottlers donated funds for local disabled children (publishing photos of said kids wearing T-shirts branded with the local bottler's name 'Spit') or when Nairobi bottlers fundraised for the Joytown Rehab Center for Cripples.[18] Beyond funds, bottlers often lent their name to and provided refreshments for local charitable walks, like one organized to end hunger in Nairobi.[19] Bottlers also aligned themselves with global organizations, such as when the bottlers in Ibadan, western Nigeria hosted ten countries (including the United States) for the second International Red Cross Fun Fair in 1965.[20] In all cases, sponsorship aligned the Coca-Cola name with worthwhile work, insulating the company against denigration.

Often, bottlers used their technical expertise to support welfare initiatives, such as when Nairobi bottlers supplied coolers to a 'Flying Doctor Service' so that blood and vaccines could be transported at a safe temperature by air, or when Bulawayo Bottlers provided a truck to transport gifts for the 'aged and orphaned.'[21] Coca-Cola's familiarity with transportation by road, in particular, played a significant role in the type of betterment work it undertook mid-century. There was a company history at play here, as well. As early as 1935, bottlers in the United States were championing road safety initiatives aimed at curbing 'highway homicide' and, in turn, making roads safer for the delivery of its products.[22] By mid-century, the notion had spread to the United Kingdom and then across Africa, where urbanization was accompanied by rising automobile accidents.[23] In 1959, Mombasa kicked off the first road safety contest on the continent, a three-tiered promotion that invited young contestants to answer questions about road signs, teenagers to field questions about bicycle travel, and adults to demonstrate their knowledge of motor vehicle rules. Thousands of people participated.[24] Before long, similar campaigns emerged from Malawi to Ethiopia, where an Addis Ababa Road Safety Weekend included Coca-Cola-branded umbrellas, coolers, and products set up at sixteen checkpoints along 100 km of highway.[25] Everywhere, road safety projects aimed to enhance public cognition around traffic rules, essential civic work that we would normally expect governments to perform.

Road safety campaigns and beauty pageants spoke to anxieties produced by urbanization. Likewise, the prizes awarded by Coca-Cola were deliberate markers of upward mobility that fit with the commodification that attended this moment. Watches, radios, guitars, and Singer sewing machines were commonly given out alongside money and Coca-Cola drinks. But by far the most regularly awarded items revolved around transport: scooters and cars, at times, but mostly bicycles.[26] As modes of mobility, bikes were heavily sought after, so much so that bottlers sometimes fashioned campaigns solely around them. 'Bike-and-Coke fever hits Luanda,' a *Coca-Cola South of the Sahara* article announced of 1964 Angola. In exchange for twenty specially numbered crowns, participants could receive brand-new bicycles.[27] So successful was that campaign that it was replicated in Monrovia, Liberia.[28] Just as beauty pageants helped shift notions of female beauty, bicycles broadened the scope of African personhood.

Though seemingly contradictory to the push for road safety, bottlers across the continent also began to sponsor road races in much the same vein as they sponsored pageants. Races including bicycles were aimed at safety, such as the Copperbelt Cycling Race, the Salisbury Cycling race, or Réunion Island's annual cycling meet, all of which were Coke branded and most of which attracted Black competitors as well as white.[29] Increasingly, Coca-Cola bottlers were involved in car racing as well, less around road safety and more around motor vehicle sport. For the most part, this seems to have been a white endeavor, likely because it was expensive and required access to items still beyond most Black Africans' reach. While the 1962 Coke-branded road race in Dar es Salaam, Tanganyika focused on control, as did a similar one in Tripoli, Libya that same year, by 1972, the races had everything to do with speed. Now known as road safaris, as in the East African Safari or the African Safari Rally, by 1978, Coca-Cola races were increasingly extreme endeavors, like when the Coca-Cola Bottlers' Motor Rally saw drivers competing on a twenty-two-hour day and night course; other races crossed national borders.[30] Speed, endurance, and bragging rights were on the lines in these events, aligning Coke sponsorship with sportsmanship as well as transnational movement by road. These cases showed the extent to which Coca-Cola's experience moving around the continent was of use. Here, as elsewhere, the movement of Coke-labeled vehicles also aligned with the emergence of filling stations. From Kano, Nigeria to Bulawayo, Southern Rhodesia, bottlers had entered into exclusive selling agreements with gas stations.[31] In a sense, Coca-Cola was working to brand the very roadways—themselves emergent at this time—that crisscross Africa.

While racing targeted older audiences, bottlers just as regularly focused their betterment activities on children, often in a deliberate attempt to activate young Black children as consumers. Such was the case in 1962 Mombasa, where bottlers sponsored a Swahili-language Punch and Judy puppet show for 250 children from the African Buxton Primary School. 'The audience was completely mystified with all the characters shown and the various voices used by the entertainer,' an internal magazine reported, 'plus the fact that the characters Punch, Judy, Jumbo, and the crocodile spoke to them in their own language.'[32] Here Coke bottlers' deployment of a local language demonstrated the very kind of savvy born of local involvement that helped capture new consumers. In 1967, the Johannesburg Bottlers of Coca-Cola likewise merged amusement with product promotion, bringing a well-known jazz band to a sponsored Christmas Festival aimed at hundreds of, as they called them, 'non-white crippled children,' distributing Coke-branded yo-yos to those in need at the same time.[33] By supporting entertainment, particularly that which was focused on society's most vulnerable citizens, Coca-Cola augmented goodwill, just as branded items spread its name recognition.

In 1972, South African Bottlers of Bloemfontein similarly enticed children by partnering with the department of education to run an essay contest, harkening back to the promotions we read about in the previous chapter. The topic of the essay: 'My visit to a soft-drink factory.' No fewer than 33,000 white, Black, and Coloured school children participated by visiting a plant and writing about their experience (with a Coke-branded pencil and ruler). The best essay in each class was sent to the final round of judgment; the winners received a trip to Kruger National Park. 'The promotion was a talking-point in Bloemfontein for months,' an article in the internal company publication *Coca-Cola Southern Africa* reported: 'It was a mammoth undertaking, but it repaid every cent of the cost and the effort.'[34] The Bloemfontein contest, like all Coke work aimed at children, included product sampling, unapologetically introducing children to Coke, Fanta, and Sprite in an era when this was understood to be permissible. Similarly, in 1974, Peninsula Beverages at the South African cape gave 3,120 free beverages to children in exchange for a donated toy for an underprivileged child as part of a partnership with the local B'nai B'rith charitable organization.[35] Sampling, here and elsewhere, had become a cornerstone to the Coke business, with its roots in the drink's earliest expansion in the US south. Give folks a taste of the product for free, the thinking went, and they would later pay for more.[36] It was not unusual to find dealers sampling thousands of drinks in a day, often in conjunction with other promotions.[37] Sampling on this scale took place in an era before the company forbid itself from marketing to children under thirteen. At this time, product-laden goodwill endeavors happily created both fun and a taste for fizz among the young and old alike.

Operating within the confines of apartheid, South African bottlers tried to capture equally children across what were then called the European and African markets. While this equanimity had a gloss of progressiveness to it, it was merely good business, something most companies were doing at the time. South African bottlers also trained themselves on acts of charity, particularly local ones that benefited the very communities in which they operated. There was savvy to this too: stable societies could be consumer societies. Charity also functioned to alleviate apartheid-era guilt without making substantive structural changes to systems of inequality. Toys for tots might feel good, but it did not radically oppose South African injustice. Still, Coca-Cola betterment schemes were not without merit. In August 1973, for instance, Export sponsored a Dolphin Learn to Swim campaign to combat drowning amongst all swaths of citizens; its goal was to reach 50,000 children from all races and all parts of the country over five years, something it was on track to do at the end of one year. Part of the campaign was a school competition. The company boasted that the top two prizes went to township schools, including one in Kwazakele, Port Elizabeth, where students had to walk over seven kilometers a day for lessons in the only nearby pool. When third place went to Sandown Primary, a white school, Export made much of the fact that the school donated its winnings to a needier Black school in Witkoppen. In this promotion and others like it, Coca-Cola Export insisted that the money it donated was clearly tracked. The company also seemed keen on showing that the bulk of its charitable donations went to Blacks where, presumably, the need was greater.[38] Coca-Cola Export and bottlers seem to have understood just how out of step South Africa already was with the rest of the continent and world in this era. By extension, they seem to have grasped that this disjuncture only raised the stakes for their company-sponsored betterment work there. Here as elsewhere they stepped in to do work we might expect of a government, in this case under circumstances where such goodwill efforts, particularly when they reached across racial lines, could easily have attracted the ire of the apartheid state.

The South African business tried to negotiate apartheid by spreading product equally in ever-novel manners. Bottlers elsewhere on the continent likewise attempted to capture youth in their own creative ways. In 1965 Lagos, bottlers participated in that year's Scout Jamboree where nearly 2,000 Nigerian boy scouts were joined by their counterparts from as near as Dahomey (now Benin), Togo, Ghana, Sierra Leone, Liberia, Zambia, and Libya, and as far away as the United States, the United Kingdom, Austria, Greece, and India. The Lagos bottler supplied ice-cold Coca-Colas as well as free transportation for local sightseeing that included a trip to a bottling plant and a screening of 'Wonderful World,' the promotional film discussed in the last chapter. Marketing materials on trucks and billboards boasted of this sponsorship.[39] The next year, the Coca-Cola Company of Nairobi partnered with Safari Air Services to host a reception for the United Missionary Air Training and Transport (UMATT) that similarly aligned the drink with a Kenyan publicity-garnering event. The brainchild of Brother Michael Stimac, an American Marist and schoolteacher, UMATT sought to introduce 2,000 Kenyan boys to aviation, aeronautics, and engineering over a three-year period by having them help fly materials to mission stations around Kenya. In partnership with Max Conrad, then the holder of the world's long-distance flight record, UMATT received wishes of 'God Speed' from local Catholic, Protestant, and Jewish clergy when it originated in St. Louis, Missouri for its transatlantic journey, as well as the literal blessing of Pope Paul VI during a stopover in Rome. In Kenya, the plane and its mission were commercially blessed by Esso Standard Limited, Kenya Shell, BP Kenya, Safari Air Services, and, of course, Coca-Cola.[40]

While UMATT represented Coke's round-about engagement with youth education, the company more often supported learning by funding schools and students directly. This took the form of cash donations, like when Uganda bottlers earmarked money for primary school fees, when local bottlers pledged to feed schoolchildren in Northern Rhodesia (now Zambia), or when the Coca-Cola Export Corporation presented funds to Inanda Seminary, the historic high school for Black South African girls.[41] In each case, bottler funds went to a local educational institution in need. In West Africa, at least some educational support was driven by the charitable wing of Coca-Cola USA. In 1960, *Overseas* reported that because of its contribution to the Phelps Stokes Fund, Coca-Cola USA was supporting a string of scholarships for West African students to study in the United States. The impressive list included students from Freetown, Liberia and Lagos, Nigeria then pursuing degrees in dentistry and engineering at Howard University, a student from Kumasi, Ghana, then studying for a degree in engineering at Drexel University, and students from Ojoto and Orajaka, Nigeria, studying agronomy at Cornell University and economic geology at the University of Chicago, respectively—all because of Coca-Cola USA's donations.[42] Most often, scholarships were driven by local bottlers for local use. Such was the case in 1963 when bottlers from the Rhodesias and Nyasaland began awarding four-year university bursaries to Black students from local high schools in order to support post-graduate training in the country.[43] A few years later, Coca-Cola Middle Africa offered bursaries for two student athletes from Nkubu Secondary School, near Meru, Kenya.[44] Across the continent—from Ethiopia to Swaziland—Coca-Cola bottlers and Coca-Cola Export established bursaries and scholarships for students. Some were part of competitions, like one in Ethiopia that ran in conjunction with a promotion, or part of a business deal, like that in Swaziland that accompanied the opening of a local plant. Others were earmarked for particular universities or particular groups of people, like Coke's donations to the Hellenic Education and Technical Institute or the Indian Centenary Scholarship Trust or its scholarships aimed explicitly at Bachelor of Science degrees at universities in Botswana, Lesotho, and Swaziland.[45] All over the continent, local bottlers underwrote their license to operate by providing avenues to university. Not only did scholarships engender goodwill, but they also helped support the creation of a professional class across the continent.

Like promoting traffic and water safety campaigns, Coca-Cola, by way of its bottlers, performed important civic work by supporting avenues for education, work we often assume governments should do, but which they often cannot or do not do. Here too Coca-Cola was helping fulfill middle-class aspirations for betterment, in much the same way that it did when its bottlers gifted washing machines, cars, televisions, and refrigerators to vendors and consumers.[46] Coolers were particularly important, as alluded to earlier. Not only was cooling technology essential for product spread, but coolers also signified the size and import of a business. Moving from a single cooler box that required ice to a narrow, electrified refrigerator and then on to a double refrigerator indicated growing prosperity, then as now. Thus, the company ran 'cooler contests,' urging bottlers to distribute as many of them as possible to dealers of appropriate size and respectability.[47] The more Coke coolers were out in the world being properly used, that is, the more that were kept free of competitor stock and being used in good faith, the more people could buy product. In turn, the more product sold, the more vendors grew.[48] It was, in this case and most others related to goodwill endeavors, a win-win situation. This, then, is the crux of Coca-Cola's betterment work, in all its diverse local manifestations: what is good for the community, however small and remote, is good for Coca-Cola. For, strong communities become consumer communities.

Beating the Boycott

In some cases, no amount of deep enmeshment could protect the Coca-Cola business from larger politics. So it was with Egypt in the late 1960s. In 1966, an Israeli plant near Tel Aviv announced that it would begin bottling Coca-Cola in that country for the first time, using concentrate shipped from Europe. Bottling began two years later.[49] In response, the Arab League—a group of Arab nations united in their shared heritage and shared opposition to Israel—initiated a boycott of Coca-Cola, giving bottlers time to divest themselves of product. By 1968, bottling operations had ceased in Bahrain, Iraq, Kuwait, Lebanon, Qatar, Saudi Arabia, and the Trucial States, in addition to Libya and Egypt. Egypt was a significant loss for the company, one that would take twelve years to reverse. During that time, Coca-Cola did not stop its concentrate shipment to Israel, staying consistent with the company's policy of doing business wherever business could be done and staying mindful of the backlash that an anti-Israel position would prompt. The company was thus after another way off the boycott list and back into the Arab League markets, which it saw as starting with Egypt. The solution would be another form of goodwill work, this time on a far larger scale than any other in this chapter. But, like the betterment schemes outlined above, it too would be a win-win proposition for the company and the country.

When the Arab League boycott began in 1968, Coca-Cola was in the midst of expansion. Not only had the company just rolled out large-scale packages and new products like Sprite,

Fanta, and Tab, but the business had also moved beyond soda. In 1960, Coca-Cola acquired Minute Maid, the American producer of concentrated juice, marking the company's first step outside of the carbonated drink market and towards becoming, as it sees itself now, a total beverage producer. The juice business not only enhanced Coca-Cola's portfolio, but it also grew the number and kinds of resources the company now had to procure. Of primary importance was, of course, citrus like oranges, lemons, and grapefruit. Citrus was grown in various locations, including South Africa, Arizona, and Florida, where the company learned the ins and outs of this temperamental agribusiness.[50] But, almost at once, there was recognition that, eventually, more citrus-producing land and concentrate factories would be needed for expansion.

Meanwhile, and differently, leaders familiar with both the Egyptian and the larger African businesses had risen in the ranks within the Coca-Cola system. Most important among them was J Paul Austin, who we first read about in Chapter 1, when he was cutting his teeth in South Africa, and who had been elected president of The Coca-Cola Company in 1962 (he would become CEO in 1966, chairman in 1970, and retire in 1981). Austin oversaw a period of unprecedented growth for Coca-Cola, leaving the company exponentially bigger and more profitable than it was when he was elected president.[51] As we read earlier, Austin believed in the power of the free market to change the world. He also believed in the power of the African business, understanding that the full breadth of the continent included Egypt. From 1968, Al Killeen, who we met in the last chapter, served as Senior Vice President of Coca-Cola Export. He too took it as a point of pride to be intimately familiar with the African market in all its complexities; he also had ties to the Egyptian business from his time on the continent. Into this climate came an Egyptian named Sam Ayoub. Ayoub began his career in municipal government in Alexandria. He later worked in banking in Cairo, New York, Bombay, and Addis Ababa, before going to Eritrea at the behest of Emperor Haile Selassie to set up Ethiopian Air there. Thereafter, he and his wife emigrated to the United States. In 1959, Ayoub joined Coca-Cola Export, becoming assistant treasurer in 1963, treasurer in 1971, and, in 1972, Vice President of Export. In 1976, he was elected Vice President and Treasurer of The Coca-Cola Company and, the following year, President of Coca-Cola Middle East. In 1980, he became Executive Vice President and Chief Financial Officer of The Coca-Cola Company.[52] In between this rise, he would be instrumental in working out a deal to get Coke back into Egypt using his, Killeen's, and Austin's contacts to pave the way.

While on the surface, Egypt's boycott of Coca-Cola was a straightforward fulfillment of the terms of the Arab League boycott, other factors were at play. First, it bears saying that not all Arab League countries participated in the boycott, immediately or eventually. Tunisia and Morocco, for instance, never ceased production of Coca-Cola. Other countries, like Djibouti and Somalia, were exempted from participation because they only joined the Arab League after Coke operations were established in their countries. While Egypt was a powerhouse in this league, it did not have to boycott Coca-Cola. So why did it? There were economic reasons that made the boycott appealing. By 1966, the year the boycott was announced, President Gamal Abder Nasser Hussein of Egypt was steering a faltering economy. Reliant on foreign aid for food and struggling to pay down its foreign debt, the country was in trouble. The country's defeat during the Six Day War of 1967 only heightened its precarious position.[53] At the same time, Nasser fashioned himself as an anti-imperialist. He would not be the first or last to see Coca-Cola, brought in alongside America's growing global presence after World War II, as an agent of imperialism. Thus, when Coca-Cola appealed to him via intermediaries with thinly veiled threats suggesting that a Coca-Cola boycott could trigger larger anti-Egypt sentiment on the part of Americans, the pleas fell on deaf ears.[54] At the same time, it did not help that Coca-Cola concentrate needed to be imported for bottling in the state-run bottling enterprise, further affecting the country's trade imbalance. In this calculus, politics and economics aligned with regional loyalty, rendering it economically sensible to follow the Arab boycott and expel Coca-Cola from Egypt.

Then, in 1970, Muhammad Anwar Sadat succeeded Nasser as president, bringing a different outlook to the country's state of affairs. According to some historians, it was in direct response to the dire state of Egyptian finances that Sadat initiated the Yom Kippur War of 1973, rightly betting that the war would bring Arab investment into the country.[55] When wartime aid proved insufficient to right the struggling nation, Sadat enacted a policy of economic liberalization known as *infitah* (or opening).[56] One goal of this policy was, explicitly, to woo foreign investment.[57] By 1973/74, Egypt was just as keen on gaining access to foreign capital as Coca-Cola was on regaining access to its market. Just as with the boycott's initiation, getting Coca-Cola back into Egypt would be driven by political and economic prerogatives.

Coca-Cola was well aware of the larger political forces at play. As Ayoub later joked about his time as CFO, Coca-Cola 'got the best information... better than the information of the State Department.'[58] Coca-Cola knowledge started at the top. For instance, from his base in Atlanta, Austin formed a close relationship with then Georgia Governor Jimmy Carter during the early 1970s, continuing this relationship once Carter was elected President of the United States in 1976 and again in 1980.[59] This was not unusual: The Coca-Cola Company has a long, well-documented record of access to the highest levels of government, in the United States as elsewhere. On the ground wherever it was, Coca-Cola always sought, as Ayoub arrogantly put it, 'the cream of the community to run our Coke operations,' meaning those folks 'with the best connections.'[60] As a network of local bottlers, Coca-Cola had large webs of information at its disposal, virtually everywhere. Coca-Cola thus had channels to both high-level and on-the-ground intelligence, even after operations had ceased in Egypt. Taking advantage of this, the company sent Ayoub into Egypt in the early 1970s in an unofficial capacity to start feeling out the situation. With his own contacts, as well as Al Killeen's, Ayoub came away with a favorable sense of the climate. On 18 June 1974, Austin sent a Telex to Claus Halle, a Senior Vice President of Export, then in Mexico, saying 'Never before have we had this climate in which to tackle the boycott problem.' Remarking on the contacts Ayoub made via Killeen, Austin wrote that this information could be trusted, since 'we are not dealing with strangers.'[61] The plan was simple: create a win-win situation. As stated in a preliminary report, Coke understood that 'To develop the Egyptian soft drink market, it is necessary to provide parallel investment in the Egyptian economy.'[62] Coca-Cola seems to have understood immediately that some sort of *quid pro quo* was in order. In September, Austin received a letter from Henry Kissinger, then Secretary of State, presumably in response to one that he had written. Thanking Austin for consulting with the US government, Kissinger wrote that 'The Department will be pleased to facilitate the approach of the Coca-Cola Company to the Government of Egypt.'[63]

From 1974, a series of internal reports investigated the potential for Coca-Cola's re-entry into Egypt, scanning the existent soda landscape.[64] When the boycott was enacted, Coca-Cola ensured that all bottles bearing its logo were removed from the market, threatening legal action against any bottler who did not comply. Bottlers continued to use their lines, since those were independently or government owned. These they now filled with Si-Cola, a local creation.[65] Pepsi, which did not do any business in Israel, also came in to fill the void created by Coke's exit. Still, Egyptians seemed to have a greater taste for cold, sweet drinks than was being met. In 1974, the potential for the Coca-Cola business seemed huge: while any entry would require significant money from the company, the possible profits made it an enticing prospect, as did the potential to open doors to the larger Arab world. According to Ayoub, as reported in *The New York Times*, the company anticipated selling a minimum of a hundred million cases in the region during its first year after re-entry, with thirty million in Egypt alone, roughly the same as 2% of the company's total volume at that time.[66]

Imagining a deal that would make both Coca-Cola and the Egyptian government happy, and working with the US government's endorsement, Coca-Cola trained its sights on a citrus project, with its Minute Maid business and expertise in mind. As early as 1952, plans had been drawn in Egypt to try to reclaim millions of acres of desert land for use; making the desert bloom was something of a pipe dream for Sadat. By the early 1970s, some of this agricultural work was under way. In 1974, a group of Coca-Cola engineers arrived in Egypt to assess the situation. Focusing on a parcel of land west of Mullak, they studied the existing irrigation systems and mapped rain water and soil composition in relation to their Florida-based expertise in order to check the feasibility of turning 15,000 acres into citrus farms.[67] While it would be hard work, the plan seemed possible.

'As an expression of the desire of The Coca-Cola Company to participate in the development and growth of your Excellency's country and the Egyptian people,' Austin wrote to Sadat in an undated letter found in the archives, 'it gives me great pleasure to attach our proposal that The Coca-Cola Company be given the opportunity to develop a project that would reclaim desert land for plant production, provide employment, and produce additional crops for both local use and export.' Austin enumerated details. Coca-Cola sought to lease 15,000 acres at a nominal fee to develop citrus, tomato, and other crops in what was called Project Ramses, named after the famed rulers of ancient Egypt. Ramses would start small, with a pilot that enabled the company to gain expertise with this particular soil, and then grow an additional 1,000 acres a year.[68] The multi-year project would come to include the creation of a concentrate plant and a renewed partnership with the government bottling company, El Nasr. It would entail some outside personnel, but far more significant numbers of Egyptian jobs (one estimate put the number of Egyptians to benefit from Coke's re-entry at 20,000).[69] In sum, the project would require $100 million, to be supplied by both foreign and local sources, as well as no less than 137,000 gallons of water per minute, which Austin requested free of charge, now and in the future. Asking that all materials and personnel needed to be imported be free from import duties and taxes while alluding to the project's revenue-generating capacity, Austin proposed a mutually beneficial deal. 'We are able to present our project on the assumption that your Excellency will be willing to waive the name of The Coca-Cola Company from the boycott list,' Austin concluded: 'With this action, the citizens of Egypt will be able to enjoy Coca-Cola, the recognized standard for quality all over the world.'[70]

For its part, the Egyptian government seems to have seen Coke as a harbinger for other businesses' entry into the country, something it desperately needed since Sadat's liberalization tactics had had only minimal success in stabilizing the economy (indeed, Ford and RCA would follow Coke).[71] While Coca-Cola could potentially bring money into Egypt, it could also be used as a bargaining chip in a larger, more important negotiation, one that would itself entail the influx of investment from the US government: peace with Israel. As early as 1968, internal

Coca-Cola documents suggest that Israel had agreed to stake the cessation of boycotts against Coca-Cola as part of any peace agreement with Egypt; certainly that was a line that Coca-Cola used in discussions with Egyptians.[72] When Coca-Cola entered into the agreement for Ramses, it did so with backing from the Overseas Private Investment Corporation (OPIC), the financial institution of the United States, as well as in conversation with the US government. Thus, when Anwar Sadat of Egypt and Menachem Begin of Israel signed their historic peace treaty with Jimmy Carter as witness in 1979, another agreement was in the works. That same year, Egypt lifted its boycott of Coca-Cola. The two processes had been entwined.

In July 1979, Coca-Cola trucks moved through Cairo and Alexandria for the first time in more than a decade. American news coverage of Coca-Cola's re-entry was triumphant. In its efforts to 'uncork the Egyptian market,' the Egyptian deal was 'Making the world Safe for Coca-Cola,' and returning 'as much a symbol [of the United States] as Uncle Sam,' to the region, newspapers announced.[73] Re-entry constituted a coup for the company. Estimates on the amount of money that The Coca-Cola Company put into the scheme vary from five to eighteen million dollars.[74] Certainly, the amount of investment was significant. But what the company received in return was equally if not far more significant. By 1983, Coca-Cola had achieved market leadership in Egypt, generating ongoing revenue.[75] At the same time, the weakened Arab boycott had indeed opened the door to production in countries from which it was once barred, even though the boycott remained in technical effect for several years.

In a strange twist of fate, the addendum to this story is that in the end, Coca-Cola withdrew from Project Ramses before any citrus harvesting could begin under its direction. It turns out that no one ever asked the Egyptian military if the land given to Ramses could be used. This came to a head when the military simply began using said land for bomb practice, much to everyone's surprise. While the army offered Ramses a portion of the originally promised land, the Department of Irrigation then got involved to reduce the amount of water that would be allocated to this scheme. The new amount offered fell below what Coca-Cola thought was necessary to turn desert into arable land. Despite pleas from Austin to Sadat himself, the situation was reportedly intractable by late 1980. Coca-Cola pulled out of Ramses, having secured its re-entry into the country and having paved the way for others to do so along the way, but without directly growing citrus.[76] I have seen it argued that the Egyptian government did not act in good faith, that in the end what it wanted was Coca-Cola's money as a kind of bribe for its license to re-enter. Though this perhaps overstates the case, that the Egyptian government should have acted in self-serving ways should not surprise us. Though we often expect that the narrative of capitalism is one of a company exploiting a foreign nation, this case reminds us that the capitalized are themselves agents, equal to if not savvier than any external corporation. I have also seen it suggested that Coca-Cola did not act in good faith, that the company never intended to follow through with Ramses, something the reams of binders and studies that went into the project seem to disprove. Still, the fact remains that Project Ramses greased the way back into Egypt for Coke and that Coke did not, in fact, do the work with Project Ramses it intended to do. Given the long view, even with lost expenditure, I imagine that Coca-Cola still felt that it was worth it.[77]

Coca-Cola wasted no time getting back to the business of goodwill work once back in Egypt. In fact, right after signing on to Project Ramses, it underwrote an academic expedition to study tombs of ancient Pharaohs, the citrus project's namesake.[78] Coke quickly took up the quotidian, too, once more showing up in all manner of daily life. How was it able to get so involved again so quickly? While negotiations were yet underway for re-entry, Coca-Cola Export sent marketing and publicity teams to Egypt to conduct the research necessary to remake Egypt into Coca-Cola country. In a forty-page report that functions as an ethnography, one group of advertising experts from McCann-Erickson unpacked the situation at hand. What they found was that Coca-Cola had its work cut out for it if it sought to remake itself as the beloved local beverage it was once seen to be. 'While it is true that one will often find an old Coke cooler still in use (filled with Si-Cola) and find remains of 11 year old signage,' they wrote, 'we take no particular comfort in this, and do not assume that there is a deep or widespread longing for Coca-Cola itself... nor that there is a very broad appreciation of the identity of Coca-Cola that goes appreciably further than using the term in simply the generic sense to indicate "a cola."' To rectify this situation, the team suggested an initial budget of over \$600,000 to be used in all sorts of ways to get back into the hearts and minds of Egyptians.[79]

Recommendations for inaugural betterment work will not surprise any reader of this chapter. There was the usual proposal for magazine contests backed by large monetary prizes, including one with an essay prompt on the theme of peace, seen as being particularly timely: 'To combine inauguration advertising with a campaign to demonstrate Coca-Cola's contribution to the economy, to forestall the canards about product impurities which will inevitably circulate, and to get "editorial" coverage, the company might sponsor an essay contest which would be carried out in cooperation with one of the leading Egyptian publications,' consultants from Doremus business communication wrote in a proposal. Then there were ideas to co-brand everything from music festivals and comic books to circuses. Marketing personnel also suggested Coke-branded plastic shopping bags, glasses, and even bottle-shaped cigarette lighters, useful in a country of such 'inveterate smokers' that would presumably gain exposure '15–25 times a day,' not just to the smoker, but to those around him (and increasingly her). On a larger scale, there were plans to outfit existing small-scale shops with 'prefabricated kiosk facades' that made Coke their flagship product. Then, there was the plan to combat the abysmal state of Egyptian traffic with reflective, Coke-branded decals meant to help the 'automobiles, buses, donkey-drawn wagons, bicycles, motorcycles, trucks, and pedicarts' that shared the road achieve greater visibility.[80] In these ways and others like them, Coca-Cola Egypt followed the company's old playbook, tried and true all over Africa. Goodwill on the largest scale—achieved through the citrus project—enabled a return to win-win betterment on the smaller one.

Change, as Always, is Afoot

During its twelve-year absence from Egypt, Coca-Cola operations continued elsewhere on the continent. Administrative regions were re-aligned, like when Middle Africa was split into East and West Africa in 1972. Following the cessation of the Egyptian boycott, Export's Africa zone office was moved to Athens, Greece, and slated to include—in the company's language—'Africa' and 'Arab African' countries, as well as South Asian ones like India and Pakistan (included because of their similarly sized economies).[81] Administrative units would change and change again, but for the time being, that Export lumped both North Africa and sub-Saharan Africa together speaks to the power of getting back into Egypt and relinking its most important northern hub of business to the rest of the continent.

All over, the business was still expanding, starting local bottling operations for the first time in Chad, Gabon, Mali, Mauritania, Uganda, and the Central African Republic during the second half of the 1970s.[82] In many places, growing demand meant that new bottling contracts were being awarded, like when Shinyanga Bottling Operations began servicing the Williamson Diamond Mine of Tanzania or when the Mount Kenya Bottling Company began producing at a capacity of 500,000 cases per annum for Kenya's Central Province.[83] Elsewhere, the business was contracting. In 1963, the Federation of Nyasaland, Northern Rhodesia, and Southern Rhodesia was dissolved; Nyasaland became independent Malawi and Northern Rhodesia became independent Zambia. Unwilling to accede to majority Black rule, in November 1965, the white Southern Rhodesian minority government issued its Unilateral Declaration of Independence from Great Britain. In response, Great Britain and the United Nations issued embargoes against the nation; South Africa, itself a white minority racist state, and Mozambique/Angola (until their independence from Portugal in 1975), did not comply. Faced with embargoes, Coca-Cola Export officially ceased operations, and over the next decade, all bottling contracts expired. All the while, local bottlers found ways to continue eking out Cokes. Concentrate was flown in under duress from South Africa, and all operations were severely tested during the war that preceded the triumph of majority rule in 1980. In 1979, the Coca-Cola Export branch office was re-opened on the eve of Zimbabwean independence, and new contracts were issued for plants in Bulawayo, Fort Victoria (now Masvingo), Gwelo (now Gweru), Salisbury (now Harare), and Umtali (now Mutare).[84]

Across both stable and unstable theaters of production, Black personnel continued to advance within the Coca-Cola system, albeit unevenly, slowly aligning both Export offices and bottling plants with African demographics. Kenya presents perhaps the best documented example of successful Black advancement at this time. Export Newsletters, sent throughout the Export Corporation, abound with instances of long-serving Black employees and their promotions. In 1970, we see that one

Badru Kara, formerly a route manager in Nairobi, was appointed Territorial Supervisor in marketing for Middle Africa. That same year, one Godfrey Tetu was appointed assistant plant manager in the Nairobi company bottling operation.[85] In 1972, Charles Mukora, an athletic coach, was appointed marketing services manager for Middle Africa.[86] Mukora would continue to rise within the system, becoming head of external affairs and public relations for Coca-Cola Middle Africa, as well as chairman of the Kenyan National Olympic Committee. In 1975, Horace Owiti became a new manager of Middle Africa, having held a variety of positions in both the Export office and on the bottler side. 'Announcing Mr. Owiti's appointment,' Export reported, 'Managing Director Mr. A A Parissis, told staff "Horace's promotion is further evidence of this Company's policy of rewarding meritorious employees, regardless of race, creed or national origin."'[87] Export records substantiate Parrissis's claim. At the same time as increasing numbers of Black employees were rewarded with advancement in Kenya, there was an undertaking to transfer the company-owned bottling plant to local ownership there.[88] Such a move necessarily entailed more employment opportunities for local talent. Along the way, employees were regularly helped with efforts to improve their education. Case in point: we see that one Eunice Mbuthia of East Africa Region was given a scholarship to train as a bilingual secretary in France in 1981.[89] Not only does this instance alert us to a possible avenue for advancement for an employee (and a female employee, at that), but it also reveals the extent to which the business was keen on broaching the language divide, particularly between English- and French-speaking nations. While Export articles and long-service lists suggest that the Coca-Cola business was still heavily populated by whites at high levels, this was changing.

Conclusion

On 25 May 1963, representatives from thirty-two countries convened in Addis Ababa, Ethiopia to form the Organization of African Unity (OAU), the continent's first post-colonial organization aimed at continent-wide unity on an independent Africa.[90] In 1972, the OAU sponsored the first ever All Africa Trade Fair; 180,000 visitors from thirty-six countries attended. Held in Kenya, the fair sought to establish trade and partnership across member states. Heads of state and royalty were on hand at the well-publicized opening, including President Kenyatta of Kenya, Haile Selassie of Ethiopia, Idi Amin of Uganda, and Queen M'amohato Bereng Seeiso of Lesotho. So too was Coca-Cola present. 'Thousands of bottles of Coca-Cola, Fanta and Sprite were served at the All Africa Trade Fair—and enjoyed by visitors from many countries,' readers of the Coke publication *In Middle Africa* were told, lest they needed reminding: 'As at every major national and international event, Coca-Cola and associated products played an important part in ensuring a friendly and hospitable atmosphere.'[91] As post-colonial independence was won across the African continent, Coca-Cola was there, cheering the way and staking ever-new positions in new political orders through betterment work aimed at protecting its license to operate. Thus it is that we find Daniel Arap Moi, the second President of independent Kenya, being photographed opening the newly formed Rift Valley Bottling plant and, on another occasion, receiving a check for 50,000 Kenyan shillings in aid for the disabled from Coke Export personnel.[92] Coca-Cola's post-colonial work harkened to its earlier goodwill work, conducted under different political orders. In its sustained commitment to ubiquity and to comingling its work with that of ruling powers, Coca-Cola had, in fact, become a kind of link between the old and new.

In 1981, Sam Ayoub, then chief financial officer for The Coca-Cola Company, reflected on the state of the business at that year's worldwide external affairs conference. Times were tough, he told attendees. Increasing costs and competition coupled with rising inflation meant that the business needed to work harder, and smarter, to continue growing at a rate higher than inflation and higher than the company's historic 12% growth. At this meeting, he introduced two systems meant to rationalize work while continuing to standardize operations across the planet, OPACS (Operational Planning and Control System) and MERIT (Managing Every Resource in Inflationary Times), which he jokingly referred to as a pyramid like those that could be found in his native Egypt. Both systems would be implemented in Africa as elsewhere over the coming years, further modernizing operations.[93] Two years later, Ayoub spoke again to a global Coke audience, this time at a worldwide marketing conference. Here he predicted the business's outlook with figures from 1982. Looking at total soft drink volume, total operating income, and total growth, it seems that from the vantage of 1983, there was still significant room for Coca-Cola to grow in Africa, in particular.[94]

By 1983, if not well before, Coca-Cola had become deeply involved in African civil life. Betterment projects that sought to alleviate social ills while securing the company's ability to operate had become a hallmark of the business across the continent, in small ways, like beauty pageants, and grand ones, like six-figure citrus deals. Twenty years earlier, in 1963, an interviewer called attention to Coke's endeavors—in particular those that brought overseas employees to Atlanta annually to be trained—as a kind of 'volunteer foreign aid program.' But, for J Paul Austin, who conceived of that and so much more, nothing about Coca-Cola's work was pure charity. Rather, it was necessary, since it fed the growth of a free world market based on free enterprise, which in turn fed the company's growth. 'With a long background in Africa,' the interlocutor wrote, 'Mr. Austin is a mine of information about the unintended benefits of American business in foreign parts,' quipping that 'the fact is that some of our most effective foreign aid comes as a reflex of programs developed by far-sighted businessmen.' There is much that is laudable about Coca-Cola's betterment work, as we saw here: promoting traffic safety, teaching children to swim, and endowing scholarships all helped Africans in ways that were either beyond the purview or the potential of local governments. Yet, this writer overstates the case: not everything Coca-Cola did on the ground was unimpeachable or without unintended consequences, in Africa as elsewhere (as we shall see in later chapters). Nor was it all guided by far-sighted businessmen. Just as often, if not more, Coke Export and Coke bottlers were guided by local players smart enough to harness the will and pocketbook of the company to their own ends. All over Africa, in ways grand and small, were Africans keen to make the company pay to operate, compelling funds for nutritional supplements for 55,000 children in Kenya or finances for rural water projects or free drinks for 10,000 people who had come to witness the granting of Hindu Rites, and so much more.[95] Make no mistake about it, Africans were agents here who repeatedly harnessed an inessential product to do the essential. It is to Coca-Cola's credit that it heeded its consumers' needs, following rather than leading the way, paying far more attention to local concerns than any local politician seemed to. But it is to Africans' credit that they bent this most iconic corporation to suit their needs. Never was the story of Coca-Cola in Africa a one-sided story, even if the other side is often hidden from our view.[96]

Despite its work enmeshing its product in all manner of life, securing its license to operate, by 1983, when Ayoub spoke, there was still much for Coca-Cola to do in Africa. Arguably, this was the case because the persistence of the apartheid state in the 1980s—more than two decades after much of the continent attained independence—presented obstacles to both freedom and growth. Just as the top of the continent preoccupied a good deal of Africa-focused energy for more than a decade, the bottom of the continent would now demand attention. For apartheid—that rotten system that endured beyond all credence towards the end of the twentieth century—needed to be reckoned with. Much like any other important moment on the continent, Coca-Cola was sure to be present, taking a central, if hidden role in the negotiations that would help transition the country, assuring the drink's security and bearing witness to the true dawn of postcolonial Africa at the same time.

5

A CATALYTIC ROLE UNTOLD

COCA-COLA AND THE UNDOING OF APARTHEID

On 11 February 1990, Nelson Mandela left prison a free man after twenty-seven years' incarceration. Weeks later, he began visiting those nations that had supported his African National Congress (ANC) in the long fight against apartheid. Abroad, Mandela worked to shore up additional support for his party's continued quest for a free and fair election in South Africa. In June, Mandela landed in the United States, stopping, among other places, in Atlanta, where he placed a wreath on Martin Luther King Jr.'s tombstone and received honorary degrees from several historically Black colleges. What he did not do in Atlanta (or elsewhere, for that matter) was accept any product or support from Atlanta's most powerful entity, The Coca-Cola Company. This snub did not go unnoticed. 'Mandela aides bar Coke,' one newspaper announced; 'An offer from The Coca-Cola Company to support Mr. Mandela's tour was rejected,' said another; 'Coke products are banned from the luxury chartered jet the ANC entourage are using,' stated one more.[1] The reason for the rebuke: Coke is not an entity 'we can do business with,' a local ANC operative explained.[2] Though Coca-Cola had disinvested from South Africa in 1986, that the beverage was still available there four years later prompted anti-apartheid protestors to boycott the company. Apartheid was waning by 1990, but activists' anti-Coke sentiment was not.

Three years later, just before being elected the first president of a free South Africa, Nelson Mandela again arrived in the United States. This time, he called for Americans to end sanctions against South Africa and to begin reinvesting in the country that he hoped to lead. Stopping again in Atlanta, he not only met openly with Coca-Cola representatives, but he also publicly thanked one in particular for 'quietly help[ing]' end apartheid. Neither events were surprising, since this time Mandela was traveling across America on a Coca-Cola jet, with his trip orchestrated, in large part, by the very company he had once scorned.[3]

This chapter is about what happened to compel this shift, both for Mandela personally and for the larger story of anti-apartheid activism and Coca-Cola that it embodies. To tell this tale, I begin in the 1970s, heady days of activism in both South Africa and the United States. This is a story that is interwoven with that of American activism, both against Coca-Cola and against apartheid. It is similarly entwined with the ascent of a new wave of youth activism in South Africa in tandem with the escalation of South Africa's civil war. In this chapter, I explain the hidden maneuvers and complex restructuring that enabled Coca-Cola's unique form of disinvestment. This singular form of disinvestment allowed Coke to do what no other company managed: keep its products in South Africa while the company positioned itself in opposition to the apartheid state. Coke's unique form of disinvestment, I demonstrate here, prepared the company to thrive anew in whatever order was to follow apartheid both in South Africa and, most importantly, on the African continent writ large.

A CATALYTIC ROLE UNTOLD

South Africa and America in the 1970s

The June 1971 cover of *Coca-Cola Southern Africa* featured the newly opened J G Strijdom Tower in Hillbrow, Johannesburg. Named after a key architect of apartheid, the tower was at once an homage to white supremacy and an engineering feat. Rising 269 meters above the street—the seventh tallest structure of its kind worldwide—the Hillbrow tower relayed thousands of phone-calls across the nation simultaneously, fast becoming an iconic landmark on Johannesburg's skyline. Five restaurants filled the top floor, all of which served Coca-Cola products.[4] With its cover spread, the publication pronounced that Coca-Cola stood at the pinnacle of a nation it had called home for nearly fifty years, aligning the beverage with the country's enduring racist regime.

In the early 1970s, the apartheid state's grip on South Africa was firmer than ever. By then, all major resistance parties had been banned, their top leadership killed, imprisoned, banished, or forced into exile. While resistance to apartheid never abated, the next, and final wave of activism would not begin in earnest until 1976. Before then, the state operated with near impunity, suppressing dissent and providing cheap, plentiful labor to thriving white-owned industry both below ground, in the mines, and above ground, in everything from telecommunication to the soft drink business. Indeed, South Africa had become one of Coca-Cola's most successful markets owing to the company's longevity and ample investment there, as well as racist political conditions that enabled it to thrive.[5]

This is the South Africa that E Neville Isdell, Coca-Cola's future CEO, entered in 1971.[6] Born in Ireland but raised from age ten in Zambia, Isdell attended the University of Cape Town, where he participated in low-level anti-apartheid activism, before returning to Zambia after graduation to work for a fledgling Coca-Cola bottler there. In Zambia, Isdell drove trucks, peddling lukewarm Fantas and Cokes in an emergent commercial landscape. In the 1970s, he was appointed to work in Johannesburg where, just as during his university days, he saw South African apartheid firsthand. He recalled the paradoxes of apartheid, visible by way of the Coke business. Despite the state's might, which was plentiful, inspectors would overlook violations in bottling plants, particularly if they related to petty apartheid, or those laws ensuring separation by race in such places as bathrooms and canteens. These laws were skirted by some Coke plants, including those eventually run by Isdell, a precedent set years earlier by J Paul Austin.

Yet, at the same time, Isdell recalls witnessing the state's fury up close. Isdell happened to be riding sales routes in Soweto on 16 June 1976, the start of what came to be known as the Soweto or children's uprising. That day, schoolchildren rose up against the state, seeing shebeens (or beerhalls), libraries, schools, and more as markers of their oppression; these they attacked with their limited means. The state responded with its full strength, teargassing, arresting, and killing children in the most widespread display of violence seen since 1960. After 16 June, nothing would ever be the same in South Africa, as the children's uprising spread. Business as usual changed for Coke that day, too. For the first time, Coca-Cola became a target of anti-apartheid resistance. On 16 June, a Coca-Cola driver was murdered while delivering product. Isdell attended the funeral, itself a space of political activism. While Isdell's presence was cautiously welcomed, that he was the only white man in attendance—and a Coca-Cola employer to boot—made him conspicuous.[7] Though Coca-Cola had long been able to negotiate apartheid while growing customers across all races, by 1976, the tides were turning for the company.

Coca-Cola was likewise becoming the target of activists in America. The rise to prominence of Reverend Leon Sullivan and his calls for Black consumer engagement drew attention to Coca-Cola's operations in the United States, particularly as they related to race. Sullivan was a Baptist minister and activist. Throughout the 1960s in Philadelphia, he called for 'selective patronage' of companies that failed to hire sufficient numbers of Black employees, urging Black consumers to harness the power of their pocketbooks. His activities were noticed by Martin Luther King, Jr. and his Southern Christian Leadership Conference (SCLC); King brought Sullivan on board to help fashion what became known as Operation Breadbasket, the economic wing of SCLC. The Chicago branch of Operation Breadbasket—its earliest success—was headed by a young seminary student named Jesse Jackson. Under Jackson, Chicago's Operation Breadbasket targeted businesses, including Coca-Cola and Pepsi Cola, that, in its estimation, did not have enough Black employees. As a result of both pressure and planned/executed boycotts, Operation Breadbasket won thousands of jobs and revenue for Black communities in Chicago.[8] Beyond Chicago, Coca-Cola, Pepsi Cola, and other companies under fire from Operation Breadbasket worked to avoid further boycotts. In southern bottling plants, this meant eliminating segregated restrooms and hiring Black bottling representatives, early gestures meant to overcome longstanding racist hiring policies and working conditions.[9]

Reverend Sullivan also played a role in drawing attention to Coca-Cola's operations overseas. In 1971, Sullivan was elected to the Board of Directors of General Motors, at the time the largest employer in South Africa. Witnessing South African apartheid through a corporate lens, Sullivan came to believe that international companies ought to take a stand against apartheid. As such, he issued what he called the Sullivan Principles in 1977 as a blueprint for corporate responsibility and opposition to apartheid. The original principles called for integration of all work and comfort spaces (including restrooms and lunchrooms), equal and fair employment and pay, training programs to encourage Black and other non-white employment and advancement, and active improvements to life outside of work for Blacks and other non-whites.[10]

Coca-Cola was reluctant to become a signatory to the Sullivan Principles, despite forceful lobbying by Sullivan himself.[11] The company's initial opposition to the principles, eventually signed by more than 100 United States corporations (including, ultimately, Coke), demonstrates the fine line it first sought to walk in South Africa. Coke's particular position reflected the views of both Coca-Cola Atlanta and Coke in South Africa, but for different reasons. That the Sullivan Principles would put the company in blatant violation of some laws presented problems for Coke South Africa, despite the fact that the company was increasingly taking a stand against apartheid. For those in America, likewise wary of wading into politics as part of a company-wide policy,[12] the stated United States' position of constructive engagement with apartheid South Africa presented a preferable option. Both wanted a way to oppose the apartheid state without going on record as having done so. At the same time, Coke claimed that signing the document would constrain the company and, conversely, that the principles were not far-reaching enough.[13]

Thus, at first, Coca-Cola implemented the Sullivan Principles without officially becoming a signatory to them, a move that, presumably, protected Coca-Cola South Africa from prosecution while keeping with the company's general apolitical ethos.[14] This wobbly position compelled the corporation to find a spokesperson able to translate its stance to a growing public, made up of shareholders, college activists, and others, who had begun calling for businesses to disinvest (end their work in South Africa) and investors to divest (stop investing in businesses who worked in apartheid South Africa).

Into this climate, Coca-Cola Atlanta hired Carl Ware. Born in rural, segregated Georgia, Ware held a BA from Clark University and had completed an internship at the Office of Economic Opportunity at Carnegie Institute of Technology. In 1974, Ware was recruited to Coca-Cola by J Paul Austin, in whose home his sister labored as a domestic worker. Ware joined the office of government affairs, becoming the first African American in this department. In this capacity, he represented Austin (and Coke) at the Opportunities Industrialization Centers of America, an organization founded by Sullivan.[15] For the next five years, Ware held a position in government affairs at Coca-Cola while serving on the Atlanta City Council, where he worked alongside Mayor Maynard Jackson to enact civil rights reforms in the city. In 1979, Ware resigned from the City Council to join Coca-Cola full time, taking over as Vice President of Special Markets for Coca-Cola USA. His charge was to expand African American and Hispanic markets through marketing and advertising.

Ware's first major test came in 1981 when Reverend Jesse Jackson, by then a well-known civil rights activist and head of People United to Save Humanity (PUSH), organized a large-scale boycott of Coca-Cola in the United States. Jackson's efforts were in response to the company's systemic racism in America, though they were informed, in part, by the company's holdout on signing the Sullivan Principles, since Jackson had just visited South Africa in 1979.[16] As Ware recently wrote, 'Coke was an easy target' for PUSH, but, he acknowledged, 'we were vulnerable because there was a lot of truth in what Jesse said.'[17] Though American big businesses were generally wary of calls for affirmative action in those days, Ware recalled, there was a growing recognition that change was coming. In 1981, Roberto Goizueta, Coca-Cola's new chairman, and Don Keough, the company's new president, tasked Ware with opening communication with Jackson. This Ware did in earnest. The result was the Coke PUSH agreement of 10

August 1981, ending the boycott. As part of the agreement, the company promised to put thirty million dollars into Black-owned businesses in the United States and committed itself to hiring Black employees up to its senior management and including its board of directors.[18] The company likewise agreed to appoint Black distributors and suppliers, to forge relationships with Black banks, to advertise in Black-owned newspapers, and to support historically Black colleges in the United States.[19] Some of Coke's promises translated to its international work, to the extent that the company now actively sought to re-examine its work overseas, in particular in apartheid South Africa, a country that was, by then, on the radar of civil rights activists in the United States. By the early 1980s, if not well before, activists working towards racial retribution in the United States were equally positioned against the apartheid state, seeing it for what it was: the last government based primarily on racial segregation. And, by 1980, Coca-Cola's presence in apartheid South Africa was well-known. Witness the fact that William M Kelley Jr., then a Coca-Cola vice president, appeared before the Subcommittee on Africa of the House Committee on Foreign Affairs on 31 July 1980 to discuss Coca-Cola's position in the fraught nation.[20]

Ware's success with PUSH advanced his career, setting him on an upward trajectory. In 1982, he was promoted to Vice President of Urban Affairs and in 1986 to Senior Vice President. In 1991, he was named Deputy Group President for Northeast Europe and Africa, where he served under E Neville Isdell. Then, in 1993, on the eve of Mandela's election, he was appointed head of Coca-Cola's Africa Group. By the time of that appointment, Ware had demonstrated that he was the right man for the right job at the right time. By the early 1980s, in addition to facing the backlash of American civil rights entities paying close attention to the company's race record, universities, businessmen, and activists were all calling for American companies to go beyond signing the Sullivan Principles. The calls now were for the company to disinvest from South Africa entirely. On the ground in South Africa, it was unclear how long the apartheid state would linger and whether its longevity was in the best interest of businesses, in any case. On both sides of the world, the company was facing pressure around race relations. Brought on board because of his ability to negotiate difficult situations, Ware was quickly deployed by Coca-Cola to be its spokesperson for all things race-related, first in the United States and then in South Africa, where he was sent to sort out Coca-Cola's work under the apartheid state. By the time he retired years later, Ware would become the highest-ranking African American employee in the company, assuaging those who claimed the company's racial makeup was inadequate by his very existence.[21] He would also play a central role in navigating and helping end apartheid in South Africa as well as setting up Coca-Cola to thrive anew in post-apartheid Africa. Yet, in the early 1980s, all that lay in the future.

Moving Towards Disinvestment

Eighteen months after the Coca-Cola PUSH agreement saved the company from an embarrassing and troubling Coca-Cola boycott in the United States, Keough and Goizueta called upon Ware to work out a similar solution to another race-related problem, this time in South Africa. The impetus for tasking Ware: a newly received report that the company had commissioned from Consumer Behavior, a market research firm headed by a Black South African, Eric Mafuna, meant to survey operations in South Africa. Titled, 'The Plantation Experience,' the report served not to assuage United States Coke leaders that their work in South Africa could withstand scrutiny, but rather to trouble them. According to the report, Coke's Minute Maid plant in the Northern Transvaal, now Limpopo province, was like an

American plantation, both in terms of management style and 'slave labor' conditions.[22] Predictably, the report arrived like a bomb. 'I remember sitting in Don Keough's office' with Goizueta, Ware recalled. 'They said to me, Carl, we want you to go to South Africa and leave no stone unturned. That was the only instruction I had. No brief.'[23] Ware remembers being told that the duo needed him to determine what the company's 'posture should be' in South Africa, suggesting that they were not willing to be directed by information from the South African office, especially in light of this recent report.[24] With growing global interest in South Africa, the stakes were now too high. What was needed was an American perspective on how the company could chart the troubled waters of late apartheid South Africa. 'I said, OK, I'm willing to do that,' Ware recalled, 'but I need to know how the rest of Africa feels about South Africa' along the way.[25]

On 4 March 1983, Ware embarked on his first trip to Africa, a twenty-two-day journey where he visited Nigeria, Kenya, Zimbabwe, and Zambia (all English-speaking nations with old, robust Coke operations), before arriving in South Africa. Traveling through those first nations, Ware felt a heartfelt connection to, as he calls it, 'the motherland,' writing lovingly of being surrounded by familiar-seeming faces in Nigeria, in particular. He was less impressed by the state of Coca-Cola operations, however, finding many to be rudimentary at best and sub-par, at worst. His distaste aside, he asked all Coca-Cola bottlers and employees what to do about South Africa. While he encountered reticence from some bottlers who feared disrupting the South African sugar industry, for the most part, the message seemed clear enough to him. As far as the majority of African Coke operatives were concerned, irrespective of race, Coca-Cola had to play a role in ending apartheid if the company wished to retain any standing on the continent. By the time Ware arrived in South Africa, he had internalized this position. Landing in

South Africa, Ware was termed an 'honorary white,' one of many absurd policies of the apartheid state meant to ensure that foreign Blacks would not be subjected to the daily perils faced by the local majority. For Ware, whose parents had been sharecroppers, arriving in apartheid South Africa, even in 1983, when many petty apartheid restrictions had been lifted, was akin to traveling back in time to the Jim Crow South.[26] Immediately, he was struck by the parallels between South Africa's present and the United States' past. And immediately, he felt charged to play a role in bettering the lives of those around him.

In South Africa, Ware connected with Coca-Cola leadership and supporting personnel on the ground, including Eric Mafuna—author of the plantation report—and Ernest Mchunu, then the highest-ranking Black Coca-Cola manager in the country.[27] From Mafuna and Mchunu, as well as the folks they connected him with, Ware started to get a sense of the magnitude of racial disparity in the country. What he saw moved him profoundly. Later, Mafuna would suggest that Ware had been sent to sweep Coca-Cola's image problems under the rug, but that once Ware saw how the apartheid state functioned first-hand, he could do no less than become an instrument for change.[28] While Ware never states that he was told to ignore operational issues in South Africa, he does say that his experiences in South Africa moved him to try to imagine a way that Coca-Cola could play a part in much-needed change.

The first place Ware looked to affect change was through the Coke business directly. Though there were not, at present, any Black-owned franchises in South Africa (just as there had not been until recently in the United States), Ware learned about two aspiring Black families already working within the Coke system: Richard and Marina Maponya, distributors for Coca-Cola in the nominally independent Bantustan of Bophuthatswana, and the Kunene family, then distributors of the product in the town of

Vosloorus, who will later become important in this story. Ware then toured the Devland Plant in Soweto, the very one that J Paul Austin had integrated and that Isdell had run.[29] He visited both small-scale operations and big plants to get a feel for how the business looked on the ground, all while starting to make connections with some anti-apartheid activists. The result: Ware came to see that while Coca-Cola was in compliance with the Sullivan Principles, broadly conceived, 'mere compliance was not enough.' 'Our business,' he later wrote, 'needed a radical overhaul' if it were to play any role in changing South Africa.[30] Keeping in mind the state of operations elsewhere on the continent while committing himself to working against apartheid, Ware began to scheme a path forward. 'As the largest private-sector employer on the continent of Africa, we knew we would have to demonstrate our abhorrence of the system of apartheid,' he wrote.[31] Still, this had to be done in a way that would not jeopardize the business, either in South Africa or on the continent. Returning to Atlanta, Ware began to create an elegant plan that would meet the complex needs he faced. His scheme would do what seemed to be impossible: allow Coca-Cola to stay in South Africa while still opposing the apartheid state.

The first part of Ware's plan was to steer The Coca-Cola Company to renew its support for the business in South Africa. At a South African bottlers' convention on 1 September 1983 in Monte Carlo, Don Keough did just that. There, the company chairman affirmed Coca-Cola's commitment to what was then Coke's tenth-biggest market and recipient of the company's single largest capital investment (150 million US dollars over three years) anywhere in the world, including the United States. Doing business in 'South Africa and southern and central Africa is a special privilege,' Keough told the assembled bottlers, 'because you are among the most successful Coca-Cola bottlers in the world.'[32] Paying homage to the South

African men who pioneered the business there, folks like Phil Gutsche and Les Forbes, Keough noted that this was not the first time the South African Coke business had faced obstacles. As before, he predicted, the business would prevail, gently prodding the assembled folks to support whatever changes Atlanta would soon send their way. That next month, Roberto Goizueta addressed a group of Johannesburg bottlers, likewise echoing the company's commitment to the country. Goizueta also affirmed the company's position regarding apartheid, which had begun to shift after Ware's trip. 'We are proud of our policy of non-interference in local politics,' he stated, 'while at the same time maintaining our commitment to the Sullivan Principles and to helping Black businessmen.'[33] For the first time, Coke leadership began to speak openly about affirmative action and about having signed the Sullivan Principles, charting a new stance: Now the company would oppose apartheid not by leaving this profitable nation, but by starting to focus on empowering those most wounded by the unjust system.

It seems that Goizueta, and corporate Coke generally, were following the lead set by local Coca-Cola management by becoming more forceful in their opposition to apartheid. Some within Coca-Cola South Africa had begun outwardly pronouncing their opposition to apartheid. In 1984, company executive Hennie Viljoen, also vice president of the Federated Chambers of Industries, helped draft a statement demanding the release of labor leaders who had been arrested. Viljoen also helped draft a letter to Senator Edward Kennedy, supporting the end of apartheid, and met with government operatives to express Coca-Cola's opposition to apartheid. Adrian Botha, another company official, likewise helped compose an anti-apartheid piece that received press attention. And, in 1985, Viljoen went on South African television to demand the release of Mandela.[34] In short, by the mid-1980s Coca-Cola South Africa staked a position against apartheid predicated on the company staying and staying involved in South African politics.

Between 1983 and his second trip to South Africa in 1986, Ware sharpened his plan for Coca-Cola based upon the belief that the best work Coca-Cola could do in South Africa was to keep working in the country. The climate on both sides of the world was not an easy one in which to do this. In 1985, Ware reported: 'In South Africa, we are in a race against both the advocates of violence and the opponents of change. In the U.S., we are in a race against traditional American impatience, the fondness for the quick fix and the dramatic gesture.'[35] In South Africa, then gripped by mass resistance to apartheid first ignited by the children's uprising, Coke's position was tenuous. There, the anti-apartheid movement was opposed to big businesses, particularly multinationals. Ware recalled first meeting Nobel Laureate Desmond Tutu, already a well-known anti-apartheid activist. At their first encounter, Ware was devastated when Tutu scoffed at the notion that the business could do anything useful for the cause except leave the country.[36] Sentiments were similar in the United States. There, American campuses were enflamed, with calls for American universities and pension funds, in particular, to sell their stocks from those companies that did business in South Africa, including Coca-Cola. For Ware, while divestment might serve as a useful moral gesture, it would not actually affect change in South Africa. 'I went all over the country speaking, explaining ... that yes, we are anti-apartheid too. Coke is. But there is a way. There is a business strategy to how you do this. Just to disinvest and pull away from South Africa without leaving some legacy of something in the way of ownership of the soft drink,' would be disastrous, Ware recalled.[37] Ware's position was that Coca-Cola must find a way to stay in South Africa in order to affect change, while somehow depriving the apartheid state of revenues from its business. Just leaving, Ware believed, would cause a market hole soon to be filled by another business. His plan, on the other hand, would allow the company to still make money and still affect change. There was a kind of business hubris to this scheme, wherein the company positioned itself to play a role in ending apartheid, which, the gamble went, would be good on both sides of the Atlantic. The trick was to convince stakeholders on both sides of the world to buy into it.

Besides gaining support from US anti-apartheid activists—which Ware attempted to do by speaking to crowds around the country—Ware's scheme was predicated on wooing South Africans working to end apartheid to embrace Coca-Cola. In reaching out to local anti-apartheid activists, Ware, and Coca-Cola, displayed a level of respect for those South Africans working to end apartheid not typical of big business. Chief among Ware's targets was Desmond Tutu, who had already shown his skepticism for Coca-Cola, but who Ware was desperate to win over. According to Ware, Tutu was set to issue a press release demanding that all US businesses leave the country when Ware asked him to pray with him. Thereupon, Tutu reversed course.[38] While we cannot know what caused Tutu to change his outlook, we do know that he did. When, shortly after their first meeting, Ware proposed that Tutu head a Coca-Cola-endowed charitable fund in South Africa (detailed below), Tutu accepted, opening the door for those working against apartheid from within South Africa to see Coca-Cola as an ally.

Beyond Tutu, Ware worked to convince high-profile anti-apartheid operatives in exile to see Coca-Cola as a friend.[39] At the time, the ANC maintained exile offices in Lusaka, Zambia, Dar es Salaam, Tanzania, and London, England. Ware was based in London in those days and would regularly meet in secret with local ANC operatives. Speaking of Thabo Mbeki, future deputy president under Mandela and then second president of a free South Africa, himself based in London, Ware recalled that they 'met frequently to discuss the Coca-Cola strategy in South Africa,' and, in particular, how business might help empower Black South Africans. At the time, the ANC subscribed to communist principles that saw big business as anathema to positive social change. Ware introduced Mbeki and others to Coca-Cola's brand of capitalism, which is predicated on the belief that if everyone up and down the value chain succeeds, the business succeeds. They found surprising common ground around how Coke could help empower people through grassroots, small-scale entrepreneurship. According to Ware, his discussions with Mbeki and others helped the ANC reframe its sense of the role that capital could play in a free South Africa. Beyond local meetings in London, Ware also speaks of traveling regularly—if quietly—to meet with other exiled ANC operatives in Lusaka and Dar es Salaam.[40] Given the danger associated with consorting with what was then regarded as a terrorist organization, Ware and Coca-Cola had to keep these visits off the books. Still, these trips helped shift the ANC's position on Coca-Cola just as they affected Coke's sense of its role in South Africa. Yet, no matter how much support Ware could muster for Coke's attempt to stay in South Africa and engage in charitable work from within the movement, it soon became clear that such a position would not be viable on the world stage.

In 1986, Leon Sullivan convened a multinational conference of chief executive officers to discuss the role of companies in ending apartheid that forever shifted the terms of debate. Ware was sent to what became known as the Leeds Conference in Kent, England to represent Coca-Cola. There, business leaders were unequivocally introduced to the full horrors of apartheid, something that Ware had seen firsthand, but that many had not. What became obvious there was that the Sullivan Principles were never going to be enough to affect change on a large enough scale. Indeed, it was becoming increasingly clear that the principles, predicated largely on issues of petty, or small-scale apartheid, had served only to reinforce the apartheid state's stronghold on society. The time for total disinvestment from the country had arrived if companies wanted to maintain their standing.[41] Whether deliberately or not, Ware had been preparing Coca-Cola for this moment. By shifting the plan he already had in the works, he now fashioned a path for the company to technically disinvest from South Africa while still continuing to sell its product in the country. This stance would allow the corporation to oppose the apartheid state for an international audience, while aligning itself with leading members of South Africa's anti-apartheid movement, all while still keeping its products available for South African consumers. It was to be Coca-Cola's own form of disinvestment.

Coca-Cola's Disinvestment

The path to Coca-Cola's full disinvestment began not by starting to leave the country, but by finding ways to stay involved there. Under Ware, Coca-Cola contributed ten million US dollars (roughly twenty-five million rand) to create a charitable fund, named the Equal Opportunity Foundation (EOF).[42] The EOF was set up to be an independent South African nonprofit aimed at helping create a South Africa beyond apartheid. Focused primarily on funding educational and empowerment projects in disadvantaged communities, the EOF's charge was to underwrite initiatives that would enable 'black leadership infrastructure' in a post-apartheid South Africa, while demonstrating The Coca-Cola Company's clear commitment to ending apartheid.[43] The EOF's Board of Directors boasted a who's who of anti-apartheid educators and activists selected by Ware. The board included Alex Boraine, head of the Institute for a Democratic Alternative for South Africa (IDASA), Allan Boesak, World Alliance of

Churches' leader and head of the United Democratic Front, the leading resistance body that emerged in the 1980s, Arthur Chaskalson, then director of the Legal Resources Center, Jakes Gerwel, rector of the University of the Western Cape, Ernest Mchunu, president of the Black Management Forum and Coca-Cola's senior Black South African employee, Yusuf Surtee, tailor and trustee of the Black South African business community with strong ties to the anti-apartheid movement, and, as its head, now Archbishop Desmond Tutu.[44] At the time of its initiation, the EOF was the largest privately funded foundation under the control of Black South Africans.[45]

The EOF was in place around the time of Sullivan's Leeds conference, when it became clear, to all multinationals, that the time for full disinvestment from South Africa had arrived. For The Coca-Cola Company, leaving South Africa broke with long-standing precedent, one not even Nazi Germany had prompted the company to invalidate. Ware recalled a momentous meeting he had early in his career with long-time Coca-Cola head and icon Robert Woodruff. At the time, Woodruff cautioned Ware that 'Coca-Cola is not a Democratic company; it is not a Republican company.' The message, as Ware later learned in government relations, was that there was, as he paraphrased it, a 'sort of unwritten law,' that Coca-Cola always stayed neutral, no matter the situation. 'Therein lies I think part of the reason for the great continuing success of The Coca-Cola company wherever we do business,' Ware opined. It also reveals why, as he put it, 'going against the South African government itself in terms of our disinvestment from South Africa,' was such risky, uncomfortable business. In order to enact this move, Coca-Cola needed a carefully worded press release to convey that it was apartheid and not South Africa that it was opposing.[46]

To craft this document, Ware called upon a man of impeccable moral credentials. Ware had recently noted that despite their blossoming friendship, Tutu had never been to the company's offices in Johannesburg. Ware used this opportunity to invite Tutu to the local office, telling him on the way that the company was about to disinvest from South Africa and asking for Tutu's blessing. The result was a press release that went, as Ware tells it, 'back and forth across the Atlantic a dozen times' by fax until its wording pleased both Don Keough and Desmond Tutu, respectively.[47] So it was that on 17 September 1986, The Coca-Cola Company announced that it was poised to disinvest from apartheid South Africa, mere weeks before the United States government passed the Comprehensive Anti-Apartheid Act, initializing American sanctions. Announcing its opposition to apartheid specifically, Coca-Cola gave itself nine months to sell its holdings in South Africa in such a way, as the company told it, as to benefit those most subjugated by the apartheid state. 'Our objective is not solely to disinvest,' Keough was quoted in *The New York Times* the next day: 'Our goal is to structure the transactions in a way that improves the prospects of black South Africans and increases their ability to invest in their country's economy.'[48] Not only was Coca-Cola the first corporation to name politics, instead of failing business conditions, as the reason for its exit, but it was also the first to commit itself to fashioning its exit in such a way that it benefited Black South Africans.[49]

In order to meet the requirements for disinvestment, Coca-Cola had to cease all company-owned operations in South Africa, which had up until then been run by Coca-Cola Export. Before disinvestment, Coca-Cola held a 30% share in Amalgamated Beverages Industries (ABI), one of the biggest distributors of soft drinks in the nation. In recent years, it had lowered its stake from 64% by selling off part of its shares to South African Breweries, arguably in anticipation of just this day.[50] Coca-Cola also had a high corporate stake in a local canning operation. The Coca-Cola Company now had to sell these holdings in order to deprive the apartheid state of any tax revenue generated by them. In 1986, Coca-Cola also owned and ran one of its concentrate plants, which served a large swath of the continent, from inside South Africa. This, too, needed to be attended to in order to meet the demands and spirit of disinvestment.

How did the company accomplish this? First, The Coca-Cola Company and Coca-Cola Export entered into an agreement with a newly created South Africa company called National Beverages Services, or NBS, in order for NBS to take over all of the company's operations in South Africa. The goal was to create as seamless a transition as possible, both operationally and ideologically. NBS was meant to function as Coca-Cola Export once had while ensuring that the company met the needs of disinvestment and United States sanctions.[51] Beyond transferring its operations to NBS, Coca-Cola relocated its Durban concentrate plant to the independent nation of Swaziland (now Eswatini). Three years after it became operational, revenues from concentrate production had doubled the small country's corporate tax revenue. This meant that, as Ware later told a group of Mount Holyoke students, 'There are now, quite literally, schools, hospitals and roads in Swaziland built with this Company's tax payments.'[52] With the concentrate plant no longer generating revenue for South Africa and without any employees in the country, the company concluded in an internal white paper that it had now 'met a traditional definition of disinvestment.' Unlike traditional disinvestment, however, it noted that its disinvestment had not hurt the very people most in need of help: Coca-Cola assessed that no former employees lost their jobs; they had simply gone to work for NBS and other 'locally-owned enterprises.' As such, the white paper concluded, 'the disinvestment process will actually improve the economic prospects of thousands of black South Africans who will be offered the chance of ownership in their country's soft drink industry.'[53] This was the third leg of Ware's disinvestment plan, after contracting with NBS and moving the concentrate plant: focusing on Black empowerment.

Since Coca-Cola was no longer officially operating in South Africa, the company had to rely upon independent bottlers and NBS to fulfill the last—and arguably most essential—part of Ware's plan: Black empowerment. ABI, the largest bottler of Coca-Cola in South Africa, led the way by offering Black employees the chance for equity participation that the white paper mentioned. On offer, 11% of its shares, once owned by Coca-Cola Export, for its employees and small retail dealers.[54] Many took advantage of this offer, most of whom were Black.[55] Beyond stocks, ABI began to offer managerial training, hoping to encourage the promotion of talent in the system.[56] At the same time, Coca-Cola bottlers and NBS began to focus on the growth of small-scale distribution systems that would take Coca-Cola into the informal, densely populated areas of the country. To be sure, such a spread worked well with emergent marketing plans aimed at capturing new, predominantly Black consumers, but it also served to empower thousands of new Black employees. In a speech from December 1988, Ware noted the 'political irony in this... business development,' proudly declaring that NBS's new 'informal distribution program has 10,000 blacks involved already' and a five-year projection of ten times that number. With robust investments in bicycles, motorbikes, and coolers— all of which harken to the spread of Coca-Cola elsewhere—the era immediately after disinvestment saw, ironically, a massive 'grassroots distribution' of Coke product and businesses into disempowered corners of South Africa.[57]

Beyond small-scale empowerment, Coca-Cola—by way of NBS and Ware—focused on several high-profile initiatives. Ware had been struck on his first trip to Africa by the absence of African—which to him meant Black African—management across the system. 'Whether you went to Kenya or Zimbabwe or

Francophone Africa or Nigeria,' he told me, there was a 'dearth of human talent,' that troubled him deeply. It was one of the first problems he sought to fix, starting first in South Africa and first with one man.[58] When Ware initially arrived in South Africa, Ernest Mchunu was already working for Coca-Cola Export; indeed, Mchunu was one of the first Coke employees Ware met. Mchunu had been headhunted from Edgar's Department Store to join Coca-Cola in 1974 as 'Black Marketing Officer,' brought on to consult about the 'Black market,' as it was called. Much of Mchunu's early work laid the groundwork for later Coca-Cola initiatives begun under Ware but, once Coca-Cola had left South Africa, continued under Mchunu, with Ware's endorsement.

Born in the 1930s in Alexandria township outside of Johannesburg, Mchunu was a self-made businessman who rose to play an important role for Coca-Cola in this era. Mchunu's earliest work for Coca-Cola involved helping spread the company's reach, both by capturing new consumers and by expanding points of sale in places like Alex. In Mchunu's early days, Coca-Cola South Africa was trying to fend off market advances from Pepsi-Cola. One way the company did this was school samplings. 'The main purpose' of these, Mchunu wrote in his memoir *Cheeky Native* in language that would undoubtedly horrify Coca-Cola leadership, 'was to "catch them young" so that they grew up addicted to the beverage.' 'This strategy worked extremely well for the company,' he concluded.[59] Mchunu was also an early advocate for promoting Black drivers, jobs that quickly came to be seen as esteemed positions. Both of these initiatives—school sampling and the emergence of Black drivers—helped insulate the company against much of the township unrest that began after the Soweto uprising and the subsequent declaration of a State of Emergency. 'Incredible as it may seem,' Mchunu wrote of Coca-Cola deliveries into the 1980s, 'most students protected our delivery trucks instead of setting them on fire as they did with anything associated with white companies or the government.'[60] Black drivers, in other words, started to give the company a gloss of Blackness. Through his work with distribution and sampling, Mchunu gained an insider view of the Black market and its potential for the company. He presented his findings at the Coca-Cola Southern Africa Bottlers' Convention in 1984 in a paper called 'The Black Market is Still the Great Unknown.' In his talk, the first of its kind given by a Black South African, Mchunu noted that Black traders in Soweto working in informal spaza shops had annual turnover rates above 350,000 physical cases and annual buying power of four million rand.[61] 'We at Coca-Cola must recognize the growing importance in our business of both the black consumer and the black businessman,' Mchunu concluded, 'as this is where our growth and our future lie.'[62] Coca-Cola Export rewarded Mchunu for his insight by promoting him to corporate social responsibility manager for Black markets.

It was in this role that Mchunu was tasked with hosting Ware on Ware's first visit to South Africa in 1983. Mchunu writes of his amazement meeting an African American businessman of such high standing who showed primary interest in the South African struggle from the position of the oppressed. Ware was equally pleased to find an employee of Mchunu's experience and stature in South Africa. The connection they formed would be important for both of them. Over the following years, Ware helped accelerate Mchunu's career: He had Mchunu appointed to Leon Sullivan's watchdog group in South Africa, representing Coca-Cola; he was responsible for Mchunu's appointments to various boards, including that of the EOF; and he enabled Mchunu to visit Coca-Cola Atlanta, among other places. For his part, Mchunu opened doors for Ware, introducing him to both anti-apartheid activists, like those who came to people the EOF board, and Black businessmen poised for empowerment.

To be sure, Ware recognized that it is one thing to want to empower Black South Africans. It is quite another to find men and women capable of rising quickly to the business challenges that Coca-Cola would present, particularly at the highest levels of ownership within the system. Mchunu played an important role in identifying those who would be empowered for these roles. First, he introduced Ware to Richard Maponya, perhaps the most famous township-raised entrepreneur in South Africa, known for growing businesses in Soweto despite apartheid-era conditions. By the time Ware arrived, Maponya and his wife owned a Soweto dairy and held Coca-Cola distribution rights in Bophuthatswana. This tangential connection to the Coke business made Maponya attractive to Ware. When Coca-Cola disinvested from South Africa, Maponya assembled a group of Black businessmen to form the company Kilimanjaro Holdings, which then bid successfully to buy a bottling plant in East London. Ware was instrumental in constructing this deal. Later, Kilimanjaro would be taken over by Fortune Holding, the company run in part by the Kunenes, the second Coca-Cola Black empowerment story.[63]

Mchunu was also the first to tell Ware about the Kunenes, often—and to their chagrin—heralded as the quintessential Coca-Cola feel-good story. The Kunene fortune began with the aptly named patriarch, Fortune Kunene, and his wife, both schoolteachers, and their seven children. In 1978, Fortune Kunene introduced soft drinks to their family's side business of running a fresh milk shop in the East Rand township of Vosloorus. In 1983, Kunene moved from retail sales to running three wholesale outlets, later adding alcohol to his inventory. From there, he and his three sons who had joined the business expanded into distribution. 'Unbeknownst to us,' Zanosi Kunene, one of Fortune's sons and eventual chairman of what became known as Fortune Holdings, the Kunenes' growth had, as he told me, 'caught the system's attention.'[64] Kunene recalls meeting Ware in the 1980s and gaining the admiration of the larger Coke universe for having grown such a robust business under such challenging circumstances.

When, in 1989, it looked as though apartheid may in fact end during their lifetime—a day they never thought they would live to see—Zanosi and two of his brothers set their sights on bettering their family via Coca-Cola. They made an appointment to visit Ware in London. There, the Kunenes registered their intent to be considered for a bottling franchise, should one become available. The problem: they had neither capital nor acquisition experience. Ware suggested they return to South Africa and meet with Coca-Cola's auditor at Ernst and Young. Kunene recalls how challenging it was to be township entrepreneurs trying to navigate a South African economy that had largely been closed to them. Initially, Coca-Cola also appeared closed to their aspirations. Kunene bitterly recalled for me the frustration of meeting with Coke only to hear that their aspirations would go unmet, year after year.[65]

While the Kunenes had proven themselves to be smart businessmen, the realities of late apartheid South Africa meant that they did not have access to the sort of capital needed to break into the bottling world. Multiple players in the system—Coke Atlanta, Ware, and existent bottlers in South Africa—would have to come together to help give them their start. Ware set the ball in motion. In the early 1990s, the Kunene brothers were summoned to Atlanta. There, they were told that Coca-Cola had identified a company for them called Coca-Cola Bottling Mpumalanga, or CCBM, near Nelspruit. Dave Cruise of Suncrush—whose family goes all the way back to the earliest days of bottling sparkling water in South Africa—wanted out. At the time, the Kunenes had amassed around two million rand for the purchase, an impressive amount of money for distributors. However, the price for CCBM, as recounted by those involved, was around seventy million rand. For the deal to go through, Coca-Cola took out a loan to back the Kunenes. The company then bought out Cruise and flipped his shares to the Kunenes, making the independent bottler Peninsula Beverages (PenBev) partners with the Kunenes.[66] Both the Kunenes and PenBev leadership recall the partnership as deeply impactful, if at times fraught.

In 1994, Zanosi arrived in Cincinnati to begin a four-month training stint in bottler operation. The Kunene family took over CCBM on 1 January 1995, with Zanosi as assistant general manager. Six months later, Zanosi became managing director.[67] The Kunene enterprise grew. In 1997, the Kunenes acquired Maponya's Kilimanjaro in East London, running it alongside PenBev, who held a minority stake in the enterprise. Then, in 2002, the Kunenes continued to go from strength to strength, merging with Phil Gutsche's South African Bottling Company (Sabco) to become Coca-Cola Fortune, then the second largest bottler of Coca-Cola in Africa. Coca-Cola Fortune later became part of Coca-Cola Beverages Africa (CCBA), now the largest bottler of Coca-Cola in Africa and the eighth largest bottler of Coca-Cola in the world.[68]

Right from the start the Kunenes brought a perspective that dovetailed with what Ernest Mchunu had reported, as well as what the ANC folks had been telling Ware: that for Coca-Cola to grow and play a meaningful role in South Africa, the company needed to focus on expanding its small-scale operations, particularly in high-density—or Black—areas. With the Kunenes on board and Coke being run internally by National Beverages, a new initiative was launched to push beyond white consumers to reach all parts of the South African market. Longtime Cape Town-area bottlers recalled an initial trip into nearby Khayelitsha township at this time. The realities of apartheid were such that they had limited experience with this—or any—township, since these emerging markets were considered to be far less profitable than, for instance, a formal supermarket in an affluent suburb. 'It was quite a day for all of us,' Managing Director of Forbes Investment Holdings Stuart McLeod recalled, 'and in a way it was an introduction to what our lives would be.'[69] That was the start of developing mom-and-pop spaza shops that would forever bring Coke red to South African townships, in the Cape, as elsewhere.

This, then, was the final portion of Coca-Cola's disinvestment: grassroots initiatives meant to provide on-ramps to economic participation for scores of Black South Africans hitherto excluded from the system. A Coca-Cola-produced video of life under disinvestment gives a sense of what this flavor of empowerment looked like. It opens with Dr. Nthato Motlana, chairman of Soweto's famed 'Committee of Ten'—a group formed in the aftermath of the Soweto uprising—then also a board member of Coca-Cola's EOF. '[P]olitical power arises as a consequence of economics,' he pronounced: 'We therefore say to our people, get off your backsides and make money.' The best way to make money, as described in this video: sell Coca-Cola. The video introduces us to a string of small-scale entrepreneurs— mostly women—for whom Coke is their economic lifeline. We meet Eunice Sibiya, Letty Mochwaedi, Simon Mboxwana, Mr. and Mrs. Gulwa, Irene Masiu, and sisters, Lynette and Hellen Masoeu: wholesalers, small-shop owners, and vending trolley operators from Klerksdorp, Bloemfontein, Soweto, and elsewhere. Their stories resonate. They all started small, with one or two crates of Coca-Cola. No matter what else they have on offer—fruits, sweets, or cooked foods—Coke is the item that draws people in, that enables their business to grow. All echo the same sentiment: without Coca-Cola, their business would not be as profitable, not be able to support upwards of ten people each. The film's narrator affirms that there are 'thousands like them,' people for whom 'disinvestment has been a success' at the expense of the South African government, deprived now of Coke-generated tax revenue.[70] Another Coca-Cola video details the rise of one particular empowerment story, Mtshselwa's Transport in Guguletu. We learn that Mr. Mtshelwa began delivering Coke products in the township in 1985, when unrest precluded white drivers from entering Guguletu. His business had since grown, with the bottler's help, to seeing him deliver upwards of 250,000 cases a year. An impending new truck acquisition is sure to drive this number up, we hear.[71] The 1989 edition of Coca-Cola's magazine *Journey* similarly explored the disproportionate impact of the product in disadvantaged portions of South Africa, in this case by looking at the small town of Jouberton, where no fewer than 625 Black entrepreneurs were making a living off of Coca-Cola.[72] While this article, much like the videos before it, casts Coca-Cola in the best possible light, a kernel remains true even under the gloss: a direct by-product of Coca-Cola's disinvestment was sustained expansion into Black consumer spaces, made possible by a sustained mobilizing of a Black workforce. Later, Coca-Cola would make much of the fact that its form of divestment empowered many South Africans, while the forms that other companies took did the opposite.[73]

While Coca-Cola became increasingly available in previously underserved corners of South Africa during the company's disinvestment, Ware attempted to stoke goodwill towards the company from on high. Under Ware's direction, Coca-Cola funded several secret meetings between the exile wing of the ANC and South African politicians and businessmen who, by the late 1980s, had begun to imagine a world beyond apartheid. Meetings of this sort have been increasingly documented by reporters and historians.[74] Until now, however, no one has ever included Coca-Cola on the list of companies involved. The reason: work like this necessarily had to be kept quiet. When

I told Ware that I had been unsuccessful in my attempt to find contemporaneous documentation about these meetings, he laid it bare: 'You won't, because we never publicized it.' Yet, now that apartheid is no more, Ware was able to state 'unabashedly' and with no small amount of pride that Coca-Cola did, under his direction, funnel funds to anti-apartheid work, including meetings that preceded the end of apartheid. Ware was particularly proud that he funded ANC members to attend the famed Dakar, Senegal meeting that took place in July 1987 between the ANC and the Institute for Democratic Alternatives in South Africa (IDASA), a group made up of mostly Afrikaners dedicated to forging a path towards democracy.[75] This meeting was significant because it demonstrated IDASA's willingness to meet with a banned organization, despite being roundly condemned by the South Africa government and facing the backlash of right-wing organizations for doing so. In retrospect, this meeting set South Africa on a path towards its eventual negotiated settlement. Dozens more meetings would take place along the way.[76] Though it was not publicized, that Coke helped enable the first one did much to enhance the company's credibility on the African stage, where Coke's involvement was an open secret. At the same time, Ware made sure to augment anti-apartheid goodwill within South Africa in smaller, and similarly quiet, ways. When Winnie Mandela's home in Soweto was demolished, he arranged for it to be refurbished at Coca-Cola's expense. Coca-Cola helped fund the anti-apartheid play *Sarafina!* and get it to Broadway. Coke funded at least one peaceful demonstration by Soweto's Committee of Ten, and more.[77]

Though largely without documentation, these activities and more were corroborated by interviews with E Neville Isdell, Rute Moyo, and Zanosi Kunene. All of this activity was off the books, meaning that while we know about it now, most people did not then. Thus it was that despite all that Coke had tried to do to make disinvestment work for most South Africans, while feeding its bottom line, the company faced backlash at the time.[78]

After Disinvestment

The most targeted criticism of Coke's particular form of disinvestment was that it was, in fact, nothing but a sham. An early proponent of this point of view was Jesse Jackson—that old thorn in the company's side—who saw the EOF (whose creation was entwined with disinvestment) as no more than a ploy to enhance the company's standing.[79] Others likewise imagined Coca-Cola's sale to NBS as little more than window-dressing meant to make it look as though the company had left the country when, in fact, it had not. In his autobiography, Mchunu casts disinvestment in just this light, calling it 'obviously a lie' that was evidence of 'the company's stroke of genius.'[80] Later, Pepsi-Cola would pick up this line as it attempted to re-enter the South African market after apartheid ended. Pepsi made much of the fact that between it and its nemesis, only one had been available for purchase during the dark days of apartheid.[81] Ware himself seems to gesture to the flimsiness of NBS's independence at a 1992 talk he gave to South African bottlers in Bermuda titled 'We Shall Return,' gesturing to the imagined day, post-apartheid, when Coca-Cola could again operate officially inside South Africa. There, Ware stated that there were many Coke folks in the audience that could not be acknowledged as such.[82] To be sure, Coca-Cola's form of disinvestment was unique. Certainly, there was never a time when consumers could not purchase Cokes in South Africa. If anything, as documented above, the company only expanded its reach during disinvestment.

Criticism of Coca-Cola's particular form of disinvestment also surfaced close to its corporate home. At the time, Tandi Gcabashe, daughter of Chief Albert Luthuli—former president of the ANC and the first African to be awarded the Nobel Peace Prize—was living in exile in Atlanta. Gcabashe was Director of the Southern Peace Education Program of the American Friends Service Committee and head of The Coke Campaign, whose very purpose was to agitate against Coca-Cola's form of disinvestment. Under the slogan 'Coke sweetens apartheid,' The Coke Campaign called for consumer boycotts of the beverage. According to the campaign, Coca-Cola's form of disinvestment was disingenuous. 'The object of disinvestment is not to change the color of people who finance apartheid,' the campaign pronounced 'but to end all financial support for apartheid. Total disinvestment must mean the cessation of all economic operations and connections, including license, trademarks, factories, suppliers and distributors.'[83] According to The Coke Campaign, all Coke had done was create a flimsy middle class. Moreover, that the beverage was still available in South Africa meant that the company was not truly disentangled from the apartheid state. We saw the result of the campaign's work in the opening to this chapter: when Nelson Mandela first arrived in Atlanta, neither the corporation nor any local ANC politicians were willing to engage with Coca-Cola.

Coca-Cola responded to The Coke Campaign with a glossy brochure meant to counter many of its concerns with the company's position, bolstered by support from Tutu, Boesak, and others. In particular, Coke took aim at the idea that Coca-Cola served only to create a 'token' middle class that could be 'easily manipulated,' as the campaign had charged. Calling such a claim 'patronizing and insulting,' the brochure cut to the crux of external opposition to Coca-Cola in South Africa at the time. At stake was the question of who gets to decide what is best for disadvantaged South Africans, well-meaning activists far away from South Africa or struggle leaders on the ground?[84] Clearly, there was a disconnect between the two.

That much of Coca-Cola's work against apartheid was kept quiet while the company only seemed to expand its reach during the late apartheid era, coupled with enduring notions that the West must know what is best for Africans, meant that by 1990, prevailing anti-apartheid sentiment outside South Africa saw Coca-Cola as part of the problem. Ware tried to work against this image problem by appealing to his friend, Tutu. In a letter dated 10 April 1989, Tutu endorses Coca-Cola's struggle credentials, presumably in response to Ware's request to do so. After congratulating Ware on becoming a grandparent for the first time—calling it a 'gooey' experience—Tutu gets serious. 'I am sorry to hear that Coca Cola is running into some trouble over its alleged dishonesty about the manner of its disinvestment from South Africa and that it is being accused of aiding and abetting the apartheid regime,' he states, noting unequivocally that '[n]othing could be further from the truth.' Against the claims that the EOF was itself a front, Tutu weighs in that he feels 'honoured' to serve on the board that is helping perform important empowerment work. Moreover, he notes that he and other board members were satisfied with the way in which Coke disinvested, closing by saying that Ware could use this letter in any way that he saw fit.[85]

What Ware did with this letter is open to question. When pressed, Ware suggested that other nations in Africa 'just knew' about his Coke-led anti-apartheid work. Eventually, that knowledge made its way to anti-apartheid stalwarts who had been banned or imprisoned during this time. Winnie Mandela herself, Ware told me, alerted her husband to Coke's goodwill in his absence.[86] Recall that on his first trip to America, Mandela scorned Coca-Cola, but on his second trip he embraced the company. Clearly, something happened between 1990 and 1993 to change, if not the entire universe of anti-apartheid operatives' view of Coca-Cola, then at least that of its figurehead, Nelson

Mandela. In 1993, when Mandela again arrived in the United States, Coca-Cola took charge of moving Mandela between New York City, Washington, Los Angeles, and Atlanta at the African National Congress's request.[87]

Coca-Cola did more than just provide access to its jet. In Atlanta, Coke arranged for Mandela to visit Clark University, Ware's alma mater, and to meet company chairman Roberto Goizueta. The company also facilitated Mandela's stay at the Ritz Carlton, making sure that Mandela—who everyone was told to call President Mandela—was amply comfortable. The television would be set to CNN or NBC, the room should be stocked with fresh fruit, a chair should be stationed outside the room for a security detail, and a waiter should arrive each morning to take Mandela's breakfast order in person, rather than by telephone, employees were told.[88] Preparations for imagined news conferences were equally thorough. If pressed, internal memos explained, Coke was to say that it was but one of several companies aiding Mandela on his trip.[89] 'Senior management of The Coca-Cola Company regularly meet with world leaders visiting the city as part of our ongoing business process,' another internal memo suggested as a talking point.[90] Yes, all acknowledged, Coca-Cola would be considering re-entry into South Africa, once sanctions were lifted. And, yes, the company did plan to use time on its plane flights to press Mandela on threats to its business in South Africa—enduring violence in townships, an excise tax against soft drinks, and the ANC's recent statements about compelling responsible behavior by businesses.[91] In the end, Coca-Cola's hospitality worked. By the time he left America, Mandela had welcomed Coca-Cola into his inner circle.

Thus it was that on 10 May 1994, Carl Ware and his wife Mary were invited to Pretoria, South Africa to witness Mandela's inauguration as the first democratically elected president of a free South Africa. Two days later they were summoned to a private meeting with President Mandela at his office in the Union Buildings. There, they were met by ANC old-timers, including Jakes Gerwel, who had left the EOF board to join Mandela as his chief of staff. The purpose of their meeting was to discuss Coca-Cola's plans to re-enter South Africa. Ware had just been appointed head of Coca-Cola Africa, so whatever he discussed was within his discretionary power. Ware explained how Coke was in the process of helping launch the first Black-owned franchise under the Kunenes and how the company was committed to, as Ware later wrote, 'dramatically increase investments in microbusinesses such as spazas, kiosks, taxi ranks, and wholesalers, thereby creating thousands of jobs and hundreds of new business owners in townships throughout the country.'[92] According to Ware, Mandela nodded his approval.

Shortly thereafter, Coca-Cola formally re-entered South Africa. 'On behalf of The Coca-Cola Company,' Carl Ware said on the occasion, 'it's good to be back home in South Africa.' Ware focused not on re-entry as such, but rather on the ways in which Coca-Cola planned to 'adapt, change, and lead,' seeking to be no less than 'an example for how to do business responsibly in a democratic South Africa.' 'Black empowerment,' he made clear, was not 'an obligation,' but rather 'a tremendous business opportunity,' echoing Coca-Cola's long-standing belief in the possibility to do good and do good business at the same time. 'Atlanta does not know best,' Ware humbly concluded. Instead, he anticipated productive dialogue on how best to change the South African business and, indeed, that of Africa generally. 'I believe we are on the threshold of an historic opportunity,' Ware pushed further: 'I say this because never before has such a unique synergy existed to move Africa and South Africa to another plateau of leadership and growth.'[93] Here, then, was the true endgame: not just getting Coca-Cola back into South Africa, but also finding a pad from which to launch a renewed expansion into Africa north of the Limpopo River. Ware's anti-apartheid work had become known. 'It was out there,' he told me. 'There was not a place in Africa, not a statehouse or president or a prime minister or a minister of finance or a commerce minister who didn't know about our work in South Africa.' As a result, as Ware led the way as head of Coca-Cola Africa on a post-apartheid continent, he was 'always received with welcome, wide-open arms everywhere I went.'[94] In the buoyant days after apartheid ended, extant Coca-Cola bottlers were themselves keen on expansion, seeing the end of South Africa's status as a pariah state as a business opportunity. The time was ripe for a new investment in not just South Africa, but also Africa generally.

Conclusion

On 28 July 1993, Nelson Mandela wrote a letter to Carl Ware expressing how he felt about both Ware and Coca-Cola. 'It is always a difficult task to find words adequate enough to express the depth of our indebtedness to somebody as special in our life as you have become, Carl,' he began. 'When the history of our struggle is properly reviewed in the near future, only then will the world be privy to fully understand your catalytic role in that struggle. We in the ANC know of countless contributions made to innumerable individuals and organizations in our country through your direct intervention. This you did, not only in your capacity as one of the decision makers within Coca Cola, but also in your own right as a conscientious human being of African descent.'[95] Ware, unsurprisingly, cherishes this letter, along with a photograph of himself and Mandela, both evidence of his role in history-making.

Not all who have lived into the post-apartheid era feel as positively about Coca-Cola. In 2016, I spoke to Tandi Gcabashe, now back at home in Durban. Despite having lived to see the end of apartheid, she continues to view Coca-Cola with derision, naming the company's form of disinvestment as a 'trick' that served to divide struggle activists. She said Coca-Cola understood this tension, so common in boycott debates, and had manipulated it in order to polarize opposition. Yes, she acknowledged, Boesak, Tutu, and Winnie Mandela had all 'bought into' Coke's position, but they had been wrong, in her estimation. She approached Nelson Mandela at Namibian independence in 1990, she told me, in order to tell him about her experience leading the boycott in exile. In her memory, he listened to her and, despite having flown into Namibia on a Coca-Cola jet, refused to return on one.[96] Perhaps this was the reason he later scoffed at Coca-Cola during his first trip to America. Yet, whatever impact Gcabashe had was not enough. In the end, Coca-Cola was able to woo Mandela, with its history of struggle credentials and its promise of post-apartheid economic growth. In her heart, Gcabashe told me, she still boycotts Coke.[97] As we will later see, she is not alone in this stance.

The story told in this chapter illustrates the tension between exiled activists and those who stayed, as well as, though to a lesser extent, the tensions between those who were imprisoned and those who were not. In addition, the tale here helps explain how the ANC accepted the idea of capital as a means for liberation, laying bare the ANC's expediency and helping us better understand why the party shifted so dramatically from communist to free market principles once empowered.[98] This story reveals, again, the power of Africans on the ground to bend Coca-Cola to their needs, something that was difficult—if not impossible—for external observers to appreciate. Finally, this narrative forces us to think about the role of sanctions and disinvestment in helping end apartheid, debates that are far from reconciled.

The story of Coca-Cola's role in the end of apartheid also stands as a rare example of The Coca-Cola Company openly taking a political stance. When I asked Ware why it is that Coke took on the fight against apartheid in quite the way it did, he offered what I have since heard to be the company line: apartheid, a system of patently unjust racism, was so deeply anachronistic and so obviously painful that it demanded the company work against it purely on moral grounds. Sure, South Africa was a hugely important market for Coca-Cola, but there was more than that. Here, Coke folks generally gesture to the company's history of working towards racial equity, seen, for instance, in a particularly beloved story of how Robert Woodruff hosted MLK's Nobel Peace Prize dinner.[99] In Ware's reckoning of his own life, it is clear that his participation as a proxy for Coke in the anti-apartheid struggle—at whatever level—was ethically motivated. 'There were human dynamics' and 'there were philosophical beliefs' that drove him to help end apartheid in any way that he could, he told me. But he never ignored the fact that his actions were likewise driven by his position as an employee of Coca-Cola. Thus, 'there was also an enlightened self-interest' in how he and the company, under his direction, operated. Ware and Coke understood full well just how important South Africa in the 1980s was. 'You could lose South Africa,' he said, 'and lose the world.'[100] In the end, Ware and the larger company believed that how Coca-Cola behaved in late apartheid South Africa, how it met the challenge both internally and globally, would determine its future, perhaps in the entire world. Closer to the point at hand, Ware and Coke understood that how Coca-Cola negotiated apartheid would determine if and how the company could thrive anew in a now fully post-colonial continent. As the door closed on the apartheid regime, as Ware ascended to the head of Coca-Cola Africa, it was this terrain—that of Africa, north of the Limpopo—that now held the company's attention afresh.

6

BELIEVE IN AFRICA

COCA-COLA IN THE NEW MILLENNIUM

In November 1992, The Coca-Cola Company announced an internal reorganization. No longer would sub-Saharan Africa be subsumed under Europe or the Middle East for administrative purposes; now, in recognition of the 'new opportunities' emerging from the continent, the forty-six countries south of the Sahara where Coke operated would stand alone under the direction of Senior Vice President Carl Ware.[1] 'The face of Africa,' a six-minute internal video produced by Coca-Cola, provided a 'profile of the African consumer' at this time. With drumbeats in the background, a buoyant narrative voice belied the stark images presented. Differences in language, culture, and terrain aside, declining disposable incomes, low literacy rates, under-developed infrastructure, insufficient electricity, and poverty persisted across the region, viewers were told. While Coca-Cola was already entrenched across Africa, the road to rendering a more stable, economically viable continent—where Coca-Cola would thrive alongside capitalism and democracy—appeared steep.[2]

Five years later, in July 1997, Carl Ware articulated Coca-Cola's refined view of its now fully post-apartheid African business at the African/African-American Summit, in Harare, Zimbabwe. Convened by Reverend Leon Sullivan and hosted by Zimbabwean President Robert Gabriel Mugabe, the summit brought together businesspeople, NGOs, politicians, and religious leaders to expand American and African partnerships. In a press release, the office of President Bill Clinton announced that though the American president could not be there, he was sending Reverend Jesse Jackson and Transportation Secretary Rodney F Slater along with the first lady Hillary Clinton in his stead.[3] Speaking at the summit, Ware established that The Coca-Cola Company—through its franchises and company-owned plants—had supported between 700,000 and one million people in Africa and sold over 600 million cases of Coke products there the preceding year. Yet, with the same region at roughly half the per capita consumption as the rest of the world, there was much room for growth. Ware reminded listeners that Coke's history in Africa was old and that its track record for staying through trying times was impressive. Coke's business in Africa was 'no experiment,' he said, but rather—gesturing to the marketing campaign of the day—'the real thing,' tried and true and set only to grow. Clearly aware of African challenges, Ware then made sure to state, in no uncertain terms, Coca-Cola's optimism about African possibilities. 'We believe very strongly that Africa's time is now,' Ware concluded: 'The trends toward political freedom and economic reform, the growing of a young, educated, urban consumer market, these trends are coming together, now, for a vibrant business in Africa. I can assure you.' He closed with the company's new African tagline, 'We believe in Africa.'[4]

In this chapter I trace Coca-Cola's renewed faith in the African continent (at times sub-Saharan and at times including North Africa) in the post-apartheid era. I map the company's recommenced spread north of South Africa, where it reinvigorated old businesses and launched new ones, often deploying South African expertise to do so. Then, I explain how the company used sport, marketing, and music to capture the hearts and minds of a continent at the dawn of the new millennium. In sum, this is a chapter about what Coca-Cola's belief in post-apartheid Africa looked like.

Back in South Africa

Coca-Cola's negotiation of late apartheid South Africa smoothed its re-entry into the country. 'After years of disinvestment in protest of the nation's apartheid policies, The Coca-Cola Company welcomed the election of the new democratic majority government,' Coke's magazine *Journey* narrated in 1995, just as 'President Nelson Mandela welcomed the Company back to South Africa.'[5] That year, while Mandela launched his landmark Reconstruction and Development Program, meant to jump-start the economy, he visited the South African Bottling Company's (Sabco) plant in Port Elizabeth, posing there for a picture with director Phil Gutsche. Speaking at the plant, Mandela appealed to big business to play its part in developing the nation while assuring Coca-Cola that his government saw the company as an ally.[6] When, later that year, Mandela's presence as the South Africa's Springboks won the Rugby World Cup became a symbol of national reconciliation, Coca-Cola was pleased to have sponsored the event. '1995 Rugby World Champions love Coca-Cola,' the company announced with an article applauding the comingling of rugby star Francois Pienaar, global icon Nelson Mandela, and Coca-Cola.[7]

The Coca-Cola Company wasted no time expanding in the new South Africa, drawing from an extensive playbook it had prepared in advance.[8] Almost overnight, 7,000 outlets were remerchandised while the southern African company division office was reseated in Johannesburg. At the same time, a thousand new kombi minibuses were outfitted to serve as taxis that both advertised and sold Coca-Cola products from internal coolers, continuing the company's expansion into previously neglected consumer markets.[9] It seemed that Pepsi, which attempted its own relaunch in the country (complete with a newly formed, much-touted African American bottling franchise) stood little chance of winning this leg of the cola wars.[10] By 1997, *The Sowetan* newspaper reported, Coca-Cola had delivered 27,000 coolers, vending machines, and ice-makers across the country, blanketing Soweto and elsewhere Coke red.[11] The company aimed to double its impact in South Africa, which already stood at $4.8 billion in annual retail turnover, with plans to raise its per capita consumption.[12] 'South Africa is sacred ground to Coca-Cola,' company CEO Doug Ivester affirmed, 'and we are determined to become one of the great success stories in South Africa's future.'[13]

Coca-Cola's commitment to South Africa was not mere talk. By early 1997, Coke was set to invest between five hundred million and 1.25 billion rand in South Africa over five years.[14] Corporate Coke also demonstrated its faith in the renewed, more inclusive South African business by supporting first Kilimanjaro Holdings—the group begun by Richard Maponya—and then the Kunene Brothers, the first Black-owned franchises on the continent. After Kilimanjaro faltered in 1994, the Kunenes and Coca-Cola jointly formed Fortune Investment Holdings. Later, Fortune Holdings acquired Vinto minerals to become Coca-Cola Bottling Mpumalanga (CCBM), which would, in turn, join Gutsche's Sabco to catapult this small family business to the forefront of Coke decisions on the continent.[15] Financial investment, dedication to the informal market, and mergers demonstrated Coke's commitment to a revamped South African business model that included far more Black participants than ever. Indeed, optimism abounded for Coke in South Africa just a few years after apartheid ended, as sales grew by as much as 35% in some parts of the country. 'What's happening now in South Africa is just a preview of things to come,' *Journey* reported, quoting Ware saying that such progress, 'bodes well for our entire system.'[16]

Here, then, was evidence of Coca-Cola's clearest endorsement of its South African business—its positioning of the country at the center of the company's overall plan for the continent, south of the Sahara, after apartheid. In 1995, Coca-Cola announced that Gutsche's Sabco—which had begun in 1940 when his father was a part-time route driver there—was set to become the company's first 'anchor bottler' on the African continent. The anchor bottler would serve as Coca-Cola Export once had, as the direct liaison between bottlers and Coca-Cola Atlanta on topics like marketing and sales. Sabco would merge with The Coca-Cola Company's bottling interests in Kenya, Tanzania, Uganda, Namibia, and Mozambique to control sixteen operating facilities (during its initial phase) from one focal point in Port Elizabeth, South Africa. Keith Kunene, of Fortune Holdings, and Reg Mengi, of Bonite Bottling in Tanzania (which we will hear more about below) were to sit on the board of directors. Gutsche said he 'was honored' to be chosen for this landmark role.[17]

Coca-Cola's faith in its South African business, thus, was intimately tied to its focus on the continent, post-apartheid. Ware spoke about this position in 1995 when he sat before a congressional hearing on trade in Africa. There, he offered members of the American government his perspective on African possibilities and challenges. The committee had already heard from then deputy president of South Africa Thabo Mbeki; Ghanaian president Jerry Rawlings was scheduled to speak the following week. Representatives from other multinationals—like

ATT and General Motors—were there, along with folks from USAID, the African Development Fund, and more. But Ware was to be 'the most popular panelist,' a representative quipped, eyeing a Diet Coke on the dais, while another jokingly thanked Coke for its ubiquity, particularly in places where water was unclean.[18] To these congressional sub-committee members, at least, Coca-Cola was welcomed as an ambassador of good product and goodwill.

With the Cold War over, Ware reported, the time had arrived to decrease African economic dependency and increase African political stability. There were policies the US government could implement to help encourage growth and the spread of development in Africa, Ware claimed. But there were also changes, he suggested, that a multinational system like Coke was particularly well-poised to affect.[19] Ware explained Coca-Cola's unique position in Africa as an engine of change, describing the business as a 'multi-local system' with 'unmatched impact on the continent,' felt as an 'employer, taxpayer, manufacturer, purchaser, hirer, and corporate citizen,' none of which is surprising to readers of this book. He also offered evidence of Coca-Cola's double-digit multiplier effect—that is, the number of people informally supported for every formal Coca-Cola job—as further proof of Coke's profound position on the continent. In this capacity, he understood the challenges ahead for the continent, he said. He offered, by way of one example, that 98% of Africans lived without ice or any form of refrigeration.[20] Rectifying this would require a chain of engagement from loans, to venture capital, to movement of goods and services, still nascent across the region, but a Coca-Cola specialty. Refrigeration would mean the spread of electricity, a developmental milestone that would do more than just allow for cool drinks, demonstrating the utility of Coke as a harbinger of more than itself. And, best of all, Ware said, Coca-Cola was just getting started.[21]

Coca-Cola's willingness to put money into Africa in the late 1990s was in line with some global trends. The company's commitment to invest $600 million over a five-year period[22] in Africa grew out of a moment when some world economists were feeling 'that Africa is not quite the hopeless case that has so often been assumed,' as one reporter noted wryly from the World Economic Forum in Davos in 1998.[23] With the Cold War and apartheid in the past, much of Africa seemed poised for growth. South Africa's economy, in particular, boomed immediately after apartheid—with American companies playing an even greater role than they had before disinvestment[24]—igniting optimism.[25] Beyond South Africa, many African countries seemed stable; many had submitted to IMF and World Bank policies around debt and were moving towards both privatization and to viewing capitalism as a tool rather than a problem. Between 1995 and 1998, the entire African continent had seen 4.5% growth.[26] Economists reckoned that this was just the start, calling Africa—as *The Washington Post* did in 1998—'the final frontier and the last emerging market.'[27] When, nine months before becoming CEO of The Coca-Cola Company, Ivester toured several countries in Africa, he came away with a similar sense of possibility for the business on the continent. At the time, sales of Coca-Cola products in Africa accounted for a meager 3% of global Coca-Cola revenue. Ivester wanted to double this number by strengthening bottlers, increasing outlets, and intensifying marketing. 'To be very candid,' Ivester noted in his speech at Davos in 1998, 'Africa has not historically been a real priority for the Coca-Cola Company.' 'But,' he said, 'over the past two years, we have come to a very different perspective.'[28]

That same year, Bill Clinton arrived on the continent to undertake the most extensive African tour of any American president to date (eleven days). Carl Ware was traveling with him, along with representatives from several other multinationals. The goal of the trip: to encourage trade with and investment in sub-Saharan Africa, both of which were underutilized. The prospects were promising. In 1996, United States investments in the region had generated a return of 31%, more than double the returns from Latin America and Asia and one and a half times the returns from the Middle East, according to Commerce Department figures.[29] Coca-Cola saw room for growth in this favorable atmosphere. For all of the company's decades of expansion on the continent, per capita consumption of its products was as low as three (in Ethiopia), twenty-nine (in Kenya), and even 155 (in South Africa), compared to 370 in the United States.[30] The continent appeared ripe for expansion. That the continent was so big and so young—estimates suggested that by 2020 there would be one billion Africans, with one in five of the world's teenagers being African—only stoked the company's enthusiasm.[31]

To the challenge—leveled even then—that growing the consumption of sugary beverages might not be in the best interest of Africans, Ivester retorted that Coke was scientifically shown to be good for hydration.[32] Later, such claims would cause problems for the company. At the time, Coca-Cola's focus on encouraging small-scale entrepreneurs and making money for investors while aligning its work with American interests would supersede what were then just incipient health concerns. By the end of the 1990s, as far as The Coca-Cola Company was concerned, Africa was the final frontier.

Belief Becomes Expansion

When Carl Ware gave his 'We Believe' speech in 1997, he detailed just how Coca-Cola was expanding its business in Africa. First, the company was investing in people by promoting successful employees across the region. Ware used individual stories to give a sense of what this looked like. He spoke of

Tunde Popoola, a Nigerian, once part of External Affairs in Nigeria and now working for the bottling operation in Zimbabwe; Charles Kagochi, a Kenyan who was learning the ropes as a field operations manager in South Africa; and Chris Inoma, a Nigerian who had just successfully completed mid-career training. Beyond single stories, Ware focused on company efforts at enhancing collective talent. The company now ran a 'Leadership for Marketing Excellence' program as well as several 'centers of learning' to identify talent. At the same time, it created an internship for South African university students as part of its 'Project Brain Gain' program, where the company pledged to hire 100 Black South African graduates annually for the next five years. 'There are literally dozens of... Kagochis', Inomas' and Popoolas' stories to tell,' Ware quipped, 'but the message I want you to remember is: Through investments in people like these, we're exploding the myths about Africans'—namely, that they cannot work across national borders—as well as myths about Africa's lackluster potential.[33]

Harnessing people power was just the first step in system growth, Ware explained. Whereas Coca-Cola in sub-Saharan Africa was then comprised of 140 plants run by both The Coca-Cola Company and franchise bottlers, the company intended to double the size of its business over five to seven years. Of particular concern to Ware was the state of many Coca-Cola facilities, which he saw as run-down and outdated. That nagging lack of cooling technology was also at the front of his mind: without proper cooling apparatuses, Coca-Cola could not flourish. To rectify these problems, the company would support the more than half a million entrepreneurs who sold Coke on corners, in markets, from trolleys, and in spaza shops by spreading marketing materials and cooling technology. Additionally, Ware explained, the company sought to collaborate with African governments, forging mutually beneficial partnerships that would enable both company growth and regional development. These collaborations were becoming increasingly possible as many African nations began liberalizing their policies and opening themselves up to free market growth.[34] The Africa unit's history around the turn of the twenty-first century was to be, as Coke's magazine *Journey* put it in 1990, 'a story about ice and electricity, about price controls and free markets, about decline and rebirth.'[35]

At the start of the twenty-first century, most outsiders were not readily investing in Africa (favorable predictions for the continent aside), so Coca-Cola had to look within to find the money and know-how to enhance its business. With apartheid over, Ware told me, Coke turned to South Africa as 'one of the strongest, most efficient, most profitable, and highly skilled bottling operations in the world.' 'Our concept,' he said, 'was to take the financial, the technical, and managerial know-how of South Africa and bring it north. Just explode the rest of the continent with that skill, financial, and technical base so that the rest of Africa in terms of the Coca-Cola system would mirror the system in South Africa.' To do so, Coca-Cola had to form joint ventures amongst The Coca-Cola Company, South African bottlers, and various African governments.[36] In some cases, this meant reinvigorating old systems. In others, it meant creating new ones. Some were to be parastatals, while others were to remain independent. But all aimed to standardize and modernize the Coke system anew.

While some brand-new bottling systems emerged at this time—Coca-Cola entered the Seychelles for the first time in 1993—for the most part, Coca-Cola was focused on bringing older systems up to date in this era.[37] The company first focused on Central and East Africa, places that, as Ware noted, were easy to fly to from Johannesburg and that had, for one reason or another, flailed in recent years. First, there was Tanzania, which was already on the way to an overhaul by the time Ware took control of Coke Africa. *Journey* would later call its story one of 'breathtaking decline and rebirth.' The business had languished under Julius Nyerere's socialist order that stymied growth. A series of lackluster bottlers did not help. Market share had plummeted from 71% to 14% during the 1980s. Then came the turnaround: just as President Ali Hassan Mwinyi's government began to encourage investment, moving the country away from its founding socialist ideals, Coca-Cola licensed four new bottlers and built four new plants, one to the tune of thirty-five million dollars. The company—by way of its bottlers—then spread thousands of electric coolers. System volume quickly quadrupled.[38] One of the most impressive new bottlers was Bonite Bottlers, based in Moshi, run under the chairmanship of Reg Mengi (who would later become one of Africa's most prominent billionaires). Mengi's attention to quality control and competitiveness made his plant recognized as, in E Neville Isdell's 1990 words, 'simply the best plant in Africa,' and earned Mengi a seat on the Sabco board.[39]

While socialist policies in Tanzania had stalled the system there, Zimbabwe's long war for independence had likewise taxed its operations. Tommy Hagan, of Mutare Bottlers, recalled that they first felt the war's effects in 1976, when sales plummeted and many rural stores closed. Despite the bottler's best attempts to keep operating as usual—delivering product into rural areas throughout—fuel shortages and attacks to delivery vehicles thwarted them. Then, of course, there was the problem of procuring raw materials. At the time, concentrate was produced in Zimbabwe, while carbon dioxide was flown in twice a week from South Africa in dry ice form. Twice a week the bottlers would rush to transport the dry ice blocks to Mutare before they melted. Simon Goldberg, also of Mutare Bottlers, likewise recalled the ingenuity needed to keep the business running when the country was at war: when an important piece of the bottling line broke on Christmas Day—one of the busiest for production—the resident engineer/problem fixer jimmied an inventive solution that required a block and a round-the-clock attendant holding it in place while oiling it, an innovative, if exhausting, solution that had to last for three full weeks.[40] Despite its lean years, Mutare Bottlers and the larger Zimbabwe business had begun to revive after 1980 in the newly liberated nation. In the 1990s, Zimbabwe was the fourth largest sub-Saharan Coke market, employing more than 23,000 people working in plants and servicing 17,000 retail outlets.[41] Still, the effects of isolation and war had taken a toll. Thus, Coke invested sixty million rand into Zimbabwe to bulk up infrastructure in the 1990s. As we already saw in the joint African/African-American summit, Ware was friendly with Mugabe, Zimbabwe's leader since 1980, which helped pave the way for reinvigoration. In this case and others like it, Ware's personal connection to an African leader would serve the company well.[42]

Ware likewise recalls contacting Yoweri Museveni to propose Coca-Cola's re-investment in Uganda. Ware speaks of meeting with Museveni in the early 1990s, when Museveni (who had seized power there in 1986), was looked favorably upon by the West as a harbinger of a new, free Africa (much like Mugabe was at the time). 'When I went in to meet with the president Museveni in Uganda,' Ware recounted for me, 'he knew of what we had done in South Africa' and he was new to the job. 'So it was not difficult for me to sit down with him and say, look, we got investors from South Africa who know what they are doing, and who will come in here with The Coca-Cola Company, invest in your country, build new bottling plants, and train Ugandans to run those plants.' According to Ware, Museveni 'loved the idea.'[43] Here was a company promising to bring infrastructure, investment, and training to his nation. With Museveni on board, Sabco entered Uganda, with Coca-Cola investing thirty million dollars in the country along the way.[44]

The story in Kenya was similar and also involved wooing government at the highest levels. While Kenya had long been a premier Coke market, the business had languished in recent years under retail price controls and 70% taxation.[45] Of particular concern to Ware was that it was often difficult to get a cold Coca-Cola there. Often, beverages were served 'warm,' or at room temperature. Under the renewed system (that now included Sabco), Kenyan bottlers made much of the fact that they were the second largest taxpayer in the country. In 1990, the government responded to this argument by lifting the price controls that had stymied the business. Coca-Cola quickly spread coolers across the nation—hoping to instill the notion of serving Coca-Cola ice cold—and implemented a renewed policy of Kenyanization that sought to reward Kenyan talent within the Coke business. Soon signs reading *Baridi*—or 'ice cold' in Swahili—could be seen throughout the country.[46]

Ware had been equally disappointed by the state of operations in Ghana, on the other side of the continent, noting his displeasure at the plants he had toured in the 1990s. As he had done elsewhere, he requested a meeting with then President Rawlins. This time, negotiations were fraught. Rawlings wanted a parastatal and to dictate the terms of the agreement—who would be involved, who would maintain control. Ware recalled telling him that was not how Coca-Cola operated. For Coca-Cola to remain in Ghana, the company insisted on maintaining management control (51% to the government's 49%). Coke would provide the initial investment and put together a team that it saw as capable of getting a new plant up and running as soon as possible. 'Fast forward eighteen months,' Ware recalled, and the plant was built.'[47] According to Ware, the success of the Coca-Cola Ghana parastatal did more than just secure and modernize Coca-Cola's business in Ghana. It cemented Ware's friendship with Rawlings, just as other agreements had likewise ingratiated Ware with leaders across Africa. At the same time, this agreement paved the way for the Ghanaian government to privatize other industries, even forming joint collaborations with South African mining firms.[48] Coca-Cola, in Ware's telling, was bringing to Africa not just product but also a fresh perspective.

In the same vein, Coca-Cola re-entered Eritrea immediately following Eritrean independence in 1991. Ware recalls chartering a plane from Nairobi to Addis Ababa and then going on to Eritrea. 'Everything was just bombed out,' he said. Aside from a lone restaurant, 'The only thing other than the restaurant that was absolutely... pristine was the old Coca-Cola bottling plant.' According to Ware, locals had protected the plant for the two years it sat vacant. As he arrived, they were busily reconnecting the power supply, so with the turn of a switch, the old machines started to run. *Journey* magazine would later call this 'the little plant that could,' jokingly noting that the equipment—the 1950s vintage Leoncino and Daino trucks, the Dunmore washer, made in Wisconsin in 1963—were so old that visiting the plant was like taking 'a trip down memory lane.'[49] Ware recalled the imposing 6'4" military-fatigue-clad figure cut by Isaias Afwerki, leader of independent Eritrea, who arrived to meet him. Though intimidated, Ware pulled from his playbook, telling Afwerke how Coke was going to not only reinvigorate the system, but also how it would train people, thereby 'developing a country through the use of the Coca-Cola apparatus.' It was not a hard sell.[50] Around the same time, the company re-energized its system in Ethiopia and then in Sudan, where it had been absent since that country's 1985 coup.[51] It would be another decade before the company re-entered Somalia in 2006. There too it would find that, despite that nation's war, the Coca-Cola plant remained in pristine condition.[52]

Like Eritrea and later Somalia, when Coke personnel talk about re-invigorating the Coke business in the 1990s, all mention

Angola, no doubt because when they went in there the country remained ensconced in a relentless proxy civil war. 'I remember flying into Angola ... in shambles,' Ware recalls. Landmines and gunfire abounded. Ware and his entourage visited a Coke plant in Luanda that was 'so bad' in terms of quality control, Ware said, he 'just couldn't drink it.' Scanning the terrain for a new location, Ware and associates arrived at the small village of Bom Jesus, sixty kilometers outside the capital. There stood the remains of an old sugar plant that happened to have access to a river that could provide much-needed water.[53] Still, nothing was easy about re-entry during wartime. As a South African sent to set up the technical side recounted, white Coke personnel were held up at gunpoint at a roadblock on at least one hair-raising occasion.[54] No doubt the presence of white South Africans fanned the flames in a country still reeling from the apartheid state's intervention in its war. According to Rute Moyo, a Zimbabwean who joined Coca-Cola southern Africa after apartheid and who cut his teeth in Angola, it would take careful work to convince the Angolans that Coke's presence was not simply a way to entrench the interests of racist whites in the country.

Moyo played a key role in helping update the Coke system in Angola. He recalls being astounded by the sight of a defunct Coke plant in Huambo. While the whole city was war-torn, the plant was 'the only building in the whole of Huambo that didn't have a bullet hole.' 'It was the most surreal experience,' Moyo told me, 'and was one of the most poignant moments for me in my career at Coke.... I realized, this must mean something.' That the plant had been protected—like its counterparts in Eritrea, Somalia, and elsewhere—suggested to Moyo that there was a latent respect for the product. Working closely with US Ambassador Donald McHenry,[55] Moyo, as he tells it, wooed the Angolans, who were charmed by the fact that he was Zimbabwean. This led the way to a parastatal born with direct investment from The Coca-Cola

Company. Moyo is quick to point out that the success of the Angola re-entry—after much heartache—was equally due to Charles Frenette, a marketer then heading Coca-Cola southern Africa.[56] Through him, the company focused on capitalizing on existing product recognition and local pride as it tried to transfer ownership to Angolans. After years of importing overpriced cans of Coca-Cola from South Africa, Moyo told me, 'the pride that [Angolans] took in actually having a plant and producing their own Coke in their own country was phenomenal.'[57]

Ware's unit's belief in African potential meant that Coca-Cola reinvigorated bottling operations across the continent. Whether they were parastatals (like Ethiopia or Angola) or independent (like Tanzania and Kenya) did not actually 'matter in the strictest sense of the word,' as Ware put it. 'We brought the same story to them' all. That story was simple: Coca-Cola, if let in and fostered, will bring infrastructure and skills development to your country. It will bring know-how from South Africa and make or remake existing businesses to meet new needs. It was not long before an enormous swath of the continent was being run out of South Africa. Moyo moved from Angola to Mozambique, while Ernest Mchunu, whom we met in the last chapter, took control of Zambia. Zimbabwean Nathan Kalumbu, who would later take over Africa from Alexander B Cummings (more on him later) before being charged with Africa, the Middle East, and Eurasia, was first tasked with running Malawi and Zambia. At the same time, the Congo fell under South African control.[58] The company pumped money into its Francophone business partners as well. It also funneled money into Nigeria, another enormous market, keeping it and Francophone West Africa in close contact with anchor bottler Sabco. Gerald Glancey, a South African technical manager, recalled traveling to these countries and more at this time, setting up bottling lines and doing governance control, making sure that every plant produced products of equal quality and taste. It was not always easy, and it was never boring, as he tells it. By the end of the twentieth century, he said, 'The whole of sub-Saharan Africa was run out of this office' in Johannesburg, South Africa.[59]

The stories of the Coke unit's reboot in much of its African business in the 1990s, as told by Coca-Cola personnel, are of course self-serving: we came, we proposed something wonderful, they jumped at the chance. Still, the fact remains that Coca-Cola re-entrenched its business in this era, whether or not it was as effortless as this narrative makes it seem. The company made no bones about working with any African leader—Ware had personal stories about many. Nor did the company pay particular attention to the political situations in which it found itself, save whether or not business would be affected. After the cause of ending apartheid, Coca-Cola no longer seemed particularly invested in any other political issue on the continent. Still, informants were all clear, everywhere Coca-Cola operated with a strict ethical standard that the company enforced through annual training and tight monitoring. Engaging in bribery or any other form of corruption was prohibited, I was told repeatedly. Mostly, the company focused on sowing goodwill for its business. According to interviewees, here it succeeded: employees recall traveling internationally without a passport, using Coca-Cola IDs as credentials, while others tell of being welcomed into Somalia with the message, we hate America, but we love Coke.[60] All make the case that Coca-Cola, already well-known across the continent, nonetheless spread widely and deeply in these years, opening doors both to privatization and infrastructure systems (including those around cooling technology), which other firms rapidly capitalized on.[61]

For its work on the post-apartheid continent, The Coca-Cola Company received praise. In 1997, The Corporate Council on Africa awarded CEO Doug Ivester its inaugural award for

Corporate Citizenship in Africa. Having invested one billion dollars on the African continent over the previous five years, Coca-Cola had seeded African entrepreneurship in unparalleled ways, the Council proclaimed. Speaking at the ceremony, then First Lady Hillary Clinton remarked, Coca-Cola is 'offering compelling examples of corporate citizenship in a democracy.' 'Do you believe in Africa?' a new video put out by the company asked that same year, before affirming, 'We believe in Africa.'[62]

The Dawn of a New Direction

As the new millennium dawned, Coca-Cola let its leased sign atop the Ponte City Apartment Tower in Hillbrow, Johannesburg expire. According to Vukani Magubane, corporate and media relations manager for Coca-Cola South Africa, the decision to cede the largest sign in the southern hemisphere to telecommunications giant Vodacom did not reflect Coca-Cola's lack of faith in South Africa or the African continent. Conversely, he said, removing the sign was part of the company's 'evolving... community-based marketing' that was no longer trying to brand from above.[63] Coca-Cola entered the new millennium poised to demonstrate its belief in all Africans in new ways. First, the company relinked the administration of North Africa and the sub-Saharan continent. Then, there was a changing of the guards. In 2001, Alexander B Cummings, Jr., a Liberian who started as deputy region manager in 1997 Nigeria, took over African operations from Carl Ware.[64] Building upon Ware's successful updating and consolidating of the system, Cummings now helped oversee and implement three campaigns—each with deep roots on the continent—meant to woo the hearts and minds of Africans in fifty-six nations from the ground up, through sports, advertising, and music. It is to these that we now turn.

Sports

Globally, Coca-Cola has supported sport for nearly as long as the business has been around. As early as 1905, Coca-Cola yoked its product to active living, first by aligning itself with America's pastime, baseball. Iconic outfielder Ty Cobb was an early and much publicized fan of the beverage. Later, when the company met opposition to its European expansion around World War II—detractors called the drink 'physically debilitating'—Coke launched a deliberate plan to brand itself the epitome of well-being, creating advertisements that pronounced as much and sending a truck stocked with Coca-Cola to trail the Tour de France. This was just the start. When the company sponsored the 1952 Summer Olympics in Helsinki—as it had every Olympics since 1928—it reaffirmed its comingling with global athletics in the post-World War II order, ensuring the continuation in this enduring, high-profile partnership.[65] Since then, Coca-Cola has supported and co-branded fitness and sporting events, big and small, around the world.

Coca-Cola's history of supporting sport in Africa is similarly long-standing. From its earliest decades in South Africa, Coca-Cola Export and individual bottlers promoted colonial pastimes like cricket, lawn bowling, surfing, and golf.[66] Coke's support of sport elsewhere on the continent reflected Africans' diverse leisure pursuits. In the 1960s and 1970s, the company and its bottlers put their name and product behind swimming in Egypt,[67] cycling in Madagascar, boxing, cricket, and netball in Kenya,[68] handball in Côte d'Ivoire, tennis tournaments in Cameroon and Swaziland, table tennis in Nigeria, and more.[69] In 1972, the company endorsed something called 'mini-basketball' in Senegal.[70] Three years later, Coca-Cola hosted an event for a new East African sport, pushball, where participants pushed a human-sized—Coke-branded—ball around. An article cheered the company's endorsement of this sport, lauding the refereeing ability of then regional director Charles Mukora and noting that there was 'plenty of Coke, Fanta and Sprite' for 'apres-pushball' on hand.[71] No matter the sport in Africa, it seems, if Coca-Cola could attach its name to it, it would.

Coca-Cola's endorsement of sport was, of course, useful as a way to spread its product and to forestall any critiques of the beverage as unhealthy. As it had with Cobbs on the other side of the world, Coca-Cola thus sought to conjoin its product with athletic pursuit in Africa, first by finding athletes who would serve as brand ambassadors. From the 1960s onward, South African golfer Gary Player stood behind Coca-Cola in print and radio ads for the remainder of his career (the company would eventually host an invitational in his name). In 1972, Kenya's sportsman of the year, runner Julius Sang, likewise became a 'roving ambassador' for the product—the first of many.[72] Beyond wooing individuals to speak on its behalf, Coca-Cola threw its weight behind festivals and tournaments that drew large numbers of participants from within and across regional boundaries. In 1965, the company sponsored the regional West African Games, then held in Ibadan, Nigeria.[73] In 1972, it promoted a boxing championship that drew from fourteen African nations.[74] The same year, Coca-Cola supported the trials for the continent-wide All Africa Games.[75] The slogan from a 1972 basketball festival in Djibouti seems to capture the essence of Coke's message in Africa throughout the decades: 'Coca-Cola: the drink for sportsmen.'[76]

While Coca-Cola supported all manner of sport, as the continent settled into the era of independence, no sport garnered as much attention as soccer/football. This is because soccer has historically been the sport of the majority of Africans, a game that needs only the barest of materials to play.[77] Supporting soccer became one way for the company to broaden its marketing reach while appearing healthy, all while securing its license to operate, as we have seen, standard operating procedure for this company. In

1975, Coca-Cola Export in South Africa undertook a three-part program to promote soccer amongst Black South Africans. The scheme involved creating and distributing five-minute training videos as well as running seminars for coaches in Bantustans and townships. But the pinnacle of the program entailed taking a group of Black South Africans from Soweto to train with leading soccer clubs in Rio de Janeiro, Brazil, all underwritten by Coca-Cola bottlers.[78] Likewise, from 1977, Coca-Cola partnered with FIFA—the Fédération Internationale de Football Association—as part of its World Football Development Program. Jointly, FIFA and Coca-Cola hosted seminars in Mauritius, Kenya, Zambia, Tanzania, and Malawi that promoted soccer as well as coaching, administration, sports medicine, and more sports-related skills. Dozens of participants lined up, while governments fell over themselves to publicly thank both FIFA and Coca-Cola Africa (and its bottlers) for providing opportunities for growth.[79] Soccer was and is so important to Africans that Coca-Cola continued to support the sport independently of its partnership with FIFA. In 1978, Coca-Cola Africa sponsored a skills development program in Kenya, for instance.[80] At roughly the same time, a young bottling employee in then Southern Rhodesia began to scheme a way for Coca-Cola to be further involved with soccer in that country, initiating what would become the most significant Coca-Cola sport partnership on the continent.

In December 1973, five days after his final school exams, Sam Musvanya joined the Delta Coca-Cola plant in Masvingo, then Southern Rhodesia. The job offer had arrived by way of his father. The reason: folks at the plant had seen Musvanya play soccer and wanted him on the plant's team. Musvanya was a hard worker and he was good with numbers. It was not long before he began to rise through the ranks. He moved from costing clerk to cost investigator, from budget accountant to management accountant, and, then, from administration manager to general manager for the plant, all by 1985. Arriving at an administrative role empowered him to later move to Mutare Bottling when Delta closed its regional plants in 2002. Musvanya would spend another twelve years there, making forty total within Zimbabwe's Coke system. When I spoke to Musvanya, he was clear that his rise reflected the wealth of training he received on the job in Masvingo, Harare, and, later, South Africa, where he was sent for regional instruction. These were tumultuous political years as Southern Rhodesia became Zimbabwe, but, in Musvanya's telling, the Coke system navigated changes with ease, continually providing opportunities for ambitious workers. As Musvanya worked his way up, he put himself in a position to contribute to more than just the business by focusing on his first love, soccer.

In 1989, Musvanya was in a marketing meeting at Delta when someone started to talk about how important soccer was in the country, despite the absence of any organized youth leagues. What did exist was sponsored by beer and cigarette companies and targeted older players. Something was missing. The idea that was raised, he told me, humbly obfuscating his lead role in the discussion, was 'that we should catch them when they are young,' focusing for the first time on high school students with a soccer tournament aimed just for them. What emerged, Musvanya elaborated, was a plan 'to groom the young people for the future of Zimbabwean football,' all by comingling soccer with Coca-Cola. Here was a way to blend product marketing with his dearest passion.[81] Musvanya headed the delegation sent by the bottler to approach the minister of education. What they found was that some structures were in place that Coca-Cola could tap into—both a program called NASH, the National Association of Secondary Heads, and a structure dividing the country's schools. 'Our aim was to get all people in secondary school throughout the country to participate in this football tournament,' identifying talent, particularly in 'rural areas,' that would otherwise go unnoticed. The final meeting took place in a hotel in the midlands. There, members of NASH, the bottlers, and Coke personnel cemented a plan for a boys-only fifteen-and-under youth tournament to be called the Coca-Cola NASH football tournament. Ten years later, when the tournament expanded to Mexico, its name was changed to Copa Coca-Cola.

The first tournament ran in 1989, spreading brand recognition alongside soccer. Matches were held first in zones, then across districts, provinces, and, eventually, at the national level. Guilford High School from Bulawayo took the inaugural title. There, a young boy named Peter Ndlovu was spotted. He would later go on to play in the English Premier League—the first in a string of Zimbabwean soccer players whose talent was identified this way.[82] In 1995, the first rural school took the championship. It was to be the first of many, each of which stood as proof, Musvanya told me, that the league was doing what it was meant to do. Four years later, the tournament became regional, with Zambia and Malawi on board. Later, South Africa would join.[83] That was just the start. As Nigeria won the Olympic gold medal for soccer in 1996 at the Summer Olympics in Atlanta, Coca-Cola praised the team and turned its corporate eye towards enhancing its soccer support on the continent.[84]

In the landscape of the re-invigorated Africa business, under Cummings, Copa only grew. In 2010, Zimbabwe added a girls' tournament, a far-sighted vision against gender discrimination, still a rarity years later.[85] That same year, when South Africa became the first African nation to host a FIFA World Cup, Coca-Cola was there to endorse it. Here was a chance for the nation and continent to prove their worth. Coke sponsored what became the cup's official song, Shakira's 'Waka Waka,' that celebrated 'This time for Africa.' In the aftermath of a successful tournament, Copa grew even more. In 2013, South Africa hosted thirteen countries in a regional tournament. Copa went from

2,000 to 20,000 teams in thirteen African markets in one year.[86] By 2014, the cup was drawing from well beyond the region. It now included participants from sixty countries worldwide. That year, Copa hosted a five-day youth camp in Brazil alongside that year's World Cup.[87] Such camps would become regular endeavors. After Brazil came Germany and then France. The purpose of the camps was to convene a handful of players from each participating country who exemplified core positive tenets associated with soccer success. Together, the young hopefuls would train with professionals. In France, Paris Saint-Germain ran the camp. The goal was not competition, but rather to learn from one another. Malefsane Meble, a senior manager of brand experience involved in Copa from South Africa since 2009, told me that the camps continued Copa's work to spread brand awareness. But, more importantly, they 'create friendship, with football as the one language that connects everyone.'[88]

Today, Copa Coca-Cola is the largest youth soccer tournament in the world, reaching more than one million youngsters.[89] I spoke to the head of one participating team in 2016. Lucky Dlamini is an educator at a rural, struggling school in Eswatini, teaching upwards of fifty children at a time in a crowded classroom. Many children come from child-headed households. Paying school fees and accessing clean water are enduring struggles. Dlamini calls his work 'a calling,' but readily admits it is a challenging one. One bright spot for him: Copa Coca-Cola. Dlamini is the school's soccer coach. Through Copa, his boys' team has access to boots, kits, and soccer balls. They have a chance to compete and, for the best, to earn university scholarships. Though they had yet to win a tournament—much coveted since the prize is a soccer-themed Coca-Cola-sponsored project—he was able to accompany a few boys to a regional training camp in South Africa the year before we spoke. It was all of their first time on an airplane and, as he tells it, not an experience they will soon forget.[90] Sure, he says, Copa brings Coca-Cola. There are product samplings and branding everywhere around the tournament.[91] But Copa is also fanning hopes and providing avenues for tangible betterment. Enthusiasm for the program is robust, he told me. And that goes for more than just Eswatini. In 2019 Kenya, for instance, that country's tournament kicked off with 5,400 participants between the ages of fifteen and twenty. That year's theme: teaching youth the importance of recycling.[92]

The spread of Copa is, in part, about the deliberate seeding of what the company calls brand love. Tournaments are blanketed Coke red. Product is sold and sampled freely. Supporting soccer is a proxy for marketing product. Yet, it is hard not to feel like branding is secondary to the sport itself. Underneath all that red is a pure love for the game of soccer. Sure, all participants I spoke to mentioned the beverage when asked about the tournament. For them, Coca-Cola was aligned with the optimism endemic to soccer enthusiasm. But, they were equally quick to say with both clarity and sophistication that Coke is good only in moderation and that the drink is not meant for children under thirteen, echoing the company's official line. Even if Coca-Cola's aim in endorsing Copa is to spread product, this thread of Coca-Cola's work in Africa—like that of so many more in this book— strikes me as another story of how Africans have responded to an opportunity for betterment by bending it to work for them. In other words, we can be cynical and say that Coke's soccer support is mere branding. Or, we can see Copa—and its like— as yet another way that Africans have beautifully bent the will of a multinational to suit their needs, this time through the beautiful game.

Crazy Marketing

In the new millennium, Coca-Cola's advertisements in Africa grew out of the same optimistic viewpoint that saw the company throw its weight behind sport—and youth sport in particular. Coca-Cola has always been a master marketer. Some argue that all the company does is market. Ashish Patel, self-described fourth-generation Kenyan-Indian and head of Label Converters, a Nairobi-based company that supplies the labels for Coca-Cola bottles throughout East Africa and beyond, put it best when I interviewed him. He said, in 'this world, it is all about image, nothing else.' In his estimation, 'a product is [simply] how you dress the product.'[93] How Coke clothed—and marketed—itself in Africa in the new millennium says an awful lot about how the company saw the continent in these years.

In 2009, on the eve of FIFA's South African World Cup, Coca-Cola South Africa debuted the new global ad campaign then supplanting the popular 'Coke Side of Life' promotion. Now, consumers were entreated to 'Open Happiness' by opening a Coke. In a world barraged with images of suffering and pain, Coca-Cola positioned its product as a portal to the converse, happiness. In South Africa, the campaign debuted with a short film by South African student director Mfundo Mkhize. Titled, 'The Ultimate Goal,' the film merges happiness with youth, soccer, and Coke.[94] 'Hello Africa,' it opens, 'It's a brand new day.'[95] Narrating a dream sequence of the ultimate soccer goal scored by an underdog in a lopsided fight—the epitome of youthful aspiration—the commercial offers a buoyant vision for young, hip, and contented Africans, keeping Coke closely aligned with soccer at the same time. Other Open Happiness commercials around the World Cup featured the relentlessly upbeat song Coca-Cola commissioned for the event from Somalian singer K'Naan. Titled 'Wavin' Flag—Coca-Cola Celebration Mix,' it too became a theme song for the tournament and for a way of life that embraces optimism and youth.[96]

Coke continued to market its brand alongside soccer and happiness in South Africa in 2014. This time, its focus was not

1. Umhloti Beach, South Africa, 1949.

2. Distribution store in the Sahara Desert, n.d.

3. Factory, Pretoria, South Africa, c. 1950.

4. Loading operations, Kimberley, South Africa, c. 1950.

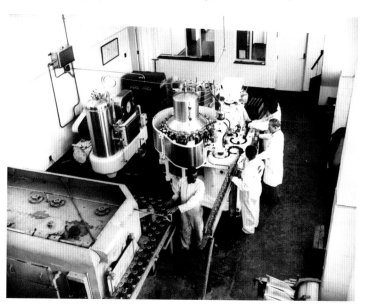

5. Bottling operations, Kimberley, South Africa, c. 1950.

6. Roadside sale, Liberia, 1952.

7. Advertisement, Congo/Zaire (now DRC), 1952.

8. In front of the Sphinx, Egypt, n.d.

9. Shop, Dar Es Salaam, Tanganyika (now Tanzania), 1953.

10. Bottling plant, Nigeria, 1954.

11. Truck route, Belgian Congo/Zaire (now DRC), 1955.

12. Factory, Nyasaland (now Malawi), 1956.

13. Joint birthday celebration for Johannesburg and Coca-Cola, South Africa, 1956.

14. Parade, Dakar, Senegal, 1957.

15. Workers transporting Coca-Cola during the construction of the Kariba Dam, 1957.

GRANT ADVERTISING (PTY) LTD.
Johannesburg
Size: Full Page   English   Control No. 40-2753
Native Press   S.F.   U.S.   February 1959

16. Miriam Makeba, South African advertisement, 1959.

17. Moroccan display at World Fair, 1958.

18. Copperbelt 'Cycle Safely' contest advertisement, 1959.

19. Coca-Cola delivery truck driving towards Nyali Bridge,
Mombasa, Kenya, 1959.

20. 'Coca-Cola refreshes you best' sign, n.d.

21. Mt. Elgon warehouse, Uganda, 1960.

22. Coca-Cola delivery to a bank, Dahomey (now Benin), 1962.

23. 'Animals of Africa'
advertisement, 1962.

24. 'Animals of Africa' display, n.d.

25. D V C Hammond, Durban plant manager, and Bob Cane, advertising manager, right, peruse the Kirstenbosch album, 1964.

26. 'Let's Know Our Country' advertisement, Liberia, n.d.

27. 'Discover Africa' contest, advertisement, n.d.

28. 'Discover Africa' contest, n.d.

29. Advertisement, Côte d'Ivoire, n.d.

30. Ghana café, n.d.

31. Coca-Cola movement by plane, Liberia, 1963.

32. Petrol station, n.d.

33. Coca-Cola Bottling Company of Mombasa, n.d.

34. Truck parade, Sierra Leone, n.d.

35. Road safety display, n.d.

36. Mr. G A Boakye, production foreman, Kumasi Plant, Ghana, n.d.

37. 'Coke Adds Life to...' advertisement, *Prize* magazine, 1980.

38. Beaded Coca-Cola bottle, n.d., South Africa.

39. Coca-Cola Johannesburg 'Rainbow Nation Campaign', South Africa, 2014.

40. Carl Ware and Nelson Mandela, n.d.

youth soccer, but the opposite. And this time, its branding was not simply a commercial, but rather an integrated marketing project. In a short video, viewers are introduced to the Gogos (Zulu for grandmothers), who are—true to their name—a team of fifty-year-olds and up who play soccer together. The oldest team member, we are told, is eighty-four. The video opens with the Gogos jogging, each wearing a green and yellow kit with a yellow doek on her head. 'As I turned older,' one Gogo narrates, 'I didn't want to become a typical grandma. So, I started the team for other grannies.' We hear that soccer is important to these women who play as much for health as comradery. One remarkable day, we hear, the Gogos were elated when a man from Coca-Cola arrived to show them the real FIFA trophy as part of Coca-Cola's famed trophy tour that traverses the continent. Later, another Coca-Cola man arrived to announce something even better. Six of the grannies would be going to the World Cup in Brazil on Coca-Cola's dime.[97] Coca-Cola would later tweet a picture of the Gogos from Brazil with the caption 'can you imagine your granny scoring the game winning goal?' Here is a campaign that was at once marketing, human interest, and light-hearted fun. In short, it was happy. And it was not the only promotion of its kind.

On the heels of the Gogos and the success that it generated, South African Coca-Cola marketers initiated another marketing plan as part of a global campaign, initiated in Brazil, called 'Crazy for Good.' Meant to spark random acts of kindness, crazy for good celebrated the ways ordinary people make the world a little better. Crazy for Good led to global celebrations of those who randomly pay tolls for others, give out money, plant trees, high five strangers, and hang swings. 'Are you crazy enough?' the campaign asked, suggesting that forthright optimism in the face of global problems was crazy, but in a good way.[98] The idea, South African marketer Marina Loubser told me, was 'based on the happiness driver of giving.' Giving makes people happy, in other words, and Coke was now firmly in the happy business. So, she described, 'We went and found all these crazy masters, we called them in South Africa, people that are doing amazing things for no benefit for themselves but just to do something great for their communities.' Having found them, Coke then celebrated them.[99]

Of all the masters, Coca-Cola marketers chose to create a video about one who best exemplified their vision for good in post-apartheid South Africa. Tom Hewitt, we hear in the video produced about him, was born in England but 'born again in Durban, South Africa,' a city then grappling with an abundance of street children. A lifelong surfer, Hewitt's mad idea was to change the trajectory of these children's lives by teaching them to surf. I wondered, he narrates, 'If I could teach these children to surf, would it change their future? Would it let them be kids again? Would it set them free?' Part practical, part spiritual, Hewitt's idea was to empower kids to feel better and be more competent all at once. The answer to his questions, shown with beautiful images of children diving into water and triumphantly rising to stand on boards, the sun twinkling behind them, was a resounding yes. By the end we learn the fate of some of his top students. One is now a lifeguard, while two more run surf schools.[100] There is something of a savior narrative to this story as packaged here. We see a white man—an outsider no less—being cheered for teaching street kids to do something that is only mildly marketable. Yet, we cannot help but still be impressed by Hewitt's project, which has grown since this video to include Mozambique and girl surfers. The fact that his work is on the periphery only makes it that much more compelling. Here it epitomizes Coke in the sense that it is both irrelevant to structural problems, but also good. At a time when robust critiques of top-down development models abound, the idea of celebrating one man helping a handful of kids strikes a chord of micro goodness, all of which is clearly in line with Coca-Cola's vision of its own impact.

South African Coke marketers did not simply celebrate crazy good. They tried to replicate it, too, by initiating their own project inspired by the San Francisco man who randomly hung swings as part of that region's campaign. The questions it asked: 'what if a swing could help an underprivileged community?' and 'could a swing grass a field?' In yet another marketing/activation co-endeavor, Coca-Cola hung swings from trees at Skeen Primary School in Alexandra township and at the Wits stadium, both in and around Johannesburg. The seats of the swings were made out of tricked-out Coke crates and loaded with android devices transformed to tally each individual swing. For every swing, Coca-Cola committed to plant one square meter of grass at Skeen, a 'much loved but run down' school. University students at Wits would be swinging in solidarity. So too could people swing virtually, with every tweet, like, and share equaling an additional swing. They even set up the swing itself to tweet. With no pre-campaign work and no support from Atlanta, the campaign hit 988,425 swings within a matter of days, reaching its goal well ahead of schedule. The video documenting the swing project is filled with all manner of South Africans happily smiling and swinging. It ends with Coca-Cola and the city of Johannesburg planting and watering sod at Skeen Primary School. Results of the promotion included, viewers are told, 500,000 more eyes on the brand, trending nationally on Twitter, and a 161% happiness increase, tallied, we learn (perhaps cheekily), by some very smart metric. An unexpected outcome, we hear, is that in the aftermath of the project's success, Beijing, New York, and Hamburg each adopted its own 'swing for change' project meant to grass other fields in South Africa.[101] Again, this is typically Coke—non-essential, light-hearted, focused at youth, a fun, feel-good endeavor with tangible, if limited, results.

Beyond Crazy for Good and beyond South Africa, Coke Africa showed its optimism for the continent in ways that aligned with the global company by picking up on an ad campaign born in Australia. In 2011, an Australian advertising executive came up with a novel—and many thought implausible—local advertisement campaign. She proposed doing something unheard of: unbranding Coke red. Instead of its trademark Spencerian Coca-Cola, traditional Coke red labels would be replaced with the phrase 'Share a Coke with...' followed by one of the 250 most popular first names in the country. Eventually, this was raised to 1,000 names. Members of the Australian team that created this groundbreaking campaign described the exhaustive work that went into launching it: one brief, five agencies pitching on it, more than twenty late-night hours with Atlanta, endless trademark headaches, twenty-five separate risk assessment meetings, one 'massive global brand exception,' 150 submissions to the marketing approvals committee, 4,000 hours of talking to Coca-Cola Amatil stakeholders individually, four weeks to find a machine to print the names on the can, 225 trademark searches to check names, 2,302 artworks, over 300,000 point-of-sale pieces nationally, and individual approval of every name by management. In the end, in a country of twenty-three million people, Coca-Cola sold over 250 million individualized personal packs.[102] This remarkable success meant that Share a Coke was rolled out in fifty countries the next year.[103]

Across Africa, Coke executives charged with implementing Share a Coke encountered similar obstacles. The first was choosing appropriate names. According to Alexander B Cummings, the goal was to 'cut across people,' meaning to choose widely from different ethnic groups so as not to alienate any one segment of a given population. Everywhere, marketing teams were used to determine what the best, in most cases, 1,000 names would be.[104] Often, marketers defaulted to youthful names. Another issue Coke faced was finding label makers willing to make these new labels. Ashish Patel in Kenya, for instance, was not willing to incur the expense it would take to make novel, presumably short-lived labels.[105] There was no doubt that the campaign presented challenges. But it was also hugely successful. After Share a Coke came Share a Feeling, with bottles that included emojis and sayings, and that was just the start. In sum, this long-lasting global campaign has been lauded as the most successful marketing campaign of all time.[106]

South African marketers understood that the heart of Share a Coke, and its success, was identity recognition. As part of their local roll-out, marketers produced what would become an award-winning local commercial that was later picked up and reshot for use around the world, from Nigeria to Russia. The ad 'Bobby' tapped into the anxiety and reward around recognition and naming that were at the heart of the Share a Coke campaign globally—hence its spread. In the commercial, a dog in Johannesburg is, presumably, trying to find a Coke bottle with his name on it.[107] The backdrop: young, hip, multiracial, and happy urban South Africa. As the dog searches everywhere from coolers at parties to store refrigerators, the Ting Tings' musical refrain tells us, 'They call me Stacey. They call me Jane... Maybe Jolisa... That's not my name, that's not my name.'[108] The dog's frantic search recalls news images of emptied coolers in supermarkets worldwide as people searched for bottles and cans with their name on them. Eventually, the pup finds his way to a rooftop in Hillbrow where four other dogs are staring in satisfaction at a 'Share a Coke with Bobby' billboard. The punchline: Bobby is a common dog name in South Africa.[109] The rumor, according to Loubser, was that Warren Buffet liked the ad so much that he played it at shareholder meetings.[110]

Five years later, Share a Coke South Africa was still focused on the politics of the campaign. Responding to a 2016 Twitter trend about how white people mispronounce Black names, 2018 Share a Coke cans arrived with phonetic pronunciations—gleaned from linguists and writers—under each South African name. Under 'Raessa' it read 'Rah-Yee-Sah.' Under Kgotso, 'Goh-tso.' And under Relebohile, 'Ree-Leh-Boo-Hee-Leh,' and so on.[111] Working with the department of Home Affairs, Coca-Cola determined the most popular names for each part of the country, culled from all eleven official South African languages. Then, the company deliberately mismatched them, so that cans in a given region reflected names least common to that region.[112] Alongside the phonetic cans, Coke released commercials where individuals told viewers how to pronounce their names. Additional YouTube videos were created to Share a Sound, by, for instance, introducing how to make a Q click. The chief creative officer for FCB Johannesburg, the ad agency that launched the campaign, noted that the goal here was to take an already successful global campaign and localize it. 'By adding the pronunciation to people's names,' he said, 'the Coca-Cola can became much more than an acknowledgment of identity—it became a teacher, a change maker.' Allowing people a chance to try to say a name 'without fear' rendered the can 'an education tool and a symbol of cultural pride,' he said.[113] Here Coca-Cola pushed beyond reflection to action, attempting to insert its product into larger, pressing questions about identity and belonging.

Coke Studio

The final leg of Coca-Cola's work in the new millennium in Africa—beyond sport and innovative marketing—was Coke Studio. First launched in Pakistan in 2007, the original Coke Studio aimed to form a bridge between an older, conservative generation and a younger, progressive one by encouraging musical collaborations across this seeming divide. An early, but much-lauded result: a seventy-year-old artist who had not produced music in two decades paired with a teen pop star to make a song that ended up topping the charts for weeks.[114] The success of Coke Studio Pakistan, like anything else in the Coke world, ensured its spread. Second came Coke Studio India. After that came Coke Studio bel Arabi and then Coke Studio Africa, based in Kenya, which covered twelve markets and produced twelve different edits in English, Swahili, Portuguese, French, and Amharic. Coke Studio South Africa followed.

Coke Studio Africa—much like its South African counterpart—is based upon a clear ideological framework. If you can get Africans together to share in each other's music and culture, it suggests, you can form pan-African bonds. 'The whole idea and what we hope,' marketing director Ahmed Rady explained to me on the day I visited a live taping of season four in Nairobi, 'is that through an entertaining, lighthearted medium we get this deeper message of bridging divides.' During each of the regular eleven weeks in a season, two artists from across the continent are brought together. They each learn a version of the other's song. They also collaborate on a new piece of music together. Footage from their week of learning and collaborating is then aired on TV, shot upon a slick, Coke red studio, culminating in on-air performances. What this means, more than anything, is exposure for artists across the continent. 'All of a sudden an artist from Uganda can do concerts in Nigeria,' Rady noted, making the money the artists receive secondary. Coke chooses musicians who understand and embrace its vision: 'We want to work with people who want to make a difference and want to work with us and love the brand as an idea,' he clarified. Alongside the weekly airings are activations that include trucks and stands where people can get a taste of mini studios. Each season also brings in an international star. The result: Coke Studio is widely popular. In 2016, 75% of teens and young adults in the countries covered by Coke Studio Africa were aware of the show and a whopping

83% of those who were aware of it watched it.[115] Like soccer and marketing, here Coke found a way to use music to spread brand awareness and love while tapping into African enjoyment. Or, conversely, Africans found a way to compel this company to support their musical endeavors.

By producing Coke Studio Africa, the team in Kenya wanted to do more than just grow pan-African connections. They wanted to send Africa's youth a deliberate message: no matter where you want to get in life, there are no shortcuts. Virtually all of the artists focused upon in season three, I learned, spoke about their individual struggles. That was deliberate. The message, Rady told me, was to tell the youth that while happiness and optimism are important, they are no replacement for hard work. 'Persistence,' he said, 'is an integral part of how you get anything.' So to be happy, you must stay focused and work hard.[116]

Conclusion

At the start of the new millennium, Coke's African marketing teams amplified earlier Coke campaigns around happiness and optimism. Nowhere is this clearer than the company's Reason to Believe campaign. Begun in Mexico in 2011, by the time it was picked up in Africa in 2012, the campaign became a way to merge the 'We believe' mentality voiced by Carl Ware with the reality of the Africa population reaching the one billion mark. Set to Steve Kekana's 'I love you Africa,' the African commercial that debuted as part of this campaign was unapologetically—perhaps even illogically—hopeful about the continent, juxtaposing stark images from elsewhere with their supposed African converse. Kekana sings 'I love you Africa' as young girls dance around him, while we read that 'there are a billion reasons to believe in Africa.' The evidence, given in juxtapositions, includes the following: 'While the world shakes and stumbles, Africa dances to a different beat;' 'For every bank bailed out, 2 million Africans send money back home;' '1 in 5 European club players is African and millions more are ready to shine;' 'As authorities try to tame the internet, Africa becomes the most mobile-connected place on the planet;' 'For every international brand trying to sell a song, 5000 African bands go live;' 'While the world turns grey, we live in full color;' and, of course, 'While the world worries about the future, 1 billion Africans are sharing a Coke.' 'All I need is right here in Africa,' Kekana croons, suggesting that despite outside appraisals to the contrary, the continent is capable of self-healing. The commercial closes with an iconic Coca-Cola bottle and a bubbling 'open happiness' tagline.[117]

'A billion reasons to believe' was positioned as a counterpoint to the steady diet of negativity that most of us consume daily from the news. 'We live in a world where every time you open the TV you are going to see a lot of bad news. You are going to see the worst,' said Rady. According to him, this is a result of newsmakers' interests and not reality. There are hundreds of good things that happen daily, he told me, but since these go unpublicized, especially in Africa, 'a very cynical generation' had come of age under a cloud of negativity. 'We,' at Coke, he clarified, 'are trying to speak to this generation and say, "listen, there are reasons to believe."' We aimed 'to say not only believe in yourself, but [also] we believe in you.' Here Coca-Cola was enacting what Ware had promised: belief in the power of Africa to forge its own happiness. And, yet, this was not mere fluff. 'We have to be clear about what kind of happiness' we endorse, Rady cautioned: 'It's not naïve happiness' that Coca-Cola promotes. Such a position would do no more than stoke complacency. 'No, no, no,' he told me, Coca-Cola encourages 'purposeful happiness,' the kind of driven optimism that can make change. How does it do this? Through soccer, marketing, music, and, of course, product. As such, Coke is the ultimate crazy for good master.[118] As the twenty-first century dawned with Coca-Cola more present in Africa than ever, the company would move to more substantive, sustainable ways to effect positive change.

7

THE BOTTOM LINE

WEIGHING COCA-COLA'S SUSTAINABILITY

In 2014, for the twentieth anniversary of the end of apartheid in South Africa, Coca-Cola marketers honored the Rainbow Nation literally, by generating rainbows above Johannesburg's skyline. By then, much of the optimism that had attended the emergence of the post-apartheid nation had waned. The government's mandate felt tenuous, the economy was faltering, and even the country's golden boy, Oscar Pistorius, had fallen from grace. Working within the Open Happiness campaign, marketers sought to refocus the national narrative, first by wrapping a building with the message 'Happy 20 years to our rainbow nation' and then by creating rainbows using—and here was the kicker—water cleaned by Coca-Cola. 'We are very excited to have discovered a way to create actual rainbows by capturing the sun at specific angles through a mist of recycled water,' the company announced.[1] This multifaceted promotion was an ambitious endeavor. A rainbow-maker was flown in from Albuquerque, New Mexico. Water personnel were consulted. Product samplings of special packages that read '#RainbowNation' were set up under the rainbow's arc.

'Moments of happiness,' as they were called, were caught on film and shared via social media. Coke also distributed sets of bottles spray-painted in all colors of the rainbow, such as a purple one sent to Archbishop Desmond Tutu as a nod to his signature robe. In the end, Coke's marketing team received five medals at Cannes for what was seen as another groundbreaking promotion.[2] Like the other optimistic campaigns of the new millennium, this one offered a saccharin message: despite all manner of hardship, Africa, via Coca-Cola, was a place of happiness and hope, a place, presumably, over the rainbow.

The promotion's success aside, all was not well for the company. As the new millennium dawned, Coca-Cola, like other companies doing business in Africa, faced a host of threats to its business, just as governments across the globe began to focus on sustainability benchmarks that needed to be met for the African continent (and elsewhere in the global south) to thrive. At the juncture of both was water, suggesting that it was no accident that clean water was central to the Rainbow Nation promotion. By the new millennium at least, water emerged as a prime threat to African life and, by extension, Coca-Cola's business there, since problems around access and cleanliness abounded across the continent. Coke understood this early on and set itself goals to stave off this threat by contributing to its solution. At the same time, lagging women's empowerment, the proliferation of waste, and energy concerns threatened African life and The Coca-Cola Company's ability to do business on the continent alike. In response, the company implemented social and environmental initiatives that sought to serve multiple bottom lines at once—those of investors, the company itself, and the continent. In this chapter, I demonstrate that while the multifaceted programs launched by Coke evolved from the company's history as an enmeshed corporate citizen, these new programs did something more. To continue to grow in Africa in the new millennium, Coca-Cola's focus on sustainability, broadly construed, complicated any neat understanding of its contemporary bottom line.

Being There as Corporate Citizen

Coca-Cola's business in Africa flourished as the continent moved into the twenty-first century. In 2009, then head of Coke's Africa unit, Alexander B Cummings, spoke to the growth of the company across Africa after the end of apartheid. Besides investing five billion dollars in the continent, with a plan to invest twelve billion more in the next decade, by then, the Coke system employed roughly 65,000 Africans, and, according to multiple studies, helped create '10–12 indirect jobs in related industries through the materials and services' the company used.[3] In 2015, then president of Coke's Africa group Nathan Kalumbu affirmed that the number employed was up to 70,000 and only set to grow.[4] Studies show that every Coca-Cola employee in Africa in turn supports between four and ten other people.[5] Back of the envelope estimates thus suggest that, by 2020, more than three quarters of a million Africans were being supported by Coca-Cola work, not to mention those working in jobs generated by secondary industries. A series of reports commissioned by the company underscore the profound social and economic impact of this reach,[6] and while we should take these with a grain of salt, independent reporting has suggested a similar story.[7]

Sanguine reports (self-generated and external) that laud Coca-Cola's impact on the continent aside, Coca-Cola's presence in Africa was never without problems—no less so now. As the company's footprint expanded in the new millennium, questions arose about the effects of the product's ubiquity. As a drink business, Coke's usage and treatment of water was of primary concern. How much water did the company use, and at what price? To what extent did Coke bottlers contribute to water depletion and pollution? Was the company doing anything to nurture women and youth workers within its system? Likewise, how much energy did the company use and was this fair, particularly in energy-strained countries? And, what became of all the waste generated by Coca-Cola products?[8]

When, in September 2000, the United Nations adopted its Millennium Declaration, it called upon partner nations to focus on measurable global development over the next fifteen years. The resulting Millennium Development Goals (MDGs) championed the eradication of poverty and diseases, as well as the promotion of education, gender equality, maternal health, environmental sustainability, and women's empowerment.[9] In so doing, the MDGs drew attention to precisely the kind of collateral effects of a company like Coca-Cola in Africa.

Coca-Cola first addressed the challenges spotlighted by the UN through its charitable wing, The Coca-Cola Foundation, founded in 1984. A 501(c)(3) separate from the company, The Coca-Cola Foundation allocates money from corporate Coke to its separate regional foundations, including the Africa Foundation. As of 2021, Coca-Cola donated roughly 1% of the previous year's operating income to charitable endeavors around the globe via the foundation, some of which are detailed in the text that follows.[10]

At the same time, Coke promoted itself as a corporate citizen, now reframed in contemporary language. The idea that a corporation could be conceived of as a citizen emerged after the 1984 publication of R E Freeman's *Strategic Management: A Stakeholder Approach*.[11] Freeman's idea that citizenship—and the social responsibility that it suggested—was beneficial to a company was broadly taken up throughout the 1990s.[12] In 1998, John Elkington's *Cannibals with Forks* brought method to theory. Elkington introduced the idea that not only could businesses engage in socially responsible work, but also that this work could—and should—be quantified through what he called 'triple bottom line' reporting, accounting that measured not only financial, but also social/ethical, and environmental bottom lines.[13] Elkington foresaw a shift where NGOs, who had traditionally avoided working with business, saw utility in business skill sets. He realized that such partnerships would be dually beneficial. While NGOs gained technical know-how, companies gained much sought-after community trust.[14] Big corporations agreed. In 2002, at the World Economic Forum in New York, for instance, CEOs from thirty-four of the largest multinational companies signed a 'Global Corporate Citizenship ... Leadership Challenge for CEOs and boards.' Coca-Cola was among them.[15]

Coca-Cola embraced the idea of itself as a corporate citizen in Africa in the new millennium. None of this was new for Coke in Africa, as is no doubt clear by this point in this book. We can trace the desire to be an integral part of society back to J Paul Austin's 1963 articulation of what he called Coke's 'voluntary foreign aid program,' where the company filled governance gaps around the world.[16] Austin also believed that Coke had more to do economically than just contribute to the bottom line: 'The free enterprise system can be imaginatively applied to combat world poverty,' he was quoted as saying in 1967.[17] Austin was interested in the planet as well, urging the company to stay committed 'to prevent[ing] any further violence to the ecology of our planet, and to promot[ing] ... environmental renewal'[18] by working as, in his words, 'a responsible corporate citizen.'[19]

As CEO of Coca-Cola from 2004 to 2008, E Neville Isdell took up the challenge set earlier by Austin under what he now termed 'connected capitalism.' According to Isdell, 'Connected capitalism is so much broader,' than classic corporate social responsibility. 'It is the creation of the Socially Responsible Corporation, which examines the company's actual footprint on society and focuses on how, as part of a core business strategy, it can reduce the negative impact.'[20] Locating its responsibility work within its central corporate strategy, Isdell suggested that Coke focus on those ills that ran alongside its primary business. The result was a nascent strategy that sought to better itself and its environs at the same time as part of a 'philosophy of mutual benefit,' another idea with deep roots in Coca-Cola's history.[21]

Isdell's successor as CEO of the company, Muhtar Kent, continued this trend in the twenty-first century, uniting connected capitalism with the UN's MDGs. Drawing upon his predecessors' work, Kent oversaw the unveiling of a series of Coca-Cola sustainability initiatives. These codified what had long been part of Coke's operations on the continent. After eighty-seven years in Africa, Nathan Kalumbu reiterated in 2015, Coke was proud to do business in every African nation in a way that benefitted both the company and Africans. 'Two of the key learnings we have taken from almost a century of serving African consumers,' he explained, 'are the importance of investing in community prosperity and the value of public-private sector partnership' since 'the strength and sustainability of our business is tied directly to the strength and sustainability of the African communities we serve.' Kalumbu further explained that not only did Coca-Cola do this because it was good for business; the company also believed that, in his words, 'partnerships across government, civil society and the private sector offer the most certain way to make a meaningful difference; [since] each partner brings unique capabilities and together we can address the vast opportunities and complex challenges that exist.'[22] Kalumbu was describing the sustainability system put forward by Kent, still in play under his successor James Quincy, termed the Golden Triangle Partnership model.[23] In this, Coca-Cola serves as the convening partner, strong enough to bring governments, global development agencies, and local NGOs to the table in order to enact sustainability projects. Through this model, a triple bottom line is served.

Vice President of International Government Relations and Public Affairs at Coca-Cola Michael Goltzman, when speaking to the Senate Committee on Foreign Relations in May 2017, described how the golden triangle functions. He explained that Coca-Cola is not interested in replacing governments, but rather that through this model, Coca-Cola offers its skills, either around systems ('logistics, supply chain, distribution and marketing expertise') or around method (water purification and recycling, for instance). It helps convene large NGOs like USAID, the Bill and Melinda Gates Foundation, the World Wildlife Fund, and many more. These, it then connects with local, small-scale implementing partners, the kinds of NGOs and nonprofits focused on one city, region, or even neighborhood. Finally, it connects itself (the private sector) and NGOs to the third triangular spoke: governments. That way, the golden triangle ensures that no one is doing work that is either at odds with or redundant to that being undertaken by governments.[24] Does this model benefit Coca-Cola and feed its expansion? Yes. The extent to which it helps sustain African communities is taken up in the next section. In sum, this model of corporate citizenship—able to better the world and business at once—became Coca-Cola's guiding principle in the twenty-first century.

Sustaining Humans

The idea that people need to live in a way that enables the biosphere to endure took hold in the twenty-first century. No longer was it acceptable to view the planet as limitless resource, seeking growth at any cost. Governments, NGOs, and businesses alike began to outline practices that demonstrated a commitment to the planet's future. In 2011, Coca-Cola named its first Chief

Sustainability Officer, Bea Perez, to account for and steer the company's work in this domain. In 2015, Perez spoke about the wobbliness of the very term 'sustainability,' noting that many continued to see it as synonymous with philanthropy. For Coca-Cola, Perez explained, sustainability meant finding a way to protect the company's continued use of limited resources by ensuring the existence of those very resources. When describing sustainability, she said, Coca-Cola, 'lean[s] more toward the words of shared value because we do believe that companies have to be honest about the self-interest that is involved.'[25] Coke made no bones about undertaking sustainability initiatives that serve the company, focusing, under Perez, first on water and women's empowerment—both central to its operating model, albeit in different ways. Coke's sustainability initiatives also came to include farming, medical distribution, youth, energy, and waste, often in overlapping ways. Perhaps unsurprisingly, the bulk of Coca-Cola's sustainability work was born in Africa, where the need was pronounced, and the business was entrenched.[26]

Delivering Drugs

In a 2010 TED Talk, philanthropist Melinda Gates recalled once wondering 'how is it that they can get Coke to... far-flung places?' and questioning, with particular regard to the distribution of medicines, 'why can't governments and NGOs do the same thing?'[27] Gates was reflecting on the fact that in many parts of the world, like Africa, it could take weeks or months for medicine to arrive and, as a result, often what is attained arrives spoiled. Just as regularly, caches of medicine rot in warehouses, either because there is no refrigeration or no organized distribution method on hand. The human cost of this inefficiency is steep.

As we already know, one of Coca-Cola's strengths is its complex distribution network that ensures that a bottle of Coke can be found virtually anywhere. For Gates and others like her, this unmatched network offered a mechanism by which nonprofits and governments might go about the task of distributing other products, particularly life-saving ones. The same year as Gates gave her talk, Coca-Cola launched Project Last Mile (PLM), a golden triangle endeavor that united Coke's systems, the Bill and Melinda Gates Foundation, USAID, the Global Fund, The Coca-Cola Foundation, governments, and more in order to move medicines and supplies the so-called 'last mile' required to get them into the hands of needy populations.[28] 'Nearly 50% of people in Africa lack access to critical medicines,' a fact sheet for the project announced, 'yet you can get a Coca-Cola nearly anywhere in the world.' The goal of PLM was to solve the one with the other, that is, use Coke's logistical expertise to enhance the 'storage, distribution, and marketing of critical medicines and medical supplies.'[29]

In 2010, PLM launched in Tanzania with a public-private collaboration bent on improving efficiency in the national supply chain. It ran training programs, collected data on 5,000 public health facilities, and 'optimized delivery routes' that served rural populations. 'The collaboration appears to be working,' Perez and colleague Guy Wollaert reported: 'Data released by the Clinton Global Initiative in 2012 showed that average delivery times have fallen from 30 days to 5.'[30] The result: In 2013, PLM expanded to Ghana, before moving to more African countries.

PLM looks different in each national setting, depending on local needs and partnerships. Drawing upon the company's marketing expertise, PLM was invited by the Global Fund and the Ministry of Health into Eswatini to help construct four-phased campaigns aimed at preventing the spread of HIV in the country, as well as addressing the treatment and care of those living with the disease there.[31] In other places, Coke's logistical know-how is harnessed. In Mozambique, PLM helped distribute items to the more than 70% of the population that lives in rural and remote areas.[32] Likewise, PLM entered Liberia following the Ebola epidemic to help rebuild the country's strained medical supply chain, using Coke's expertise around allocation and distribution.[33] In South Africa, PLM has been a key partner involved in the creation of what are called 'pick-up points,' that assist the National Department of Health's centralized distribution program for people living with HIV and other chronic illnesses. Between 2016 and 2018, nearly 1.3 million patients were enrolled in this program by way of 1,950 facilities and 450 pick-up points.[34]

In Ghana and Nigeria, it is Coke's know-how around cold technology that matters. In Nigeria, PLM launched a program to help maintain the cold chain equipment (CCE) necessary to store vaccines and medicines. The need there was dire. In 2018 Lagos state, a fact sheet explains, only 60% of primary health care centers had functioning CCE, with many working only about 65% of the time. In comparison, the Nigerian Bottling Company (NBC) served roughly 25,000 roadside vendors in the same state, each with its own refrigerator, which it was able to keep working 98% of the time.[35] Through a PLM collaboration, Coca-Cola helped create a pilot maintenance program overseeing approximately 500 CCE; it then trained 124 technicians to monitor the systems once they were in place, thereby creating long-term solutions. PLM projects are unique collaborations meant to harness Coca-Cola's expertise in Africa to serve timely, local needs.[36] To wit: in June 2021, Coca-Cola announced that it was giving two million dollars to PLM to help roll out Covid-19 vaccines in the nations where it has projects.[37]

Nurturing Talent

While PLM focuses on health, Coca-Cola's other sustainability endeavors target segments of African populations. All offer a similar framework: provide on-ramps to economic participation in order to empower people through capitalist systems. Project Nurture, for instance, focused on small-scale farmers in East Africa. An $11.5 million collaboration among The Coca-Cola Company, the nonprofit Technoserve, a local Coca-Cola bottler, and the Bill and Melinda Gates Foundation, Project Nurture ran from 2010 to 2014 with the goal of 'uplifting' 50,000 small-scale farmers in Uganda and Kenya. As the demand for juice grew globally, analysts at Coca-Cola realized that there was a worldwide deficit of mangoes and passion fruit. Project Nurture helped fill this void by supporting mango and passion-fruit farming that met the company's high agricultural standards, the results of which were then sold to Coca-Cola bottlers and others. Farmers were trained in agronomy and organized into business groups before being connected to markets ready for their produce.[38] Minute Maid Mango, launched in 2010 in Kenya and 2011 in Uganda, was the first product to use locally sourced juice—more than 36,000 metric tons. Farmers had a ready outlet for their produce (doubling most of their incomes), while the Coke business saved the cost of importing fruit.[39] A Harvard Kennedy School study affirmed the positive results of the project. Project Nurture, it concluded, 'contributes to business and development goals that creates economic opportunity for farmers, offering them additional income and the stability, resilience, health, education, and other benefits that come with it. Those benefits, in turn, enable farmers to supply high-quality fruit on a consistent basis, contributing to supply chain security and business growth.'[40] The key to the project's success, according to this report: partnerships that harnessed individual needs and expertise.[41]

Coca-Cola has also addressed youth empowerment in Africa as part of its sustainability work. Coke's MENA Scholars program, begun in 2011, is a collaboration among The Coca-Cola Company, Indiana University's Kelley School of Business, and the US Department of State. Through MENA, 100 college-aged students from North Africa, the Middle East, and Asia are brought to the US for an immersive month-long business school program. The students then return home with enhanced knowledge and capability to launch their own enterprises. In 2015, half of the 390 MENA scholars were women.[42]

Additionally, Coca-Cola launched what it calls YES, or Youth Empowered for Success, in 2015. Formed as a partnership with Mercy Corps, Harambee, Microsoft, and the Coca-Cola Foundation, YES began as an attempt to provide business skills training to—at first go—25,000 youth in Kenya, Uganda, Nigeria, Liberia, Tunisia, and South Africa. Central to the YES program is a scalable curriculum accessible on transportable tablets.[43] In Kenya and South Africa, the YES program is visible at YES Hubs, Coke-branded kiosks that provide free internet access. Susan Mboya, head of The Coca-Cola Foundation, describes the YES initiative's four components: 'recruiting, training, providing access to jobs, and then what we call enabling, which is things like mentoring and providing access to finance,' some of which is done by way of NGO partners. Importantly, the YES Hubs are easily set up in marginalized areas.[44]

I visited the pilot YES Hub in Ruaka, Kenya, a bright-red Coke-branded kiosk. The proprietor, Steve Okire, had previously run a car wash on site. His entrepreneurial spirit made him a good match for the program from the company's point of view, just as he readily took to the idea of expanding his car wash to include, as it did when I visited, a restaurant, internet stations, a meeting space, and, most significantly, solar-powered internet connectivity. Okire explained to me that he liked the idea of creating a safe space for local youth, which he defined as nineteen- to twenty-seven-year-olds; there were plenty around, as we were near the university. The hub was also useful for other groups to meet, including his church club. At the hub, a few cents for every soda sold went into a kitty to help needy students, while other outreach programs collected clothes for children. Visitors accessed a basic business skills curriculum, free of charge, on available tablets. When I was there, the internet was temporarily down and the tablets were being refurbished. Still, everyone I spoke to was optimistic that this was but a short-term glitch in an otherwise strong model of conjoined business and sustainability work.[45]

By far the bulk of Coca-Cola's sustainability efforts over the last decade have targeted women, a result of the growing recognition across the sustainability world that if you empower women, you uplift societies.[46] The centerpiece of these efforts: the company's 5x20 program, launched by Muhtar Kent at the Clinton Global Initiative in 2010 with the ambitious goal of empowering five million women worldwide by 2020.[47] 'There's an issue,' a 2014 5x20 infographic proclaimed: 'Women do 66% of the world's work but only earn 10% of the world's income. Yet they invest 90% of their income into family and community.'[48] The problem? A series of obstacles that impede women's full economic participation. 'Such barriers,' a 5x20 report listed, 'include lack of asset ownership, unequal compensation, and difficulty accessing formal labor markets, financial services, and networks.'[49] They also included minimal cultural and social support, unequal protection under the law, and lack of access to basic necessities, like power and water.[50] While 5x20 could not tackle all of these, it could—and did—bring Coke's expertise around economic participation to a wide range of golden triangle initiatives.

5x20 worked within the Women's Empowerment Principles set forth by the United Nations in 2010 and signed onto by the company.[51] That meant that the program's definition of empowerment hinged upon access to specific criteria: 'business skills, financial services, assets, and support networks of peers and mentors.'[52] These tenets were already partially built into the

Coke system. Perhaps that is why Coca-Cola was one of the first private sector companies to attempt anything like 5x20. In doing so, the global team charged with steering the program studied previous empowerment attempts to figure out what worked. Then, the team determined how to scale its programs at the magnitude of five million.[53] When, in 2016, the UN Secretary General declared women's economic empowerment to be an international goal, Coca-Cola was already being lauded for being well on its way towards meeting its target.[54]

While 5x20 began in four pilot markets (South Africa, Brazil, India, and the Philippines), before eventually expanding to 100 countries, more than a third of Coca-Cola's 5x20 efforts happened in Africa, where the need at the so-called bottom of the economic pyramid was marked.[55] Zoomed out, 5x20 was a catchall name for a broad range of programs that, like Project Last Mile, considered local realities. As golden triangle endeavors, they partnered with large and small NGOs. Some 5x20 programs were also supported by The Coca-Cola Foundation, but these were only those projects that did not intersect with the company's business, thus maintaining a firewall between the foundation and business.[56] All kept their sights trained on the idea of empowering five million women. To be counted in this tally, the company reported, 'women must: be at least 16 years old; participate in at least one 5by20 enabling activity; face barriers addressed by 5by20 program; and be either a current or a prospective entrepreneur.'[57]

Initially, 5x20 worked with women who were already embedded within the company's value chain. The women chosen were not directly employed by Coca-Cola, but rather were those whose private enterprises intersected with the business in some way. This meant they were farmers, retailers, recyclers, and distributors, aligning the 5x20 program with Coke's notion that the company's sustainability work ought to be close to its core business.[58] Other 5x20 projects dovetailed with other Coca-Cola-driven sustainability work, such as those that were part of Project Nurture, mentioned earlier, or those that were aligned with water and energy projects, mentioned later. Others intersected with artisans, including those women who repurpose or 'upcycle' Coke refuse, discussed later in this chapter. Eventually, 5x20 also came to include programs beyond the company's value chain.

An important launching pad for 5x20 were micro/manual distribution centers (MDCs), small, independently run depots that serve as waypoints between bottlers and points of sale. In 2017, there were approximately 3,500 MDCs worldwide, primarily in Africa.[59] MDCs are the backbone of the Coke business, particularly in Africa, since it is through MDCs that bottlers deliver product that then makes its way—by truck, car, tuk-tuk, handheld cart, and more—to the most remote parts of the continent.[60] MDCs serve the kind of micro-outlets that might buy but one or two crates at a time, like a township spaza or a rural shop. In 2010, Coca-Cola's internal research found that a striking 86% of MDCs were female owned and operated, making MDCs the perfect starting point for 5x20 initiatives.[61]

I visited several MDCs in my research. They were colorful, packed enterprises, where towering stacks of crates filled with red Coca-Cola, green Sprite, orange Fanta, and more lined the walls. Some had trucks, carts, and tuk-tuks nearby. All had a buzz of activity around them, with employees coming and going. One I saw in Ngong, Kenya, serviced a sizable radius (thirty km), while another I visited in Tema, Ghana, catered to but one densely populated neighborhood (though it delivered to no fewer than 200 vendors there).[62]

The MDCs I saw were run by savvy businesswomen. All had similar stories of growth and empowerment through Coca-Cola. In a bustling Lagos neighborhood, I met Alhaja Lawal, an MDC operator with an oft-repeated Coca-Cola success story.[63] Standing in her generator-cooled office, Lawal and I chatted. Lawal had been in business thirty-two years, she told me. In her early days, she sold only foodstuffs. She described how she had grown what began as five crates of Coca-Cola, given to her as a bottler promotion to supplement her food business, into a robust retail and wholesale enterprise, now selling thirty-five to forty thousand cases a month and employing twenty-five people. Lawal talked of the training and support she received along the way from the Nigerian Bottling Company that enabled her to overcome obstacles. 'What have you used your revenue from Coke to do?,' my assistant asked in Yoruba. Without missing a beat, she replied: 'I sent my children to school.' Lawal was proud to recount how she raised and educated four children, one of whom was home just then from university, sheepish in the shadow of her mother's praise.[64]

In Ngong, Kenya, I heard a similar story from M K Maina, another successful MDC operator. Maina had opened her depot in 1998 with modest retirement savings. She began with 450 crates. When I visited her, she was moving thirty to fifty thousand crates a month. She employed twenty-three people to use her trucks and tuk-tuks across a wide radius, working out of her now two depots. Like Lawal, Maina spoke about the personal benefits from working with Coke. 'Coca-Cola really means a lot to me,' she explained as we stood in a valley of red crates: 'I haven't gotten other money from elsewhere. What has built my business, the retail profits I've made, I've put them back into the business so that is what brought this to where it is today.' Additionally, she said, 'I'm also building my family with the same money,' proudly showing me a cell phone picture of an impressive family home, now under construction, before explaining how, most importantly, her profits had enabled her to send all her children to university.[65]

The women who run MDCs are, in many ways, the elite within the 5x20 world. Simply becoming an MDC is a sought-after position.[66] The bulk of 5x20 recipients, by comparison, operate on a much smaller scale. Of those within the Coca-Cola supply chain, most are small-scale retailers. In the densely populated, low-income neighborhood of Imbaba, Cairo, I met women who ran telephone-booth-sized shops. Some had innovative baskets that served as dumbwaiters, delivering goods vertically up high-rise buildings. Being out of the house, earning a modest income generated by their small enterprises, and being trained by NGOs had changed their lives. Their stories were similar. Missing, sick, or deceased husbands, children and school fees, and lack of options—felt more acutely in a place where women are often bound to the home—had limited these women's options. 5x20, working through partners, had changed that by creating opportunities for women who, without exception, were active participants in their own betterment.[67]

Most of the women I met in Imbaba had but primary education and basic reading and writing skills. Still, this was enough to seek out training. All described entering economic relationships aware of what was at stake. Even while I roamed the neighborhood with Coca-Cola personnel and members of the implementing NGO, other women approached us, hoping to get into a 5x20-type program, firstly, to attain a cooler. In Imbaba, as elsewhere, women received their first cooler box on loan from bottlers. This helped protect the cooler (from, say, needy relatives) as well as the company's investment. After hitting certain milestones, a woman would own her cooler, giving her an asset from which to further grow her business. As elsewhere, the size of any given cooler (from a small box that takes ice and must be carried up to a double glass door refrigerator) correlates with the size of a business, creating visible benchmarks. And, as elsewhere, the drink was just the anchor around which other items—fresh fruit and eggs, crisps, and sundry—were sold.

I heard similar stories in Ghana, Kenya, Zimbabwe, and South Africa. Compared with Egypt, female entrepreneurship is more common in sub-Saharan countries. Still, women echoed similar impediments to growth. Some had had other meager jobs, like cleaning or knitting, before 5x20. Others had long been in retail but lacked the means and know-how to grow their businesses. Many had side enterprises, painting nails, cutting hair, or making food, but they needed a boost to stabilize their endeavors. Time and again, I saw 5x20 programs addressing these and other problems, in part because across Africa, Coca-Cola is largely respected and seen as a desirable product that credentializes people and businesses, thus helping create economic sustainability for otherwise fledgling enterprises. Most women I spoke to had more than tripled the money they had been living on since joining 5x20.

How 5x20 programs functioned differed depending on any number of factors. On the ground, April Jordan from corporate Coca-Cola's communication office told me, 'the local teams through our Coca-Cola offices work with partners locally to determine the best way to reach women, what is the need in that market, and how can they put together programs that would be helpful.' The key word here is 'local,' where training fits the needs and timeline at hand: 'It might be several months of courses that happen a few days a week where the women learn everything from accounting to how to better market themselves, how to manage employees, how to budget appropriately,' and other sorts of business training, she explained.[68]

In South Africa, a program called 'Bizniz in a Box' gave women modular containers that became spaza shops. Women could eventually own these outright upon meeting pre-determined milestones. By 2020, Coke reported that more than eighty women owned their own shops, while 700 more had been trained through this 5x20 initiative. Likewise, a program called

Educating Nigerian Girls in New Enterprises, or ENGINE, shepherded nearly 13,000 sixteen-to-nineteen-year-old girls through business training and into the formal economy, roughly half of whom then joined Coke's value chain.[69] Everywhere, women spoke about the mentoring they received and how that made a difference to their long-term success. Most talked about the next milestone they hoped to meet, professionally. Bathini Tati, a successful spaza owner I met in Meadowlands, South Africa, for instance, described how she hoped to acquire a larger cooler and, later, expand her operation to include a carwash.[70] Everywhere, women told me about their dreams for their future and, without fail, their hopes for their children.

Once 2020 drew to a close amidst the Covid-19 pandemic, Coca-Cola announced that it had exceeded its goal by empowering more than six million women worldwide. At final tally, 5x20 claimed to have enabled 6,073,117 women, 33.7% of whom were in Africa, figures that are quantified (and verified independently) in its final, March 2021 report. That puts the number of empowered African women at 2,045,964.[71] Having surpassed its target, Coke nevertheless pledged that 'women's economic empowerment continues to be a major global challenge and core priority for The Coca-Cola system, both internally and externally,' offering ongoing support for underprivileged women and promising to have women in half of the company's positions of power by 2030, an equally important goal.[72]

Coca-Cola's 5x20 publications paint a positive, successful story. The company's assessments focus, unsurprisingly, on the kind of narrow narrative of betterment I have just described. In part, this is because my visits to 5x20 programs were facilitated by Coca-Cola bottlers, The Coca-Cola Company itself, and local partners. This meant that I was, by design, taken to meet thriving women who were, presumably, primed to speak to me. Was there unevenness across 5x20? Were there women for whom participation did not lead to success? As with any project of this scale, the answer must be, yes. Likewise, we may wonder, is this type of empowerment—rooted squarely in economic participation—the best and only form of empowerment? This is tricky to answer and is certainly beyond the purview of a company to fret about. Still, it is hard not to be impressed by the magnitude of the overall project, just as I found it hard not to be moved by the passion of those who work within the 5x20 world, from the corporate top to implementing partners. Likewise, the successful micro-businesses headed by strong, smart women, and the hardworking saleswomen I met impressed me. Sure, some had small gripes: not enough attention was being paid by bottlers, more resources were needed, that sort of thing. Yet, ultimately, each of the women I met was focused, more than anything, on her and her children's future and, importantly, on acquiring the tangible means to affect it positively. Far from being naïve about their involvement with 5x20, the women I met were clear-eyed about their use of Coca-Cola to sustain their own lives.

Without doubt, 5x20 programs served the company by enhancing the respectability of selling Coke. At the same time, the growth of MDCs and retail outlets is good for business. The more outlets, the more sales. Yet, as we shall see below, the more sales, the more other problems—like those surrounding resources—rise. In other words, Coke's ubiquity, exploded in the twenty-first century and given new gloss by its entwinement with female empowerment, taxed Africa in new and profound ways, in turn prompting new needs.

Protecting Environmental Resources

Water

Sustainability goes beyond nurturing people to protecting the environment. For a drink business, the most precious resource is water, which Coca-Cola has long understood. Since the early decades of the twentieth century, the company has studied water patterns around the world as well as purification methods to ensure that it has ample water and the ability to clean said water to its high standards.[73] Beginning in the early 2000s, Coca-Cola started coming under fire for using more than its fair share of water, procuring water at an unfairly low cost, and contributing to water pollution, allegations well-documented elsewhere.[74] In 2004, the company thus undertook its first global water risk assessment to grasp the breadth of the problem, determining that the threats to the company were physical, regulatory, and reputational.[75] It was clear that escalating water use throughout the value chain alongside company growth and changes from global warming had made water a major threat to the Coke business, not to mention to the globe, in the new millennium.

In response, in 2009 the company (in tandem with the foundation) built on earlier, smaller water programs to launch a series of projects that focused on company water use both inside and outside of its plants. In so doing, Coca-Cola aligned itself with global sustainability trends, such as the United Nations' call for universal access to 'safe and affordable drinking water' by 2030.[76] This was a steep goal for Africa, where there were roughly 300 million people without access to clean water in 2010.[77] As with women's empowerment, Coca-Cola brought its golden triangle partnership model to bear on the questions around water in Africa over the last decade.

Everywhere—Africa included—Coca-Cola first focused on what happened with water inside its plant walls. This meant paying attention to water efficiency. Over the last decade, the company has reduced the liters used per final product by 19% globally, though in areas where returnable bottles remain, like Africa, the amount of water used is likely higher, since water is required to clean bottles.[78] The company then focused on the estimated 39% of system-wide production volume that came from 'high or extremely high water stressed regions,' 21% of which came from company-owned plants rather than franchises.[79] These are precisely the places that draw global ire, given the poor optics of drawing water from regions of the world in most need of it.[80] The company launched partnerships in such areas—some described in the text that follows—that aimed to replenish the environment as well as procure new water sources. Finally, the company began working towards what it called water neutrality—that is, putting equal parts usable water out into the world as that which it uses.

Conceived of as being a quick metric to measure progress, as a concept, water neutrality meant to highlight Coke's balancing act as a consumer and steward of water. At individual bottling plants, water stewardship includes running wastewater through any number of cleaning treatments so that the water expelled could support wildlife. At the Maame Bottling Facility I visited in Accra, Ghana, for example, this is visualized by what is called 'activated sludge,' wastewater treatment that feeds into fishponds. The swimming catfish evidence the safety of the water.[81] These kinds of fishponds are common at factories across Africa as quick visualizations of responsible water use. In 2015, Coke announced that it had achieved water neutrality, in part from work like this.[82] Still, five years later, a company water footprint analysis showed that 93% of Coke's 'total blue water footprint' resided in its supply chain, primarily on the farms that grow the ingredients used in its beverages. In other words, much work needed to happen outside factories.[83]

When approaching water threats outside of its production plants, Coke's work has been focused on Africa, where the need is extreme. There, the bulk of Coca-Cola's efforts falls under the umbrella, RAIN, or Replenish Africa Initiative. Launched in 2009 with a sixty-five-million-dollar commitment from The

Coca-Cola Foundation and managed by the Global Environment & Technology Foundation (GETF), RAIN aimed to improve water access and, thus, African lives. Over a decade of golden triangle work, RAIN worked with more than 300 partners in more than 4,000 communities across forty-one countries.[84] RAIN worked from the premise that while water is a human right and should itself be free, water delivery and water purification incur expense. Understanding this up front meant that RAIN created projects embedded in capitalist systems that sought to minimize the cost for consumers at the bottom of the economic pyramid. RAIN projects also lead with need, not technology, I heard from Greg Koch, Senior Director of Water Stewardship at Coke, as well as Monica Ellis, Chief Executive Officer of GEFT. There are thousands of ways to clean water and multiple methods to source it, but for any given RAIN project to work long-term, any methods deployed had to be appropriate for local conditions. Often this meant avoiding the most state-of-the-art technology, since those tend to be difficult to maintain (witness the beauty of relatively simple activated sludge, mentioned previously).

Members of the global team driving RAIN also explained to me that the water problem is vast, ranging from shortages and access issues to cleanliness and related health and hygiene concerns. They noted that water infrastructure is expensive work that requires a political will that is hard to muster anywhere in the world. Additionally, they noted that the water-borne diseases that kill and sicken millions annually need not exist, since humans know how to purify water. Yet, cleaning water does not have the same cachet as other humanitarian work. It should, they said, since labor around accessing water is time-consuming, profoundly limiting possibilities.

Water stewards at Coke embraced what Coca-Cola has long known: that any successful endeavor must align with local needs and be collaborative. Thus, RAIN projects brought together a dizzying array of partners, including governments, global NGOs, development organizations, local community organizations, local bottlers, non-revenue-generating water boards, and other stakeholders, including corporate Coca-Cola and the company's individual business groups. As with other golden triangle endeavors, RAIN used Coca-Cola's expertise in management systems, logistics, and marketing as it built upon the company's convening power and deep enmeshment across Africa.

RAIN focused on what it called WASH—water supply, sanitation, and hygiene—as well as the productive use of water and watershed protection. Some RAIN projects responded to ecological degradation, such as one in southern Morocco that sought to rehabilitate date palm plantations by improving water use and protecting watersheds, or another focused on repairing catchment areas in South Africa to enhance the land's capability to retain water.[85] A project in Somalia sought to extend water into the dry period to boost drought resistance.[86] Other RAIN programs targeted farmers, such as those that ran in Ghana, Mali, and Malawi, or another in Kenya, which worked to augment crop yield and increase subsistence sales.[87] Still more RAIN projects dug wells and boreholes, created reservoirs, and repaired hand pumps, as ones in Liberia, Cameroon, and Senegal did.[88]

A different group of RAIN projects focused on extending existing water systems into areas of the continent that had up until then lacked piped water. In one case this meant laying pipes that reached into the outskirts of Bamako, Mali, and in another, doing the same in the peri-urban area Balkuy, outside Ougadougou, Burkina Faso.[89] Similar access projects were undertaken in Mauritania and Rwanda, as well as Somaliland, where the focus was on improving access to water within IDP settlements in Hargeisa.[90] I visited one such Coca-Cola project in Beni Warkan, Minya, Upper Egypt, about 300 km from Cairo. Coke's work there fell under a local company commitment, begun in 2011, to develop 100 of the poorest villages in Egypt as part of a golden triangle partnership. In this case, development meant refurbishing the existing, but much deteriorated, 1960s-era health clinic and school, enhancing health and wellness education, and extending water access. I spent a day in the village, speaking to everyone from the Cairo-trained obstetrician who devotes herself to contraceptive and reproductive education; the dentist who provides low-price treatment; the headmaster of the 2,000-pupil school, who proudly showed off the school's computer lab—alongside the more mundane, but important, windows, desks, and books that now populate what had once been an abandoned building; and people who now have water taps in their homes.

It is impossible to overstate the emotion around water access. The women I spoke to—and they were all women; the men were scarce—described the burden of having between four and seven children to care for, besides elderly and infirm relatives. They teared up as they recalled waiting as much as twenty years for water taps in their homes—some of which had no roofs—and the time it took previously to fetch water. The indignities around such deprivation were clear. The Coca-Cola team and related NGO representatives I was with stressed that they rarely brought outsiders to visit projects like this so that the recipients' dignity and privacy is maintained. When I visited, this village of 18,000 people was now fully connected to water that was regularly tested to be within safe drinking parameters. Nothing about this project was branded Coca-Cola.[91]

Besides extending taps, many RAIN projects centered around building water kiosks—small structures of different shapes and sizes—from which purified and raw (untreated) water was both sold and provided to communities in areas of the continent without piped water. Before such kiosks existed, people either traveled long distances to access water or captured rainwater, both temperamental and potentially dangerous methods of acquisition. Alternatively, many Africans did—and still do—source water from vendors, such as tanker deliveries in Ghana, water trucks in Somalia, or 'donkey water' in parts of Kenya's Rift Valley, so named because donkeys pull the carts from which water is sold. Often, this water is low-quality and overpriced. A broad swath of RAIN projects set up kiosks to bring water closer to needy populations while ensuring that the water available is purified.[92]

I visited two RAIN water health centers (WHC) in Ghana, one in rural Pakro, one and a half hours north of Accra, and another in peri-urban Ablekuma, closer to the capital city. At both, I met with implementing partners and other stakeholders, including the queen mother and acting chief of Pakro, who provided the land for the WHC. Both WHCs are constructed out of metal and glass, purposefully see-through to mimic the transparency of the operation, I learned. Both have ample logs and records, which anyone can review. And both serve as meeting spots, where the community converges. While both WHCs look similar, the water they treat requires different processes.

In Pakro, the WHC draws river water from a kilometer away in the service of more than 5,000 residents; raw water is used to flush newly built loos in a nearby school, another Coca-Cola-sponsored project. To prepare it for safe use, the water is sent through four stages of purification that rid it of total dissolved solids (TDS), color, microbes, and pathogens. The system is run by a trained operator, who logs daily purchases. Every day, people bring clean jerry cans for refilling, which costs a fraction of what it would elsewhere. The operation is monitored by trained service personnel, who oversee functionality and make sure the water stays within parameters for safe consumption set by WHO and FDA. The entire WHC is sanitized once a month. Since the WHC was established, the queen mother explained, cases of bilharzia and other water-borne illnesses have plummeted in the region. The next step, I heard, was to begin thinking about piping water directly to people's homes.[93]

At Ablekuma, the WHC treats borehole water, which naturally contains higher TDS than river water, by putting it through a six-stage purification process that includes reverse osmosis and ultraviolet light to blast any viruses, bacteria, or pathogens. A backup generator guards against power outages, while chlorinated water is available for consumers to clean dirty cans before refilling. The operation is run by a female operator and monitored for safety and consistency. In total, it services 20,000 people, some of whom travel up to two kilometers to purchase water, while others get their water delivered by tricycles. The water sold to consumers is a quarter of market price and up to high safety standards.[94]

The implementing partner from Ablekuma—Waterhealth—deployed the same technology I saw in Liberia, as part of RAIN's attempt to blunt the impact of the Ebola epidemic in West Africa. There, Ebola treatment units, as they were called, enhanced access to sanitation with some twenty-two million liters of safe, clean water, provided free of charge during the epidemic.[95] These WHCs were only one part of Coca-Cola's multi-prong response to the Ebola outbreak, Alexander B Cummings—himself a Liberian—proudly told me. Besides donating personal protective equipment, the company kept its plants operating and its staff paid in Liberia, Guinea, and Sierra Leone despite a dramatic drop in business during the crisis. Most importantly, through outreach, water, and training, Coke helped make sure no associate or family member was lost to Ebola across all three nations.[96]

On the other side of the continent, I visited a series of RAIN kiosks similarly structured around local requirements and ingenuity. In the flower-growing village of Naivasha, a peri-urban area 100 km northwest of Nairobi, there were an estimated

100,000 people living in low-income areas beyond the reach of formal water service at the time I went. Without government-run water programs, people were accessing water from the nearby lake, threatening the area ecosystem, or from boreholes. Often, those accessing water were young boys who left school to turn a profit via donkey carts. The ground water in the region—while plentiful—is dangerous; it contains excessive amounts of fluoride that, if consumed, as it was and, in some cases, continues to be, causes fluorosis, a medical condition that turns teeth brown and weakens bones. RAIN's 'Water & Sanitation for Naivasha's Peri-Urban Poor,' which ran from 2012 to 2014, attempted to meet these multifaceted needs in five settlements.

I visited one settlement—Mirera—two years after the project there had officially ended to meet with various stakeholders, including the project manager from the key partner in this RAIN initiative, Water and Sanitation for the Urban Poor (WSUP), a registered not-for-profit who works with mandated government institutions to help them deliver a service. Here, WSUP teamed with implementing partner Naivasha Water, as well as the small-scale independent provider, Mirera Suswa. The project centered around existing boreholes, one drilled by Kenya Railway in 1946 and another drilled by a colonial farmer on the Marula Estate Farm in 1951, both of which had been purchased by Mirera Suswa. From these old boreholes, RAIN laid pipes to seven newly created storage tanks. These tanks in turn fed a network of eighteen kiosks spaced approximately fifty to one-hundred meters apart. Each kiosk served approximately 2,000 homes.[97]

In this model, the water is purified on the spot, at each kiosk, using filters created and sold by the Catholic Diocese of Nakuru (another settlement where this project operated). In 1998, the diocese built upon research from Tanzania to work on ways to reduce fluoride in water, witnessing firsthand the devastating effects of fluorosis endemic to the Rift Valley. The result: low-cost filters made from animal bones, purchased from residents, that, when crushed and made into a powder, create a bone-char that successfully captures fluoride. In 2012, the diocese formed the Nakuru De-fluoridation Company (NDC) to sell its filters.[98] Each filter looks like a blue water tank that sits upon a concrete-block kiosk.

In Mirera, each kiosk is run by a female operator, as part of 5x20. Formerly, I heard, many of these women had eked out livings by brewing changaa, the local beer. Now, under RAIN and 5x20, their water kiosks served as starting points for other economic ventures. One woman I met was still just barely getting by, selling water and small amounts of other products, like soap and salt, along with two crates of Coke. Yet, others I spoke to were doing much better, selling a whole range of items alongside their water kiosks, like tampons, Pampers diapers, washing detergent, cocoa, and more.[99] Coke estimated that 159 women and youth were empowered by this particular RAIN initiative.[100] It was not uncommon to pair 5x20 with RAIN. Coca-Cola reported that some 400,000 women were empowered as part of RAIN-related projects.[101]

A significant number of RAIN projects focused on sanitation, too. An estimated two-thirds of sub-Saharan households lack ready access to soap and water, according to a recent report. RAIN initiatives aimed to improve sanitation, some by building toilets, like in Rwanda, and others by constructing small modular units that repurposed water for sanitation purposes, such as in Ghana and Nigeria. Some 1,200 RAIN sanitation efforts were aligned with schools, as was the case in Zambia, Botswana, Benin, and Malawi. There, according to Coke's final report, 'clean water access, sanitation facilities, handwashing stations and hygiene training' had the effect of 'reduced risks of disease and absenteeism,' all while increasing the overall performance of children.[102]

Assessing the success of RAIN projects, Coke reported that in just over a decade, 1.1 million Africans had access to improved sanitation, while more than 450,000 hectares of land had improved water management. The company also announced that it had exceeded water neutrality. In 2020, 170% of the water used in its finished products was replenished in nature. The company then set new goals for 2030 that included enhancing regenerative water use, focusing on climate adaptations, working further to improve access to water and sanitation, focusing on women and girls, enhancing watershed health, and expanding to focus on water in agriculture, particularly in water-stressed regions.[103]

Waste

Most RAIN projects lack any Coke branding, blending into the scenery. Conversely, the most visible marker of Coca-Cola's imprint on the planet is its wrapping, the cans and bottles that, if littered, mar the landscape and, if trashed, clog landfills and waterways. A common refrain among Coca-Cola personnel is that packaging remains one of the key global threats to the business. In an ideal scenario, soda would be sold without any package at all. Witness the birth of the Freestyle fountain machine that blends Coca-Cola products on the spot. While touted for its innovative design and technology, the Freestyle has the added benefit of enhancing the sale of fountain beverages, which require but a cup for enjoyment. An additional fact about the Freestyle: the Georgia factory that produces the machine is run off methane gas siphoned from a nearby landfill, a green innovation. Promising as they may be, at present, the expensive Freestyle machines are only available in Asia, Europe, and North America.[104] And, in any event, it is hard to imagine the fountain business eclipsing packaged beverages.

Coca-Cola has long been aware that packaging presents sustainability challenges. In part, this is because soda products are easily spotted items in a sea of refuse, making drink companies ready targets for environmental ire. 'We don't deny that the bright red can and the familiar bottle are a part of the problem,' J Paul Austin responded to criticisms in 1970. 'And we've been taking steps designed to reduce their numbers in places where they don't belong.'[105] In 1970s America, taking steps meant mounting campaigns against littering and in favor of using (and returning) two-way glass bottles, where they were still in use. Coca-Cola was similarly singled out for over-contributing to the refuse problem in South Africa in the early 1980s. There too the corporation responded, initially, with deflection, saying its products were just more visible than others. And there too the company initially fell back upon its philanthropic work, noting its support for the Keep South Africa Tidy Association and placing blame at the feet of consumers unwilling to dispose of products properly.[106]

When Coca-Cola began producing one-way, disposable packaging, consumer demand for convenience and heavy marketing drove the production of these packages, thereby replacing returnable glass bottles (RBGs) with cans and, eventually, PET (polyethylene terephthalate), or plastic bottles. No longer bound to return glass bottles to a store to retain a deposit, consumers were free to dispose of cans and plastic bottles however they wished, driving up the visible refuse problem. In response, Coca-Cola began contributing to nonprofits that worked to enhance the rate and efficiency of recycling initiatives in the United States and, eventually, elsewhere in the world.[107]

In America, recycling initiatives initially strove to get consumers to separate their trash and municipalities to enact curbside recycling pick-up. Beyond those two processes, it remains necessary to get recyclables to be re-used instead of simply dumped in landfills. This is a two-pronged problem. One, people do not recycle all items that could be recycled. Secondly, a vast amount of trash that people think they recycle does not actually make it into anything but the ground. According to the the Environmental Protection Agency, in 2017, only about 35% of all waste in America was recycled or composted. Within that figure, only 8% of plastic was recycled.[108] Some experts estimate that as much as 70% of recyclable material ends up in landfills or trash heaps around the world.[109]

How and why American recyclable material does not ultimately get recycled is a complicated story. In part, it has to do with the way items are discarded at the source, since even small amounts of cross-contamination can cause problems down the line. Secondly, the MERFs, or material recovery facilities that process would-be recyclables for end-production use, are easily clogged and are themselves places of contamination. Most importantly, the cost to separate a ton of recyclables is often far greater than the worth of said material, particularly when it comes to PET. PET is useful for making items like fleece and car mats. Yet, recycled PET (rPET) is always up against virgin PET in terms of cost. The cost of virgin PET, in turn, is related to the cost of oil, from which it is made. If the cost of oil is low, so too is the cost of virgin PET, making the almost always higher cost of rPET prohibitive.[110] It is far cheaper to just dump plastic in landfills.

Up until recently, China regularly saved the day for much of the world by buying its trash. Some was repurposed, but more often it landed up in landfills and trash heaps, often in the poorest parts of the world. In 2017, China announced a ban on recyclables, followed by a ban on all waste importation.[111] The result: a dire need to find a better way to deal with the growing global trash problem, much of which continues to be shipped to parts of the world least able to deal with it. The problem of refuse, and in particular plastic waste, remains a thorn in the side of the drinks business. As activists point out repeatedly,

Coca-Cola, and others, contribute disproportionately to the world's plastic problem, bearing, as many see it, disproportionate responsibility for its cure.[112] Coca-Cola has responded to this challenge by backing various NGOs that aim to 'close the loop' from use to reuse, many of which are trying to find innovative solutions to the problems posed by plastic (one of which is detailed later).[113] The company has also thrown time and energy into creating green bottles, a portion of whose PET comes from plants, thereby absorbing CO_2 in their creation. Coca-Cola is also working on a paper bottle.[114] Critics of Coca-Cola call these actions and others like them 'greenwashing,' meant to make the company look good while doing little to root out the problem.[115]

The story of packaging and waste in Africa is somewhat different than that in the global north. Unlike in the United States, the bulk of Coca-Cola sales in Africa comes from returnable glass bottles. This raises the question of whether glass is preferable, from an environmental point of view. An RBG has a theoretical lifespan of as much as twenty-five to forty uses.[116] Yet, not all glass bottles make it back to the bottler for reuse. I recall walking in KwaMashu township in KwaZulu Natal when a local medicine man offered his wares in empty Coke bottles, far from a rare sight. The glass figures in Ngwenya Glass works, near the border between Eswatini and South Africa, similarly advertise, 'In my previous life I was a Coke bottle,' no doubt to the chagrin of the bottler who described to me ongoing schemes to reclaim empty bottles.[117] Still, if it can be captured, unlike plastic, glass is endlessly recyclable, at least in theory. In practice, it is often not easily recyclable, for a variety of reasons, including color.[118] Glass is also heavier than plastic, which means that transporting glass bottles requires more fuel than is the case for their lighter counterparts, important in many parts of Africa where the distance from bottler to point of sale is great. Additionally, RBGs are made from sand, itself a resource, and require washing, which uses water, placing additional burdens on the environment. Thus, the answer to whether glass or plastic is more sustainable differs depending on time and place.

Whether or not RBGs are better for the planet, one-way plastics are on the rise in Africa, as elsewhere, alarming environmentalists.[119] Still, the waste, energy, and recycling people I spoke to within the Coke system—whether based in the United States, Europe, or Africa—were techno-optimists, sure that there are solutions to the problems posed by packaging waiting to be found. Some explained to me that landfills can be seen as kinds of mines, capable of being plumbed for, among other things, energy found in emitted gasses.[120] Already, as mentioned previously, this technology is being used to power the Freestyle factory in Georgia. Speaking about waste in Africa, specifically, many put their faith in enterprises like PETCO, the industry-created collaboration driving recapturing and recycling efforts in South Africa to great effect.[121]

PETCO is a nonprofit PET Recycling Company, which was established in 2004 as a voluntary consortium of South African food-grade PET resin users to self-regulate the recycling of plastic bottles. From the start, Coca-Cola was a key partner driving the process of, de facto, subsidizing in-country recycling and trying to close the loop from use to reuse. The ongoing threat that the government will attempt to regulate PET spurs it on, showing a prime example of how corporate citizens self-regulate in lieu of government mandate.

A decade into its inception, PETCO drove an 822% increase in recycling tonnage in South Africa, helping lower CO_2 levels and reduce landfill shortage, thrusting recycling efforts over 50%.[122] To put this in perspective, various studies estimate that parts of Europe and the United States rarely exceed 30% recycling of post-consumer waste; only the most committed nations surpass 50%.[123] As Casper Durandt, who served as both chairman of PETCO and technical manager for Coca-Cola South Africa when we spoke, explained to me, 'Recycling only works when the money works. So, in the case of PET bottles, we need to put the money in to make it work.'[124] Putting in the money often entails balancing available bottles with demand for PET for use as fiber, PETCO's Business Development Manager and sustainability economist Alistair Schorn told me. PETCO does this by working with a network of trash collectors and end-use facilities.

One such end-use plant is MPACT, the only bottle-to-bottle recycling plant on the African continent. At this plant, PET is broken down, washed, and repurposed into plastic pellets for use in food-grade products. Food-grade resin, as it is known, is then blended with virgin PET to create recycled bottles. MPACT employs 150 people at its plant and, in collaboration with PETCO, creates tens of thousands of employment opportunities for trash collectors.

The PETCO/MPACT model is at the forefront of PET use globally. After demonstrating that its robust system has the capacity to close the loop on packaging, it was exported to Kenya, where it drove up recycling rates 35% in two years. Similar programs have been established in Ethiopia and Tanzania.[125] I saw advertising for other like-minded enterprises in Zimbabwe in 2017 and witnessed other smaller Coca-Cola-driven recycling schemes in Ghana, Rwanda, and Nigeria.[126] Everywhere, I heard the same story: without Coca-Cola and other resin users subsidizing recycling, there simply was not the political will to enact it, particularly in the many parts of the continent without any sort of municipal rubbish infrastructure.

It bears saying, as well, that Africans have long dealt with Coca-Cola refuse in their own ways. As early as 1965, Hausa bead makers in northern Nigeria were using green Coca-Cola bottles to make much sought-after green Bida beads, alongside beer bottles for brown beads and Pond's face cream bottles for clear ones. 'There really isn't anything the Coca-Cola people can do about it,' the company's *Coca-Cola Overseas* stated in feigned frustration, 'although they are the ones who have to pay for the bottles!'[127] Like the expensive glassware available at Ngwenya, Africans continue to repurpose Coke glass in unforeseen ways.

Coca-Cola caps, wrappers, and cans have likewise long been raw materials for artisans, generating a boggling range of trinkets for purchase at road-side shops and 'chic Afrique' boutiques across the continent and beyond. In the corporate Coca-Cola archive in Atlanta, I first heard the ironic term 'Coke crap' for such items, but for me they are charming evidence of on-the-ground recycling. The more apt term for such items, heard more often in the Coke world, is 'upcycled,' a word that notes when something has been repurposed to be of greater use than its initial inception. Some 5x20 programs embrace such upcycling, partnering with the (mostly) women behind them, as well.[128]

That is not all that happens to Coke refuse. In Johannesburg, I met Mbongeni Buthelezi, an acclaimed artist who uses a hair dryer to heat discarded plastic wrappers from PET bottles to create subtle portraits, sold the world over.[129] He explained to me that, as a struggling artist, he looked in the trash heaps around his home for usable mediums from which to create.[130] In Ghana, a children's center walls are built using sand-filled PET bottles as so-called eco-bricks.[131] In Uganda, fishermen use empty Coke bottles as buoys for their nets.[132] And in Soweto, 'skylights' using empty plastic bottles bring light into shack homes. When we look at how Africans re-use Coke refuse, we find no shortage of ingenuity.

To be sure, acquiring material for these and other projects can be difficult, dangerous work, particularly if it requires picking from trash heaps. Coca-Cola is clear that it does not support landfill picking, which is dangerous and unhygienic. Through

PETCO, Coke does support roadside pickers. If you get up early enough in, say, Johannesburg, you will see armies of mostly young men walking the streets, trolleys in tow, carefully poring over roadside trash. These waste- or trolley-preneurs arose to meet a need they saw. If they could rifle through people's trash, they could find valuable plastic, glass, and cans that could then be exchanged for money. PETCO noticed these workers and sought to incubate income opportunities for them as it too recognized the use of such roadside picking. In 2016, Durandt put the number of folks doing this type of work at around 40,000, with about 18% of them scavenging on landfills and the remaining majority working roadside.[133] In 2017, I heard that the number was 60,000.[134] Coca-Cola and PETCO support those pickers who go through rubbish outside the point of consumption, though they are clear that this work is difficult and degrading; the average trolleypreneur was making about 200–250R a day in 2016, hardly a livable wage.[135] But, in the absence of available employment as well as other viable methods of trash collecting, Coke and PETCO are nevertheless trying to empower these collectors. Together, they provide reflective vests, safer trolleys, and plastic collection bags; PETCO pays pickers on debit cards and trains them in basic business skills in further attempts to bring dignity to this work. They also work with some collectors to acquire baling machines, thereby scaling up their operations. PETCO, and through it, Coca-Cola, capitalizes on pickers' labor to make recycling work just as trolleypreneurs better themselves via the process.[136]

Energy

Entwined with questions of Coca-Cola refuse are questions around Coke's energy use. In 2013, the company established global sustainability targets that included reducing its global CO_2 emissions by 25% by 2020, which it has said it achieved. In

2020, the company set a new goal of another 25% reduction in absolute greenhouse gas emissions by 2030 and, thereafter, a goal of net-zero emissions by 2050. To reach these milestones, the company has established a multi-tiered program that addresses each step in its value chain. According to self-reporting, the bulk of Coca-Cola's carbon footprint comes from its supply chain, leading to its investment in sustainable farming practices and other outreach programs.[137] Elsewhere, Coca-Cola tries to source renewable energy (for manufacturing), focuses on fuel efficiency (for distribution), and replace and enhance energy devices in its plants and coolers.

The challenges of carbon emissions reduction in Africa are hampered by the same obstacles that thwart waste reduction on the continent: unstable regulatory environments, the predominance of small—and therefore less efficient—plants, and underdeveloped provider sectors. In most parts of the continent, bottlers have their own generators to supplement erratic energy grids. In some places, there are small-scale solar initiatives that provide supplemental energy to plants.[138] Additionally, some bottlers have set up cogeneration schemes, where fuel burned powers the plant with little loss in transfer, while the fumes from the fuels produce the CO_2 needed in beverages.[139]

The question of reducing CO_2 in Africa is tied up in general energy problems on the continent, as it is in many parts of the world. In 2015, the United Nations set a goal to see 'affordable, reliable, and modern energy' sources available globally by 2030, an uneasy target for Africa.[140] As of 2017, nearly one third of Africans lacked access to electricity and more than half relied on biomass for basic energy needs.[141] While Coca-Cola is not in the business of electrifying the world, it has used its convening power—in golden triangle initiatives—to tackle some of these problems, most visibly with its EKOCENTERS, mentioned in the preface to this book.

Coca-Cola's EKOCENTERs are, in their bright-red glory, the epitome of the company's sustainability work on the continent. At their full capacity, EKOCENTERS are kiosks that do the following: sell Coca-Cola products alongside a wide range of sundry in a shop; create a community center; purify and sell local water supplies; provide renewable energy and internet capability; and empower the women who work at the shop and water tap, while delivering ancillary jobs, such as maintaining water and energy infrastructure. Coca-Cola first launched the EKOCENTER in 2013 South Africa, using the innovative 'slingshot' technology that, ultimately, proved unsustainable.[142] It relaunched in 2016, in Rwanda, with a partnership among Pentair, Ericsson, MedShare, and Phillips, along with Solarkiosk, TIGO Rwanda, and local brewer Bralirwa, whose core business is beer brewing but who bottles Coca-Cola in Rwanda. The center was launched to much fanfare by Paul Kagame (President of Rwanda) and Odette Uwamariya (Governor of its Eastern Province), alongside Coke CEO Muhtar Kent, Randy Hogan (the CEO of Pentair), Reverend Jesse Jackson, and Erica J Barks-Ruggles (the American Ambassador to Rwanda). That year, Coca-Cola placed over 100 EKOCENTERS on the African continent.[143]

One of its creators calls the EKOCENTER a kind of ecosystem, able to encapsulate mercantile, social, and medical needs.[144] This was visible to me when I attended the 2016 launch in Rwanda. Beside the kiosk is a seating area with room for sixty people, space for small-scale food vendors, pit latrines with sanitation stations, and a telecommunications tower. Adjacent is a free-standing water pump that provides both raw municipal water and water that has been purified by reverse osmosis to meet WHO standards. Behind that is a medical clinic frequented by 100–200 people daily.

The water pump, kiosk, and telecom tower are powered by a solar system, which yields enough power to run the water pump, hold some for backup for the healthcare center, and sell excess to small-scale entrepreneurs. The fees received help maintain the device, which is monitored remotely, but fixed locally by trained mechanics. At the time I visited, the kiosk was generating €4,000 monthly revenue. Both the water pump and the kiosk are run by 5x20-trained women entrepreneurs.

In the days surrounding the 2016 launch, I spoke to dozens of people involved in making the flagship Ruhunda EKOCENTER a reality, from employees of convening partners to corporate Coca-Cola personnel, directors of the Coca-Cola Foundation, 5x20 stewards, and more. I also talked to the 5x20 women who work the water kiosk and local shop. What struck me was the emotion behind my conversations. Without fail, I heard stories—often tearfully told—around the ethics and importance of bringing water, energy, connectivity, and empowerment structures to Africa. And without exception, I heard the same refrain: though there were many partners involved in this ambitious project, Coca-Cola had convened it. 'What would you do if Coke stopped doing this work?,' I asked one director who, like so many others involved in the project, struck me as something of an activist for its cause. 'Who else might continue a project like this?,' I pressed. No answer came to mind.

Conclusion

In his 2015 examination of Coca-Cola's ecological impact, *Citizen Coke: The Making of Coca-Cola Capitalism*, Bartow J Elmore levels what is a common critique at the company. Elmore writes that while Coke has undoubtedly done good work, primarily around water, it has done so at little cost to itself. According to his research, Coca-Cola's investment in water projects in 2010 was but a 'drop in the bucket' compared to the company's net profit that same year, making it appear to be but 'partial payments for services rendered.' Elmore further asserts that the tax breaks Coca-Cola receives from its green initiatives outweigh costs and muddy the question of whether communities 'are giving more than they get' when it comes to Coca-Cola.[145]

At the same time, while a decade plus of RAIN work reached approximately six million Africans, that is but a fraction of the number of people in need of clean water.[146] We could make similar claims about the insufficiency of other initiatives in this chapter given the scale of need. And, yet, as Monica Ellis explained, RAIN remains the single largest sustained effort to tackle water problems in Africa.[147] The same might be said of Coke's other projects. This, in turn, prompts us to query—as many do—whether governments, rather than a business, should be driving sustainability initiatives. Zoomed out even farther, we could ask if all this green work is but what critics call greenwashing, looking good without doing much.

We are primed by the times we live in to be cynical, thinking the worst of big business. And, there is undeniable truth in the excesses and limitations of capitalism. On the ground across the continent, I saw a company committed to sustaining its business by protecting its license to operate, much as Elmore suggests. But I also saw scores of Coca-Cola employees and partners committed to sustainability, who set long-term, quantifiable goals for helping empower women; clean water; promote healthy communities; source ample energy, and more, primarily by pulling together stakeholders and investing time, money, and resources to effect change.[148] I spoke to no one who was in it just to make the company look good; if anything, the folks who work in Coke-driven sustainability initiatives are exceedingly dedicated, making the business somewhat beside the point. Similarly, I spoke to no Africans moving blindly into exploitative relationships; all were clear about what they were doing and why, and all expressed a sense of control over their fate. These savvy agents were making full use of a company to gain purchase on their futures. At the same time, while it seems theoretically preferable to have elected officials beholden to their populace doing this work, in practice, many African governments have demonstrated that they often cannot or will not do so.

There is a sense, then, that the sustainability projects Coca-Cola has spent the last decade undertaking in Africa are akin to the missionary endeavor of an earlier era. Here is a global entity working with local insiders to make substantive changes, secure in its faith in the goodness and health of its mission. And here are communities, willfully seeking to reap the rewards of participation, even if it comes at a cost. There is, thus, an uneasy compromise at play. On the one hand, you have a business doing work that no one else can or will do, much of it positively life-altering, some of it serving to obfuscate the role of governments. On the other hand, you have increased consumption of a product that itself yields ecological and biological stress. That, then, is the final drumbeat beneath the sustainability work I saw, questions I take up in the conclusion: how much can the planet and human body endure, and at what cost?

CONCLUSION

In the opening minutes of the 1980 comedy *The Gods Must be Crazy*, a pilot tosses an empty Coca-Cola bottle out of an airplane and into the Kalahari Desert, inadvertently upending life for the San who find it.[1] 'It was the strangest and most beautiful thing they had ever seen,' a faux documentarian narrates, adding that these childlike 'little people,' as they are dubiously presented to us, 'wondered why the gods had sent it to them.' After initial confusion, the San begin experimenting with the bottle, using it to make music, prepare food, cure animal skins, and more. 'Every day they discovered a new use for the thing,' we hear, because 'it was harder and heavier and smoother than anything they'd ever known.' It appeared to be, in fact, 'the most useful thing the gods had ever given them.' Overnight, this 'thing they had never needed before became a necessity.' But like the Biblical apple, the promise of the unmistakable hobble skirt bottle quickly turns curse, as competition breeds new emotions like anger and greed. Before long, the San retitle the beautiful bottle 'the evil thing' and scheme to return it to the gods.[2]

'There's no message' to this slapstick comedy, South African writer/director Peter Uys said in 1985, downplaying criticisms of the film's condescending portrayal of the San and its nonexistent reckoning with apartheid. What motivated him, he said, was the

259

question of whether 'a tribe' could come to covet a product like Coca-Cola, which he saw as emblematic of modern throwaway society while still being 'a beautiful thing, if you've never seen glass before.' The film was wildly successful.[3]

Read through the lens of the history of Coca-Cola in Africa, Uys's film becomes parable. In the early twentieth century, Coca-Cola bottles all but arrived from the sky in much of Africa. They were not, as we recall, immediately welcomed. Like the mythical San of the film, many wondered what to make of this drink. This was not irrational. Coca-Cola is not a necessity, as many would-be consumers understood. As elsewhere, Coca-Cola needed to harness its corporate wing and local bottlers to create an African consumer base with a taste for its products and a willingness to pay for them. Such efforts worked. Before long—as in the film—many Africans came to see this thing that they had never before needed as indispensable. It helped that as Coke grew, so did its attendant contributions to employment, industry, infrastructure, agriculture, sport, the arts, and other components to industrialized life in the Capitalocene. This too was deliberate. For, as is no doubt clear at this stage of this book, Coca-Cola understood full well that entwining its inessential product with the essential anchored it. Yet, that is not all it took to ensure Coca-Cola's presence on this continent.

This book has demonstrated that Coca-Cola's durability is the result of becoming African over its more than 100 years on the continent. The stories herein, about localization, diversification, and responsiveness, have shown some manifestations of this Africanization. As such, this book has made the case for reading this corporation's presence in Africa as neither evidence of American consumer over-reach nor African duplicity, but rather something more iterative and, ultimately, more interesting. This is not to say that African players directed the entirety of Coca-Cola's story in Africa or to assert that the ever-growing presence of a drinks business is good for the continent. Nor is it to claim a singular African stance or a uniform experience. If anything, this book has tried equally to point out the limitations of Coca-Cola's adaptations to underscore the unevenness of the company's localness.

Still, considering the history and footprint of Coca-Cola in Africa as a result of Africanization (however incomplete) places Africans front and center, reminding us that the capitalized are agents able to assert power over, in this case, a multinational corporation. At the same time, some of the most defining moments of this era are cast in new light: racist political and capitalist structures; the end of colonialism and apartheid; the rise of industrialized, consumer classes; the invention of Africa; efforts at sustainability and empowerment; and more look different when refracted through the bottle. Synthesized as part of a biography, the narrative in this book also suggests the utility of a pan-African scope. Here, echoes of history come up against exceptions to render visible both similarities and differences across the continent. At the same time, the very nature of a continent-wide examination delineates gaps requiring future investigation. The story of Coke in Africa reveals much, in other words, including what it is we do not know.

The history told herein shows how Coca-Cola became visible nearly everywhere—its red dotting landscapes far and wide— and seamlessly enmeshed in the fabric of life, becoming what philosopher Slavoj Žižek calls the 'perfect commodity,' both object and desire for the object at once. Echoing Marx, Žižek explains that around the globe Coke became more than itself.[4] We see this clearly in Africa. Coke is a fizzy brown drink, but it is also other types of soda, clean water, jobs, soccer, music, happiness, and more. This is partly because of the drink's (and its siblings') pleasing and consistent flavor, well-honed by quality assurance and commitment to detail. But that alone does not

suffice as explanation. As Žižek reminds us, the strength of the
Coke brand hinges on more than taste, a 'mysterious something
more' that cannot be detected by 'chemical analysis.'[5]

Within the Coke system, this amorphous something is called
brand love, its import clear to more than a few cheater brands.
These would-be competitors may taste and look like any number
of Coca-Cola products, but that alone is rarely enough to unseat
king Coke. Take, as an example, Mo Cola in Tanzania. The
brainchild of billionaire Mohammed Dewji, Mo Cola tries to
capture market share from Coca-Cola with rival drinks that taste
good and cost less than Coke products. The problem, as the
founder put it in 2016, was that Coke has 'this amazing formula'
that constrains Mo Cola's potential.[6] Folks at corporate Coke see
the issue differently: even if rivals could replicate Coke's formula
precisely, they tell me, competing beverages could still never
surpass the aura around the real thing.

As another example, witness the 2016 Johannesburg break-up
of a counterfeit Valpre water operation, one of Coke's signature
spring water brands. When police happened upon the outfit,
hundreds of thousands of seemingly genuine Valpre bottles were
being filled with hose water filtered through a rag. News coverage
of the story showed the authentic-looking fillers, seals, and Coca-
Cola-branded labels for the decidedly inauthentic water. That the
bottles were bound primarily for informal shops frequented by
marginalized South Africans speaks to problems around equity
in water consumption and perhaps helps explain the longevity
of the fraud.[7] The bust had, in fact, happened by chance. No
complaint had driven police into the makeshift factory. In other
words, the fakes had been accepted as real. Until they were not.

More than a century after Coke landed in Africa, it is not
enough to look or taste like a Coca-Cola product. The real thing
matters. Coke worked hard to ensure this threshold through its
multi-pronged efforts at localness, just as Africans labored to

force the corporation to suit their evolving needs. All the while, Coca-Cola focused on its growth, forever eyeing the horizon. Yet, partway through the twenty-first century, whatever notion of continued expansion the company may have once harbored has come up against human and planetary limits unlike others it faced before. These very real borders around consumption and production now stand before Coca-Cola and its future in Africa. They are the same boundaries, I suggest in closing, that may impede all our futures.

Bodily Boundaries

The hard truth for a beverage company is that humans can only drink so much. Coca-Cola tracks intake of its products through per capita consumption rates that measure growth and guide national investments. It is these metrics that show how much room there is for increased consumption in most parts of Africa, for instance.[8] Unspoken is, how much will be enough? Or, put better, at what point is too much?

While ingesting non-alcoholic fluids sounds benign, not all drinks are equally healthy. Coca-Cola once pronounced that all beverages aid in hydration, but these days most people can recognize that a bottle of sugary, carbonated water hydrates, but only at a cost. This leads to what Kirsti Iivonen, an expert on organizational structures and business ethics, has called the 'strategic sustainability paradox' at Coca-Cola's core: on the one hand, the company promotes healthy, youthful, active living; on the other, its central product, Coke red, is chock full of sugar and caffeine, putting it at odds with the very image the company promotes.

Iivonen explains that the company—like others in its position—navigates this contradiction by creating a 'complex and intricate web of defensive responses that seek to portray harmony and obfuscate responsibility.'[9] Here she is denigrating the kinds of initiatives that have been detailed in this book. Sociologist David Fig has written likewise, explaining how this works in South Africa specifically, where he describes corporate social responsibility efforts—such as those detailed in the previous chapter—as but greenwash, meant to render objectionable actions palatable. He has been particularly critical of work like 5x20, whose success is predicated on enhancing product consumption. By creating what he terms 'irresistible notions of partnership, accommodation, win–win situations, synthesis and compromise' that woo the public, companies like Coca-Cola 'distract[...] the gullible into believing that business has a serious sustainability agenda.'[10] Both Iivonen and Fig give voice to the critique raised at the end of last chapter: that Coca-Cola's good work comes at a cost. Nowhere is this corporate paradox clearer than in Coca-Cola's dealing with sugar, one of the two biggest threats to the company today.

As a widely consumed substance of dubious health benefits, sugar had until recently escaped the same level of attention as alcohol and tobacco, other so-called sin products. Yet, by the early twenty-first century, the global rise of noncommunicable diseases (NCD) prompted increased scrutiny on sugar intake. Soaring rates of obesity and dental caries, among other ailments, suggested that sugar—which had, by then, infiltrated a wide range of food and drink products—needed attention. In 2015, the World Health Organization (WHO) issued guidelines calling for a steep universal reduction in sugar intake since NCDs were now the leading cause of mortality, totaling 68% of world deaths in 2012.[11] To blunt this figure, the WHO recommended limiting free sugar intake—which includes soda—to less than 10% total energy, with a strong suggestion to get that number below 5%.[12] Importantly for Africa, the WHO stated that nearly 75% of all NCDs occurred in countries designated as low and middle

CONCLUSION

income. Importantly for Coke, it voiced a growing concern that free sugars that took the form of 'sugar-sweetened beverages' (SSBs) were a particular problem. Not only did they lead to higher caloric intake, but their empty calories also inhibited eating healthier foods, creating the perfect scenario for weight gain, unhealthy consumption, and heightened risk of NCDs.[13]

Public health researchers describe this phenomenon in South Africa, a wealthy African country where soaring sugar consumption in the second half of the twentieth century landed the nation eighth highest in terms of sugar intake globally in 2011.[14] By 2017, the average South African was ingesting about ninety-nine grams (or twenty-three and a half teaspoons) of added sugar a day, four times the WHO 2015 recommendation.[15] Sugar, these researchers theorized, was a colonial activity that had infiltrated both 'the economy... and diets over an extended historical period,' laying claim to both and spawning attendant troubles.[16] And those complications were vast. A 2013 study on sugar-related morbidity and mortality in South Africa tallied approximately 2,000 incidents of amputations from diabetes and 800 incidents of blindness from diabetes per year, with NCDs accounting for 40% of total deaths.[17]

These same researchers also determined that, while South Africans had once ingested sugar from a wide range of products, by 2012, a full third was coming from soft drinks alone, echoing the WHO's finding that SSBs were disproportionately to blame for the sugar crisis, in this case in South Africa. This was not hard to imagine. In 2017, a single 330 ml soda contained one to two teaspoons more sugar than the WHO recommended imbibing in a day.[18] Anecdotally, the outward face of poverty in South Africa looked like a typical low-income meal, a loaf of white bread and a two-liter bottle of Coca-Cola, an all-too-common, if nutritionally empty, sight. Most disturbing, as a rich country, South Africa stood as a bellwether for the continent should per capita consumption levels of liquid sugar rise alongside GPDs. 'Sugar,' researchers concluded, 'should be portrayed as the "new tobacco"' and treated as such.[19]

South African sugar scholars thus followed in the footsteps of others worldwide to lend their support to a tax on SSBs, proposed by the government in 2016.[20] From the government's point of view, such a tax would serve both health and fiscal needs. Not only could it disincentive sugar consumption, but such a tax could also augment government coffers. As happened elsewhere (like in parts of the United States, Great Britain, and Mexico), when SSB taxes were proposed and/or implemented, there was immediate push-back from beverage producers, including Coca Cola.[21]

How did Coke resist? First, Coke focused attention on its corporate social responsibility work, the very initiatives that were documented in the previous chapter, as evidence of its fundamental commitment to health. Parallel to this, Coca-Cola initially denied that sugar was to blame for any ills, at its most nefarious by funding scientific studies and nonprofits that suggested that diet rather than sugar drove obesity and type two diabetes.[22] After these tactics were exposed as astroturfing—that is, muddying the source of knowledge to serve a predetermined end—Coca-Cola changed strategies again. Sugar taxes are regressive, some Coca-Cola executives began claiming instead, since they shift the financial burden onto those least able to carry it, normally consumers and small business owners.[23] Eventually, this line of thought also petered out, as Coke executives began to realize that fighting such taxes was likely futile. Instead, in South Africa, the company began calling for the sugar tax to be born equally across the industry, starting at the point of raw cane sale. Such an alignment would ensure that sugary yogurt, coffee, and juice drinks, not to mention chocolate and other sweets, were taxed on par with sugar-sweetened sodas. Some sugar researchers agreed with this line of thinking, as well.[24] Ultimately, the sugar tax was implemented in April 2018 under the Health Promotion Levy, the first sugar tax on the African continent, and one of the first of its kind to base the tax on grams per sugar and not product type.[25]

In the noise surrounding the sugar debate, the voices of regular Africans are hard to come by in any quantifiable way. Anecdotally, I asked everyone I interviewed and encountered—from men who work bottling lines to women who hawk cold Cokes by the roadside to folks with no clear relationship to the soda industry—how they felt about sugar. Most expressed similar sentiments. They were aware that large amounts of sugar were bad for them and, when asked about young children, were adamant that they did not allow them to consume sugary sodas, save on special occasions. It is possible that my interviewees were trying to tell me what they assumed I wanted to hear. Yet, given that most of my other questions were around the proliferation of the Coca-Cola business, I was inclined to take them at their word. Differently, I heard from some Coca-Cola personnel about push-back they received around diet versions of Coke. Their research indicated that some consumers were wary of paying the same amount for a product that contained fewer sought-after calories.[26] How do we align these sketches—while admittedly incomplete—with evidence of rising levels of liquid sugar consumption in Africa? At most, they suggest an unevenness to consumer education around sugar alongside the all too human tendency to consume a known sin product. Simultaneously, when it comes to soaring sugar intake, we do well to remember that the problem is physiological and, ultimately, not unique to Africa.[27]

Still, for all the handwringing around Coca-Cola's greenwashing and astroturfing, in the second decade of the twenty-first century, it started to look like maybe sugar was not going to cause Coca-Cola's downfall after all. Coca-Cola had seen the writing on the wall when it came to sugar and had begun acting accordingly.

Right around the time sugar taxes were being passed globally, Coca-Cola shifted gears. First, the company began shrinking packages, since smaller sizes meant fewer calories per serving. Then, the company reaffirmed its commitment not to market to children under thirteen years old.[28] Concurrently, the company continued rolling out lower- and zero-calorie versions of its drinks, while expanding into the still, or non-carbonated, beverage market. By 2016, fourteen of Coke's twenty-billion-dollar brands were still, while in the US, soda consumption plummeted to a thirty-year low, an indication, some said, of what was coming globally.[29] Most importantly, the company began noiselessly retooling the formulas of some of its cornerstone products, including Sprite in Australia and Fanta in Europe, mostly without any repercussions. 'Coca-Cola has quietly been removing sugar from its drinks—and no one seems to care,' journalist Chase Purdy penned in 2017, suggesting that 'In hindsight, the corporate fuss over sugar was misplaced.'[30]

When asked in 2016 whether the company was 'actively trying to reduce sugar,' then president and COO James Quincey did not miss a beat. 'Absolutely,' he said, we are pushing 'reformulations around the world to bring the added sugar down in a number of our famous brands but also innovating new zero sugar versions' in the hopes of 'helping drive the business in revenue with less sugar through reformulation, innovation, and smaller packages.'[31] Rather than fight the growing anti-sugar tide, Coca-Cola had decided to ride it.

From a marketing standpoint, Coca-Cola addressed sugar concerns differently, by introducing an advertisement campaign that, for the first time, subsumed signature Coke red within a newly named 'One Brand.' At its Paris launch in early 2016,

Coca-Cola's Chief Marketing Officer Marcos de Quinto explained that the novel global marketing strategy would bring Coca-Cola, Diet Coca-Cola, Coca-Cola Zero, and Coca-Cola Life together as part of a newly packaged single brand.[32] These would be celebrated under a creative campaign called 'Taste the Feeling,' which would roll out worldwide that year.[33]

Taste the Feeling recentered marketing around Coca-Cola products' taste, with hundreds of images and ten new television commercials, which used original music and close shots of bubbling beverages to play upon viewers' senses. The ads celebrated the universality of everyday moments and everyday struggles, suggesting, via diverse vignettes, that a cold Coke—of any kind— adds something inimitable to life's little episodes. The drink, with or without the sugar, embodies the very taste of them.[34] When One Brand arrived in Zimbabwe in May 2016, Coke's Marketing Activations Manager, Vee Chibanda, explained the company's thinking for an African audience. 'The new "One Brand" approach will bring together all Coca-Cola Trademark products,' she said, in order to 'reinforc[e] our commitment to offer our consumers' choice with more clarity and show how everyone can enjoy the specialness of an ice-cold Coca-Cola, with or without calories, based on their taste, lifestyle and diet.'[35] Coca-Cola was there for all consumers, regardless of their position on sugar.

Taken to its logical end, the One Brand campaign promotes the idea that Fanta or Coke Zero or Sparkling Valpre are all 'Coke,' extending Žižek's understanding of the commodity and changing Coke red into something of a mascot, rather than the company's bread and butter. Reflecting on this unprecedented shift, financial analyst Asit Sharma mused in 2016, 'It's not hard to suspect deep ambivalence among The Coca-Cola Company's management about the company's flagship product.'[36] For the first time in its history, signature Coke red appeared as just another part of Coca-Cola's brand.

In Africa, the rise of One Brand also correlated with a landmark reorganization of the company on the continent, which saw the bulk of the business amalgamated from a central base. In November 2014, The Coca-Cola Company announced its intention to merge with two South Africa bottlers—SAB Miller and Coca-Cola Sabco—to form Coca-Cola Beverages Africa (CCBA), creating the largest bottler in Africa. Controlling twelve markets (and 40% of volume sales in Africa), with plans to expand further, CCBA became the eighth-largest bottler worldwide. Philipp H Gutsche, son of Philipp Rowland Gutsche—whom we met back in Chapter 1—would chair the Board of CCBA from his headquarters at the Lakeside Plant in Port Elizabeth, South Africa.[37]

When I met Phil Gutsche on a placid May morning in 2017, we opened the day with ice-cold Coke reds, pulled from a hidden refrigerator in the corner of his office. It was his second soda of the day. Gutsche was happy to walk down memory lane with me, proudly showing off the company's accounting books from the 1940s and recounting early memories of running around with Richard Cook (Alan Cook's older brother), of Sparletta fame. 'It's amazing, if you think of it,' Gutsche considered, 'where I came from. From 450,000 cases,' when he began as a temporary worker during his school holidays, to their recent figures, 'just short of a billion.' 'It's progress,' he declared contentedly.

When our talk turned to sugar, Gutsche was nonplussed. He recalled the early excise tax that nearly crippled his father's fledgling Sabco before Sparletta was formed to save the day.[38] The current sugar tax was similar, he noted. Putting his utmost faith in the African business, sure to be the dominant consumer bloc by 2030, he declared that, ultimately, sugar was but a speedbump. 'In business you hit walls. It's like sailing,' he said, turning the conversation to his other passion besides Coca-Cola. He asked rhetorically, 'when you've got a headwind,' what do you do, before answering for me: 'You duck.'[39] When faced with changing consumer tolerance for liquid sugar globally, Coca-Cola met the moment by understanding the moment. The company worked to lower sugar content in all manner of ways, while moving into beverages that sidestep the issue of sugar altogether. In other words, the company ducked. When it comes to the other issue pressing the company today—the planet's limits—the solution may not be so simple.

Planetary Boundaries

The hard truth for any beverage company is that the planet can only sustain so much. If a company consumes ever-increasing amounts of fruit, water, energy, and sugar in its production process, at some point these resources will be depleted. Recall Coca-Cola's past responses to projected fruit deficits. In those cases, the company turned to fostering farmers in order to increase the amount of available ingredients, a clever, if ultimately temporary, solution. At the same time, if a company produces ever-more unusable waste—be it plastic, aluminum, or glass—at some point Earth will be burdened beyond repair.

Of course, companies are not the sole drivers bringing humans up against planetary confines. But they are crucial ones in the twenty-first century. 'The capitalism that structures the contemporary global economy,' historian Julie Livingston pens, 'is the most significant engine of this dynamic, its organizing telos, and peddler of [the] narcotic' she calls 'self-devouring growth.' Livingston explains how late capitalism depends upon increasingly self-destructive modes of consumption. 'Ever more intensive forms of capitalist consumption animate a system that will harm everyone,' she explains from her vista in Botswana, 'even those whose consumption mainly remains aspirational.'[40] In Livingston's analysis, it is precisely capitalism's logic of insatiable growth at any cost (exemplified by large multinationals) that has brought humanity—even those who participate only minimally in global systems—up against what Earth can maintain.

In 2009, scientists delineated just what Earth's limits look like. They articulated nine planetary boundaries that regulate Earth's resilience and, if respected, assure the continuation of life. Two boundaries—climate change and biosphere integrity—were noted as 'core' ones on which the others depended. These were among the four areas that already exceeded the proposed safe limit for continued life on earth (the other two were biogeochemical flows and land-system change), according to this model. Teasing out safe zones as well as areas where humanity had already breached the danger threshold, the planetary boundary framework was not a political or business document. Yet, scientists and scholars, particularly those affiliated with the Stockholm Resilience Center, have worked within its framework to promote actionable responses to global problems for governments and businesses alike over the last fifteen years.[41]

Like those of other multinationals, Coca-Cola's sustainability initiatives around water, carbon use, and waste were conceived of and articulated within the planetary boundaries framework. Yet, despite scientific understandings of how close humans are to working ourselves out of existence, techno-optimism abounds within the Coca-Cola system. From Coca-Cola's point of view, there is no reason to despair, since there will undoubtedly be technological solutions to the problems posed by technological advancement.

What does Coca-Cola's techno-optimism look like? Folks within the Coca-Cola system point first to the potential for green economies to create new forms of employment, explaining, for instance, how solar systems in Eswatini and Ghana grow jobs and meet environmental needs at once. They applaud the longer vantage point demanded of companies that are serious about sustainability—setting goals a decade out instead of, say, quarterly, as companies are generally wont to do—for promoting bolder environmental business plans. In Africa, Coca-Cola's techno-optimists focus specifically on novel solutions born of necessity and opine that, because of them, the global south could very well 'leapfrog' the global north, skipping paths taken elsewhere in the world and thus providing new roadmaps for growth. Here, they point to things like EKOCENTERS as potentially exportable models of change with the power to meet hidden environmental needs. They suggest that even the most hopeless environmental spaces—landfills—could be mined for use, as is already being done with the factory that creates Freestyle machines, for instance. More than anything, Coca-Cola's techno-optimists put their faith in circular or closed-loop models that feed into themselves, endlessly reusing in order to reduce. Here, they highlight innovative systems like cogeneration schemes that combine heat and power to fuel factories and provide necessary CO_2 at once as well as bottle-to-bottle plastic recycling plants that use little to no virgin PET in their never-ending production of food-grade plastic.

It is alluring to imagine that the ills spawned by capitalism's expansion can be solved by further expansion of capitalism, that the planetary boundaries can be addressed without reckoning with the very systems that brought humanity up against them. To do so is, on one level, to enter capitalism's self-affirming worldview. To be sure, Coca-Cola, like other companies, has not escaped criticism for the way it has used the planetary boundary concept for just this reason, with some further saying that corporations have merely employed the framework as cover to do work that should belong to governments or other, presumably disinterested, stakeholders.[42] These critiques are ultimately critiques of capital itself, rooted in a worldview that wants engagement free from monetary concerns, a position that is arguably more aspirational than practical.

Still, to investigate and perhaps even get behind corporate attempts at sustainability is not just being gullible. It is embracing deliberate hope and putting faith in human ingenuity.[43] It is understanding that corporations are made up of humans, many if not most good-intentioned. It is seeing that large-scale problems demand global players. And, it is recognizing that just because corporations have contributed to problems does not preclude their ability to contribute equally to solutions. Our perch late in the Capitalocene, amidst the Covid Era, has rendered visible the limits of individual governments and made clear the need for the kinds of collaboration that yield integrated, localized systems, the very sort that a company like Coca-Cola excels at. Yet, this same moment has brought all of us (albeit unequally) up against the boundaries that a business like Coca-Cola seems to abut. Ultimately, this moment has forced us to interrogate what will be possible and what will be essential to humanity's survival on the other side, including asking: will a beverage company?

***

In the 2010 television advertisement 'Sleepwalker,' which debuted during that year's American Super Bowl, a white man emerges from sleep in the African savannah. Wandering about, eyes closed, he stumbles under the gaze of a cheetah, inadvertently startling a herd of elephants, before skirting the edge of a precipitous drop. Driven by his subconscious thirst, he pays no mind to the danger he faces on his somnambulant mission. Blindly, he steps into a dugout canoe, stepping out just as a hippopotamus takes the boat into its mouth. Purposefully, the wandering protagonist enters a rustic hut, where he finds an electric refrigerator stocked with bottles of Coke red. In the warm glow of the humming machine, he pulls out a glass hobble skirt bottle. Making it back to camp, he drinks happily from the perspiring bottle, absentmindedly petting a jackal to his side, while giraffes prance in the background. Eyes still closed, he smiles as the 'Open Happiness' tagline appears.[44]

It is 'an odd little waking dream of an ad,' *Time* magazine television critic James Poniewozik wrote upon its release in 2010.[45] In this advertisement, Coca-Cola is fully at home in the African veldt while humans—shown through a half-dressed white everyman—are sleepwalking through their consumption, blind to the world around them and, perhaps, to the consequences of their actions.

Well before Sleepwalker's 2010 release, Coca-Cola was at home in Africa. And, in the decade-plus since it came out, we can conclude that humanity and Coca-Cola have both woken up to the consequences of consumption and the dangers of denial. Both have faced the reality that the overconsumption of sugar entails. Both have glanced the planet's limits and charted paths to try to course correct. The question we must ask, in closing, is whether these changes could possibly be enough for Coca-Cola in Africa or, for that matter, for all of us.

ACKNOWLEDGMENTS

Endings evoke beginnings with reminders of what it took to get from one to the other.

Thank you to Jeanne Penvenne, who I first met as a freshman in college, and who, over a glass of wine two decades later, made an introduction that set this project in motion. To my other forever mentors—Emmanuel Akyeampong, Carolyn Hamilton, and Suzanne Blier—thanks for contributing at key moments and in key ways.

Thank you to my students and colleagues at the University of Pennsylvania, who have indulged my talking about Coca-Cola for the last few years, and to Val Ross, in particular, for reminding me at the onset that any multi-year project ought to be enjoyable. Thanks to Lauris Olson, for the gifted Coca-Cola cookbook and general library support, as well as Fayyaz Vellani, Adam Mohr, Matthew Osborn, Stacy Kastner, Jake Rutkowski, and the rest of my colleagues in the Marks Family Center for Excellence in Writing, for their friendship.

Thank you to the many friends who shared images, documents, memories, and upcycled items of and about Coca-Cola from their research and travel in Africa, as though participating in a scavenger hunt. Lee Cassanelli's reminiscences about Coke in Somaliland, Peter Decherney's photographs from Ethiopia and

ACKNOWLEDGMENTS

Kenya, Maya Jasanoff's pictures from the Congo River, Abena Osseo-Asare's images from Ghana, and more ensured that Coke in Africa was never far from my mind.

Thank you to the personnel at The Coca-Cola Company who were open to this endeavor and who, in turn, opened the company up to me, especially the dedicated team of archivists in Atlanta (Jamal Booker, Ted Ryan, Ginny Van Winkle, and Sarah Rice), as well as the dozens of people within the Coca-Cola universe who helped me access the people, places, and materials I needed to write this book. I am particularly grateful to the more than 200 people up, down, and adjacent to the Coca-Cola value chain in Africa who gave me their time and, especially, to those who shared privately held materials with me.

Thank you to the funding bodies that enabled my research: Atlanta University Center's Robert W. Woodruff Library, the Huntsman Program, the Kleinman Center for Energy Policy, Penn Global, and the University of Pennsylvania's School of Arts and Sciences. Thank you to the archivists at the Atlanta Research Center, Emory University, the National Archives of Ghana, and the New York Public Library for their assistance. And thank you to my research assistants, all dazzling students at the time we worked together: Alexander Bendix, Ghita Chraibi, Kaustubh Deo, Gian Paul Graziosi, Justin Kogotho, Shubham Poddar, and, especially, my intrepid co-travelers, Folatomi Alli-Balagun and Halima Said.

My family in South Africa always provides refuge and support. Joni Brenner and Scott Hazelhurst did that and then some, particularly when we turned the Eswatini portion of my research into a family road trip. For that and so much more, I thank them.

To my children, Benjamin, Sophie, and Vivienne, I offer the most thanks for bringing everything into focus and for tolerating my absences. So too do I thank my mother, Pam, for her continued support, and my late father, David, for always delighting in my pursuits. My greatest expression of gratitude goes to my husband, Chad, who inadvertently launched this project by sending me a news article and who has been its biggest champion since. Nothing I do would be possible without him.

NOTES

INTRODUCTION

1. Chinua Achebe, *Things Fall Apart* (New York: Anchor Books, 1994), 6. For more recent literary references see Chimamanda Ngozi Adichie, *Half a Yellow Sun* (New York: Random House, 2008), 206; and Chris Abani, *Graceland* (New York : Farrar, Straus, and Giroux, 2004), 1. Interestingly, 'The People's Drink,' *Coca-Cola: Refreshing Nigeria Through the Years* (The Coca-Cola Company, c2005), 38, offers the following view on Coca-Cola and kola: 'Over the years,' this commemorative booklet, notes, 'the triad of Coca-Cola, Fanta and Sprite has served as a symbol of the famed hospitality of the average Nigerian,' so much so that, 'A chilled bottle of' one had 'become in most homes the standard and convenient alternative to "kola nuts," the symbolic welcome offering to every valued guest.'

2. Edmund Abaka, *Kola is God's Gift: Agricultural Production, Export Initiatives, and the Kola Industry of Asante and the Gold Coast, c. 1820–1950* (Suffolk: James Currey, 2005), 2. See also Shantel George, work in progress on the history of the kola nut, explained here: <http://www.international.ucla.edu/Institute/article/186740> Accessed 7 June 2018.

3. Abaka, *Kola is God's Gift*, 5 and 125. For more on the kola nut, see Judith A Carney, 'African Traditional Plant Knowledge in the Circum-Caribbean Region,' *Journal of Ethnobiology* 23, No. 2 2003, 167–185; Judith A Carney and Richard Nicholas Rosomoff, *In the Shadow of Slavery: Africa's Botanic Legacy in the Atlantic Word* (Berkeley: University of California Press, 2009); Paul E Lovejoy, *Caravans of Kola: The Hausa Trade, 1700–1900* (Ahmadu Bello University Press, 1980); and Robert Voeks and John Rashford, eds., *African Ethnobotany in the Americas* (New York: Springer-Verlag, 2013).

4. See Paul E Lovejoy, 'Kola in the History of West Africa,' *Cahiers D'études Africaines*, 20, No. 77–78, 1980, 97–134; and Martin Ford, 'Kola Production and Settlement Mobility among the Dan of Nimba, Liberia, *African Economic History*, 20, 1992, 51–63.

5. Abaka, *Kola is God's Gift*, 18.

6. See Carney, 'African Traditional Plant Knowledge,' 167–185. See also Shantel George.

7. F A Fluckiger, 'The Pharmacognosy of Kola,' *American Druggist and Pharmaceutical Record*, 25, No. 3, 10 August 1894, 99–100, in Caswell A Mayo and Thomas J Keenan, eds., *Volume XXV: July–December 1894* (New York: American Druggist Publishing Company, 1894).

8. Fluckiger, 'The Pharmacognosy of Kola,' 99. Also Abaka, *Kola is God's Gift*, ix, 125, and 128.

9. Jean Barbot quoted in P E H Hair, Adam Jones, and Robin Law, eds. *Barbot on Guinea: The Writings of Jean Barbot on West Africa, 1678–1712* (The Hakluyt Society, London, 1992) 188, cited in Carney, 'African Traditional Plant Knowledge,' 180.

10. Abaka, *Kola is God's Gift*, 128.

11. A M F J Palisot-Beauvois, *Flore d'Oware et de Benin en Afrique*, 4 ième Livre (Paris, 1805), cited in Abaka, *Kola is God's Gift*, 129.

12. Abaka, *Kola is God's Gift*, 129–130.

13. Frederick Allen, *Secret Formula: How Brilliant Marketing and Relentless Salesmanship Made Coca-Cola the Best-Known Product in the World* (New York: Harper Collins, 1994), 26.

14. 'That nut from Africa,' *New York Times*, 3 November 1895, 11.

15. Charles C Yarbrough, 'Therapeutics of Kola,' *Journal of the American Medical Association* 33 (19) 1899, 1148–1149.

16. Armand Gautier with A J Rice-Oxley, translator, *Diet and Dietetics* (Philadelphia: Lippincott, 1906), 276.

17. Bartow J Elmore, *Citizen Coke: The Making of Coca-Cola Capitalism* (New York: W.W. Norton, 2015), 20.

18. Mark Pendergrast, *For God, Country, & Coca-Cola: The Definitive History of the Great American Soft Drink and the Company That Makes It*, Third Edition (New York: Basic Books, 2013), 21; Allen, *Secret Formula*, 23. See also: C E Johanson and M W Fischman, 'The Pharmacology of Cocaine Related to its Abuse,' *Pharmacological Reviews* March, 41 (1) 1989, 3–52.

19. Pendergrast, *For God, Country, & Coca-Cola*, 21.

20. *Ibid.*, 21.

21. *Ibid.*, 23.

22. Elmore, *Citizen Coke*, 54.

23. E J Kahn, Jr., *The Big Drink: The Story of Coca-Cola* (New York: Random House, 1960; orig. 1950), 101.

24. Allen, *Secret Formula*, 47.

25. Elmore, *Citizen Coke*, 54

26. *Kola is God's Gift*, 134.

27. Kahn, *The Big Drink*, 101.

28. 'Coke Adds Life,' <https://commons.marymount.edu/locjowett/coke-adds-life/> Accessed 4 January 2022.

29. Darcy S O'Neil, *Fix the Pumps: The History and Recipes of the Soda Fountain* (Art of Drink: 2009), 47–53.

30. Tristan Donovan, *Fizz: How Soda Shook Up the World* (Chicago: Chicago Review Press, 2014), 4.

31. Anne Cooper Funderburg, *Sundae Best: A History of Soda Fountains* (Bowling Green: Bowling Green State University Press, 2002), 6. See Joseph Priestley, *Directions for Impregnating Water with Fixed Air in Order to Communicate to It the Peculiar Spirit and Virtues of Pyrmont Water, and Other Mineral Waters of a Similar Nature* (Reprinted by American Bottlers of Carbonated Beverages, Washington DC, 1945).

32. Donovan, *Fizz*, 8.

33. Cooper Funderburg, *Sundae Best*, 7.

34. Hunter Oatman-Stanford, 'Medicinal Soft Drinks and Coca-Cola Fiends: The Toxic History of Soda Pop.' April 10, 2014. <https://www.collectorsweekly.com/articles/the-toxic-history-of-soda-pop/> Accessed 2 July 2018.

35. Donovan, *Fizz*, 25–31.

36. Oatman-Stanford, 'Medicinal Soft Drinks and Coca-Cola Fiends.' See also O'Neil, *Fix the Pumps*, 9.

37. Donovan, *Fizz*, 30.

38. O'Neil, *Fix the Pumps*, 4.

39. Donovan, *Fizz*, 19.

40. A Wolf, G A Bray, and B M Popkin, 'A short history of beverages and how our body treats them,' *The International Association for the Study of Obesity*, Obesity Reviews 9 (2007), 159.

41. Cooper Funderburg, *Sundae Best*, 21.

42. Bray and Popkin, 'A short history of beverages,' 159.

43. Cooper Funderburg, *Sundae Best*, 43.

44. 'Cool Iced Drinks... American Soda Fountain, Ice Cr'm Sodas &tc. FJ Bryne, Chemist,' *Bulawayo Chronicle*, 11 February 1899, 3.

45. *Cape Times*, 18 December 1901, 13.

46. See, for example, *Rand Daily Mail*, 31 January 1903, 17; *Rand Daily Mail*, 24 March 1910, 2; *Rhodesia Herald*, 13 May 1910, 2; and *Mafeking Mail and Protectorate Guardian*, 16 September 1911, 3.

47. *The Lagos Standard*, 4 June 1913, 8.
48. See *Uganda Herald*, 30 January 1920, 9; *Sierra Leone Weekly News*, 14 August 1920, 6; *Nigerian Pioneer*, 2 September 1921, 18; *Gold Coast Leader*, 17 April 1920, 3; and *Dar Es Salaam Times*, 3 July 1920, 6.
49. 'Coca-Cola: 125 Years Of Making Friends,' *African Business*, 18 December 2011. <https://african.business/2011/12/economy/coca-cola-125-years-of-making-friends/> Accessed 18 April 2018.
50. Dan Baxter, Communications Director, EMEA, The Coca-Cola Company, email communication with the author, 14 July 2017 confirmed that it is often said that Coke is largest employer on the continent (at +/- 70,000 employees) even though no third party has established this in writing to his knowledge; Therese Gearhart, President, Southern Africa, Coca-Cola, author interview, Johannesburg, 5 July 2016; Alex Cummings, 'Tomorrow is Starting Now,' Speech at Africare Dinner, 3 November 2009, Coca-Cola Archives. Gearhart said that Coke routinely reports a multiplier of four, just to be safe, but that studies show the number is more like seven to ten. Cummings' speech put it at ten-twelve.
51. The Coca-Cola Company: Brands, <https://www.coca-colacompany.com/brands?gclsrc=aw.ds&gclid=Cj0KCQiA8ICOBhDmARIsAEGI6o363MAUzz1yu8-3X1LjXW0cOcdgp6i2RWCWBb_oOwT_t6p3PxCZ43saAmL8EALw_wcB&gclsrc=aw.ds> Accessed 18 April 2018.
52. Jo Guldi and David Armitage, *The History Manifesto*, Cambridge University Press. <http://historymanifesto.cambridge.org/read/> Accessed 5 June 2021.
53. Arjun Appadurai, 'Introduction: Commodities and the Politics of Value,' in *The Social Life of Things: Commodities in Cultural Perspective*, ed. Arjun Appadurai (Cambridge: Cambridge University Press, 1986), 15; Daniel Miller, 'Coca-Cola: A Sweet Black drink from Trinidad,' in *Material Cultures: Why Some Things Matter*, ed. Daniel Miller (Chicago: University of Chicago Press, 1998), 169; Slavoj Žižek, 'The Pervert's Guide to Ideology,' directed by Sophie Fiennes, 2012.
54. See, for instance, Robert J Foster, *Coca-Globalization: Following Soft Drinks from New York to New Guinea* (Palgrave MacMillan, 2008); and Paul Zimmet, 'Globalization, Coca-Colonization and the Chronic Disease Epidemic: can the Doomsday scenario be averted?' *Journal of Internal Medicine* 247 (3) 2000: 301–310.
55. See, for a good overview of these positions, Jon Miller and Lucy Parker, *Everybody's Business: The Unlikely Story of How Big Business Can Fix the World* (London: Biteback Publishing, 2013).
56. Pietra Rivoli, *The Travels of A T-Shirt in the Global Economy: An Economist Examines the Markets, Power, and Politics of World Trade*, 2nd Edition (Hoboken: John Wiley and Sons, Inc., 2009), xi.

57. Anne Hoy, *Coca-Cola: The First Hundred Years* (Atlanta: The Coca-Cola Company, 1986), 116. See also 'An Oasis in the Sahara Desert,' *Coca-Cola Overseas*, February 1961, 14, No. 1, 28.

58. 'Happenings around the world,' *Coca-Cola Overseas*, April 1954, 7, No. 2, 28.

1. ALL THAT SPARKLES

1. 'The Coca-Cola Africa Story,' (Windsor: Coca-Cola Africa, c 2002), 6. Coca-Cola Archives.

2. *Ibid.*, 14. See also 'Now in China,' *The Coca-Cola Bottler* 20, No. 6, September 1928, 36; and G Lynn Coggin, *ABI: Over Sixty Years as a Bottler of Coca-Cola* Book One: 1923–1975 (Johannesburg: ABI, 2005), 9.

3. See, for instance, 'African Trade and Commerce,' *African World and Cape-Cairo Express*, 29 April 1905, 593–594.

4. 'All those who have travelled in the tropics know by experience,' an advertisement in *The African World and Cape-Cairo Express* of 8 July 1911, 519, explained, 'that the use of water for drinking purposes must in all cases be accompanied by measures of a precautionary character. The water has, in most instances, to be submitted to various purifying processes, such as filtration or boiling, and even then, absolute safety is not guaranteed. Manufactured aerated water has, in consequence, been almost universally adopted.' On 'do it yourself' water filtration systems, see: 'A Portable "Home" Soda Water Factory' *African World and Cape-Cairo Express*, 8 July 1911, 519; 'Flugel & Co's Automatic Aerated Water Machine' *African Mail*, 11 July 1913, 415; and 'A Complete Sodawater Factory,' *African World and Cape-Cairo Express*, 29 April 1911, 783.

5. Coggin, *ABI: Book One*, 76.

6. 'List of Licensees,' *Cape Town Gazette*, 4 May 1869 No. 4, 117 names Mulvihal as a licensee of one 'Dublin Inn.' Thereafter, Mulvihal and family started a mineral water plant, establishing a connection between hotels and water bottling at the Cape. Adverts for 'Mulvihal's, suppliers of Dry Ginger Ale and Club Soda to the House of Parliament' began to appear in newspapers. For an example, see *The Cape Times*, 18 September 1882, 2. See also Michael Walker, *The Old Hotels of Cape Town 1890–1911: A History Long Forgotten, Seldom Told* (South Africa: St. James, 2015), 36. The Mulvihals were not the only ones. In 1852, Samuel Wordon started the first soda factory in Cape Town, which he later passed on to his son, also Samuel. When the younger Wordon ran into business difficulty in 1891, he partnered with Thomas Henry Pegram, changing the company's name to Pegram's Limited; this would later be absorbed by Schweppes, after it arrived on the continent. Coggin, *ABI: Book One*, 76.

7. Lastovica and Lastovica's examination of bottles list a string of Mulvihal productions. Ethleen Lastovica, with Albert Lastovica, *Bottles & Bygones: A Guide for South African Collectors* (Cape Town: Don Nelson, 1982). See also 'Vasco Natural Mineral Water, To be Obtained at all Bars, Sale Distributing Agents, T Mulvihal and Sons,' *The Cape Times*, 22 June 1904, 6; 'DISA Water: A South African Natural Mineral Water. Absolutely Pure. Absolutely Genuine. Bottled from the original spring, near Parow, Cape Colony. Strongly recommended by the medical profession. Much superior to any water at present on the Market. Blends Perfectly with Whisky. Agents, T. Mulvihal & Sons, Ltd.,' *The Cape Times*, 17 December 1910, 8; and 'Boys for mineral water factory, apply, immediately, T. Mulvihal and Sons, Canterbury-street,' *The Cape Times*, 23 December 1913, 2. Vasco is also referenced in The *South African Medical Record*, 23 December 1911.

8. In 1870, Ritchie Lawrence opened the first mineral water factory in Kimberley, servicing the needs of the diamond mines there. From 'Kimberley: Diamond Capital of the World,' *Coca-Cola Overseas*, December 1953, 6 No. 6, 32.

9. Anthony Turton, Craig Schultz, Hannes Buckle, Mapule Kgomongoe, Tinyiko Malugani & Mikael Drackner, 'Gold, Scorched Earth and Water: The Hydropolitics of Johannesburg,' *Water Resources Development*, 22, No. 2 (2006), 313–335.

10. A H Bleksley, *Johannesburg Gezondheids Comite, Sanitary Department* (Johannesburg: Standard and Digger's News Printing and Publishing Company, 1896).

11. Kirby Manià, 'Diving the Reef: Water Metaphors in the Work of Ivan Vladislavic,' *English in Africa* 43 No. 2 (Aug. 2016), 63–89.

12. Coggin, *ABI: Book One*, 76. For more information on this era, including about some of the immigrants who set up water factories at this time like W K Mager and Meyer Lange, see the following: Douglas A Simmons, *Schweppes: The first 200 Years* (Springwood Books Ltd., 1983); *Partners in Progress: A Tribute to the Coca-Cola Bottlers of South Africa by the Coca-Cola Export Corporation, Southern African Area* (foreword by Fred Meyer, publication details unknown), South Africa Box I, 'Bibliography II: Prior to 1977,' Coca-Cola Archives; and 'South Africa's "Mr. Coca-Cola" still smiles at 100,' January 2007 <http://www.africanjewishcongress.com/wcrsa3.htm> Accessed 11 June 2018. See also *Queenstown Press*, 20 July 1894; *Pharmaceutical Journal*, 29 June 1905, 75; and *Chemist and Druggist: The Newsweekly for Pharmacy*, Volumes 42–43, 9 September 1883, 384 and 29 July 1893.

13. 'Niagra Steam Mineral Water Works, Goldberg and Zeffert Proprietors,' *Rand Daily Mail*, 25 May 1903, 15; See also Dr. A C van Vollenhoven and

A J Pelser, 'A report on a Cultural Heritage Impact Assessment for the Proposed Biomass-to-Electricity Plant on the Farm Boschkop 543 Jr, Close to Bronkhorstspruit, Gauteng Province, for Core Earth Resources,' October 2008, 1–15; and Lastovica and Lastovica, *Bottles & Bygones*.

14. See 'Aerated Water Manufacturers,' *Rand Daily Mail*, 6 May 1903, 10; 'The Niagra,' *Rand Daily Mail* 10 August 1904, 10. On Van Riebeek, see 'Van Riebeek: The Famous Natural Mineral Water,' *Rand Daily Mail*, 5 September 1904, 5. In 1928, Schweppes took control of Van Riebeek Natural Mineral Water Company according to Coggin, *ABI: Book One*, 77.

15. For names, see declaration of prices list *Rand Daily Mail* 25 September 1905, 1; *Rand Daily Mail* 5 June 1908, 1; and *Rand Daily Mail*, 16 September 1909, 1. See also 'Appollinaris Water,' *Diamond Fields Advertiser*, 18 May 1906, 5.

16. See 'The Newcastle Cold Storage, Ice, and Mineral Water Manufacturers is in the market and can be purchased as a going concern,' *Rand Daily Mail*, 31 March 1904, 12; and 'Great sale of a Mineral Water factory,' *Rand Daily Mail*, 2 May 1904, 2.

17. When Schweppes arrived to set up shop in Durban, the company published an advertisement in the *Rand Daily Mail* warning 'All persons... against using the name of "SCHWEPPES" or any Colourable Imitation thereof.' From *Rand Daily Mail*, 14 February 1903, 12. In 1904, Mr. Gert Jacos of the Spes Bone Mineral Waterworks was accused of bottling his own water in bottles belonging to, and bearing the name of, the Albion Mineral Water Works, something that was not uncommon. From 'Analysis Wanted: Mineral Water Case,' *Rand Daily Mail*, 13 October 1904, 6.

18. See, on petrol use, 'Apology,' *Rand Daily Mail*, 4 December 1909, 2; a public warning against destruction of Albion bottles, *Rand Daily Mail*, 21 May 1914, 8; 'West Rand: Mineral Water Case: A question of trade marks,' *Rand Daily Mail* 19 April 1928, 4; 'Alleged false trade description: Mineral Water Manufacturers Prosecuted,' *Rand Daily Mail* 21 May 1914, 8; and Lastovica and Lastovica, *Bottles & Bygones*, 26.

19. 'The Coca-Cola Africa Story;' Coggin, *ABI: Book One*, 7. Coggin puts the date at 1925.

20. Zolakone was the registered trademark of William Handley, an Englishman who had emigrated to New Zealand in 1875 and worked in a mineral water factory there before establishing this branded aerated drink, which quickly took off, particularly in Australia <http://www.aucklandmuseum.com/collection/object/am_humanhistory-object-829912> Accessed 18 July 2020. See also 'The Brewer's Exhibition,' *Chemist and Druggist*, 23 October 1893, 690. By 1900, advertisements for Zolakone were appearing as far afield as Wales.

21. Ads found in *Cape Times*, 17 December 1909, 6; 21 December 1909; 31 December 1909; 4 January 1910; 5 January 1910; 11 January 1910.

22. As early as 1901, an advertisement in the *Cape Times* implored readers to 'Meet your friends at the American Soda Fountain, where cold beverages and the famous "Ice Cream Soda" are dispensed,' calling ice cream soda 'just the real thing' on a hot day, *The Cape Times*, 18 December 1901, 13. By October 1905, *The Rand Daily Mail* was likewise promoting 'American Soda Fountains,' for its readers. See, as a few examples, 'For the business man: Johannesburg Morning Market,' *Rand Daily Mail*, 11 October 1905, 3, which mentions an 'American Soda Fountain;' and 'Princes Café Coronation Buildings Germiston, THE place for Grills, Luncheons, Dinners, Breakfasts and Light Refreshments, American Soda Fountain, Ices, Strawberries & Fruit Salads DAILY. A fine assortment of the very Best Chocolates. For a real good meal, Princes Café, Cannot be beaten,' *Rand Daily Mail*, 24 March 1910, 2.

23. Walker, *The Old Hotels of Cape Town 1890–1911*, 36.

24. *Ibid.*, 59–61; Also, Lawrence Green, *A Taste of South-Easter: Memories of unusual Cape Town characters, queer shops and shows, old bars, hotels and cafes and the panorama of the streets.* <https://archive.org/stream/ATasteOfSouth-easter/ATasteOfSouth-easter_djvu.txt> Accessed 21 July 2022.

25. Coggin, *ABI: Book One*, 9.

26. Roy Jones, 'Coca-Cola Refreshes the World,' *Coca-Cola Overseas*, October 1961, 14, No. 5, 3–6.

27. Coggin, *ABI: Book One*, 9. There is confusion on this date, put alternately at 1932 (wherein it would have been Export, not the foreign department, who was in charge). All the evidence suggests that 1928 is the accurate date.

28. *Rand Daily Mail*, 21 November 1928, 16.

29. *Rand Daily Mail*, 28 November 1928, 16.

30. *Rand Daily Mail*, 11 January 1929. And again on 1 February 1929.

31. *Rand Daily Mail*, 25 January 1929, 5.

32. *Rand Daily Mail*, 21 November 1928, 16.

33. *Rand Daily Mail*, 28 November 1928, 16.

34. *Rand Daily Mail*, 21 November 1928, 16.

35. *Ibid.*

36. *Rand Daily Mail*, 25 January 1929, 5.

37. *Partners in Progress*, 2.

38. Coggin, *ABI: Book One*, 9.

39. *Ibid.*

40. *Partners in Progress*, 2.

41. While the Coca-Cola Company would soon build its own bottling plants, its earliest history in the country saw it relying on the apparatuses and expertise

of extant mineral water makers, many of whom had been around since the earliest days of sparkling beverage production. Coggin, *ABI: Book One*, 7.

42. *Ibid.*, 11. See also *Roots: Forbes*, unpublished Peninsula Beverages document, Peninsula Beverages private collection.

43. Dave Lewis, Chairman, Forbes Holdings, author interview, Peninsula Beverages, Cape Town, 12 July 2016.

44. E Neville Isdell, former Coca-Cola CEO, author interview by telephone, 30 March 2016.

45. Coggin, *ABI: Book One*, 12.

46. *Partners in Progress*, 5 and 13.

47. *Ibid.*, 9, 24, 26, and 27. See also Coggin, *ABI: Book One*, 13; and 'Kimberley: Diamond Capital of the World,' *Coca-Cola Overseas,* December 1953, 6 No. 6, 32. Additional material about Worcester Minerals received from Renaye Kramer, email correspondence with author, September 2018.

48. *Partners in Progress*, 8. See also Coggin, *ABI: Book One*, 1–27.

49. *Partners in Progress*, 10; Also Coggin, *ABI: Book One*, 18.

50. *Partners in Progress*, 12–13; Also Coggin, *ABI: Book One*, 16.

51. *Partners in Progress*, 12–13. On William Hyde Jr., Princeton Alum, see William Donald Hyde, Jr. <https://africanbusinessmagazine.com/uncategorised/coca-cola-125-years-of-making-friends/> Accessed 12 June 2018.

52. Coggin, *ABI: Book One*, 18.

53. *Ibid.*, 19.

54. *Ibid.*, 18–20.

55. *Ibid.*, 17; *Partners in Progress*, 12.

56. While Gutsche Sr. had assumed this job to be temporary, just part of the wartime interruption, a fortuitous trip to an international Coca-Cola conference in Atlanta in 1948 awakened him to what future this beverage may hold in the post-World War II, blooming days of apartheid. Amidst the fever to give out franchises, Gutsche was granted one, getting his family's foot in the door. Coggin, *ABI: Book One*, 17. Corroborated by Philipp H Gutsche, Chairman, Coca-Cola Beverages Africa, author interview, Lakeside Plant, Port Elizabeth, 15 May 2017.

57. Coggin, *ABI: Book One*, 17.

58. Philipp H Gutsche, author interview.

59. *Ibid.*

60. Dave Lewis, author interview. Confirmed by Alan Cook, bottler, author interview at his home, Johannesburg, 21 May 2017; and Philipp H Gutsche, author interview.

61. Letter from T J Cook to Fred Meyer re: The Life of a South African Bottler, 11 July 1983, Alan Cook private collection (hereafter Cook collection).

62. 'Sparletta: South Africa's National Soft drink,' 18 March 1981, Cook collection.

63. Letter from T J Cook to Fred Meyer, 11 July 1983.

64. 'Sparletta: South Africa's National Soft drink,' 18 March 1981.

65. 'Sparletta: our product,' Presented by TJ Cook, at the 25th Anniversary Annual General Meeting, 25 May 1976, Cook collection.

66. 'Sparletta: our product.'

67. Letter from J Paul Austin to Sparletta, 30 March 1966, Cook collection.

68. 'Sparletta: our product.'

69. After Suncrush, a company headed for three generations by the Hamilton family with deep roots in the early water production, joined Sparletta, by 1976, ten out of forty-nine privately owned plants that bottled Sparletta belonged to it. See news about this anniversary, *Natal Memory*, 26 May 1976, Cook collection.

70. Don Keough, speech from 1 September 1983, South Africa Bottlers' Convention at Monte Carlo, Coca-Cola Archives.

71. Coggin, *ABI: Book One*, 23–24.

72. Letter from T J Cook to Fred Meyer, 11 July 1983.

73. Coggin, *ABI: Book One*, 28.

74. In the 1920s and 1930s, the Export Corporation created a new package of Coca-Cola bottles for shipment overseas, which helped spread knowledge of the business. Anne Hoy, *The First Hundred Years* (Atlanta: Coca-Cola, 1985), 90.

75. 'Between Ourselves: Training Means Success,' *Coca-Cola South of the Sahara*, 8, No. 13 May 1962, 3.

76. G Lynn Coggin, *ABI: Over Sixty Years as a Bottler of Coca-Cola, Book Two: 1976–2000* (Johannesburg: ABI, 2005), 56–57.

77. Ira Emery, 'A new factory is opened in Johannesburg,' South Africa, *Coca-Cola Overseas*, June, 1952, 5 No. 3, 2–3.

78. 'Johannesburg builds miniature plant first,' *Coca-Cola Overseas*, December 1950, 3 No 6, 32.

79. Emery, 'A new factory is opened in Johannesburg, South Africa,' 2–3.

80. 'Between Ourselves: Training Means Success,' 3.

81. Les Forbes, 'The Tricycle Boys of Vanderbijl Park,' *Coca-Cola Overseas*, October 1952, 5, No. 5, 26–33.

82. J H Smit, 'In Praise of Secondary Industry: a report from South Africa,' *Coca-Cola Overseas*, February 1949, 2 No. 1, 26.

83. 'Coca-Cola Cold Case Manufacturing in South Africa,' *Coca-Cola Overseas*, February 1956, 9 No. 1, 22–23.

84. D O Jones, 'Dealer Visits to Cape Town Plant,' *Coca-Cola Overseas*, August 1949, 26.

85. Smit, 'In Praise of Secondary Industry: a report from South Africa,' 26.

86. Jones, 'School Sampling in South Africa: A step by step report on how to capture the youth market,' 9.

87. Ira Emery, 'Come to the Fair,' *Coca-Cola Overseas* August 1949, 25–26.

88. Ira Emery, 'Dingaan's Day in South Africa,' *Coca-Cola Overseas*, June 1950, 3, No. 3, 4.

89. Frederick Allen, *Secret Formula: How Brilliant Marketing and Relentless Salesmanship Made Coca-Cola the Best-Known Product in the World* (New York: Harper Collins, 1994), 342–43. See also Mark Pendergrast, *For God, Country, & Coca-Cola: The Definitive History of the Great American Soft Drink and the Company That Makes It*, Third Edition (New York: Basic Books, 2013), 261.

90. E Neville Isdell with David Beasley, *Inside Coca-Cola: A CEO's Life Story of Building the World's Most Popular Brand* (New York: St. Martin's Griffin, 2011), 215.

91. H C Patterson, 'The Golden City: My Return to Johannesburg, South Africa,' *Coca-Cola Overseas*, February 1952, 5 No. 1, 26.

92. *Coca-Cola* Overseas, April 1957, 10, No. 2, 2.

93. South Africa Timeline (created c. 2011), Box 1, 'South Africa,' Coca-Cola Archives.

94. See, for example, Hendrik Moleme, who, in 2015 had been with Sabco in Port Elizabeth for over fifty years. *Sabco: Proud of Our Heritage* (Sabco, 2015), 15.

95. Coggin, *ABI: Book One*, 29.

96. *Ibid.*, 31.

2. FROM CAPE TO CAIRO

1. 'Coca-Cola as Sold Throughout the World,' *The Red Barrel*, February 1929, 8 No. 2, 16.

2. Russell McCracken, 'The overseas story, part II,' *Coca Cola Overseas*, October 1948, 1 No. 3, 11.

3. For more, see 'The $4,000 Bottle: Coca-Cola Goes to War,' in Mark Pendergrast, *For God, Country & Coca-Cola: The Definitive History of the Great American Soft Drink and the Company That Makes It*, Third Edition (New York: Basic Books, 2013), 184–200.

4. E J Kahn, *The Big Drink: The Story of Coca-Cola* (New York: Random House, 1960; orig. 1950), 17. For background, including research and drafts, see E J Kahn papers, New York Public Library.

5. *Ibid.*, 16.

6. Roy S Jones, 'Coca-Cola Refreshes the World,' *Coca Cola Overseas*, October 1961, 14 No. 5, 1–6.

7. Pendergrast, *For God, Country & Coca-Cola*, 197.
8. 'Bottlers' Convention in Atlantic City,' *Coca-Cola Overseas*, June 1948, 1 No. 1, 29.
9. Pendergrast, *For God, Country & Coca-Cola*, 200–213.
10. Jones, 'Coca-Cola Refreshes the World,' 6.
11. Duke Ludwig, 'New Coca-Cola Plant in Casablanca: Inauguration by Prince Moulay Hassan Marks Great Progress in Morocco,' *Coca-Cola Overseas*, April 1951, 4 No. 2, 2.
12. Marcel De Reul, 'A Message from Casablanca,' *Coca-Cola Overseas*, June 1949, 26.
13. Ludwig, 'New Coca-Cola Plant in Casablanca,' 1–2.
14. 'New Coca-Cola Plant in Safi, Morocco,' *Coca-Cola Overseas*, October 1951, 4 No. 5, 22–23.
15. F G Van De Walle, 'Tangier, Morocco's Oldest City,' *Coca-Cola Overseas*, August 1963, 16 No. 4, 16–18.
16. When the King of Morocco visited the United States in 1958, Pendar accompanied him. See E J Kahn, Jr. *The Big Drink*, 38.
17. Letter from J Paul Austin to Mr. J G Zimmerman, 20 March 1952 recounts Pendar's complaints about his treatment and asks Export to advocate on his behalf in front of the World Court. Austin files, Coca-Cola Archives; Letter from Marcel de Reul to Gardner Tillinghast, 13 February 1950. Reul was from the Northwest African Division of Coca-Cola in Morocco, and shared a French article stating just this: 'Kenneth Pendar's presence in Morocco and in North Africa is an insult. It is, furthermore, very dangerous, because Kenneth Pendar could be here only for the purpose of fomenting anti-French intrigue hand in hand with the nationalists.' Morocco Box 1, 'Government control, Customs, Laws, 1948–76,' Coca-Cola Archives. For more, see 'Trade in Morocco is Protested Here,' *New York Times*, 30 October 1950, 35.
18. Kahn, *The Big Drink*, 38, writes, 'Quite a few Europeans have wildly concluded that most foreign operatives are American spies' passing secret messages in Coca-Cola advertisements, an implausible assertion that nonetheless reveals the cloud that hung over Coke men around World War II. See also Kenneth Pendar, Ex-Vice Consul, obituary, *New York Times*, 8 December 1972, 48.
19. Letter from Francis Girardin to Dr. C A Shillinglaw, 22 March 1951, Morocco Box 1, 'Government Control, Customs, Laws, 1948–76,' Coca-Cola Archives.
20. Letter from Marcel de Reul to J G Zimmerman, 29 April 1949, Morocco Box 1, Miscellaneous Legal, 1948–52, Coca-Cola Archives.
21. Letter from Francis Girardin to Dr. C A Shillinglaw, 22 March 1951.

22. Letter from Afred Sevab to Stephen Ladas, 25 October 1947. Additional supportive material in same file, Morocco Box 1, 'Health regulations, 1947–63,' Coca-Cola Archives.

23. Letter from A M Eshaya to Mr. C H Gordon, 14 March 1949, Morocco Box 1, 'Government Control, Customs, Laws, 1948–76,' Coca-Cola Archives.

24. Pepsi relished the fact that it seemed to dodge the bulk of the boycott in Morocco, according to Kahn, *The Big Drink*, 37.

25. Letter from A M Eshaya to Cliff Shillinglaw, 26 September 1951, Morocco Box 1, 'Government Control, Customs, Laws, 1948–76,' Coca-Cola Archives. See also Kahn, *The Big Drink*, 37.

26. Draft unsigned letter by Gardner Tillinghast, 1 March 1951: 'I have also been concerned about our evident unpopularity with most North Africans and many other Moslems. This is connected frequently with a policy of the United States to further European colonial ambitions, especially those of France.' Morocco Box 1, 'Government Control, Customs, Laws, 1948–76,' Coca-Cola Archives.

27. Letter from Clifford H Gordon to Mr. Tillinghast, 10 January 1950, Morocco Box 1, 'Government Control, Customs, Laws, 1948–76,' Coca-Cola Archives.

28. Ludwig, 'New Coca-Cola Plant in Casablanca,' 2.

29. Letter from Marcel Del Reul to Frank Harrold, 5 February 1952, Morocco Box 2, Coca-Cola Archives.

30. *Ibid.*

31. The three carefully defined categories were juice, sodas (carbonated beverages that contained a set amount of fruit juice), and lemonades (sodas made exclusively with lemons). Memorandum from The Coca Cola Export Corporation Re: New Moroccan Soft Drink Regulations, 17 January 1961. Morocco Box 1, 'Government Control, Customs, Laws, 1948–76,' Coca-Cola Archives.

32. Letter from Alexander Makinsky to Dr. Julius G Zimmerman, 15 February 1962; Letter from Alexander Makinsky to H B Nicholson Jr., 8 March 1961; and Letter from Northwest Africa Region of Coca Cola Export Corporation to Mr. O Johnson, 26 January 1961. Morocco Box 1, 'Government Control, Customs, Laws, 1948–76,' Coca-Cola Archives.

33. Letter from FG Van der Walle to Alex Makinsky, 11 June 1958. Morocco Box 2, 'Photographs,' Coca-Cola Archives.

34. Memorandum on the manufacturing of concentrate in Morocco, 9 February 1954, Morocco, Box 1, 'Health regulations, 1947–63,' Coca-Cola Archives.

35. Aristo Bentivoglio, 'Coca-Cola Launched in Libya,' *Coca-Cola Overseas*, October 1962, 15 No. 4, 24.

36. Gene Savard, 'Egyptian market continues healthy growth: Circumstances, hard word, right people make carbonated beverage history in Cairo,' *Coca-Cola Overseas*, December 1949, 2 No. 6, 20.

37. *Ibid.*

38. 'Cairo: A record being repeated in other Egyptian cities,' *Coca-Cola Overseas*, June 1949, 32.

39. 'Alexandria: A modern note in the land of pyramids,' *Coca-Cola Overseas*, June 1948, 1 No. 1, 32–33.

40. Savard, 'Egyptian market continues healthy growth,' 20.

41. 'Cairo: A record being repeated in other Egyptian cities,' 32.

42. Savard, 'Egyptian market continues healthy growth,' 20.

43. 'Alexandria: A modern note in the land of pyramids,' 32–33.

44. 'Cairo: A record being repeated in other Egyptian cities,' 32.

45. 'Despite all obstacles,' *Coca-Cola Overseas* reported to its global audience of Coke personnel, there was a moral to the Egyptian story, which it summed up as follows: 'Coca-Cola being what it is, namely a quality product' meant that 'a bottling operation based on adequate investment and organization is a profitable enterprise even under adverse conditions, anywhere in the world, not only for the bottler and the dealers, but also for all those who are directly or indirectly living from or connected with the operation.' Savard, 'Egyptian market continues healthy growth,' 20.

46. Cover with caption, 'Near a Giza pyramid as a time-scarred sphinx looks on, a modern Egyptian beauty accepts a welcome bottle of Coca-Cola from the driver of her red-tasseled camel,' *Coca-Cola Overseas*, June 1964, 17 No. 3.

47. Eric Mansel, 'At Salisbury, Southern Rhodesia, plant expansion for new equipment,' *Coca-Cola Overseas*, April 1958, 11 No. 2, 15.

48. Coke's presence in Sudan was bumpy. It was there until 1969, withdrew and then returned in 1992. It withdrew again in 1997.

49. Coca-Cola *Export Newsletter*, No. 2, March 1957.

50. Timelines, Coca-Cola Archives.

51. See *Export Newsletter*, No. 1, January 1957, No. 1; *Export Newsletter* No. 45, March 1969; and *Export Newsletter*, No. 57, June 1972.

52. E Neville Isdell, former Coca-Cola CEO, author interview by telephone, 30 March 2016. See also E Neville Isdell, with David Beasley, *Inside Coca-Cola: A CEO's Life Story of Building the World's Most Popular Brand* (New York: St. Martin's Griffin, 2011).

53. Letter from Marcel de Gallaix to Julius Zimmerman, 21 June 1948. Morocco Box 1, 'Health Regulations, 1947–1963' Coca-Cola Archives.

54. See <https://agleventis.com/brief-history-timeline/> Accessed 18 July 2018. Additional information on the Leventis family was attained during

author interviews and conversations with the following people in Lagos, Nigeria, in May 2017: George Polymenakos, Country Manager, Coca-Cola Hellenic Bottling Company; Bhupendi Suri, Managing Director, Coca-Cola Nigeria; Clement Ugorji, Vice President for Public Affairs, Communication, and Sustainability, West Africa; and Sade Morgan, Legal, Public Affairs and Communications, Coca-Cola Hellenic Bottling Company.

55. Letter from A G Leventis to Permanent Secretary of Ministry and Commerce, Received 2 December 1953, 'Coca-Cola Manufacture, 1953–56,' RG7-1-15, PRAAD, National Archives of Ghana.

56. Eric Mansel, 'At Salisbury, Southern Rhodesia, plant expansion for new equipment,' *Coca-Cola Overseas*, April 1958, 11 No. 2, 15.

57. Notes, May 31, 1954, 'Coca-Cola Manufacture, 1953–56,' RG7-1-15, PRAAD, National Archives of Ghana. As of 2003, the Coca-Cola Bottling Company of Ghana (created 1997) became part of the Equatorial Coca-Cola Bottling Company. Today, all Ghanaian bottling takes place in Accra, with depots at Accra, Kumasi, Takoradi, and Tamale, in addition to 160 mini-distribution centers. See Phoebe Calver, 'Equatorial Bottling Company in Ghana: Delivering Sustainable Business in the Community,' *Africa Outlook*, 29 June 2018, 1–18.

58. 'Third Nigerian Plant Opened in Ibadan' *Coca-Cola Overseas*, October 1962, 15, No. 4, 33; *Refreshing Nigeria through the years,* internal publication, NBC archives, Lagos, Nigeria; and photos, Nigeria Box, 'Nigeria: Misc. Overseas 12/54-6/93,' Coca-Cola Archives.

59. The 1956 inauguration of the French-owned Abidjan plant included a local parade of Coca-Cola trucks and 'a float on which an African orchestra played popular tunes around a giant "Coca-Cola" bottle surrounded by attractive African cover girls,' in front of French government officials as well as representatives of the army, church, and civil administration. F Van De Walle, 'Abidjan, Ivory Coast, West Africa: First Coca-Cola Bottling Plant in Ivory Coast Territory' *Coca-Cola Overseas*, June 1957, 10 No. 3, 32. See also: F Van de Walle, 'Coca-Cola Bottler at Dakar, Senegal,' *Coca-Cola Overseas*, June 1957, 10 No. 3, 22.

60. B J Laporte, 'Plant opens in Matadi, Congo,' *Coca-Cola Overseas*, October 1961, 14 No. 5, 7; Franco Ferrari, 'H.I.M. Haile Selassie I Inaugurates New Plant at Addis Ababa, Ethiopia,' *Coca-Cola Overseas*, October 1959, 12, No. 5, 27; 'Around world expansion in Italy, Costa Rica and Kenya,' *Coca-Cola Overseas*, December 1961, 14 No. 6, 22.

61. 'Coca-Cola at Dar Es Salaam in Tanganyika,' *Coca-Cola Overseas*, April 1953, 6 No. 2, 20.

62. K G Eldridge, 'Umtali... Gem of Rhodesia,' *Coca-Cola Overseas*, February 1953, 6 No. 1, 32–33.

63. Ray Renaud, 'King Size "Coke" in Dar Es Salaam Tanganyika, East Africa,' *Coca-Cola Overseas*, June 1957, 10 No. 3, 2–3.

64. It is captioned to note that though such 'colourful' and packed commercial spaces 'are a route-salesman's nightmare,' because of the presence of enterprising women 'the trade is there.' *Coca-Cola South of the Sahara*, October 1960, 8 No. 7, 6.

65. 'Establishment of Warehouse ups sales ten-fold, Uganda,' *Coca-Cola Overseas*, October 1961, 14 No. 5, 22.

66. D F Leggate, '"Plus Profits" and Extra Service to Customers at Filling Stations of Salisbury, Southern Rhodesia,' *Coca-Cola Overseas*, December, 1952, 5 No. 6, 8. See also Ira G Emery, 'In the Belgian Congo,' *Coca-Cola Overseas*, October, 1955, 8 No. 5, 32.

67. *Coca-Cola Overseas*, December 1951, 4 No. 6, 32.

68. Simon Goldberg, Allen Lang, and Tom Hagan, all of Mutare Bottling Company, author interview by telephone, Zimbabwe, 22 May 2017.

69. K G Eldridge, 'Umtali... Gem of Rhodesia,' 32–33.

70. *Ibid.*

71. Simon Goldberg, Allen Lang, and Tom Hagan, author interview.

72. E Neville Isdell, author interview.

73. 'Republic of Liberia enjoys Coca-Cola,' *Coca-Cola Overseas*, June 1953, 6 No. 3, 20–23.

74. Gerald Glancey, Joe Van der Walt, and Nakampe Molewa, all longtime Coca-Cola Business Unit employees, in conversation with author, Coca-Cola offices, Parktown, Johannesburg, 4 July 2016.

75. G H Smith-Wright, 'Rhodes Centennial Exhibition,' *Coca-Cola Overseas*, June 1954, 7 No. 3, 9.

76. B J Laporte, 'Her Majesty the Queen Visits Nigeria,' *Coca-Cola Overseas*, June, 1956, 9 No. 3, 27.

77. A E Killeen, 'More intensive merchandising needed,' *Coca-Cola Overseas*, February, 1955, 8 No. 1, 29.

78. *Ibid.*

79. S H Desch and F H Cheadle, 'Brakpan Samples Thru Its White Coolers: South African Bottler Conducts Highly Successful Home Campaign Combining Cold Bottle Sampling, Direct Sale and Coupon Redemption,' *Coca-Cola Overseas*, February 1952, 5 No. 1, 16–22.

80. Simon Goldberg, Allen Lang, and Tom Hagan, author interview.

81. D O Jones, 'School Sampling in South Africa: A step by step report on how to capture the youth market,' *Coca-Cola Overseas*, June 1949, 9.

82. 'Bulawayo uses a "sound" system of sampling,' *Coca-Cola Overseas*, June 1953, 6 No. 3, 32.

83. Ira G. Emery, 'A sampling event at Johannesburg,' *Coca-Cola Overseas*, October 1958, 11 No. 5, 7.

84. Letter to the editor, *Coca-Cola Overseas*, June 1949, 31. According to its author, one C J Manussis, the 'publication... and all the information contained therein is of great interest, especially to us out here miles away from civilization.'

85. 'South African Bottlers Magazine,' *Coca-Cola Overseas*, June 1951, 4 No. 3, 30–31.

86. Howard F. Wilds, Jr., 'Production school in Trinidad: Answers to long-felt need for members of bottler organization,' *Coca-Cola Overseas*, August 1949, 8–9 and 28–29.

87. 'Overseas engineers and chemists attend area meeting in New York,' *Coca-Cola Overseas*, August 1960, 13 No. 4, 20.

88. See, for instance, *Export Newsletter*, No. 2, March 1957.

89. 'Training program,' *Coca-Cola Overseas*, June 1948, 1 No. 1, 25.

90. Ira G Emery, 'South African Bottlers Conference,' *Coca-Cola Overseas*, December 1950, 3 No. 6, 26.

91. F G Van de Walle, 'Northwest African Bottlers' Meeting,' *Coca-Cola Overseas*, June 1959, 12 No. 3, 21.

92. H S Chilingerian, 'Near East Bottlers Hold Meeting in Cairo,' *Coca-Cola Overseas*, October 1961, 14 No. 5, 29.

93. R H Pasea, 'South African Sales Meeting at Johannesburg,' *Coca-Cola Overseas*, February 1959, 12 No. 1, 26.

94. Mortimer Sheppard, 'Coca-Cola in Egypt,' *Coca-Cola Overseas*, December 1955, 8 No. 6, 2.

95. 'South African Regional Sales Meeting,' *Coca-Cola Overseas*, February 1957, 10 No. 1, 28.

96. D J Walker, 'African sales meeting held in Johannesburg,' *Coca-Cola Overseas*, December 1960, 13 No. 7, 6.

97. 'Plant Management and Productions School at Johannesburg,' *Coca-Cola Overseas*, December 1958, 11 No. 6, 27.

98. 'Central African Route Managers Training Course,' *Coca-Cola Overseas*, December 1958, 11 No. 6, 28.

99. Letter to the editor, *Coca-Cola Overseas*, June 1949, 31; Documents 2C/8/53-17/10/56, 'Coca-Cola Manufacture, 1953–56,' RG7-1-15, PRAAD, National Archives of Ghana.

100. D Meijer, 'Maintaining Quality in the South African Area,' *Coca-Cola Overseas*, October 1955, 8 No. 5, 10–12.

101. *Export Newsletter* 2, March 1957.

102. *Export Newsletter* 4, July 1957.

103. *Export Newsletter* 11, September 1958. That year, Austin was joined by his vice president Al Killeen in touring Salisbury, Kampala, Dar es Salaam, Nairobi, and Mombasa.

104. H B Nicholson, 'Milestones,' *Coca-Cola Overseas*, June 1953, 6 No. 3, 1.

105. D J Walker, 'Coca-Cola South of the Sahara,' *Coca-Cola Overseas*, October 1961, 14 No. 5, 17.

106. 'A Unique business,' *Coca-Cola Overseas*, December 1952, 5 No. 6, 1.

107. *Time Magazine*, 15 May 1950, Vol. LV, No. 20, cover.

108. Letter from C A Shillinglaw to Dr. W Schatelig, 4 December 1957. Morocco Box 1, 'Morocco: Health regulations, 1947–63,' Coca-Cola Archives; Undated internal document on Charity and Ramadan, Egypt Box 1, Coca-Cola Archives; GC Baylis, 'Johannesburg Entertains Youngsters,' *Coca-Cola Overseas*, April 1959, 12, No. 2, 4; See also Tom Oliver, 'Moslems Celebrate the Feast of Eid in Johannesburg,' *Coca-Cola Overseas*, October 1959, 12 No. 5, 7.

109. 'Coca-Cola at Dar Es Salaam in Tanganyika, East Africa,' *Coca-Cola Overseas*, April 1953, 6 No. 2, 20–22.

110. D J Walker, 'Coca-Cola South of the Sahara,' 17.

111. 'Flight S.033,' *Coca-Cola South of the Sahara*, 1961, Vol. 8, Jan. 1961, No. 8, 26. For more on this, see 'Crash of Douglas DC-4-1009 in El Badary,' <https://www.baaa-acro.com/country/egypt?page=5> Accessed 8 April 2019.

3. KNOW YOUR COUNTRY

1. Independence came earlier to North Africa (Egypt, 1922, Libya, 1951, Tunisia, 1956, Morocco, 1956; Algeria followed in 1962). Ghana became the first sub-Saharan nation to attain independence in the twentieth century in 1957. In 1960, seventeen other countries gained independence. A further list of independence dates is below.

2. Laurence Lafore, 'Elephants Have the Right of Way,' *Harper's*, November 1958, 72–77.

3. 'Happenings around the World,' *Coca-Cola Overseas*, April 1958, 11 No. 2, 29.

4. The other well-known brands were General Motors, Singer Sewing Machines, and Parker Pens, according to a study reported on in 'Happenings around the World,' *Coca-Cola Overseas*, April 1958, 11 No. 2, 29.

5. 'Home Again from Cannibal Land: Mrs. W. B. Seabrook visits father at Coca-Cola home office,' *The Red Barrel*, July 1930, 28.

6. Johnson speaks lovingly about lions, noting that he only had to kill a handful in self-defense, waxes poetic about pygmies' childlike simplicity, and proudly reports that he and his wife brought three gorillas back to Kansas to raise as pets: 'Hunting Big game in Africa With Camera Instead of Guns Martin Johnson: Famed Wild Animal Photographer, Describes Adventure in Radio Interview,' *The Red Barrel*, August 1931, 22–25. Elsewhere, he described how he and his wife traveled with Coke syrup in order to make their own Coca-Cola on the spot. For more on the Johnsons, see <https://safarimuseum. com/> Accessed 18 July 2021.

7. The film was shown in thirty-one countries. Original music was performed by a fifty-six-piece orchestra in Rome. Three camera crews traveled 190,000 miles in fourteen months to capture the included footage in this Jam Handy production, dated 1959. 'Wonderful World seen by millions,' *Coca-Cola Overseas*, April 1961, 14 No. 2, 13; and 'Wonderful world of Coca-Cola: A behind the scenes story of an unforgettable new motion picture,' *Coca-Cola Overseas*, June 1959, Vol. 12, No. 3, 29. For more, see also Amanda Ciafone, *Counter-Cola: A Multinational History of the Global Corporation* (UCLA Press, 2019), 102.

8. 'Wonderful World seen by millions,' 13.

9. The film was screened in Salisbury in 1960. See *Coca-Cola South of the Sahara*, Special supplement, October 1960, 8, No. 7, 25.

10. D S Dyer, 'For your information: What is advertising,' *Coca-Cola South of the Sahara*, March 1966, southern edition, 4 No. 1, 4.

11. Many people have written at length about Coca-Cola as marketing genius. See, for instance, E J Kahn, Jr., *The Big Drink: The Story of Coca-Cola* (New York: Random House, 1960 [first published 1950]), 147; Mark Pendergrast, *For God, Country, & Coca-Cola: The Definitive History of the Great American Soft Drink and the Company That Makes It*, Third Edition (New York: Basic Books, 2013), 157–58; and Frederick Allen, *Secret Formula: How Brilliant Marketing and Relentless Salesmanship Made Coca-Cola the Best-Known Product in the World* (New York: Harper Collins, 1994).

12. David N Jones, 'Implanting Favorable Impressions: consumer and reminder advertising interpret concepts of Coca-Cola to World Market,' *Coca-Cola Overseas*, June 1948, 1 No. 1, 27.

13. Will Grant, 'Freedom and Advertising: Worldwide business creates desire for better living,' *Coca-Cola Overseas*, April 1949, 2 No. 2, 6.

14. This campaign seems to be straight out of Pierre Bourdieu's *Distinction: A Social Critique of the Judgement of Good Taste* (New York: Routledge, 1979). One such ad reads as follows: 'Friendly host to travelers. Sign of good taste in over 100 countries. There's a pleasant air of expectancy at any airport—as you

wait for the plane that is to carry you off, or the one that is arriving with family or friends. And while you're waiting there's time for ice-cold Coca-Cola—sparkling, delicious, refreshing! Wherever you are—ask for Coca-Cola—sign of good taste,' *Coca-Cola Overseas*, August 1959, 12, No. 4, last page.

15. Jones, 'Implanting Favorable Impressions,' 27.

16. Joe Rintelen, 'New Ideas: Theme of 1957 Pattern Advertising Campaign,' *Coca-Cola Overseas*, October 1956, 9 No. 5, 18–21.

17. 'Coca-Cola in Africa Narrative,' Coca-Cola Archives.

18. Examples of major ad campaigns, in print: 'The pause that refreshes' in *Coca-Cola Overseas*, October 1955, 8 No. 5; advertisement for 'At meal time, Coca-Cola refreshes you best' in *Coca-Cola South of Sahara*, April 1964, 1 No. 3; advertisement for 'Things go better with big, Big Coke. Enjoy life! Enjoy Coke!' in *Coca-Cola South of the Sahara*, March 1966, southern edition, 4, No. 1; also in *Coca-Cola Overseas* December 1965, 18. No. 6; advertisement for 'Things go better with Coca-Cola. Coca-Cola refreshes you best' in *Coca-Cola Overseas* October 1965, 18 No. 5; and advertisement for 'Sign of good taste in over 100 countries' in *Coca-Cola Overseas*, August 1959, 12 No. 4.

19. 'Our Ghana Bottlers: The National Bottling Company,' *Coca-Cola South of the Sahara*, Special Supplement, October 1960, 8 No. 7, viv.

20. Liberia became independent in the nineteenth century. South Africa became independent from England in 1910, exited the Commonwealth in 1960, attained majority rule in 1994. Egypt, 1922; Libya, 1951; Sudan, 1956; Tunisia, 1956; Ghana, 1957; Guinea, 1958. 1960 was the year of independence, for the following countries: Cameroon, Togo, Madagascar, DR Congo, Somalia, Benin, Niger, Burkina Faso, Côte d'Ivoire, Chad, Central African Republic, Congo, Gabon, Senegal, Mali, Nigeria, Mauritania. 1961: Sierra Leone. 1962: Rwanda, Burundi, Algeria, Uganda. 1963: Kenya. 1964: Tanzania, Malawi, Zambia. 1965: Gambia. 1966: Botswana, Lesotho. 1968: Mauritius, Swaziland, Equatorial Guinea. 1974: Guinea-Bissau. 1975: Mozambique, Cape Verde, Comoros, Sao Tome and Principe, Angola. 1976: Seychelles. 1977: Djibouti. 1980: Zimbabwe. 1990: Namibia. 1993: Eritrea.

21. While Killeen rose through the ranks at Coca-Cola, he would take his knowledge of work on the ground in Africa with him. Likewise, South African born J H Smit, who had worked for Export since 1940, similarly helping to steer the company's expansion mid-century, would in 1969 be elected Vice President of Export. Both Killeen and Smit took their experience in Africa to the larger Coca-Cola Export Corporation, once more demonstrating the import of the business in Africa to the larger story of Coca-Cola's global work. See *Export Newsletter* 65, 1969.

22. Lowell Lehman, 'An Interview with Albert E. Killeen: Marketing is What Our Business is all About Around the Globe,' *Refresher USA* IV, 1976, 9–10.

23. 'Operation customer in Middle Africa,' *Export Newsletter* 40, Dec 1967.

24. 'Fact, not Fiction,' *Coca-Cola South of the Sahara*, July 1963, 8 No. 17, 33.

25. Lehman, 'An Interview with Albert E Killeen,' 9–10.

26. 'A E Killeen Speeches,' 29:21, Coca-Cola Archives.

27. Lehman, 'An Interview with Albert E Killeen,' 11–12

28. Aristo Bentivoglio, 'Coca-Cola Launched in Libya,' *Coca-Cola Overseas*, October 1962, 15 No. 4, 24.

29. 'Camera shots around the world,' *Coca-Cola Overseas*, December 1962, 15 No. 6, 31.

30. 'Coca-Cola popular in West Africa,' *Coca-Cola Overseas*, February 1960, 13 No. 1, 10.

31. 'Camera shots around the world,' *Coca-Cola Overseas*, April 1963, 16 No. 2, 24.

32. 'Holiday in Ghana/Convention in Caracas,' *Coca-Cola Overseas*, February 1965, 18 No. 1, 9. For another example, the *Daily Graphic*, 5 March 1957, includes a page ad wishing Ghana a prosperous future. Below that, there is an ad 'Let CC put you at your sparkling best.' 2711, PRAAD, National Archives of Ghana.

33. D J Cord, 'Dakar, Gateway of West Africa,' *Coca-Cola Overseas*, April 1963, 16 No. 2, 30.

34. 'Usumbura: Capital of New African Nation,' *Coca-Cola Overseas*, December 1962, 15 No. 6, 28.

35. Peter Hunt, 'Corporation holds first public relations forum,' *Coca-Cola Overseas*, June 1963, 16 No. 3, 12.

36. 'Staying in Congo: Business in Congo Increases Despite Disturbances,' *Export Newsletter* 24, November 1960, 2. See also 'Kept Plant Going All Through Congo Crisis,' *Coca-Cola South of the Sahara*, October 1960, 8 No. 7, 27.

37. 'Sales up in Congo despite unrest' in 'Happenings around the world,' *Coca-Cola Overseas*, June 1961, 14 No. 3, 28.

38. 'Working for Coca-Cola in Africa has disadvantages—and advantages,' *Export Newsletter* 27, May 1961, 9.

39. B J Laporte 'Plant opens in Matadi, Congo,' *Coca-Cola Overseas*, October 1961, 14 No. 5, 7.

40. Ira Emery, 'Princess Opens Swazi Plant,' *Coca-Cola Overseas*, August 1963, 16 No. 4, 8.

41. D T Nkosi, 'Plant stockholder marries princess, Swaziland,' *Coca-Cola Overseas*, June 1964, 17 No. 3, 30.

42. 'On the Overseas Scene,' *Coca-Cola Overseas*, April 1965, 18 No. 2, 30.
43. 'On the African Scene: Zulu Paramount Chief Gets Official Residence,' *Coca-Cola Overseas*, August 1965, 18 No. 4, 6.
44. 'Export officials discuss growth plans,' *Coca-Cola Overseas*, February 1964, 17 No. 1, 3. See also 'Sprite comes to Africa, Asia,' *Coca-Cola Overseas*, December 1964, 17 No. 6, 30.
45. 'Export officials discuss growth plans,' *Coca-Cola Overseas*, February 1964, 17 No. 1, 3.
46. Ray Renaud, 'King Size "Coke" in Dar Es Salaam Tanganyika, East Africa,' *Coca-Cola Overseas*, June 1957, 10 No. 3, 2.
47. 'Export officials discuss growth plans,' 3.
48. See ad for 'At meal time, Coca-Cola refreshes you best' in *Coca-Cola South of the Sahara*, April 1964, 1 No. 3.
49. 'Area sales meeting, 1960,' *Coca-Cola South of the Sahara*, October 1960, 8 No. 7, 16.
50. *Ibid.*, 13.
51. 'Leopold bottlers train African salesmen,' *Coca-Cola South of the Sahara*, October 1960, 8 No. 7, ii–iv.
52. Aristo Bentivoglio, 'Around world expansion continues: New plants opened in Italy, Costa-Rica, Kenya; Venice one is remodeled,' *Coca-Cola Overseas*, December 1961, 14 No. 6, 22.
53. R W Cormack, 'L M Chaponda, A Director of Nyasaland Bottling Company,' *Coca-Cola Overseas*, October 1963, 16 No. 5, 32.
54. 'Camera shots around world: Nairobi,' *Coca-Cola Overseas*, December 1964, 17 No. 6, 29.
55. 'Espin Mlandle: Man of Action,' *Coca Cola South of the Sahara*, April 1964, 1 No. 3, 15–16.
56. 'Zulu Prince at Plant Party,' *Coca-Cola Overseas*, April 1965, 18 No. 2, 9. According to Export Newsletter 55 from Dec. 1971, Hlongwana started at Coca-Cola Export in 1941 as production *induna* (Zulu for headman).
57. An example of a local product is Krest in South Africa.
58. A A Parissis, '"Animals of Africa" campaign acclaimed,' *Coca-Cola Overseas*, October 1961, 14 No. 5, 10.
59. 'Camera shots around the world, Uganda,' *Coca-Cola Overseas*, April 1962, 15 No. 2, 31.
60. 'Animals of Africa Campaign,' *Coca-Cola South of the Sahara*, February 1964, 1 No. 2, 16.
61. 'Animals of Africa,' *Coca-Cola South of the Sahara*, May 1962, 8 No. 13, 18.
62. 'Orphaned cubs find home in Johannesburg Zoo,' *Coca-Cola Overseas*, February 1962, 15 No. 1, 15.

63. '"Animals of Africa" kits to be presented to zoo curators,' *Coca-Cola Overseas*, December 1962, 15, No. 6, 13.

64. E Neville Isdell, former Coca-Cola CEO, author interview by telephone, 30 March 2016.

65. 'Additional $22,400 Donated for Wild Life of Africa,' *Export Newsletter* 33, June 1962, 4.

66. 'Coca-Cola Co. takes 100 kids to game park,' *Coca-Cola South of the Sahara*, May 1962, 8 No. 13, 12–13.

67. Ray Renaud, 'Kruger National Park,' *Coca-Cola Overseas*, April 1967, 20 No. 2, 6–7.

68. 'Camera shots around the world,' *Coca-Cola Overseas*, August 1963, 16 No. 4, 26.

69. Jamal Booker, '1961 Animals of Africa Launch in South Africa,' 8 May 2012 <https://www.coca-colacompany.com/stories/1961-animals-of-africa-launch-in-south-africa> Accessed 15 June 2019.

70. 'Pigeons launch "birds of Africa" campaign,' *Coca-Cola Overseas*, December 1962, 15 No. 6, 11–12.

71. '"Birds of Africa" Land at Mauritius,' *Coca-Cola Overseas*, August 1965, 18 No. 4, 7.

72. I have written about collecting as ownership. See Sara Byala, *A Place that Matters Yet: John Gubbins's MuseumAfrica in the Postcolonial World* (University of Chicago Press, 2013).

73. Ira Emery, 'African Flora Benefits from Card Campaign,' *Coca-Cola Overseas*, October 1964, 17 No. 5, 16.

74. See Mahmood Mamdani's *Citizen and Subject: Contemporary Africa and the Legacy of Colonialism* (Princeton: Princeton University Press, 1996).

75. 'They know their country, South Africa,' *Coca-Cola Overseas*, April 1968, 21 No. 2, 24.

76. Letter from J P Austin to A Killeen, date not clear, 'Biography Files,' Coca-Cola Archives.

77. Photograph ES002024, 'Coca-Cola Overseas,' Coca-Cola Archives.

78. 'Middle Africa Knows,' *Coca-Cola Overseas*, February 1969, 22 No. 1, 27.

79. Photograph ES004938, 'Coca-Cola Overseas,' Coca-Cola Archives.

80. '"Discover Africa" a Successful Campaign in Ghana,' *In Middle Africa*, December 1970, 2, 15. Photographs DD02717 and 2718, 'Coca-Cola Overseas,' Coca-Cola Archives.

81. 'Uganda: Cradle of the Nile,' *Coca-Cola Overseas*, 1970, 23 No. 4, 8–13.

82. 'Exploring the edge of the world,' *Coca-Cola Overseas*, October 1968, 21 No. 5, 8–10.

83. 'East of Eden,' *Coca-Cola Overseas*, June–July 1970, 23 No. 2, 2–9.

84. Correspondence among Harold Weaver, Al Killeen, and J Paul Austin shows that Coca-Cola supported Weaver's production of 'Africa's Big Game' that, as one letter put it, 'has been used extensively around the company.' Unsigned letter from J P Austin to A E Killeen, cc Weaver, May 15, 1972, J Paul Austin files, Box 2 'South Africa,' Coca-Cola Archives.

85. W Labuschagne 'Cheetah,' *Coca-Cola Overseas*, 1971, 24 No. 2, 19–21; Gillian Lawrence-Brown, 'Animals of Kenya,' *Coca-Cola Overseas*, 1970, 24 No. 3, 14–23. An internal Coca-Cola timeline for Kenya includes information on the Big, Big Five Contest: 'Another part of the Big, Big Five Contest involved participants collecting sets of animal heads printed on the plastic inserts of Coca-Cola bottle tops. Anyone who collected a set of 5 bottle tops won a major prize, two leopard or lion heads won the contestant free Coca-Cola. 20 lucky people won major cash prizes.' Kenya timeline, Coca-Cola Archives.

86. Jacob Dlamini, 'To Know the African Wild was to Know the African Subject: What training as a field guide taught Jacob Dlamini about Culture, Nature, Power, and Race,' *The Johannesburg Review of Books*, 1 July 2019 <https://johannesburgreviewofbooks.com/2019/07/01/to-know-the-african-wild-was-to-know-the-african-subject-what-training-as-a-field-guide-taught-jacob-dlamini-about-culture-nature-power-and-race/#respond> Accessed 7 July 2019. See also Jacob Dlamini, *Safari Nation: A Social History of the Kruger National Park* (Athens: Ohio University Press, 2020).

87. 'Kariba Dam on Zambesi River to make Largest Man-Made Lake' *Coca-Cola Overseas*, June 1957, 10 No. 3, 4–9.

88. See International Rivers https://www.internationalrivers.org/campaigns/kariba-dam-zambia-zimbabwe Accessed 25 July 2022; 'Kariba Dam's Operation Noah,' 20 January 2022, *Zambian Observer* <https://zambianobserver.com/kariba-dams-operation-noah/> Accessed 25 July 2022; and Terence M. Mashingaidze, 'Beyond the Kariba Dam induced displacements: The Zimbabwean Tonga's struggles for restitution, 1990s–2000s,' *International Journal on Minority and Group Rights* (2013) 20 no. 3: 381–404.

89. 'Kariba Dam on Zambesi River to make Largest Man-Made Lake,' *Coca-Cola Overseas*, 4–9.

90. 'Kariba: Colossus of Africa': *Coca-Cola South of the Sahara*, October 1960, 8 No. 7, 9.

91. Cameron Day, 'Things go better with Coke,' *Coca-Cola South of the Sahara*, June 1965, 1 No. 10, 2–3.

92. Coca-Cola in Africa Timeline, Coca-Cola Archives. See also, 'Coca-Cola advertised in 57 languages,' *Coca-Cola Overseas*, October 1960, 13 No. 5, 14.

93. 'African Jingles in various vernaculars,' Coca Cola Archives.

94. 'Round and About with Coke,' *Coca-Cola South of the Sahara*, July 1963, 8 No. 17, 16. For one of many instances of sign advertisers, see an advertisement for metal outdoor signage in *Coca-Cola South of the Sahara*, June 1965, 1 No. 10, 13.

95. 'Happenings around the world' records a translation of a portion of an article which appeared in the Italian newspaper, *Corriere di Modena*. *Coca-Cola Overseas*, August 1953, 6 No. 4, 30. Corroborated in Kahn, *The Big Drink*, 39.

96. See Bourdieu, *Distinction*.

97. Homi Babha, 'Of Mimicry and Man: The Ambivalence of Colonial Discourse' in *The Location of Culture* (New York: Routledge Classic, 2004). Achille Mbembe makes a similar case with regard to the postcolony, noting that either/or binaries are not useful to understand lived experiences. Achille Mbembe, 'Provisional Notes on the Postcolony,' *Africa* 62 (1), 1992, 3–37.

98. *Coca-Cola Overseas*, June 1962, 15 No. 3, 33. This image is captioned as coming from *The Philippines Herald* in Manila.

4. THE LINK BETWEEN OLD AND NEW

1. 'Coca-Cola and the Community,' *In Middle Africa*, 1973, 17, 14.

2. Ghana serves as a prime example: When independence was won there, newspapers abounded with advertisements for rival carbonated beverages such as Vogeler's Curative Compound, Krola, which had a rainbow line of flavors, Muscatella, and other sparkling drinks. See, on Vogeler's: *Daily Graphic*, 13 August 1951, Accession No. 99, Classification NP1 13; On Krola: *Daily Graphic*, 1 February, 1957 and, on its rainbow family, *Daily Graphic*, 27 February 1957, 2, Accession No. 99, Classification NP1 31. 2715; For quinine tonic, raspberry, ginger ale, ice cream soda, Muscatella, lemonade, ginger beer, cola, club soda, strawberry ice cream soda, see: *Daily Graphic*, 15 March 57 Accession No. 99, Classification NP1 31, all National Archives of Ghana.

3. John Brinton, 'Coca-Cola in Upper Egypt,' *Coca-Cola Overseas*, 6 No. 1, February 1953, 21. On this work as deliberate, see 'For your information: Public Relations Pointers,' *Coca-Cola South of the Sahara*, 3 No. 2, June 1966, 5.

4. 'Colorful Coon Carnival: an old slave custom,' *Coca-Cola South of the Sahara*, 1 No. 3, April 1964, 6; 'Fort Victoria: Town and Country Fair,' *Coca-Cola South of the Sahara*, southern edition, 4 No. 1, March 1966, 8.

5. 'Malawi Republic Celebrations,' *Coca-Cola South of the Sahara*, Northern Edition, 4 No. 1, March 1967, 11.

6. 'Newcomer to Letaba Fleet,' *Coca Cola Southern Africa*, December 1971, 10.

7. 'Nairobi cinema opens with "Coke" promotion,' *Coca-Cola South of the Sahara*, 1 No. 3, April 1964, 28.

8. 'Coke for Kiddies Club,' *Coca-Cola Southern Africa*, August 1973, 4. Photograph DD02916, 'Coca-Cola Overseas,' Coca-Cola Archives.

9. J L Siebert, 'Climax of the South Africa film festival in Bloemfontein,' *Coca-Cola Overseas*, October 1960, 13 No. 5, 10.

10. 'On location with "Mr. Moses",' *Coca-Cola South of the Sahara*, June 1964, 1 No. 4, 10.

11. Cover image, *Coca-Cola South of the Sahara*, Northern Edition, March 1967, 4 No. 1.

12. 'One of Cetewayo's indunas of the period 1879 enjoys a Coke in 1963,' *Coca-Cola South of the Sahara*, July 1973, 8 No. 17, 26; 'Coca-Cola on location,' *Coca-Cola Overseas*, October 1963, 16 No. 5, 4.

13. A A Parrisis, 'Year of Enthusiasm and Initiative by Bottlers,' *In Middle Africa*, December 1970, 2, 3.

14. '"Miss Federation" sets "Coke" Sales Booming,' *Coca-Cola South of the Sahara*, special supplement, October 1960, 8 No. 7, 22.

15. 'Happenings around the world,' *Coca-Cola Overseas*, April 1961, 14 No. 2, 27. The winner from Kitwe was Emily Bwalya; Photos of EA Pageant 1962 and Miss Ghana Pageant 1962, 'General Africa,' Coca-Cola Archives.

16. D J Walker, 'African Beauties chosen in contest,' *Coca-Cola Overseas*, February 1962, 15 No. 1, 22.

17. Dorothy Driver, 'Drum Magazine (1951–9) and the Spatial Configurations of Gender,' in *Text, Theory, Space: Literature and History in South Africa and Australia*, edited by Kate Darian-Smith, Liz Gunner, and Sarah Nuttall (London: Routledge, 1996): 231–242.

18. 'Ruanda-Urundi: The heart of Africa' *Coca-Cola South of the Sahara*, Special supplement, October 1960, 8 No. 7, 18; 'Christmas Cheer for Cripples,' *In Middle Africa*, 1977, 25, 1.

19. 'Walking for Money: Freedom from Hunger,' *In Middle Africa*, 1972, 15, 6; 'Coca-Cola for Development Walk,' *In Middle Africa*, 1975, 19, 1.

20. 'Red Cross fair in Nigeria,' *Coca-Cola Overseas*, April 1965, 18 No. 2, 25.

21. 'Thank you South Africa,' *Coca-Cola South of the Sahara*, June 1966, 3 No. 2, 3; 'Coke Cooler Does Double Duty,' *Coca-Cola Overseas*, February 1968, 21 No. 1, 23.

22. 'Highway Homicide,' *Red Barrel*, December 1935, 14 No. 2, 2.

23. 'Road Safety Contests Continue in the UK,' *Export Newsletter* 25, January 1961, 2.

24. D J Pilgrim, 'Mombasa Road Safety Contest,' *Coca-Cola Overseas*, February 1959, 12 No. 1, 20–21.

25. 'Road Safety Contest,' *Coca-Cola South of the Sahara*, Northern Edition, March 1967, 4 No. 1, 8; 'Activities in Addis Ababa,' *In Middle Africa*, 1972, 14, 7. See also Photograph 028679, 'Malawi,' Coca-Cola Archives.

26. D J Pilgrim, 'Mombasa Road Safety Contest,' 20–21; 'Road Safety Contest,' 8; 'Awards for Salesmen in Abidjan,' *In Middle Africa*, 1972, 14, 6.

27. 'Bike-and-Coke fever hits Luanda,' *Coca-Cola South of the Sahara*, 1964, 1 No. 3, 18; Photographs DD01617 and DD01684, Coca-Cola Archives.

28. 'Fanta puts Monrovia on Wheels,' *Coca-Cola South of the Sahara*, December 1964, 1 No. 7, 11.

29. Photograph ES000697, Coca-Cola Archives; A D Campbell, 'Salisbury Cycle Race,' *Coca-Cola Overseas*, February 1962, 15, No. 1, 20. This Salisbury race was open to all. One Samuel Muhurure won the race. On Réunion, see: 'African Scene,' *Coca-Cola Overseas*, June 1969, 22 No. 4, 14.

30. 'Coca-Cola Bottlers' Rally,' *In Middle Africa*, 1978, 27, 6. See also 'South African Rally,' *Coca-Cola Overseas*, February 1969, 22 No. 1, 16–19; Lionel Cork, 'Safari of Speed in East Africa,' *Coca-Cola Overseas*, October 1962, 15 No. 4, 26–27; and '12th East African Safari,' *Coca-Cola South of the Sahara*, June 1964, 18. See also Photograph labeled 'Daressalaam Control, 1962,' 'Coca-Cola Overseas,' Tanzania 5, Coca-Cola Archives.

31. 'Bottlers in West Africa tie up with service stations,' *Coca-Cola South of the Sahara*, December 1964, 1 No. 7, 26; 'For your information: Use of Service Stations,' *Coca-Cola South of the Sahara*, April 1964, 1 No. 3 2–3; and 'Kiosks at Bulawayo filling stations,' *Coca-Cola South of the Sahara*, June 1966, 3 No. 2, 16.

32. 'Punch and Judy Show in Mombasa for the kids,' *Coca-Cola South of the Sahara*, May 1962, 8 No. 13, 28.

33. 'Around and About with Coke,' *Coca-Cola South of the Sahara*, southern edition, March 1966, 4 No. 1, 15.

34. '"My visit to a soft-drink factory" essay: Here are the winners,' *Coca Cola Southern Africa*, August 1972, 2.

35. '"Bring a Toy and Get a Coke,"' *Coca-Cola Southern Africa*, March 1974, 4.

36. Mark Pendergrast, *For God, Country, & Coca-Cola: The Definitive History of the Great American Soft Drink and the Company That Makes It*, Third Edition (New York: Basic Books, 2013): 29.

37. Photograph of customers waving to departing sampling team, 'Coca-Cola Overseas,' Zimbabwe 1, Coca-Cola Archives. On sampling 5,000 a day, see '"Miss Federation" sets "Coke" Sales Booming,' and, on heavy sampling, 'African Dealers Picnic,' both *Coca-Cola South of the Sahara*, special supplement, October 1960, 8 No. 7, 22 and 26; on sampling 10,000

in Durban, see 'Around and About with "Coke,"' *Coca-Cola South of the Sahara*, January 1961, 8 No. 8, 26.

38. 'The "Learn to swim" campaign.' *Coca-Cola Southern Africa*, August 1973, 2.

39. 'Scouts Jam Lagos,' *Coca-Cola Overseas*, October 1965, 18 No. 5, 12.

40. 'Airborne Missionaries,' *Coca-Cola Overseas*, April 1966, 19 No. 2, 26–27.

41. 'Bottlers News,' *Coca-Cola Overseas*, October 1966, 19 No. 5, 28; 'Zambia Study Tour,' *In Middle Africa*, 1973, 17, 17; On Inanda, see *Coca-Cola Southern Africa*, October 1973, 3; J Paul Austin files, Box 2, 'Export SA Waterford School,' Coca-Cola Archives.

42. '"Coca-Cola" popular in West Africa,' *Coca-Cola Overseas*, February 1960 13 No. 1, 10.

43. 'African Bottlers Provide Scholarships,' *Coca-Cola Overseas*, February 1964 17 No. 1, 12.

44. 'A helping hand for police and schoolboys,' *In Middle Africa*, 1972, 14, 22.

45. '1963 Awards for Students,' *Coca-Cola South of the Sahara*, July 1963, 8, No. 17, 19; 'Scholarships to Universities,' *Coca-Cola South of the Sahara*, southern edition, June 1967, 4 No. 2, 6; 'For a Better Education,' *Coca Cola Southern Africa*, April 1972, 3; and Letter from J P Austin to A Killeen, 17 August 1972. J Paul Austin files, Box 1 'South Africa,' Coca-Cola Archives.

46. '1972 National Cooler Contest,' *Coca-Cola in Southern Africa*, April 1973, 4; 'Winning Smiles in Kenya,' *In Middle Africa*, 1973, 17, 12; Photographs DD03094, DD03291, DD02892, Coca-Cola Archives.

47. 'Johannesburg Plant's Cooler Contest,' *Coca-Cola Overseas*, June 1966, 19 No. 3, 19; 'Queen for a Day: Cooler Contest,' *Coca-Cola Southern Africa*, December 1971, 11.

48. '1972 National Cooler Contest,' 4.

49. According to company records, Israeli bottlers had been reaching out since 1949, but a trade imbalance precluded any arrangement until now. Egypt, Box 1, Egypt file, Coca-Cola Archives.

50. 'In Letaba, South Africa, Juicing Plant Aids Citrus Industry,' *Coca-Cola Overseas*, December 1961, 14 No. 6, 28–29; 'Rooted in Optimism: Rebuilding the Groves,' *Journey: The Magazine of the Coca-Cola Company*, February 1988, 1 No. 4, 16–19; and 'Fact Sheet: Citrus Technology of the CC Company,' Egypt, Box 1, 'Egypt-1977, News Media Conf,' Coca-Cola Archives.

51. According to Austin's obituary in *The New York Times*, 'When he [Austin] was named president in 1962, the company had earnings of $46.7 million on sales of $567 million. When he retired in 1981, Coca-Cola was 10 times that size with net income of $481 million on revenues of $5.9 billion.' 'J P Austin Dead,' *The New York Times* 7 December 1985. <https://www.nytimes.

com/1985/12/27/us/jp-austin-dead-coca-cola-leader.html> Accessed 6 August 2019.

52. *Export Newsletter* 93, 1976.

53. The Six Day War of 1967 is also known as the June War, the Arab-Israeli War of 1967, and the Third Arab-Israeli War.

54. Letter from J P Austin to Eugene Black, 24 June 1968, J P Austin Files, Egypt File 6, Coca-Cola Archives.

55. The Yom Kippur War is also known as the Ramadan War, the October War, the 1973 Arab-Israeli War, and the Fourth Arab-Israeli War.

56. Andrew Jarnagin, 'When Coca-Cola Grows Citrus on the Nile, Who Wins? Revisiting the End of the Arab Boycott in Egypt,' *Grand Valley Journal of History*, 2016, 4 No. 1, Article 4. <http://scholarworks.gvsu.edu/gvjh/vol4/iss1/4> Accessed 6 August 2019.

57. See Roger Owen and Şevket Pamuk, *A History of Middle Eastern Economies in the Twentieth Century* (Cambridge: Harvard University Press, 1999); and John Waterbury, *The Egypt of Nasser and Sadat* (Princeton: Princeton University Press, 1983).

58. 'Sam Ayoub: the rebel with a brand new cause,' *The Atlanta Constitution*, 23 January 1986.

59. 'J P Austin Dead,' *The New York Times*.

60. 'Sam Ayoub: the rebel with a brand new cause.'

61. Telex from J P Austin to C M Halle, 18 June 1974. J P Austin files, Egypt 15.1, Coca-Cola Archives.

62. 'Preliminary plan,' J P Austin, Egypt File 1 of 6, Coca-Cola Archives.

63. Letter from Henry Kissinger to J P Austin, 18 September 1974, JP Austin files, Egypt 4, Coca-Cola Archives.

64. Miguel Macias, Pedro Araya, and Tully Dawson, 'Soft Drink Report on Egypt,' J P Austin Egypt files file 4, Coca-Cola Archives; See also letter from Henry Kissinger to J P Austin, 18 September 1974.

65. Memo: re trademark infringement, 14 August 1968, Egypt File 6, Coca-Cola Archives.

66. Michael Jensen, 'Coca-Cola is pressing efforts to uncork Egyptian markets,' *The New York Times*, 29 March 1978, Coca-Cola Archives.

67. 'Egypt Trip Report File,' J P Austin Egypt files, Egypt 2, Coca-Cola Archives.

68. Undated and unsigned draft letter from J Paul Austin to Anwar El Sadat, J P Austin Egypt Files, Coca-Cola Archives.

69. 'Sadat's Open Door brings Triumphant Coke back to Egypt,' *Advertising Age*, 22 October 1979. Coca-Cola Archives.

70. Undated and unsigned draft letter from J Paul Austin to Anwar El Sadat.

71. 'RC Cola, Lockheed wooing Egyptian Companies,' *Atlanta Journal*, 13 November 1979. Coca-Cola Archives.

72. Memo: re trademark infringement.

73. 'Coca-Cola, the soft drink that has become as much a symbol as Uncle Sam,' *The Washington Post*, 17 July 1979; 'Making the world safe for Coca-Cola,' *The Atlanta Constitution*, 30 September 1977, both Coca-Cola Archives; Michael Jensen, 'Coca-Cola is pressing efforts to uncork Egyptian markets,' *The New York Times*, 29 March 1978.

74. 18 million: 'Sadat's Open Door brings Triumphant Coke back to Egypt,' *Advertising Age*, 22 October 1970; Ten million: Jarnagin, 'When Coca-Cola Grows Citrus on the Nile, Who Wins?.' Five million: Nathaniel Harrison, 'Things go poorly for Coca-Cola project to grow fruit in Egypt,' *Christian Science Monitor*, 28 January 1981.

75. Coca-Cola News Release, 9 February 1983. Coca-Cola Archives.

76. Harrison, 'Things go poorly for Coca-Cola project to grow fruit in Egypt.'

77. Jarnagin suggests that Egypt was after a bribe and that Coca-Cola was not acting in good faith either. Jarnagin, 'When Coca-Cola Grows Citrus on the Nile, Who Wins?'

78. Michael Jensen, 'Coca-Cola is pressing efforts to uncork Egyptian markets.' See also, 'Coke to Pour 400,000 into Nile River Expedition,' *Atlanta Constitution*, 16 November 1977.

79. McCann-Erickson, Inc. to The Coca-Cola Export Corporation, Findings on the state of Egypt, 29 March 1978, Egypt, Box 1, File Booklet, Coca-Cola Archives.

80. Doremus and Company, Supplementary recommendations, Egypt Box 2, Egypt, Introduction to Egyptian Market, 1979, Coca-Cola Archives.

81. 'Reorganizing Africa,' *Export Newsletter* 57, June 1972; 'Move for Zone Office,' *In Middle Africa*, 1975, 19, 3.

82. 'The Coca-Cola Africa Story,' (Windsor: Coca-Cola Africa, c 2002). Coca-Cola Archives. Exact dates, as reported here: Chad (1971), Gabon (1972), Mali and Mauritania (1974), Uganda (1975), Central African Republic (1980).

83. 'Widening Markets,' *In Middle Africa*, 1976, 22, 4.

84. Coca-Cola in Africa timeline, 6. Coca-Cola Archives.

85. 'Stepping Stones,' *Export Newsletter* 50, September 1970, 4.

86. 'Stepping Stones,' *Export Newsletter* 58, September 1972, 7.

87. 'Krest Bitter Lemon for Kenya,' *In Middle Africa*, 1975, 20, 2.

88. 'A Commitment to Local Ownership,' *In Middle Africa*, 1978, 27, 2.

89. 'People in the News,' *The Thirst Breaker: A Newsletter for the Bottlers of the East Africa Region*, February 1981, 8.

90. The OAU would eventually come to include fifty-three African states before it was dissolved and replaced by the African Union in 2002.

91. 'Coke goes to the trade fair,' *In Middle Africa*, 1972, 15, 3.

92. Photograph, *The Thirst Breaker: A Newsletter for the Bottlers of the East Africa Region*, February 1981, 3; Photograph T08538, Coca-Cola Archives.

93. 'Making your Financial Contribution,' Remarks for Sam Ayoub, Chief Financial Officer, The Coca-Cola Company, Worldwide External Affairs Conference, Pine Isle, 11 November 1981. Ayoub speeches, Coca-Cola Archives.

94. 'Financial Report by Sam Ayoub,' Worldwide Marketing Conference, 21 February 1983, Los Angeles, Ayoub speeches, Coca-Cola Archives.

95. 'School feeding program,' *In Middle Africa*, 1973, 17, 15; 'Walk for Water,' *In Middle Africa*, 1976, 22, 3; 'They Feel No Pain,' *Coca-Cola South of the Sahara*, June 1964, 16–17.

96. 'Says Columnist John Chamberlain: "Foreign Aid Program" of Coca-Cola Beats Anything Washington Offers...,' *The Coca-Cola Bottler*, March 1963. Coca-Cola Archives.

5. A CATALYTIC ROLE UNTOLD

1. 'Mandela Aides Bar Coke,' *The Chicago Tribune*, 14 June 1990; 'Mandela Tour Organizers Say They Reject Coke's Offer to Help,' The Associated Press, 13 June 1990, Wednesday, PM cycle; and 'White press upset with Mandela's treatment in U.S.,' *United Press International*, 28 June 1990, Thursday, BC cycle.

2. 'ANC won't let Coke cash in on Mandela visit,' *United Press International*, 13 June 1990, Wednesday, BC cycle. See also, John Kirby Spivey, 'Coke vs. Pepsi: The Cola Wars in South Africa During The Anti-Apartheid Era,' Thesis, Georgia State University, 2009, 40; Eleanor Randolph, 'Mandela's Stops During U.S. Tour Reflect ANC Political Concerns,' *The Washington Post*, 17 June 1990, Sunday, Final Edition; Jesse Greenspan 'Nelson Mandela Comes to America: As the world mourns the death of Nelson Mandela, we take a look back at the "pop star's welcome" he received upon first visiting the United States in 1990,' 31 August 2018 (updated), <https://www.history.com/news/nelson-mandela-comes-to-america> Accessed 26 July 2022; and Mark Pendergrast, *For God, Country, & Coca-Cola: The Definitive History of the Great American Soft Drink and the Company That Makes It*, Third Edition (New York: Basic Books, 2013), 370.

3. Correspondence 1993 June–July, Mandela, Nelson's visit to Atlanta 1993, Box 30, Folder 17, Africa Group 1991–1999 from Series 5, 'The Coca-Cola Company 1938–2004,' Carl Ware Papers, Robert W. Woodruff Library of

the Atlanta University Center, Archives Research Center, Atlanta University Center. On 'quiet help,' see Pendergrast, *For God, Country, & Coca-Cola*, 370. See also S A Reid, 'Nelson Mandela in Atlanta: Collecting a Nest Egg for a New South Africa,' *The Atlanta Constitution-Journal*, 12 July 1993 <https://www.ajc.com/news/national/nelson-mandela-atlanta-collecting-nest-egg-for-new-south-africa/OCXFaTXsvAvnTNfzNVeqsO/> Accessed 18 July 2021.

4. 'Coke makes the top,' *Coca-Cola Southern Africa*, June 1971, 4.

5. E Neville Isdell with David Beasley, *Inside Coca-Cola: A CEO's Life Story of Building the World's Most Popular Brand* (New York: St. Martin's Griffin, 2011), 48.

6. *Coke in Middle Africa*, Dec 1971, 55.

7. E Neville Isdell, former Coca-Cola CEO, author interview by telephone, 30 March 2016.

8. 'Operation Breadbasket: biography,' Stanford: The Martin Luther King, Jr. Research and Education Institute, 23 October 1962 <https://kinginstitute.stanford.edu/encyclopedia/operation-breadbasket> Accessed 25 July 2022.

9. Spivey, 'Coke vs. Pepsi,' 29.

10. 'The Sullivan Principles,' Boston University Board of Trustees <https://www.bu.edu/trustees/boardoftrustees/committees/acsri/principles/> Accessed 25 July 2022.

11. Letter from Leon Sullivan to J Paul Austin, 13 June 1977, South Africa Box 2, South African Documents and Books, South Africa 1986, Coca-Cola Archives.

12. Letter from Ian Wilson to J Paul Austin, 8 January 1980, South Africa Box 2, South African Documents and Books, South Africa 1986, Coca-Cola Archives.

13. Archival materials show the hesitation around Sullivan from both the US and SA sides: Janet Pecha to J William Pruett, Research report on American Corporations in South Africa, 8 June 1978; Memo from F J Meyer, division manager, southern Africa to all members of staff, 28 February 1979; and outline of presentation to stockholder groups proposing that the company sign the Sullivan Principles, 27 February 1980, all South Africa Box 2, South African Documents and Books, Coca-Cola Archives.

14. Memo from Eric Churchward to Joe Wilkinson, 13 March 1980; Document on the Sullivan Principles Issue: A Synopsis, both South Africa Box 2, South African Documents and Books, Coca-Cola Archives. Coca-Cola did become a signatory around 1980.

15. Carl Ware with Sibley Fleming, *Portrait of a Businessman: One generation from Cotton Field to Boardroom* (Macon: Mercer University Press, 2019), 85.

16. Spivey asserts that Jackson's boycott was about the Sullivan principles, 'Coke vs. Pepsi,' 28. This is implied but not fully substantiated elsewhere. See John F. Burns, 'Jesse Jackson Takes Spirited Message to South Africa,' *The New York Times*, 24 July 1979, A8.

17. Ware with Fleming, *Portrait of a Businessman*, 107.

18. 'Accord Ends Coke Boycott,' *The New York Times*, 11 August 1981, D15; and 'Coca-Cola to sell South African Assets, Marking end of political balancing act,' *Wall Street Journal*, 18 September 1986.

19. Ware with Fleming, *Portrait of a Businessman*, 111.

20. William M Kelley Jr., Testimony before the Subcommittee on Africa of the House Committee on Foreign Affairs, 31 July 1980. South Africa Box 3, Coca-Cola Archives.

21. Recently, Ware has spoken again about the persistence of racial inequality at Coca-Cola: Matt Kempner, 'Coke's Former Go-To Executive on Race Sees Diversity Gap at Company,' *Atlanta Journal-Constitution*, 30 August 2019 <https://www.ajc.com/news/coke-former-executive-race-sees-diversity-gap-company/oU3myIrL4VQTYb1JWiYa2J/> Accessed 12 July 2022.

22. Ware with Fleming, *Portrait of a Businessman*, 121. See also note from Eric Mafuna, Folder 5: Manuscript: Seizing Opportunities, printed draft with revisions, by John Head, 2009–10, Carl Ware Papers.

23. Carl Ware, former head of Coca-Cola Africa, author interview by telephone, Atlanta, GA, 9 October 2015.

24. Ware with Fleming, *Portrait of a Businessman*, 119.

25. Carl Ware, author interview, 9 October 2015.

26. Ware with Fleming, *Portrait of a Businessman*, 137.

27. *Ibid.*, 139

28. For more on the backstory, see notes from Eric Mafuna captured in the Carl Ware Papers. Mafuna writes that Ware was meant to sweep everything under the rug, but instead demanded change, which earned him street credibility. He also explains the forces Ware was up against: 'Ex-South African managers operating out of the Atlanta HO of KO system attempted to defend the South African Minute Maid system against the prevailing political/social system. They sought to soften the edges of a grossly embarrassing situation by diverting attention to C Ware's alleged mishandling of the assignment, ie Carl and Davies ought to have visited the facility, in person, to verify wild claims made in Mafuna's report. What the South African expatriates failed to take into account was that the report had been thoroughly worked through and sanitized by Burson-Masteller executives—prior to it being shared with Atlanta leadership.' Elsewhere he explains, 'C Ware took a principled stand against the attack by South African expatriates—the latter had sought to lobby

some of the senior leadership but to no avail. C Ware walked out of his job late afternoon and it took the top leadership to persuade Ware to reconsider his decision. Ware was subsequently re-instated as the undisputed project leader of the South African situation. He was also mandated to visit South Africa to oversee the implementation of a list of far reaching recommendations based on his organizational assessment assignment. Needless to say, that there was considerable consternation and resistance (from local white managers) to the Carl Ware/Davies mission to South Africa in the months that followed. This resistance was later to be replaced by red carpet.' Note from Eric Mafuna, Folder 5: Manuscript: Seizing Opportunities, printed draft with revisions, by John Head, 2009–10, Carl Ware Papers.

29. Ware with Fleming, *Portrait of a Businessman*, 140.

30. *Ibid.*, 141.

31. *Ibid.*, 120.

32. 'Keough talk to SA Bottlers,' from Convention of South African Bottlers on 1 September 1983 in Monte Carlo, Don Keough Speeches, Coca-Cola Archives.

33. 'Remarks by Roberto C. Goizueta,' Johannesburg Bottler's Banquet, 13 October Roberto Goizueta Speeches, Coca-Cola Archives.

34. Letter from Anthony Tortorici, director of public affairs, to opinion leaders, legislatures, and administrators, unveiling new project. Coca-Cola Archives.

35. 'South Africa: Public Issues Review Committee,' speeches with agenda, meeting minutes, and correspondence, printed draft, 19 December 1985, Box 16, Folder 4, Memoir, Undated, Carl Ware Papers.

36. Ware with Fleming, *Portrait of a Businessman*, 152.

37. Carl Ware, author interview, 9 October 2015.

38. Ware with Fleming, *Portrait of a Businessman*, 151.

39. Minutes from meeting with Ware, 21 March 1986, Series 107, 260–262, Office of the President's Advisory Committee on South Africa, Emory University Archives.

40. Carl Ware, author interview, 9 October 2015.

41. Ware with Fleming, *Portrait of a Businessman*, 171.

42. Letter from J W M Makhene to Carl Ware, 13 July 1987, Box 29, Folder 10, Equal Opportunity Foundation 1987–1991, Africa Group 1991–1999 from Series 5, 'The Coca-Cola Company 1938–2004,' Carl Ware Papers.

43. 'South Africa—Public Issues Review Committee,' speeches with agenda, meeting minutes and correspondence, printed draft, 1985 December 19, Box 16, Folder 4, memoir, undated, Carl Ware Papers.

44. Also on the board: Sebolelo Mohajane, an activist from IDASA, Professor Pali Francis Mohanoe of the University of the North, and A Thembela,

rector from Zululand University. Letter from J W M Makhene to Carl Ware, 13 July 1987, Carl Ware Papers. See also, André Kraak, 'Private Sector Investment in Black Education and Training: Rescuing South African Capitalism from Apartheid's Crisis,' *Comparative Education*, 1989, 25 No. 2, 197–218 <https://www.jstor.org/stable/3099383> Accessed 18 November 2019.

45. Ware with Fleming, *Portrait of a Businessman*, 154. The book also claims that Sheila Sisulu, Gertrude Mncube, and Ebrahim Bhorat were named to the board.

46. Carl Ware, former head of Coca-Cola Africa, author interview at Coca-Cola headquarters, Atlanta, GA, 8 March 2016.

47. *Ibid.*

48. Barnaby J. Feder, 'Coke plans Pretoria Pull Out,' *The New York Times*, 18 September 1986, D1.

49. Bill Sing, 'Coca-Cola Acts to cut all ties with S. Africa,' *The Los Angeles Times*, 18 September 1986. For precedent, see NYT story, above.

50. Feder, 'Coke plans Pretoria Pull Out.'

51. NBS was meant to serve as a kind of placeholder structured specifically to, as an internal Coca-Cola document reported, 'maintain the employment practices established by Export, and to adhere to the code of conduct set forth in the Comprehensive Anti-Apartheid Act of 1986.' Box 28, Folder 6, American Friends Service Committee 1984–1986, Disinvestment from South Africa 1982–1989, Africa Group 1991–1999 from Series 5, 'The Coca-Cola Company 1938–2004,' Carl Ware Papers.

52. 'South Africa,' talking points, Mount Holyoke College, South Hadley, MA, printed 27 February 1989, Carl Ware at Mt Holyoke: Box 16, Folder 6, Carl Ware Papers.

53. 'Disinvestment as a Means to Black Empowerment,' Box 28, Folder 6, American Friends Service Committee 1984–1986, Disinvestment from South Africa 1982–1989, Africa Group 1991–1999 from Series 5, 'The Coca-Cola Company 1938–2004,' Carl Ware Papers.

54. This share offering was considered controversial at the time. See 'If Coke has its way, Blacks will soon own the Real Thing,' *Business Week* 23 March 1987; and 'SA Firm stirs a controversy with plan to sell shares to Blacks,' *The Wall Street Journal*, 19 October 1987.

55. Sixty percent of retailers and seventy-five percent of employees who purchased shares were Black, as reported by Ware in 1989 Box 16, Folder 6: 'South Africa,' talking points, Mount Holyoke College, South Hadley, MA, printed 1989 February 27, Carl Ware Papers. See also: Box 28, Folder 6, American Friends Service Committee 1984–1986, Disinvestment from South

Africa 1982–1989, Africa Group 1991–1999 from Series 5, 'The Coca-Cola Company 1938–2004,' Carl Ware Papers.

56. 'We Shall Return,' South African Bottlers' Convention, speech with letters, emails, powerpoint presentation and other materials, printed drafts #1–3, Bermuda 1992 August 4, Box 7, Folder 13, Carl Ware Papers.

57. 'South Africa Presentation,' Public Issues Review Committee, speech with meeting schedule, agenda, and minutes, printed draft 1988 December 15, Box 16, Folder 3, Memoir, Undated, Carl Ware Papers.

58. Carl Ware, author interview, 9 October 2015.

59. Ernest Mchunu, *Cheeky Native: A Practical Experience in Managerial and Leadership Excellence* (Reach Publishers, Wandsbeck: 2010) 96.

60. *Ibid.*, 97.

61. *Ibid.*, 135.

62. *Ibid.*, 139.

63. Dave Lewis, Chairman, Forbes Holdings, Peninsula Beverages, author interview, Peninsula Beverages, Cape Town, 12 July 2016.

64. Zanosi Kunene, Chairman of Coca-Cola Fortune, author interview, Kunene House, Johannesburg, 18 May 2017.

65. *Ibid.*

66. 'New Bottling Venture,' *Outlook Africa*, First Quarter, 1995, 1 No. 1 First Quarter, 1995. Box OS16, Folder 15, Carl Ware Papers.

67. Zanosi Kunene, author interview, 18 May 2017.

68. About the CCBA Group <https://www.ccbagroup.com/about-us/> Accessed 25 July 2022.

69. Stuart McLeod, Managing Director, Forbes Holdings, author interview, Peninsula Beverages, Cape Town, 16 July 2016; and Dave Lewis, Chairman Forbes Holdings, author interview, Peninsula Beverages, Cape Town, 12 July 2016.

70. INT199VIDEO, Coca-Cola Archives.

71. KO-002679, Coca-Cola Archives.

72. *Journey: The Magazine of the Coca-Cola Company*, September 1989, 3 No. 2, 9–13.

73. See, for instance, William Raspberry, 'No Way to Disinvest,' *The Washington Post*, 14 November 1986 that suggested, 'General Motors' pullout from South Africa, widely hailed by anti-apartheid here, might end up doing more harm than good,' a view attributed to Rev. Allan Boesak. See also, 'Aftermath of the Exodus: US Firms' Departure from South Africa hasn't helped Blacks,' *US News & World Report* 1 May 1989, that similarly stated, 'disinvestment has largely failed to achieve its proponents' lofty aims.'

74. Willie Esterhuyse, *Endgame: Secret Talks and the End of Apartheid* (Cape Town: Tafelberg, 2012).

75. Carl Ware, author interview, 9 October 2015.

76. Esterhuyse, *Endgame*, documents many. See also Allister Sparks, *Tomorrow is Another Country: The Inside Story of South Africa's Road to Change* (Chicago: University of Chicago Press, 1996), which does likewise.

77. Carl Ware, author interview, 8 March 2016. For a glimpse of other Coke work see, 'Archbishop Tutu Visits Atlanta Headquarters,' *Journey: The Magazine of The Coca-Cola Company*, August 1988, 2 No. 1, 23.

78. Carl Ware, author interview, 8 March 2016.

79. Feder, 'Coke plans Pretoria Pull Out;' and Ware with Fleming, *Portrait of a Businessman*, 159.

80. Mchunu, *Cheeky Native*, 187.

81. Carl Ware, author interview, 9 October 2015. After a ten-year absence, Pepsi returned through a partnership with prominent African Americans (including Shaquille O'Neal, Danny Glover, and Johnnie Cochran) under the umbrella, New Age Beverages.

82. 'We Shall Return,' Carl Ware Papers.

83. Letter from Tandi Gcabashe to Carl Ware, 22 April 1987, Box 28, Folder 10, American Friends Service Committee 1984–1986, Disinvestment from South Africa 1982–1989, Africa Group 1991–1999 from Series 5, 'The Coca-Cola Company 1938–2004,' Carl Ware Papers.

84. 'Why is CC Sold in SA?' South Africa Box 2, South African Documents and Books, South Africa 1986, Coca-Cola Archives.

85. Letter from Demond Tutu to Carl Ware, 10 April 1989, Box 28, Folder 3, Correspondence 1989–2004, Africa Group 1991–1999 from Series 5, 'The Coca-Cola Company 1938–2004,' Carl Ware Papers.

86. Carl Ware, author interview, 8 March 2016.

87. Memo from Carl Ware to John Hunter, 15 June 1993, Re: Nelson Mandela, Box 30, Folder 17, Carl Ware Papers.

88. Memo from Madeline Dickens to 'distribution,' on Ritz Carlton letterhead, re President Mandela's visit. Box 30 Folder 18, Carl Ware Papers.

89. Q and A about Mandela plus guest list. Box 30 Folder 18, Carl Ware Papers.

90. Memo from Linda K Peek to Goizueta, Ware, Hunter and Ivester re Mandela. Box 30 Folder 17, Mandela visit, 28 June 1993. Carl Ware Papers.

91. Memo from Carl Ware to John Hunter, 15 June 1993.

92. Ware with Fleming, *Portrait of a Businessman*, 214–217.

93. South Africa Bottlers' Convention, Remarks by Carl Ware, 5th Draft, June 7, 1994, Box 16, Folder 1, Series 2 Writings by Ware 1977–2011, Carl Ware Papers.

94. Carl Ware, author interview, 8 March 2016.

95. Letter from Nelson Mandela to Carl Ware, 28 July 1993, Box 28, Folder 3, Correspondence 1989–2004, Africa Group 1991–1999 from Series 5, 'The Coca-Cola Company 1938–2004,' Carl Ware Papers.

96. Tandi Gcabashe, former head of The Coke Campaign, author interview by telephone, South Africa, 20 May 2016.

97. *Ibid.*

98. Pendergrast includes this quote from Richard Maponya: 'I think Nelson is coming to see that what is holding us back now is not apartheid but money.' *For God, Country, & Coca-Cola*, 370.

99. See, for instance, Jim Burress, 'The Time Coca-Cola got White Elites in Atlanta to Honor Martin Luther King, Jr.,' 4 April 2015, NPR <https://www.npr.org/sections/codeswitch/2015/04/04/397391510/when-corporations-take-the-lead-on-social-change> Accessed 12 July 2021.

100. Carl Ware, author interview, 9 October 2015.

6. BELIEVE IN AFRICA

1. 'And then there were five,' *Journey: The Magazine of the Coca-Cola Company*, December 1992, 6 No. 3, 5.

2. 'The Face of Africa: A profile of the African consumer,' Video KO-0003389, Coca-Cola Archives.

3. Statement by the Press Secretary, For Immediate Release, Fourth African/African-American Summit, 18 July 1997 <https://clintonwhitehouse6.archives.gov/1997/07/1997-07-18-press-secretary-statement-on-africa-african-american-summit.html> Accessed 27 March 2020.

4. 'We Believe in Africa Speech,' Carl Ware, African/African-American Summit, 27 July 1997, Harare, Zimbabwe, Ware Speeches, Coca-Cola Archives.

5. 'Freedom, Opportunity, and Coca-Cola,' *Journey: The Magazine of the Coca-Cola Company*, February 1995, 8 No. 2, 8–11.

6. 'President Nelson Mandela Makes Visit to Coca-Cola Bottling Plant in Port Elizabeth,' *Outlook Africa*, First Quarter, 1995, 1 No. 1, 1, Box OS16, Folder 15, Carl Ware Papers, Robert W. Woodruff Library of the Atlanta University Center, Archives Research Center, Atlanta University Center. Also, Daryl Wilson, Managing Director, Nairobi Bottler, Coca-Cola Sabco, author interview, Nairobi, Kenya, 7 June 2016.

7. '1995 Rugby World Champions love Coca-Cola,' *Outlook Africa*, Second Quarter, 1995, 1 No. 2, Box OS16, Folder 15, Carl Ware Papers.

8. 'The Building of a New Nation: Implications for Coke' lays out, over 142 pages, detailed phases that would attend reentry, South Africa Misc., Coca-Cola Archives.

9. 'Taxis go better with Coca-Cola: it's the best Coca-Cola deal on wheels,' *Outlook Africa*, First Quarter, 1995, 1 No. 1, Carl Ware Papers.

10. 'Coca-Cola vs. Pepsi: Showdown in South Africa,' *Atlanta Constitution*, 4 October 1994. Pepsi launched a new campaign using Danny Glover and Shaquille O'Neal, who planned to pump fifteen million dollars into newly formed Egoli Beverages LP. Egoli was run by Ian Wilson, a white South African and former Coca-Cola employee who had by then been in the United States for twenty years. This article quotes Wilson as saying, 'Coca-Cola "doesn't have an organization that is representative of the spirit of black cooperation between African-Americans and black South Africans, but we do."' South Africa Misc., Coca-Cola Archives. See also: 'Getting the fizz back,' *Finance Week,* South Africa, page 2, which shows an image of a bottle in bed with the caption, 'waking up the cola champ.' Also see Mark Ashurst, 'South Africa: Return to the global economy is beginning to show,' *Financial Times* (London, England) 22 January 1998, which reports, 'Pepsico, the US-listed food and beverage group, quit South Africa in May for the fourth time since 1948. It blamed its departure on the dominant position of Coca-Cola's local distributor for the collapse of New Age Beverages in which it held a 25 per cent stake.' All South Africa Box 3, South Africa Clips 1998, Coca-Cola Archives.

11. 'Coca-Cola keeps promise,' *The Sowetan*, 11 March 1997, South Africa Box 3, South Africa Clips 1998, Coca-Cola Archives.

12. Press release: Investment in South Africa, 3 February 1997; 'SA wants double the fizz in SA market,' *The Sunday Times*, 8 December 1996; and 'Coke set to pour hundreds of millions into SA,' *Business Time*, 2 February 1996. All South Africa Box 3, South Africa Clips 1998, Coca-Cola Archives.

13. Press release, 3 February 1997.

14. This investment was covered in the following papers: *Business Day*, 4 February 1997; *Sowetan Business*, 4 February 1997; *The Citizen* (South Africa), 4 February 1997; *Bloomberg*, 3 February 1997; and *Gulph News*, 4 February 1997. All South Africa Box 3, South Africa Clips 1998, Coca-Cola Archives.

15. News Release: 'Coca-Cola Forms Joint Venture in South Africa,' 23 September 1994. South Africa Box 3, South Africa Clips 1998, Coca-Cola Archives.

16. 'Freedom, Opportunity, and Coca-Cola,' *Journey: The Magazine of the Coca-Cola Company*, February 1995, 8 No. 2, 10.

17. News Release: 'Coke names anchor bottler for Africa,' 7 November 1995. South Africa Box 3, South Africa Clips 1998, Coca-Cola Archives.

18. Committee on International Relations within House of Representatives, Hearing on trade and investment opportunities in Africa. Joint hearing with sub-committee on international policy and trade and the sub-committee on

Africa, 8 March 1995; Captured in videos KO-0003085, KO-0003088, KO-0003087, KO-0003086, KO-0003085, Coca-Cola Archives.

19. *Ibid.*
20. 'The Face of Africa: A profile of the African consumer,' video KO-0003389, Coca-Cola Archives.
21. Committee on International Relations within House of Representatives, 8 March 1995.
22. Martha M Hamilton and Lynne Duke, 'Africa's Potential as Trade Partner Attracts Corporate Interest,' *The Washington Post*, 23 March 1998, A14.
23. Philip Bowring, 'An Upbeat New Look at Africa,' *International Herald Tribune*, 3 February 1998, 8.
24. Hamilton and Duke, 'Africa's Potential as Trade Partner Attracts Corporate Interest.'
25. Mark Ashurst, 'South Africa: Return to the global economy is beginning to show,' *Financial Times* (London, England), 22 January 1998.
26. Bowring, 'An Upbeat New Look at Africa.'
27. Hamilton and Duke, 'Africa's Potential as Trade Partner Attracts Corporate Interest.'
28. Constance Hays and Donald G. McNeil, Jr., 'Putting Africa On Coke's Map; Pushing Soft Drinks on a Continent That Has Seen Hard, Hard Times,' *The New York Times*, 26 May 1998, D1.
29. Hamilton and Duke, 'Africa's Potential as Trade Partner Attracts Corporate Interest.'
30. *Ibid.*
31. 'Believe in Africa,' video KO-0002150, Coca-Cola Archives.
32. Hays and McNeil, Jr., 'Putting Africa On Coke's Map.'
33. 'We Believe in Africa Speech,' Carl Ware. On training centers see *Journey: The Magazine of the Coca-Cola Company*, March 1993, 6 No. 4, 17.
34. Carl Ware, former head of Coca-Cola Africa, author interview at Coca-Cola headquarters, Atlanta, GA, 8 March 2016.
35. 'A tale of two markets,' *Journey: The Magazine of the Coca-Cola Company*, March 1990, 3 No. 4, 9.
36. Carl Ware, author interview, 8 March 2016.
37. South Africa Box 3, South Africa Clips 1998, Coca-Cola Archives.
38. 'Tanzania: Starting from Scratch,' *Journey: The Magazine of the Coca-Cola Company*, March 1990, 3 No. 4, 12.
39. 'Where quality comes first,' *Journey: The Magazine of the Coca-Cola Company*, March 1990, 3 No. 4, 13.
40. Simon Goldberg, Allen Lang, and Tom Hagan, all of Mutare Bottling Company, author interview by telephone, Zimbabwe, 22 May 2017.

41. 'Coca Cola in Zimbabwe: turning the corner,' *Journey: The Magazine of the Coca-Cola Company*, December 1991, 5 No. 3, 16–19; See also 'Coca Cola set to double business in Zimbabwe/Atlanta,' *The Herald*, South Africa Box 3, South Africa Clips 1998, Coca-Cola Archives.

42. Carl Ware, author interview, 8 March 2016.

43. *Ibid.*

44. 'Coca-Cola to invest 30 million in Uganda,' *Reuters*, 12 July 1996, South Africa Box 3, South Africa Clips 1998, Coca-Cola Archives.

45. 'The importance of being Kenyan,' *Journey: The Magazine of the Coca-Cola Company*, March 1990, 3 No. 4, 11.

46. 'A tale of two markets,' 9.

47. Carl Ware, author interview, 8 March 2016. See also 'Coke Opens Bottling Plant in West Africa,' *Associated Press*, 7 November 1996, and similar coverage in the *Atlanta Constitution*. South Africa Box 3, South Africa Clips 1998, Coca-Cola Archives.

48. Carl Ware, author interview, 8 March 2016.

49. 'The Little Plant That Can: Coca-Cola Returns to Eritrea,' *Journey: The Magazine of the Coca-Cola Company*, June 1992, 6 No. 1, 20–22.

50. Carl Ware, author interview, 8 March 2016.

51. 'Back in Sudan,' *Journey: The Magazine of the Coca-Cola Company*, December 1992, 6 No. 3, 28.

52. Gerald Glancey, Joe van der Walt, and Nakampe Molewa, all longtime Coca-Cola Business Unit employees, in conversation with author, Coca-Cola offices, Johannesburg, 4 July 2016.

53. Carl Ware, author interview, 8 March 2016.

54. Gerald Glancey, Joe van der Valt, and Nakampe Molewa, author interview.

55. Donald McHenry was the US Ambassador to the UN from 1979–81. He later became a director of The Coca-Cola Company.

56. For more on Charles Frenette, see *Journey: The Magazine of the Coca-Cola Company*, Third Quarter 1997, 10 No. 1, 17.

57. Rute Moyo, Managing Director, Shanduka Beverages, author interview, Harare, Zimbabwe, 23 May 2017.

58. Nathan Kalumbu, former president Eurasia and Africa group, Coca-Cola, author interview, Harare, Zimbabwe, 23 May 2017.

59. Gerald Glancey, Joe van der Valt, and Nakampe Molewa, author interview.

60. *Ibid.*

61. Rute Moyo, author interview.

62. 'Believe in Africa,' video KO-0002150, and 'Believe in Africa' (shorter version), video KO-0002462, Coca-Cola Archives. See also Mark Pendergrast, *For God, Country, & Coca-Cola: The Definitive History of the Great American*

Soft Drink and the Company That Makes It, Third Edition, (New York: Basic Books, 2013), 419.

63. Matthew Burbidge, 'Ponte says "yebo" to new neon sign' 10 April 2000, *Independent Online* <https://www.iol.co.za/news/south-africa/ponte-says-yebo-to-new-neon-sign-34200> Accessed 20 April 2020.

64. For more on Cummings, see Press Release: 'The Coca-Cola Company Chief Administrative Officer Alexander B. Cummings to Retire,' 7 December 2015 <https://www.coca-colacompany.com/press-releases/coca-cola-chief-administrative-officer-alexander-b-cummings-to-retire> Accessed 20 April 2020.

65. See E J Kahn, Jr., *The Big Drink: The Story of Coca-Cola* (New York: Random House, 1960 [orig. 1950]), 166–169. Coke had been sponsoring the Olympics since 1928: Pendergrast, *For God, Country, & Coca-Cola*, 452.

66. See, for example, Ira Emery, 'English cricket team visits South Africa,' *Coca-Cola Overseas*, October 1957, 10 No. 5, 20; and 'Golfing on Three Continents,' *Coca-Cola Overseas*, February 1963, 16 No. 1, 2.

67. 'Olympic Swimmers in Cairo,' *Coca-Cola Overseas*, February 1966, 19 No. 1, 12.

68. 'Sports Desk,' *In Middle Africa*, December 1970, 2, 20.

69. 'Sports Desk,' *In Middle Africa*, 1972, 14, 21; 'Sports Desk,' *In Middle Africa*, 1972, 15, 18; and 'Swaziland Bottler Supports Local Sports,' *Coca Cola Refresher Southern Africa*, September 1974, 4.

70. 'Sports Desk,' *In Middle Africa*, 1972, 14, 21; 'Sports Desk,' *In Middle Africa*, 1972, 15, 18.

71. 'Pushball,' *In Middle Africa: A newsletter for Bottlers*, 1975, 19, 4.

72. 'Sport in Kenya,' *In Middle Africa*, 1973, 17, 5.

73. 'Camera Shots from Around the World,' *Coca-Cola Overseas*, October 1965, 18 No. 5, 32.

74. 'Sports Desk,' *In Middle Africa*, 1972, 14, 17.

75. 'Sport in Kenya,' *In Middle Africa*, 1973, 17, 5.

76. 'Basketball in Djibouti,' *In Middle Africa*, 1972, 15, 18.

77. See Peter Alegi, *African Soccerscapes: How a Continent Changed the World's Game* (Athens: Ohio University Press, 2010).

78. 'Sponsorship of black soccer,' *Coca-Cola Refresher Southern Africa*, March 1975, 1.

79. 'Fifa Coca-Cola World Football Development Program,' *In Middle Africa*, 1977, 4.

80. 'Following up FIFA/ Coca-Cola coaching,' *In Middle Africa*, 1978, 27, 11.

81. Sam Musvanya, Copa founder, author interview, Harare, Zimbabwe, 22 May 2017.

82. Alvin Madzivanzira, 'Copa Coca-Cola 2016 edition launched,' *The Patriot*, 26 May 2016 <http://www.thepatriot.co.zw/old_posts/copa-coca-cola-2016-edition-launched/> Accessed 20 April 2020. See also <https://www.youtube.com/watch?v=hpNoUKBnUZo> on Peter Ndlovu, accessed 20 April 2020.

83. Sam Musvanya, author interview.

84. 'Believe in Africa,' video KO-0002150, Coca-Cola Archives.

85. Sam Musvanya, author interview.

86. Ahmed Rady, Marketing Director for East, Central, and West Africa, Coca-Cola, author interview, Nairobi, Kenya, 10 June 2016.

87. Sam Musvanya, author interview.

88. Malefsane Mbele, senior IMC manager Coca-Cola, author interview by telephone, Johannesburg, South Africa, 26 July 2016.

89. Press release: 'COPA Coca-Cola National Championship Commences' <https://www.coca-colaafrica.com/press-centre/copa-coca-cola-national-championship-commences#> Accessed 20 April 2020.

90. Sanele Jele, 'Coca-Cola Sends Three Pupils to Pretoria HPC,' *Swazi Observer*, 11 October 2016 <https://www.pressreader.com/swaziland/swazi-observer/20161011/282969629579143>; and Ntokonzo Magongo, 'Coca-Cola Duo Back from Pretoria,' *Times of Swaziland* <http://www.times.co.sz/sports/104640-copa-coca-cola-duo-back-from-pretoria.html> both Accessed 20 April 2020.

91. Lucky Dlamini, Regional Materials Planner, Coca-Cola Refreshments, author interview, 7 July 2016, Mbabane, Swaziland.

92. 'Thousands register for 2019 Copa Coca Cola,' *Daily Nation*, 18 May 2019 <https://www.nation.co.ke/sports/football/Youth-register-for-2019-Copa-Coca-Cola/1102-5121528-an2le8z/index.html> Accessed 20 April 2020.

93. Ashish Patel, CEO, Label Converters Ltd., author interview, Nairobi, Kenya, 7 June 2016.

94. 'Coca-Cola launches "Open Happiness" in South Africa by celebrating soccer through the lens of youth,' *Media Update*, 25 May 2009 <https://www.mediaupdate.co.za/marketing/16189/coca-cola-launches-open-happiness-in-south-africa-by-celebrating-soccer-through-the-lens-of-youth> Accessed 20 April 2020.

95. 'The Ultimate Goal' <https://youtu.be/oDfSr6CiZq8> Accessed 20 April 2020.

96. 'Open Happiness Campaign Finds Ways to Celebrate Life's Simple Pleasures,' *Media Update*, 15 April 2010 <https://www.mediaupdate.co.za/marketing/24681/open-happiness-campaign-finds-resonating-ways-to-recognise-lifes-simple-pleasures> Accessed 20 April 2020.

97. 'The Gogos,' CCCO_60_222_E_H_Full high res.mp4, Coca-Cola South Africa Archives.

98. Duncan Mcleod, 'Coca-Cola Crazy for Good,' *Inspiration Room*, 23 January 2013. http://theinspirationroom.com/daily/2013/coca-cola-crazy-for-good/ Accessed 20 April 2020.

99. Marina Loubser, Brand Manager, Coca-Cola South Africa, author interview, Johannesburg, 6 July 2016.

100. 'The Crazy Master: A Short Story,' Coke_Crazy_Doccie_20Feb2013.mov, Coca-Cola South Africa Archives.

101. 'Swing for Change,' SFG.mp4, Coca-Cola South Africa Archives.

102. 'How we pulled off Share a Coke' <https://www.youtube.com/watch?v=0wnJpTpbJPE> Accessed 20 April 2020.

103. 'Share a Coke' <youtube.com/watch?v=4JmKVXgAFNA> Accessed 20 April 2020.

104. Alexander B Cummings, former head of Coca-Cola Africa, author interview, Atlanta, 8 October 2015.

105. Ashish Patel, author interview.

106. Alexander B Cummings, author interview.

107. For more see: <https://www.youtube.com/watch?v=DNhbrCwu7Bk> The dog's name is Jules, a border collie/pit bull mix. No actors were used; all participants were part of real 'crews' from downtown Johannesburg.

108. The Ting Tings, 'That's Not My Name,' *We Started Nothing*, 2008.

109. 'Bobby Ad.' CCR_SAC_2014_MASTER_FR_60s.mov, Coca-Cola South Africa Archives.

110. Marina Loubser, author interview.

111. Helena Wasserman, 'Coke wants you to get these South African names right, including Masixole and Tiann,' *Business Insider SA,* 3 December 2018 <https://www.businessinsider.co.za/coke-wants-you-to-get-these-south-african-names-right-2018-12> Accessed 20 April 2020.

112. 'How Coca-Cola's Phonetic Can Introduced South Africa to South Africa,' *Little Black Book* <https://lbbonline.com/news/how-coca-colas-phonetic-can-introduced-south-africa-to-south-africa/> Accessed 20 April 2020.

113. Wasserman, 'Coke wants you to get these South African names right, including Masixole and Tiann.'

114. Ahmed Rady, author interview.

115. *Ibid.* See also Ilyse Liffreing, 'Inside the growth of Coca-Cola's music show in Africa,' Digiday, 7 August 2017 <https://digiday.com/marketing/inside-coke-studios-growth-africa/> Accessed 20 April 2020; and Ashley Cook, 'Coca-Cola and Music: a Case Study,' *Music Business Journal*, Berklee School of Music, <http://www.thembj.org/2017/05/coca-cola-and-music-a-case study/> Accessed 27 July 2022.

116. Ahmed Rady, author interview. Also, Monali Shah, Head of Integrated Marketing Experiences, Coke Studio, Nairobi, Kenya, in conversation with author, June 2016.

117. 'I love you Africa,' part of 'Billion Reasons to Believe' campaign <https://www.youtube.com/watch?v=rb6yctYKfhs> Accessed 20 April 2020.

118. Ahmed Rady, author interview.

7. THE BOTTOM LINE

1. Sharon Keith, quoted in Press Release, 'Coca-Cola Creates Rainbows to Celebrate,' Biz Community, 22 April 2014 <https://www.bizcommunity.com/Article/196/12/112473.html> Accessed 20 April 2020.

2. Marina Loubser, Brand manager, Coca-Cola South Africa, author interview, Johannesburg, 6 July 2016; See also 'Coca-Cola Wins at Cannes Lions for its Rainbow Nation Activation,' 20 June 2014, *Media Update* <https://www.mediaupdate.co.za/marketing/66011/coca-cola-wins-at-cannes-lions-for-its-rainbownation-activation> Accessed 29 July 2021.

3. Alexander B Cummings, 'Tomorrow is Starting Now,' Speech at Africare Dinner, 3 November 2009. Cummings Speeches, Coca-Cola Archives.

4. Nathan Kalumbu, 'Africa's Time of Progress,' 9 June 2015 <http://www.coca-colacompany.com/stories/opinion-africas-time'> Accessed 16 June 2017. This same number was cited by Dan Baxter, Communications Director, EMEA, The Coca-Cola Company, email communication with the author, 14 July 2017.

5. Therese Gearhart, President, Southern Africa, Coca-Cola, author interview, Johannesburg, 5 July 2016.

6. Price Waterhouse Cooper UK, 'The Coca-Cola System's Contribution to National Development Goals in South Africa,' November 2012, commissioned by Coca-Cola; Price Waterhouse Cooper UK, 'The Coca-Cola System's Contribution to National Development Goals in Tanzania,' June 2013, commissioned by Coca-Cola; and R. Adedoyin Salami and Ayodele Olalekan Teriba, 'Economic Impact of the Coca-Cola System on Nigeria,' Lagos Business School, Pan African University, published by Coca-Cola Nigeria Ltd. On whether commissioned studies can be trusted, see S Steele, G Ruskin, M McKee, et. al., 'Always read the small print: a case study of commercial research funding, disclosure and agreements with Coca-Cola,' *Journal of Public Health Policy* 2019, 40, 273–285.

7. See, for example, Ahmed Driouchi, 'Coca-Cola's impact on Morocco,' Al Akhawayn University and the University of South Carolina, 2000; Douglas Woodward and Sandra J. Teel, 'Doing business in South Africa,' *Business and Economic Review* Jul–Sep 1999, 45 4, 3–9; Maurice McLeod, 'In Swaziland,

Coca-Cola has the power to make democracy the real thing,' 21 November 2013, *The Guardian*. <http://www.theguardian.com/commentisfree/2013/nov/21/swaziland-coca-cola-democracy-king-mswati> Accessed 2 January 2015; and Oxfam America, 'Exploring the links between International Business and Poverty Reduction: The Coca-Cola Value Chain Impacts in Zambia and El Salvador,' undated.

8. Jennifer Ann Ragland, Senior Director, Government and Stakeholder Relations, Coca-Cola, in discussion with author, Atlanta, GA, 13 July 2017.

9. The United Nations Millennium Development Goals <https://www.un.org/millenniumgoals/> Accessed 20 September 2020.

10. For more on The Coca-Cola Foundation, see <https://www.coca-colacompany.com/shared-future/coca-cola-foundation> Accessed 20 September 2020.

11. R E Freeman, *Strategic Management: A Stakeholder Approach* (Boston: Pitman, 1984).

12. Kim Davenport, 'Corporate citizenship: A stakeholder approach for defining corporate social performance and identifying measures for assessing it,' *Business and Society*, June 2000, 39 No. 2, 210–219.

13. John Elkington, *Cannibals with Forks: The Triple Bottom Line of 21st-Century Business* (Hoboken: John Wiley & Son, 1999).

14. Wayne Norman and Chris MacDonald, 'Getting to the Bottom of the "Triple Bottom Line,"' *Business Ethics Quarterly*, 2004, 14 No. 2, 243–262.

15. Dirk Matten and Andrew Crane, 'Corporate Citizenship: Toward an Extended Theoretical Conceptualization,' *The Academy of Management Review*, January 2005, 30 No. 1, 166–79.

16. John Chamberlain, '"Foreign Aid Program" of Coca-Cola Beats Anything Washington Offers...' *The Coca-Cola Bottler*, March 1963. Coca-Cola Archives.

17. 'The Battle on Poverty,' *Philadelphia Inquirer*, 31 December 1967. Biography files, Austin, Coca-Cola Archives.

18. 'J Paul Austin speaks out to save mother earth: Ecology on the Move,' *The American Soft Drink Journal*, August 1972, 20. Biography files, Austin, Coca-Cola Archives.

19. J Paul Austin, 'Environmental renewal or oblivion,' address to Georgia Bankers, 26 April 1970. Austin speeches, Coca-Cola Archives.

20. E Neville Isdell, with David Beasley, *Inside Coca-Cola: A CEO's Life Story of Building the World's Most Popular Brand* (New York: St. Martin's Griffin, 2011), 219.

21. E Neville Isdell, 'World Reach: Local Impact. The Expanding Role of Soft Drinks Around the World,' *Future Smarts*, 13 December 1993, 93. Coca-Cola Archives.

22. Nathan Kalumbu, 'Africa's Time of Progress,' June 2015 <http://www.cocacolacompany.com/stories/opinion-africas-time> Accessed 16 June 2017.

23. Hamish Banks, 'The business of peace: Coca-Cola's contribution to stability, growth, and optimism,' *Business Horizons*, 2016, 59, 455–461.

24. Michael Goltzman, then Vice President of International Government Relations and Public Affairs, The Coca-Cola Company, Testimony for the record before the Senate Committee on Foreign Affairs, 4 May 2017.

25. John Elsasser, 'Coca-Cola's Chief Sustainability Officer Bea Perez on Trust, Transparency, and Shared Values,' *Tactics*, 25 December 2015, 15.

26. Author conversations: Bea Perez, Chief Sustainability Officer, The Coca-Cola Company, Ruhunda, Rwanda, 12 June 2016; Don Dussey, Senior Public Affairs and Communication Manager, Central, East, and West Africa Business Unit, Rwanda, 12 June 2016; Nkechi Odiari, Public Affairs and Communication, Coca-Cola Nigeria, May, 2017; Norah Odwesso, Public Affairs and Communication, Nairobi, Kenya, June, 2016; Ifeoma Okoye, Regional Public Affairs Manager, Coca-Cola Hellenic Bottling Company, Nigeria, May, 2017; Camilla Osborne, Communications Manager, Coca-Cola Southern Africa, Johannesburg, South Africa, 2016–2017; Aysia Sheik, Public Affairs: Sustainability, Coca-Cola South Africa, Johannesburg, South Africa, July 2017; Priscilla Urquhart, Public Affairs and Communications, Peninsula Beverages, Cape Town, South Africa, 2016 and 2022; Emily Waita-Macharia, Public Affairs, Communications, and Sustainability, Coca-Cola Central, East, and West Africa, Ltd., Nairobi, Kenya, June, 2016; and Anne Wangalachi, Public Affairs and Sustainability Manager, Coca-Cola Central, East, and West Africa, Ltd., Nairobi, Kenya, June, 2016.

27. Melinda Gates, 'What Non-Profits can Learn from Coca-Cola,' TEDx Exchange, December 2010 <https://www.ted.com/talks/melinda_gates_what_nonprofits_can_learn_from_coca_cola?language=en> Accessed 19 January 2015.

28. PLM followed an earlier attempt to use Coke's networks to distribute medicines. See Sarika Bansal, 'Making a Medicine as Easy to Find as a Can of Coke,' *The New York Times*, The Opinionator, 3 July 2013.

29. PLM Fact Sheet, undated. All PLM fact sheets and one pagers shared by GETF.

30. Beatriz Perez and Guy Wollaert, 'Soda pop and vaccines leveraging consumer supply chains to promote public health and economic uplift,' *Voices on Society: The Art and Science of Delivery*, McKinsey Publishing 2013, 24. Additionally, they noted that 'Patients are getting the right vaccination 80 percent of the time, up from 50 percent two years earlier.'

31. Swaziland one pager, PLM. Coca-Cola had long done work spreading awareness about illnesses, as described by Dr. Chris Kirubi, for example. Dr. Chris Kirubi, Chairman, Nairobi Bottlers, author interview, Nairobi, 7 June 2016.

32. Mozambique one pager, PLM.

33. Liberia one pager, PLM. Also, Michael Goltzman, Vice President of International Government Relations and Public Affairs, The Coca-Cola Company, author interview by SKYPE, 16 March 2016.

34. South Africa one pager, PLM.

35. Nigeria one pager, PLM.

36. For an overview of PLM, see Shirin Ahmed, Leslie Curry, and Erika Linnander, 'Project Last Mile: Applying Coca-Cola's Expertise to Improve Delivery of Life-Saving Medicines,' Yale Global Health Leadership Institute, Yale University, New Haven, CT, 2015.

37. 'Project Last Mile supports the rollout of Covid-19 vaccines in Africa' <https://www.youtube.com/watch?v=jF2I5Y934ls> Accessed 27 July 2022.

38. For details on Technoserve, see <https://www.technoserve.org/our-work/projects/project-nurture/> Accessed 12 May 2021. See also, John Miller and Lucy Parker, *Everybody's Business: The Unlikely Story of How Big Business Can Fix the World* (London: Biteback Publishing, 2013) 3–27.

39. Project Nurture Messaging Fact Sheet, 2014.

40. Beth Jenkins and Lorin Fries, 'Project Nurture: Partnering for Business Opportunity and Development Impact,' 2013, The CSR Initiative at the Harvard Kennedy School, Cambridge, MA, 4.

41. For information on a sister program, see Amy C Edmondson and Jean-Francois Harvey, 'Haiti Hope: Innovating the Mango Value Chain,' Harvard Business School, 10 January 2016, 616-040.

42. Banks, 'The business of peace: Coca-Cola's contribution to stability, growth, and optimism.'

43. Michael Goltzman, Testimony for the Record, 4 May 2017.

44. Susan Mboya, President, The Coca-Cola Foundation, author interview by telephone, Nairobi, Kenya, 5 June 2016.

45. Steve Okire, NBL Yes! hub operator, author interview, Ruaka, Kenya, 8 June 2016. Also, Ronald Okello, Experiential Marketing, Nairobi Bottlers Limited, Sabco, in conversation with author, Nairobi, Kenya, 8 June 2016.

46. Miller and Parker, *Everybody's Business*, 334. See also: *Coca-Cola 5x20: Unleashing the Power of Women Entrepreneurs*, Report prepared by Babson, December 2016 <https://www.coca-colacompany.com/content/dam/journey/us/en/policies/pdf/sustainability/the-coca-cola-company-5-by-20-report-december-2016.pdf> Accessed 27 July 2022.

47. See Clinton Foundation events information here: <https://www.clintonfoundation.org/clinton-global-initiative/meetings/annual-meetings/2010> Accessed 27 July 2022.

48. 5x20 Infographic, 2014, citing: UNICEF, *Gender Equality: The Big Picture*, 2007, and Phil Borges, *Women Empowered: Inspiring Change in the Emerging World*, 2007.

49. *Coca-Cola 5x20: Unleashing the Power of Women Entrepreneurs*, 2016.

50. *Coca-Cola 5x20: A Decade of Achievement,* March 2021, 5 <https://www.coca-colacompany.com/content/dam/journey/us/en/policies/pdf/sustainability/coca-cola-5by20-report-march-2021.pdf> Accessed 29 July 2021.

51. *Ibid.*, 4.

52. 5x20 Data Release, 12 April 2016.

53. *Coca-Cola 5x20: Unleashing the Power of Women Entrepreneurs*; *Coca-Cola 5x20: A Decade of Achievement*, 4.

54. Miller and Parker, *Everybody's Business*, 384. As of its 2016 Sustainability Update, Coca-Cola announced that it had empowered 1.7 million women, nearly half of whom fell in the catchall 'Europe, Middle East, and Africa' category <http://www.coca-colacompany.com/2016-sustainability-report>. According to *Coca-Cola 5x20: Unleashing the Power of Women Entrepreneurs*, the Company earned significant international recognition for 5by20, including the Catalyst Award (New York 2013), 'Best Global Initiative for Women's Empowerment,' awarded at the Women in Leadership Economic Forum (Dubai, December 2014), and 'Women's Empowerment Principles Leadership Award (2014),' given by Women's Empowerment Principles, a joint initiative of UN Women and the UN Global Compact.

55. 'Coca-Cola 5x20 map' <http://www.coca-colacompany.com/5by20/5by20-map> and 'Coca-Cola 5x20 by the numbers,' <http://www.coca-colacompany.com/stories/sustainability/2017/infographic-5by20-bythenumbers-2017> which says that 48% come from a combined 'Europe, Middle East, and Africa.' In first years, 78% of 5x20 were in Africa and Eurasia. See also 'Unleashing the Power of Women Entrepreneurs,' pages 5 and 45, Accessed 21 July 2021. Communications Director April Jordan noted that as of 2015, about 60% of empowered women came from Africa, April Jordan, author interview by telephone, Atlanta, GA, 10 March 2016.

56. April Jordan, Communications Director, Coca-Cola, author interview. Supported by reports on 5x20 as well.

57. 'Coca-Cola Surpasses 5x20 Economic Empowerment Goal,' 8 March 2021 <https://www.coca-colacompany.com/news/coca-cola-surpasses-5by20-goal> Accessed 29 July 2021.

58. April Jordan, author interview. See also: 'Coca-Cola's Micro-Distribution Model,' <https://thesupplychainlab.blog/2019/09/30/update-coca-colas-micro-distribution-model/> Accessed 30 July 2021.

59. April Jordan, author interview.

60. For more, see Jane Nelson, Eriko Ishikawa and Alexis Geaneotes Executive Summary, 'Developing Inclusive Business Models: A Review of Coca-Cola's Manual Distribution Centers in Ethiopia and Tanzania,' Harvard Kennedy School and International Finance Corporation (of the World Bank), 2009.

61. 'Coca-Cola Surpasses 5x20 Economic Empowerment Goal.'

62. 5by20 Visits, Accra, Ghana, 12 May 2017. Also, Lariena Adjaayi, Public Affairs and Communications Assistant, Coca-Cola Equatorial Africa, Ltd., in conversation with author, Ghana, May, 2017.

63. Coca-Cola produced MDC Lagos sheet about Alhaja Lawal. Also, Emeka Mba, Public Affairs and Communications, Coca-Cola Nigeria, Ltd., in conversation with author, Lagos, Nigeria, 10 May 2017.

64. Alhaja Lawal, MDC operator, author interview, Lagos, Nigeria, 9 May 2017. I also visited Alhaja Olabukola, MDC Operator at Olabukola Ventures, Lagos, Nigeria, 9 May 2017.

65. MK Maina, MDC operator, author interview, Ngong, Kenya, 8 June 2016. Also, Victoria Macharia, 5BY20 Coordinator, Women's Economic Empowerment, Nairobi Bottlers Limited, Coca-Cola Sabco, in conversation with author, Nairobi, Kenya, 8 June 2016.

66. Aspirant MDC owner, author interview, South Africa, 4 July 2016.

67. 5x20 participants, author interviews, Imbaba, Egypt, 17 May 2016. Also, Ghada Makady, Public Affairs Director, Coca-Cola, author interview, Cairo, Egypt, 19 May 2016; Karima Elibachy, Public Affairs and Communication, Coca-Cola Egypt, 17 May 2016; and Rana Gamali, Director, Public Affairs and Communication, Coca-Cola Egypt, in conversation with author, Cairo, Egypt, 16 May 2017.

68. April Jordan, author interview.

69. *Coca-Cola 5x20: A Decade of Achievement*, 9.

70. Bathini Tati, 5x20 participant, author interview, Meadowlands, South Africa, 5 July 2016.

71. 'Coca-Cola Surpasses 5x20 Economic Empowerment Goal,' 8 March 2021 <https://www.coca-colacompany.com/news/coca-cola-surpasses-5by20-goal> Accessed 29 July 2021. Numbers verified by Ernst and Young. See also *Coca-Cola 5x20: A Decade of Achievement*, 7.

72. 'Coca-Cola Surpasses 5x20 Economic Empowerment Goal.' Also, on women workers, Bryn Morse, HR Director, Peninsula Beverages, author interview, Cape Town, South Africa, 12 July 2016; and Desiree Johannes, Employee

Relations Manager, Peninsula Beverages, Cape Town, South Africa, 11 July 2016.

73. J Paul Austin, 'Environmental renewal or oblivion,' Address by Austin to Georgia Bankers 16 April 1970, Austin Speeches, Coca-Cola Archives. In 1962, for another example, *Coca-Cola South of the Sahara* reported that 'almost 900,000,000 gallons of water were purified in overseas bottling plants' that year. 'Between ourselves: Training Means Success,' *Coca-Cola South of the Sahara*, May 1962, 8 No. 13, 3.

74. Bartow J Elmore, *Citizen Coke: The Making of Coca-Cola Capitalism* (New York: W.W. Norton, 2015), 155–192.

75. Monica Ellis, CEO of the Global Environment and Technology Foundation (GETF), author interview by telephone, 6 September 2017.

76. For UN water goals, see <https://www.un.org/sustainabledevelopment/water-and-sanitation/> Accessed 10 July 2017.

77. 'Statistics,' Water Aid Global <http://www.wateraid.org/what-we-do/the-crisis/statistics#crisis> Accessed 10 July 2017; and JMP, WHO, and UNICEF, 'Progress on Drinking Water, Sanitation and Hygiene,' 2017 <https://washdata.org/> Accessed 17 July 2017.

78. 'Refresh the World: Make a Difference: 2020 Business and Environmental, Social and Governance Report,' 21, Version 4, 14 June 2021 <https://www.coca-colacompany.com/content/dam/journey/us/en/reports/coca-cola-business-environmental-social-governance-report-2020.pdf#page=21> Accessed 1 August 2021.

79. *Ibid.*

80. Coca-Cola's overuse of water was called into question in Cape Town during the water crisis there. See, for example, Steve Kretzmann and Raymond Joseph, 'Coca-Cola and Cape Town's sweetheart Day Zero deal: How big business ignored the water restrictions and got away with it,' Ground Up, <https://www.groundup.org.za/article/coca-cola-and-cape-towns-sweetheart-day-zero-deal/> Accessed 1 July 2021.

81. Maame Bottling Facility operators, author interview, Accra, Ghana, 12 May 2018. Also, Rodrigue Bila, Regional Franchise Director, West and Equatorial Africa, Coca-Cola, author interview, Accra, Ghana, 11 May 2017.

82. John Schwartz, 'Coca-Cola Expects to Reach Its Water Replenishment Goal 5 Years Early,' *The New York Times*, 25 August 2015; Also, Greg Koch, Director of Global Water Stewardship for Coca-Cola, and Serena Levy, Communications Director, Environment, author interview, Atlanta, GA, 7 March 2016.

83. 'Refresh the World: Make a Difference,' 23.

84. *Ibid.*, 25.

85. 'Morocco (L'ALCESDAM): Reforestation in Southern Morocco,' October 2016 fact sheet; and 'South Africa: Four Returns in the Port Elizabeth Catchment Area Program,' March 2017 fact sheet.

86. 'Somalia (IRD): Somalia Drought Resistance Program,' May 2017 fact sheet.

87. 'Ghana and Mali (CARE): Scaling Water Smart Agriculture through Pathways, Program: Replenish Africa Initiative,' March 2017 fact sheet; 'Mali (SETRA): Community Water Supply, Sanitation and Small-Scale Agriculture,' February 2016 fact sheet; and 'Kenya (The Nature Conservancy (TNC) II): The Upper Tana-Nairobi Water Fund,' March 2017 fact sheet.

88. 'Cameroon (Plan): Water and Sanitation for Schools and Communities in Akonlinga and Gaschiga Councils,' February 2016 fact sheet; 'Liberia: Improving Access to Potable Water and Adequate Sanitation in Health Facilities,' May 2017 fact sheet; and 'Senegal: Potable Water Supply to Rural Communities,' February 2016 fact sheet.

89. Greg Koch, author interview. Also 'Burkina Faso (WaterAid): Improving Access to Water in Peri-Urban Ouagadougou,' March 2017 fact sheet; and 'Mali (SETRA): Community Water Supply, Sanitation and Small-Scale Agriculture,' February 2016 fact sheet.

90. 'Somalia (IRD): Somalia Drought Resistance Program,' May 2017 fact sheet.

91. 100 villages aid recipients, author interviews, Beni Warkan, Egypt, 18 May 2016; and Ghada Makady, author interview.

92. For instance, 'Somaliland (TS): Haraf-Ayaha Water Supply Project Program: Replenish Africa Initiative,' April 2017 fact sheet.

93. Visit and interviews at Pakro Water Health Center, 11 May 2017.

94. Visit and interviews at Ablekuma Water Health Center, 11 May 2017.

95. 'The Coca-Cola Africa Foundation Continues Its Ebola Relief Efforts Through Clean Water Access,' *Modern Ghana*, 2 September 2015 <https://www.modernghana.com/news/597130/the-coca-cola-africa-foundation-continues-its-ebol.html> Accessed 20 July 2021. Also, Prashant Kulkarni, Business Head, WaterHealth, and Krishna Rao, Chief Technical Officer, West Africa, WaterHealth, in conversation with author, Ghana, 11 May 2017.

96. Alexander B Cummings, Head of Coca-Cola Africa, author interview, Atlanta, 8 October 2015.

97. Mirera Suswa, Small Scale Independent Providers, author interview, Mirera, Kenya, 9 July 2016; James Kariuki Wandimi, Project Manager, WSUP (Water and Sanitation for the Urban Poor), author interview, Naivasha, Kenya, 9 July 2016; And Geoffrey Mwai, Public Affairs and Communications, Coca-Cola Kenya, Nairobi, Kenya, in conversation with author, July 2016.

98. Eli Dahi, 'Africa's U-Turn in Defluoridation Policy: From the Nalgonda Technique to Bone Char,' research report Fluoride, October–December

2016, 49(4 Pt 1): 401–416. <https://www.fluorideresearch.org/494Pt1/files/FJ2016_v49_n4Pt1_p401-416_pq.pdf> Accessed 28 July 2021.

99. 5x20 participants, author interviews, Mirera, Kenya, 9 July 2016. Also, Victoria Macharia, 5BY20 Coordinator, Women's Economic Empowerment, Nairobi Bottlers Limited, Coca-Cola Sabco, author interview, Nairobi, Kenya, 8 June 2016.

100. 'Coca-Cola Africa Foundation Fact Sheet: Kenya (WSUP): Naivasha Water and Sanitation for the Urban Poor,' February 2016 fact sheet.

101. 'Refresh the World: Make a Difference,' 25.

102. *Ibid.*

103. *Ibid.*, 20, 22, and 25.

104. Rudi Sueys, Global Manager of Sustainability, Coca-Cola, author interview online, Atlanta, GA, 17 July 2017; and Bruce Karas, VP Environmental Sustainability, Coca-Cola, author interview, Atlanta, GA, 20 July 2017. See also 'Meeting Evolving Tastes and Customizing Experiences for People: Coca-Cola Freestyle,' 24 August 2018. <https://www.coca-colacompany.com/news/meeting-evolving-tastes-with-less-waste> Accessed 1 August 2021.

105. Austin, 'Environmental renewal or oblivion.'

106. 'The True Facts about Littering in South Africa,' *Coca Cola Intercom: Internal Newsletter of the Southern and Central Africa Division of the Coca-Cola Company*, October 1981, 1 No. 4, 7.

107. Coke is a corporate sponsor of nonprofits like 'Keep America Beautiful,' 'The Recycling Partnership,' and 'The Closed Loop Fund.'

108. 'National Overview: Facts and Figures on Materials, Wastes and Recycling,' <https://www.epa.gov/facts-and-figures-about-materials-waste-and-recycling/national-overview-facts-and-figures-materials> Accessed 20 July 2021.

109. Erin McCormick, Bennett Murray, Carmela Fonbuena, Leonni Kijewski, Gokce Saracoglu, Jamie Fullerton, Alastair Gee, and Charlotte Simmonds, 'Where does your plastic go? Global investigation reveals America's dirty secret,' <https://www.theguardian.com/us-news/2019/jun/17/recycled-plastic-america-global-crisis> Accessed 20 July 2021.

110. Paul Bowen, Director, and Carlos Pacheko, Manager, both Global Environmental Sustainability, Coca-Cola, author interview, Atlanta, GA, 12 July 2017.

111. Kenneth Rapoza, 'China Quits Recycling as Trash as Sustainable Start-up Makes Strides' <https://www.forbes.com/sites/kenrapoza/2021/01/10/china-quits-recycling-us-trash-as-sustainable-start-up-makes-strides/?sh=4332d4915a56> Accessed 20 July 2021.

112. See <https://www.plasticpollutioncoalition.org/> and this in particular, 'Earth Island Institute Files Lawsuit Against Coca-Cola for False Advertising,' 8 June 2021 <https://www.plasticpollutioncoalition.org/blog/2021/6/8/earth-island-institute-files-lawsuit-against-coca-cola-for-false-advertising> Accessed 20 July 2021.

113. Bruce Karas, author interview.

114. 'Coca-Cola Unveils Paper Bottle Prototype,' 6 November 2020 <https://www.coca-colacompany.com/news/coca-cola-unveils-paper-bottle-prototype> Accessed 20 July 2021.

115. Z Boz, V Korhonen, and K S Claire, 'Consumer considerations for the implementation of sustainable packaging: A review,' *Sustainability*, 2020 12 No. 6, 2192.

116. This is a debated number. Some scholarly articles suggest as little as eight re-uses (R Stefanini, G Borghesi, A Ronzano, *et. al.*, 'Plastic or glass: a new environmental assessment with a marine litter indicator for the comparison of pasteurized milk bottles,' *Int J Life Cycle Assess,* 2021, 26, 767–784, while I heard up to forty at various plants.

117. Mpumelelo Makhubu, Corporate Affairs Director, Swaziland Beverages, author interview, 7 July 2016. Makhubu said that the bottlers do not think that their glass is used at Ngwenya, despite what the place advertises. Still, he described empowering women pickers to help return missing empties for re-use.

118. Glass needs to be separated by color. It also, if thrown into a single stream, can contaminate other recyclables. See 'The glass recycling problem: what's behind it and what to do' <https://greatforest.com/sustainability101/the-glass-recycling-problem/> Accessed 1 August 2021.

119. At least one bottler, Peninsula Beverages in South Africa, has returnable plastic bottles. Greg Morse, Manufacturing Director, and Rodney McKinley, General Manager, both Peninsula Beverages, author interviews, Cape Town, South Africa, 11 July 2016; Also, visit to Peninsula Beverages in July 2022.

120. Dr. Casper Durandt, Executive Director, Sustainability, Coca-Cola, author interview, Johannesburg, South Africa, 6 July 2016. Also, Cornelia Folz, Associate Director, Environment, Coca-Cola Europacific Partners and Yui Kamikawa, Senior Manager, Environmental Sustainability, author interview by telecom, Atlanta, 13 July 2017; and Bethel Yeboah, Public Affairs and Communications Manager, Equatorial Coca-Cola Bottling Company, author interview, Accra, Ghana, 12 May 2017.

121. See Sara Byala, 'Water, Waste, Energy: Lessons from Coca-Cola in Africa,' Policy Digest written for the Kleinman Center for Energy Policy, 8 March 2018.

122. 'Petco Facts and Statistics for 2016, updated March 2017.' See also Witt Wells, 'South Africa's PET Plastic Recycling Rates Close in on European Standards,' 11 April 2017 <www.coca-colacompany.com/coca-cola-unbottled/south-africa-recycled-2-billion-pet-bottles-in-2017> Accessed 27 July 2021.

123. Kristen Linnenkoper, 'Latest Recycling Stats for South Africa,' *Recycling International*, 12 August 2019 <https://recyclinginternational.com/business/latest-recycling-stats-for-south-africa/27327/> Accessed 28 July 2021; and Alex Gray, 'Germany Recycles More than any other Country,' *World Economic Forum*, 18 December 2017 <https://www.weforum.org/agenda/2017/12/germany-recycles-more-than-any-other-country/> Accessed 28 July 2021.

124. Dr. Casper Durandt, author interview.

125. 'Refresh the World,' 32.

126. Joyce Ahiadorme, Public Affairs and Communications, Voltic Recycling, Accra, Ghana, in conversation with author, 10 May 2017.

127. 'Bida People Make a Beeline for Bottles,' *Coca-Cola Overseas*, February 1965, 18 No. 1, 32.

128. April Jordan, author interview; Dorothy Mwangu, Community Affairs, Senior Manager, Coca-Cola, South Africa, in conversation and email communication with author, July 2016. See also '5x20: Gifts that Give Back' <https://us.coca-cola.com/store/goods/5by20-artisan-goods> Accessed 1 August 2021.

129. 'South African South African-born Mbongeni Buthelezi uses waste to create rare art form,' *Africanews*, 27 November 2017 <https://www.africanews.com/2017/11/27/south-african-born-mbongeni-buthelezi-uses-waste-to-create-rare-art-form//> Accessed 20 July 2021.

130. Mbongeni Buthelezi, artist, author interview, Johannesburg, South Africa, 4 July 2016.

131. Author visit, Ghana, 2017. See also, on the Kokrobite Children's Center outside Accra, 'Architect Builds Library with 4,500 recycled Plastic Bottles,' 13 July 2021 <https://newsbeezer.com/romaniaeng/architect-builds-library-with-45000-recycled-plastic-bottles-for-ghanas-poor-children/> Accessed 1 August 2021.

132. Research assistant Kaustubh Deo notes in August 2015 that in the Jinja Province, Uganda, fishermen used empty Coke bottles filled with water as buoys for their nets.

133. Dr. Casper Durandt, author interview.

134. Alistair Schorn, head of business and marketing development, PETCO, author interview at PETCO and during visit to MPACT, 17 May 2017. Also, Nicholas Schild, General Manager: Polymers, MPACT, Johannesburg, in conversation with author, 17 May 2017.

135. Information from Casper Durandt and Alistair Schorn, author interviews.

136. Alistair Schorn, author interview. See also, for the experiences of pickers themselves, Claire Mawisa, 'Waste not, Want not...' 26 June 2016 <http://carteblanche.dstv.com/waste-pickers/> Accessed 1 August 2021.

137. 'Refresh the World,' 35 and 39.

138. Coca-Cola, 2016 Sustainability Report <https://www.coca-colacompany.com/content/dam/journey/us/en/policies/pdf/sustainability/2016-sustainability-report-the-coca-cola-company.pdf> Accessed 1 August 2021. Also, Felix Gomis, Ghana Business Unit Manager, The Coca-Cola Bottling Company of Ghana, Ltd., Accra, Ghana, author interview, 12 May 2017.

139. Adam Metelski, Director, Quality, Safety, and Environment, Coca-Cola, author interview by telephone, 17 August 2017.

140. 'United Nations Sustainable Development Goals: Goal 7,' adopted 2015 <http://www.un.org/sustainabledevelopment/energy/> Accessed 31 July 2017.

141. Gwénaëlle Legros, Ines Havet, Nigel Bruce, and Sophie Bonjour, 'The Energy Access Situation in Developing Countries: A Review Focusing on the Least Developed Countries in Sub-Saharan Countries,' November 2009 <https://cleanenergysolutions.org/resources/energy-access-situation-developing-countries-review-focusing-least-developed-countries-sub> Accessed 27 July 2022.

142. The original EKOCENTER used slingshot technology made by Dean Kamen, inventor of the Segway, inside a twenty-foot-wide solar-powered shipping container. It opened in August 2013 in Heidelberg, South Africa.

143. EKOCENTER infographic in Coca-Cola's 2016 Sustainability Report.

144. Sebastian van der Vegt, EKOCENTER Communications Leader, author interview, Atlanta, 9 March 2016. Also, Simon Bartlett, Partnership and Marketing Director, EKOCENTER, in discussion with author; Dan Baxter, Communications Director, EMEA, The Coca-Cola Company, in discussion with author; Bob Okello, Group Execution Manager, Coca-Cola EKOCENTER, presentation; and Dorcas Onyango, Director, Program Implementation & Partnerships Management, Coca-Cola, presentation, all Ruhunda, Rwanda, 12 June 2016.

145. Elmore, *Citizen Coke*, 186–187; 192.

146. 'Refresh the World,' 25.

147. Monica Ellis, author interview.

148. 'Coca-Cola Making a Play for African Markets with Concession Stands,' 25 November 2016 <https://www.marketplace.org/2016/11/25/coca-cola-making-play-african-market-concession-stands/> Accessed 20 July 2021.

CONCLUSION

1. In the film, the San are referred to as bushmen, a colonial-era misnomer for the indigenous inhabitants of the region.
2. Peter Uys, *The Gods Must Be Crazy*, 1980.
3. Judy Klemesrud, "'The Gods Must Be Crazy" A Truly International Hit,' *The New York Times*, 28 April 1985 <https://www.nytimes.com/1985/04/28/movies/the-gods-must-be-crazy-a-truly-international-hit.html> Accessed 22 September 2021.
4. Slavoj Žižek, 'The Pervert's Guide to Ideology,' directed by Sophie Fiennes, 2012.
5. *Ibid.*
6. CNN Money, 'Africa's youngest billionaire wants to take on Coke with "Mo Cola",' 24 March 2016 <http://www.wptz.com/money/africas-youngest-billionaire-wants-to-take-on-coke-with-mo-cola/38670546> Accessed 4 January 2022.
7. SABC news, 'Fake bottled water has been uncovered in Johannesburg' <https://www.youtube.com/watch?v=A-c18tJSbAk> Accessed 4 January 2022.
8. According to The Coca-Cola Company's 2009 Annual Review, 'An important measure of our growth potential is per capita consumption—the average number of our beverages that people consume each year in a given market.' In the graphic shown, only two African countries are in the highest level of consumption—more than 225 8 oz serving of product. One more African country is between 125 and 225. More than half the countries have less than 25. By comparison, all of North America was above 250. 8–9, <http://transparency.coca-cola.ro/content/dam/journey/us/en/private/fileassets/pdf/2012/12/2009_annual_review.pdf> Accessed 20 July 2021. See also Allyn L. Taylor and Michael F. Jacobson, 'Carbonating the World: The Marketing and Health Impact of Sugar Drinks in Low- and Middle-Income Countries,' *Center for Science in the Public Interest*, 2016.
9. Kirsti Iivonen, 'Defensive Responses to Strategic Sustainability Paradoxes: Have Your Coke and Drink it Too!,' *Journal of Business Ethics*, 2018, 148, no. 2, 322.
10. David Fig, 'Manufacturing Amnesia: Corporate Social Responsibility in South Africa,' *International Affairs*, 2005, 81 No. 3, 617.
11. World Health Organization, 'Guideline: Sugars intake for adults and children,' 5 March 2015, 7 <https://www.who.int/publications/i/item/9789241549028> Accessed 4 January 2022.
12. In Alex Myers, David Fig, Aviva Tugendhaft, Jessie Mandle, Jonathan Myers, and Karen Hofman, 'Sugar and health in South Africa: Potential challenges

to leveraging policy change,' *Global Public Health, Global Public* 2013, 99. They write, '"Free" sugars refer to "monosaccharides and disaccharides added to foods by the manufacturer, cook or consumer, and sugars naturally present in honey, syrups, fruit juices and fruit concentrates."' They cite: World Health Organization (WHO), 'Guideline: Sugars intake for adults and children (Draft guidelines on free sugars released for public consultation),' 2013, 3 <http://www.who.int/mediacentre/news/notes/2014/consultation-sugar-guideline/en/> Accessed 12 May 2022.

13. World Health Organization, 'Guideline: Sugars intake for adults and children,' 4–13.

14. W W Koo and R D Taylor, 'Outlook of the U.S. and world sugar markets, 2010–2020,' Agribusiness & Applied Economics, Fargo: Center for Agricultural Policy and Trade Studies, North Dakota State University, 2011, 1–19.

15. 'Sugar and Health in South Africa,' 8.

16. Alex Myers, David Fig, Aviva Tugendhaft, Jonathan E Myers & Karen J Hofman, 'The history of the South African sugar industry illuminates deeply rooted obstacles for sugar reduction anti-obesity interventions,' *African Studies*, 2017, 76 No. 4, 476.

17. 'Sugar and health in South Africa,' 2.

18. 'The history of the South African sugar industry,' 483.

19. 'Sugar and health in South Africa,' 14.

20. South Africa began considering a tax on sugar-sweetened beverages in 2016. Nicholas Stacey, Ijeoma Edoka, Karen Hofman, Elizabeth C Swart, Barry Popkin, Shu Wen Ng, 'Changes in beverage purchases following the announcement and implementation of South Africa's Health Promotion Levy: an observational study,' *The Lancet*, 4 April 2021, 5 No. 4, e200-e208 <https://www.thelancet.com/journals/lanplh/article/PIIS2542-5196(20)30304-1/fulltext> Accessed 3 January 2003.

21. For more on global taxes, see: Global Food Research Program, 'Sugary drink taxes around the world.' University of North Carolina at Chapel Hill, 2020 <https://globalfoodresearchprogram.web.unc.edu/>; and 'Countries that have taxes on sugar-sweetened beverages,' Obesity Evidence Hub <https://www.obesityevidencehub.org.au/collections/prevention/countries-that-have-implemented-taxes-on-sugar-sweetened-beverages-ssbs> Accessed 3 January 2022.

22. Anahad O'Connor, 'Coca-Cola Funds Scientists Who Shift Blame for Obesity Away From Bad Diets,' *The New York Times*, 9 August 2015, A1.

23. Neil Craven, 'Coca-Cola boss claims sugar tax is bad for consumers and will act as a distraction from efforts to switch to lower calorie products,'

This is Money, 9 July 2016 <https://www.thisismoney.co.uk/money/markets/article-3682348/Coca-Cola-boss-Jon-Woods-claims-sugar-tax-bad-consumers-act-distraction-efforts-switch-lower-calorie-products.html> Accessed 11 August 2021.

24. Letter from David Fig to the Treasury and the SA Revenue Service, 'Resubmitted for the finance standing committee hearings on Wednesday,' in 'Re: Comment on Proposals contained in the rates and monetary amounts and amendment of revenue laws bill,' aimed at amending the Customs and Excise Act 91 of 1964, 30 March 2017. Shared with author by David Fig.

25. Michael Essman, Lindsey Smith Taillie, Tamryn Frank, Shu Wen Ng, Barry M. Popkin, Elizabeth C. Swart, 'Taxed and untaxed beverage intake by South African young adults after a national sugar-sweetened beverage tax: A before-and-after study,' May 25, 2021. *PLoS Med* 18(5): e1003574.

26. Coca-Cola South Africa employees, in conversation with author, Johannesburg, 19 May 2017.

27. Sugar consumption has risen five-fold in 100 years, according to 'Sustainable Economics: The Bitter Aftertaste of Sugar,' *Morgan Stanley Research*, March 2015, <https://static.latribune.fr/463077/etude-morgan-stanley-impact-diabete-sur-l-economie-mondiale.pdf> Accessed 29 November 2021

28. See 'Does Coca-Cola Market its products to children?' <https://www.coca-colacompany.com/faqs/does-coca-cola-market-to-children> Accessed 19 November 2021. See also: Allyn L Taylor and Michael F Jacobson, 'Carbonating the World.'

29. John Kell, 'Soda Consumption Falls to 30-Year Low In The U.S.,' 29 March 2016, *Fortune Magazine* <https://fortune.com/2016/03/29/soda-sales-drop-11th-year/> Accessed 4 January 2022.

30. Chase Purdy, 'Coca-Cola has quietly been removing sugar from its drinks—and no one seems to care,' *Quartz*, 15 May 2017 <https://qz.com/983760/coca-cola-ko-has-quietly-removed-sugar-from-some-of-its-sodas-and-no-one-seems-to-care/> Accessed 11 August 2021.

31. 'Coca-Cola COO: Boosting Revenue, Cutting Calories,' *Bloomberg Daybreak*: 'Americas,' 26 October 2016, 8:32 am EDT <https://www.bloomberg.com/news/videos/2016-10-26/coca-cola-coo-boosting-revenue-cutting-calories> Accessed 11 August 2021.

32. Coca-Cola Press Release, 'Coca-Cola Reveals New One Brand Packaging,' Mexico City, 18 April 2016 <https://www.coca-colacompany.com/press-releases/coke-reveals-one-brand-packaging> Accessed 11 August 2021.

33. Only in South Africa was this called Taste the Experience because of existing copyright. 'Coca-Cola Announces "One Brand" Global Marketing Approach,' Coca-Cola Australia, 19 January 2016, <https://www.coca-colacompany.

com/au/media-centre/media-releases/coca-cola-announces-one-brand-global-marketing-approach> Accessed 11 August 2021. Also, Jaco Nel, General Managing, Marketing, Peninsula Beverages, author interview, Cape Town, South Africa, 12 July 2016.

34. See, for example, this Coca-Cola One Brand commercial <https://www.youtube.com/watch?v=ARKXUSp9NRI> Accessed 10 June 2022.

35. 'Coca-Cola Launches "One Brand" Strategy,' *The Herald*, 18 May 2016.

36. Asit Sharma, 'Why soda taxes will help Coca-Cola: Would you believe that if more cities follow Philadelphia and institute a soda tax, Coca-Cola will benefit? Read on,' *The Motley Fool*, 5 July 2016 <https://www.fool.com/investing/2016/07/05/why-soda-taxes-will-help-coca-cola.aspx> Accessed 11 August 2021.

37. 'SABMiller, The Coca-Cola Company and Coca-Cola Sabco to form Coca-Cola Beverages Africa,' 27 November 2014 <https://www.sabmiller.com/media/media-releases/the-coca-cola-company-sabmiller-and-coca-cola-sabco-to-form-coca-cola-beverages-africa> Accessed 18 July 2021.

38. For more on Sabco see: <http://www.cocacolasabco.com/pages/our-company> Accessed 18 July 2021.

39. Philipp H Gutsche, Chairman, Coca-Cola Beverages Africa, author interview, Lakeside Plant, Port Elizabeth, 15 May 2017.

40. Julie Livingston, *Self-Devouring Growth: A Planetary Parable* (Durham: Duke University Press, 2019), 6.

41. Will Steffen, Katherine Richardson, Johan Rockström, Sarah E. Cornell, Ingo Fetzer, Elena M. Bennett, Reinette Biggs, Stephen R. Carpenter, Wim de Vries, Cynthia A. de Wit, Carl Folke, Dieter Gerten, Jens Heinke, Georgina M. Mace, Linn M. Persson, Veerabhadran Ramanathan, Belinda Reyers, and Sverker Sörlin, 'Planetary boundaries: Guiding human development on a changing planet,' *Science, American Association for the Advancement of Science*, 13 February 2015. See also <https://www.stockholmresilience.org/research/planetary-boundaries.html> Accessed 20 July 2022. On businesses engaging with the framework see, for example, the World Business Council on Sustainable Development.

42. Speaking about the corporate use of the planetary boundary framework with regard to freshwater, for example, Maik Heistermann, from the Institute of Earth and Environmental Science at the University of Potsdam, suggests that 'policy and management choices should be made by the affected stakeholders instead of being imposed by whatever water-related global trade mechanism.' Maik Heistermann, 'HESS Opinions: A planetary boundary on freshwater use is misleading,' *Hydrol. Earth Syst. Sci.*, 21, 3455–3461, 2017.

43. See Michael Shellenberger and Ted Norhaus, *Breakthrough: from the death of environmentalism to the politics of possibility* (Boston: Houghton Mifflin Harcourt, 2007). See also Rebecca Solnit, who has written extensively on hope, including *Hope in the Dark: Untold Histories, Wild Possibilities* (Chicago: Haymarket Books, 2019).

44. 'Coca-Cola "Sleepwalker" Super Bowl,' 8 February 2010 <https://www.youtube.com/watch?v=euiqoVaQcBQ> Accessed 4 January 2022.

45. James Poniewozik, 'The Best and Worst Super Bowl Commercials of 2010,' *Time magazine*, Sunday, 7 February 2010 <http://content.time.com/time/specials/packages/article/0,28804,1960734_1960750_1960791,00.html> Accessed 4 January 2022.

SELECT BIBLIOGRAPHY

Abaka, Edmund, *Kola is God's Gift: Agricultural Production, Export Initiatives, and the Kola Industry of Asante and the Gold Coast, c. 1820*–1950. Suffolk: James Currey, 2005.

Abani, Chris, *Graceland*. New York: Farrar, Straus, and Giroux, 2004.

Achebe, Chinua. *Things Fall Apart*. New York: Anchor Books, 1994.

Adichie, Chimamanda Ngozi. *Half a Yellow Sun*. New York: Random House, 2008, 206.

Ahmed, Shirin, Leslie Curry, and Erika Linnander. 'Project Last Mile: Applying Coca-Cola's Expertise to Improve Delivery of Life-Saving Medicines.' Yale Global Health Leadership Institute. Yale University, New Haven, CT, 2015.

Alegi, Peter. *African Soccerscapes: How a Continent Changed the World's Game*. Athens: Ohio University Press, 2010.

Allen, Frederick. *Secret Formula: How Brilliant Marketing and Relentless Salesmanship Made Coca-Cola the Best-Known Product in the World*. New York: Harper Collins, 1994.

Appadurai, Arjun. 'Introduction: Commodities and the Politics of Value,' in *The Social Life of Things: Commodities in Cultural Perspective*, ed. Arjun Appadurai. Cambridge: Cambridge University Press, 1986).

Bhabha, Homi. 'Of Mimicry and Man: The Ambivalence of Colonial Discourse' in *The Location of Culture*. New York: Routledge Classic, 2004.

Bleksley, A H, *Johannesburg Gezondheids Comite, Sanitary Department*. Johannesburg: Standard and Digger's News Printing and Publishing Company, 1896.

Booker, Jamal. '1961 Animals of Africa Launch in South Africa,' 8 May 2012 <https://www.coca-colacompany.com/stories/1961-animals-of-africa-launch-in-south-africa> Accessed 15 June 2019.

SELECT BIBLIOGRAPHY

Bourdieu, Pierre. *Distinction: A Social Critique of the Judgement of Good Taste*. New York: Routledge, 1979.

Boz, Z, V Korhonen, and K S Claire, 'Consumer considerations for the implementation of sustainable packaging: A review.' *Sustainability*, 2020 12 No. 6, 2192.

Byala, Sara. *A Place that Matters Yet: John Gubbins's MuseumAfrica in the Postcolonial World*. Chicago: University of Chicago Press, 2013.

―――― 'Water, Waste, Energy: Lessons from Coca-Cola in Africa,' Policy Digest written for The Kleinman Center for Energy Policy, 8 March 2018.

Calver, Phoebe. 'Equatorial Bottling Company in Ghana: Delivering Sustainable Business in the Community.' *Africa Outlook*, 29 June 2018, 1–18.

Carney, Judith A. 'African Traditional Plant Knowledge in the Circum-Caribbean Region,' *Journal of Ethnobiology* 23, No. 2 2003, 167–185.

―――― and Richard Nicholas Rosomoff. *In the Shadow of Slavery: Africa's Botanic Legacy in the Atlantic Word*. Berkeley: University of California Press, 2009.

Ciafone, Amanda. *Counter-Cola: A Multinational History of the Global Corporation*. UCLA Press, 2019.

Coggin, G Lynn. *ABI: Over Sixty Years as a Bottler of Coca-Cola* Book One: 1923–1975. Johannesburg: ABI, 2005.

―――― *ABI: Over Sixty Years as a Bottler of Coca-Cola, Book Two: 1976–2000*. Johannesburg: ABI, 2005.

Comaroff, John L. 'Images of Empire, Contests of Conscience: Models of Colonial Domination in South Africa.' *American Ethnologist*, 1989, 16 No. 4, 661–685.

Cooper Funderburg, Anne. *Sundae Best: A History of Soda Fountains*. Bowling Green: Bowling Green State University Press, 2002.

Dahi, Eli. 'Africa's U-Turn in Defluoridation Policy: From the Nalgonda Technique to Bone Char.' Research report Fluoride. October–December 2016, 49(4 Pt 1): 401–416. <https://www.fluorideresearch.org/494Pt1/files/FJ2016_v49_n4Pt1_p401-416_pq.pdf> Accessed 28 July 2021.

Davenport, Kim. 'Corporate citizenship: A stakeholder approach for defining corporate social performance and identifying measures for assessing it.' *Business and Society*, June 2000, 39 No. 2, 210–219.

Dlamini, Jacob. *Safari Nation: A Social History of the Kruger National Park*. Athens: Ohio University Press, 2020.

―――― 'To Know the African wild was to Know the African Subject: What training as a field guide taught Jacob Dlamini about Culture, Nature, Power, and Race.' *The Johannesburg Review of Books*, July 1, 2019 <https://johannesburgreviewofbooks.com/2019/07/01/to-know-the-african-wild-was-to-know-the-african-subject-what-training-as-a-field-guide-taught-jacob-dlamini-about-culture-nature-power-and-race/#respond> Accessed 7 July 2019.

SELECT BIBLIOGRAPHY

Donovan, Tristan. *Fizz: How Soda Shook Up the World*. Chicago: Chicago Review Press, 2014.

Driver, Dorothy. 'Drum Magazine (1951–9) and the Spatial Configurations of Gender,' in *Text, Theory, Space: Literature and History in South Africa and Australia*, edited by Kate Darian-Smith, Liz Gunner, and Sarah Nuttall (London: Routledge, 1996): 231–242.

Elkington, John. *Cannibals with Forks: The Triple Bottom Line of 21st-Century Business*. Hoboken: John Wiley & Son, 1999.

Elmore, Bartow J. *Citizen Coke: The Making of Coca-Cola Capitalism*. New York: W.W. Norton, 2015.

Essman, Michael, Lindsey Smith Taillie, Tamryn Frank, Shu Wen Ng, Barry M. Popkin, Elizabeth C. Swart. 'Taxed and untaxed beverage intake by South African young adults after a national sugar-sweetened beverage tax: A before-and-after study,' 25 May 2021. *PLoS Med* 18(5): e1003574.

Esterhuyse, Willie. *Endgame: Secret Talks and the End of Apartheid*. Cape Town: Tafelberg.

Fig, David. 'Manufacturing amnesia: Corporate Social Responsibility in South Africa.' *International Affairs*, 2005, 81 No. 3, 599–617.

Fluckiger, F A. 'The Pharmacognosy of Kola,' *American Druggist and Pharmaceutical Record*, 25, No. 3, August 10, 1894, 99–100 in Caswell A Mayo and Thomas J Keenan, eds., *Volume XXV: July-December 1894*. New York: American Druggist Publishing Company, 1894.

Ford, Martin. 'Kola Production and Settlement Mobility among the Dan of Nimba, Liberia, *African Economic History*, 20, 1992, 51–63.

Foster, Robert J. *Coca-Globalization: Following Soft-drinks from New York to New Guinea*. Palgrave MacMillan, 2008.

Freeman, R E. *Strategic Management: A Stakeholder Approach*. Boston: Pitman, 1984.

Gautier, Armand with A J Rice-Oxley, translator, *Diet and Dietetics*. Philadelphia: Lippincott, 1906.

Green, Lawrence. *A Taste of South-Easter: Memories of unusual Cape Town characters, queer shops and shows, old bars, hotels and cafes and the panorama of the streets*. <https://archive.org/stream/ATasteOfSouth-easter/ATasteOfSouth-easter_djvu.txt> Accessed 21 July 2022.

Guldi, Jo and David Armitage. *The History Manifesto*. Cambridge University Press. <http://historymanifesto.cambridge.org/read/>.

Heistermann, Maik. 'HESS Opinions: A planetary boundary on freshwater use is misleading,' *Hydrol. Earth Syst. Sci.*, 21, 3455–3461, 2017.

Hoy, Anne. *Coca-Cola: The First Hundred Years*. Atlanta: The Coca-Cola Company, 1986.

Iivonen, Kirsti. 'Defensive Responses to Strategic Sustainability Paradoxes: Have Your Coke and Drink it Too!' *Journal of Business Ethics*, 2018, 148, no. 2, 309–327.

Isdell, E Neville with David Beasley. *Inside Coca-Cola: A CEO's Life Story of Building the World's Most Popular Brand*. New York: St. Martin's Griffin, 2011.

Jarnagin, Andrew. 'When Coca-Cola Grows Citrus on the Nile, Who Wins? Revisiting the End of the Arab Boycott in Egypt.' *Grand Valley Journal of History*, 2016, 4 No. 1, Article 4. <http://scholarworks.gvsu.edu/gvjh/vol4/iss1/4> Accessed 6 August 2019.

Johanson, C E and M W Fischman, 'The Pharmacology of Cocaine Related to its Abuse,' *Pharmacological Reviews* March, 41 (1) 1989, 3–52.

Koo, W W and R D Taylor. 'Outlook of the U.S. and world sugar markets, 2010–2020,' Agribusiness & Applied Economics, Fargo: Center for Agricultural Policy and Trade Studies, North Dakota State University, 2011, 1–19.

Kraak, André. 'Private Sector Investment in Black Education and Training: Rescuing South African Capitalism from Apartheid's Crisis.' *Comparative Education.* 1989, 25 No. 2, 197–218, <https://www.jstor.org/stable/3099383> Accessed 18 November 2019.

Kretzmann, Steve and Raymond Joseph. 'Coca-Cola and Cape Town's sweetheart Day Zero deal: How big business ignored the water restrictions and got away with it,' Ground Up, <https://www.groundup.org.za/article/coca-cola-and-cape-towns-sweetheart-day-zero-deal/> Accessed 1 July 2021.

Lafore, Laurence. 'Elephants Have the Right of Way,' *Harper's*, November 1958, 72–77.

Lastovica, Ethleen with Albert Lastovica. *Bottles & Bygones: A guide for South African collectors*. Cape Town: Don Nelson, 1982.

Legros, Gwénaëlle, Ines Havet, Nigel Bruce, and Sophie Bonjour. 'The Energy Access Situation in Developing Countries: A Review Focusing on the Least Developed Countries in Sub-Saharan Countries,' November 2009 <https://cleanenergysolutions.org/resources/energy-access-situation-developing-countries-review-focusing-least-developed-countries-sub> Accessed 27 July 2022.

Livingston, Julie. *Self-Devouring Growth: A Planetary Parable*. Durham: Duke University Press, 2019.

Lovejoy, Paul E. *Caravans of Kola: The Hausa Trade, 1700–1900*. Ahmadu Bello University Press, 1980.

——— 'Kola in the History of West Africa,' *Cahiers D'études Africaines*, 20, No. 77–78, 1980, 97–134.

Mamdani, Mahmood. *Citizen and Subject: Contemporary Africa and the Legacy of Colonialism*. Princeton: Princeton University Press, 1996.

SELECT BIBLIOGRAPHY

Manià, Kirby. 'Diving the Reef: Water Metaphors in the Work of Ivan Vladislavic.' *English in Africa* 43 No. 2 (Aug. 2016), 63–89.

Mashingaidze, Terence M. 'Beyond the Kariba Dam induced displacements: The Zimbabwean Tonga's struggles for restitution, 1990s–2000s.' *International Journal on Minority and Group Rights* (2013) 20 no. 3: 381–404.

Matten, Dirk and Andrew Crane. 'Corporate Citizenship: Toward an Extended Theoretical Conceptualization.' *The Academy of Management Review.* January 2005, 30 No. 1, 166–179.

Mbembe, Achille. 'Provisional Notes on the Postcolony.' *Africa* 62 (1), 1992, 3–37.

McCormick, Erin, Bennett Murray, Carmela Fonbuena, Leonni Kijewski, Gokce Saracoglu, Jamie Fullerton, Alastair Gee, and Charlotte Simmonds. 'Where does your plastic go? Global investigation reveals America's dirty secret.' <https://www.theguardian.com/us-news/2019/jun/17/recycled-plastic-america-global-crisis> Accessed 20 July 2021.

Mchunu, Ernest. *Cheeky Native: A practical experience in Managerial and Leadership Excellence.* Reach Publishers, Wandsbeck: 2010.

Miller, Daniel. 'Coca-Cola: A Sweet Black drink from Trinidad,' in *Material Cultures: Why Some Things Matter*, ed. Daniel Miller. Chicago: University of Chicago Press, 1998.

Miller, Jon and Lucy Parker. *Everybody's Business: The Unlikely Story of How Big Business Can Fix the World.* London: Biteback Publishing, 2013.

Myers, Alex, David Fig, Aviva Tugendhaft, Jessie Mandle, Jonathan Myers and Karen Hofman. 'Sugar and health in South Africa: Potential challenges to leveraging policy change,' *Global Public Health*, 2013, 98–115.

Myers, Alex, David Fig, Aviva Tugendhaft, Jonathan E Myers & Karen J Hofman. 'The history of the South African sugar industry illuminates deeply rooted obstacles for sugar reduction anti-obesity interventions,' *African Studies*, 2017, 76 No. 4, 475–490.

Norman, Wayne and Chris MacDonald, 'Getting to the Bottom of the "Triple Bottom Line,"' *Business Ethics Quarterly*, 2004, 14 No. 2, 243–262.

Oatman-Stanford, Hunter. 'Medicinal Soft Drinks and Coca-Cola Fiends: The Toxic History of Soda Pop.' 10 April 2014. <https://www.collectorsweekly.com/articles/the-toxic-history-of-soda-pop/>

O'Neil, Darcy S. *Fix the Pumps: The History and Recipes of the Soda Fountain.* Art of Drink: 2009.

Owen, Roger and Şevket Pamuk. *A History of Middle Eastern Economies in the Twentieth Century.* Cambridge: Harvard University Press, 1999.

Pendergrast, Mark. *For God, Country, & Coca-Cola: The Definitive History of the Great American Soft Drink and the Company That Makes It*, Third Edition. New York: Basic Books, 2013.

SELECT BIBLIOGRAPHY

Priestley, Joseph. *Directions for Impregnating Water with Fixed Air in Order to Communicate to It the Peculiar Spirit and Virtues of Pyrmont Water, and Other Mineral Waters of a Similar* Nature. Reprinted by American Bottlers of Carbonated Beverages, Washington DC, 1945.

Rivoli, Pietra. *The Travels of A T-Shirt in the Global Economy: An Economist Examines the Markets, Power, and Politics of World Trade,* 2nd Edition. Hoboken: John Wiley and Sons, Inc., 2009.

Shellenberger, Michael and Ted Norhaus. *Breakthrough: from the death of environmentalism to the politics of possibility.* Boston: Houghton Mifflin Harcourt, 2007.

Simmons, Douglas A. *Schweppes: The first 200 Years.* Springwood Books Ltd., 1983.

Solnit, Rebecca. *Hope in the Dark: Untold Histories, Wild Possibilities.* Chicago: Haymarket Books, 2019.

Sparks, Allister. *Tomorrow is Another Country: The Inside Story of South Africa's Road to Change.* Chicago: University of Chicago Press, 1996.

Spivey, John Kirby. 'Coke vs. Pepsi: The Cola Wars in South Africa during The Anti-Apartheid Era.' Thesis. Georgia State University, 2009.

Stacey, Nicholas, Ijeoma Edoka, Karen Hofman, Elizabeth C Swart, Barry Popkin, Shu Wen Ng. 'Changes in beverage purchases following the announcement and implementation of South Africa's Health Promotion Levy: an observational study.' *The Lancet,* 4 April 2021, 5 No. 4, e200–e208.

Steele S, Ruskin G, McKee M, *et al.* 'Always read the small print: a case study of commercial research funding, disclosure and agreements with Coca-Cola.' *Journal of Public Health Policy* 2019, 40, 273–285.

Stefanini, R, G Borghesi, A Ronzano, *et al.* 'Plastic or glass: a new environmental assessment with a marine litter indicator for the comparison of pasteurized milk bottles.' *Int J Life Cycle Assess,* 2021, 26, 767–784.

Steffen, Will, Katherine Richardson, Johan Rockström, Sarah E. Cornell, Ingo Fetzer, Elena M. Bennett, Reinette Biggs, Stephen R. Carpenter, Wim de Vries, Cynthia A. de Wit, Carl Folke, Dieter Gerten, Jens Heinke, Georgina M. Mace, Linn M. Persson, Veerabhadran Ramanathan, Belinda Reyers, and Sverker Sörlin. 'Planetary boundaries: Guiding human development on a changing planet,' *Science, American Association for the Advancement of Science,* 13 February 2015.

Turton, Anthony, Craig Schultz, Hannes Buckle, Mapule Kgomongoe, Tinyiko Malugani & Mikael Drackner, 'Gold, Scorched Earth and Water: The Hydropolitics of Johannesburg,' *Water Resources Development,* 22, No. 2 (2006), 313–335.

SELECT BIBLIOGRAPHY

Voeks, Robert and John Rashford, eds., *African Ethnobotany in the Americas*. New York: Springer-Verlag, 2013.

Walker, Michael. *The old hotels of Cape Town 1890–1911: A History Long Forgotten, Seldom Told*. South Africa: St. James, 2015.

Ware, Carl with Sibley Fleming. *Portrait of a Businessman: One generation from Cotton Field to Boardroom*. Macon: Mercer University Press, 2019.

Waterbury, John. *The Egypt of Nasser and Sadat*. Princeton: Princeton University Press, 1983.

Wolf, A, G A Bray, and B M Popkin. 'A short history of beverages and how our body treats them,' *The International Association for the Study of Obesity*, Obesity Reviews 9 (2007), 159.

Yarbrough, Charles C. 'Therapeutics of Kola,' *Journal of the American Medical Association* 33 (19) 1899, 1148–1149.

Zimmet, Paul, 'Globalization, Coca-Colonization and the Chronic Disease Epidemic: can the Doomsday scenario be averted?' *Journal of Internal Medicine* 247 (3) 2000: 301–310.

Žižek, Slavoj, 'The Pervert's Guide to Ideology,' directed by Sophie Fiennes, 2012.

INDEX

Note: Page numbers followed by "*n*" refer to notes.

351

INDEX

INDEX

INDEX

INDEX

INDEX

INDEX

INDEX

Mozambique, 62–3, 225–6
'Mr. Moses' (film), 116
Mt. Kilimanjaro, 105
Mugabe, Robert Gabriel, 182
Mukora, Charles, 138, 200
Mullak, 131
Mulvihal, Thomas, 23, 26, 285n6
Museun, Patience, 105–6
Museveni, Yoweri, 192
Musvanya, Sam, 201–2
Mutare Bottlers, 67–8, 191–2
Mutare Bottling, 202

Nairobi, 63, 76, 98
    Kenyatta Day celebration
        (1973), 113
Nairobi Bottlers, 99, 118
Naivasha, 243–4
Naivasha Water, 244
Nakuru De-fluoridation Company
    (NDC), 245
NASH, 202–3
National Arts and Crafts
    Committee, 99
National Beverages Services,
    162–3, 315n51
'Native Market', 74
NBC. See Nigerian Bottling
    Company (NBC)
NBS. See National Beverages
    Services
NCD. See noncommunicable
    diseases (NCD)
Ndlovu, Peter, 203
Near East Bottlers, 74
Nectrona, 25
Nelspruit, 167

New Brighton, 97
New Mexico, 217
New York Times, The (newspaper),
    131, 161, 308–9n51
New York, 32, 73, 209
New Yorker, The (magazine), 56
New Zealand, 25
Ngong, 231, 232
NGOs, 182, 221, 223
Ngugi, Peter, 96
Ngwenya Glass works, 249, 252
Nigel, 32, 37
Niger (River), 2, 63
Nigeria, 11, 63, 203, 226
Nigerian Bottling Company
    (NBC), 64–5, 226, 232
Nile, 84
nitida, 3
Nkrumah, Kwame, 91
Nkrumah, Samia Yaba, 91
Nkubu Secondary School, 124
non-alcoholic fluids, 263
noncommunicable diseases (NCD),
    264–5
Nooth, John Mervin, 8
North Africa, 51, 55, 90, 136,
    298n1
northern Nigeria, 65, 251
Northern Rhodesia (Zambia), 49,
    124, 137
Northwest African Bottlers'
    Meeting (1959), 74
Nyasaland (Malawi), 49, 63, 137
Nyasaland Bottling Company, 96

October War. See Yom Kippur War
OK Bazaars, 27

360

INDEX

INDEX

INDEX

INDEX

INDEX

WHO. *See* World Health Organization (WHO)

Wild Life Protection Society (Southern Africa), 100

Williamson Diamond Mine of Tanzania, 137

Wisconsin, 194

Witbank Mineral Water Company, 32

Witkoppen, 122

Wits stadium, 209

Witwatersrand, 23–4

Wollaert, Guy, 225

Wonderful World (film), 84, 88

Woodruff, Robert, 52–3, 179

Worcester Minerals, 32

World Bank, 108, 187

World Economic Forum (1998), 186

World Economic Forum (2002), 221

World Football Development Program, 201

World Health Organization (WHO), 264–5

World War II, 11, 41–2, 86, 199
impacts on Coca-Cola, 33–5, 52–5

World Wildlife Fund, 223

WSUP. *See* Water and Sanitation for the Urban Poor (WSUP)

Xhosa, 110

Yale University, 9

Yarbough, Charles, 4–5

YES, 228

Yom Kippur War (1973), 129, 309n55

YouTube, 212

Zambesi River, 108

Zambia, 62–3, 157, 201

ZAR Sanitary Commission, 23

Zimbabwe, 10–11, 62, 66, 120, 137, 191–2
housed a festival to honor Cecil Rhodes, 69
One Brand arrived in, 269
Route Managers Training Course in, 74
Ware's visit to, 152

Žižek, Slavoj, 12–13, 261–2

Zolakone, 25, 287n20

Zulu, Elliot, 97